MEDIATING TWO WORLDS

distributed
by
INDIANA
UNIVERSITY PRESS

Amerika Terra Incógnita (America, Unknown Land, *Diego Rísquez, Venezuela, 1988*)

Mediating Two Worlds

Cinematic Encounters in the Americas

Edited by John King, Ana M. López, Manuel Alvarado

BFI PUBLISHING

First published in 1993 by the
British Film Institute
21 Stephen Street
London W1P 1PL

Copyright © British Film Institute 1993
Individual contributions copyright © author 1993

British Library Cataloguing-in-Publication Data.
A catalogue record for this book is available from the British Library.

ISBN 0–85170–333–X
        0–85170–334–8 Pbk

Cover design: Dean Hoad
Cover photograph: *Angel de Fuego* (Dana Rotberg, Mexico, 1992)

Set in 10/11·5pt Plantin by
Fakenham Photosetting Ltd, Fakenham, Norfolk
Printed in Great Britain by
The Trinity Press, Worcester

Remembering Nissa Torrents

CONTENTS

ACKNOWLEDGMENTS

The editors would particularly like to thank, for their invaluable advice and support: Edward Buscombe, Luiz Fernando Santoro, Rafael Roncagliolo, Joelle Hüllenbroek, Markku Salmi. Without the wonderful photographs in the BFI's Stills, Posters and Designs Collection, and the help of their staff, the book could not have been so well illustrated. The Institute of Latin American Studies, University of London generously made available a grant to cover the cost of printing these stills. The British Academy provided funds for research in Latin America. Ignacio Durán offered the hospitality and resources of IMCINE, the Mexican Film Institute.

We are also grateful to the following for their permission to reprint material:

Ana M. López, 'Are all Latins from Manhattan? Hollywood, Ethnography and Cultural Colonialism' – a longer version appeared in Lester Friedman (ed.), *Unspeakable Images* (University of Illinois Press, 1991).

Ana M. López, 'Tears and Desire: Women and Melodrama in the "Old" Mexican Cinema' – previously published in *Iris* no. 13 Summer 1991.

Kathleen Newman, 'National Cinema After Globalisation: Fernando Solanas's *Sur* and the Exiled Nation', in *Quarterly Review of Film Studies*, forthcoming.

Chon A. Noriega, 'Internal Others: Hollywood Narratives "about" Mexican Americans' – parts of this essay were previously published in 'Citizen Chicano: The Trials and Titillations of Ethnicity in the American Cinema, 1935–1962' in *Social Research: An International Quarterly on the Social Sciences* vol. 58 no. 2, Summer 1991, pp. 418–38.

Margarita de Orellana, 'The Circular Look: The Incursion of North American Fictional Cinema 1911–1917 into the Mexican Revolution', in *La mirada circular: el cine norteamericano de la revolución 1911–1917* (México: Joaquín Mortiz, 1991).

Robert Stam, 'Cross Cultural Dialogisms: Race and Multi-Culturalism in Brazilian Cinema' – previously published in *Iris* no. 13, Summer 1991.

Editorial Note

The editors have deliberately not attempted to obscure the diverse origins of the contributions by imposing a uniform spelling system; instead the different spelling and authorial footnoting systems of the USA and the UK have been maintained.

NOTES ON CONTRIBUTORS

Manuel Alvarado is Head of Education in the Research Division of the British Film Institute. He is the author and editor of numerous books about the mass media and about education. His most recent books include a collection edited with Oliver Boyd-Barrett, *Media Education: An Introduction* (1992), and *The Screen Education Reader* (1993), edited with Edward Buscombe and Richard Collins.

Timothy Barnard is a film promoter and an independent film scholar living in Toronto. He has organised a number of Latin American film retrospectives and is the editor of *Argentine Cinema* (1986). In 1988–9 he lived in Cuba and worked for the newspaper *Granma*. Time to research and write the essay in this volume was funded by the Ontario Arts Council.

Julianne Burton-Carvajal is Professor of Literature at the University of California at Santa Cruz. She has been a steadfast promoter of Latin American cinema for many years and her archival, curatorial and scholarly work has been central to the development of English-language scholarship of Latin American film. Her most recent books are *The Social Documentary in Latin America* (1990) and *Cinema and Social Change in Latin America: Conversations with Filmmakers* (1986).

Edward Buscombe is Head of Book Publishing at the British Film Institute. He is the editor of *The BFI Companion to the Western* (1988). His most recent publications include *Stagecoach* (1992) in the BFI's Film Classics series and *The Screen Education Reader* (1993), which he co-edited with Manuel Alvarado and Richard Collins.

James Dunkerley is Professor of Politics at Queen Mary and Westfield College, University of London, and runs the Masters Programme at the Institute of Latin American Studies. He is the author of numerous books on the history and politics of Latin America. His most recent books are *Power in the Isthmus* (1988) and *Political Suicide in Latin America* (1991).

Thomas Elsaesser is Professor in the Film and Television Sciences Department at the University of Amsterdam. Having published widely in the field of Cinema Studies his most recent books include the prizewinning *New German Cinema: A History* (1989) and the edited collection *Early Cinema: Space, Frame, Narrative* (1990).

Jean Franco is Professor of Comparative Literature at Columbia University. Widely regarded as the most influential English-speaking critic of Latin American cultural history and theory, she wrote the path-breaking *The Modern Culture of Latin America* in the late 1960s. Her most recent work is *Plotting Women: Gender and Representation in Mexico* (1989), and she is completing a study on border culture.

Rosa Linda Fregoso is an Assistant Professor in the Women's Studies and Chicano Studies Programs at the University of California at Davis. Her book, *The Bronze Screen: Chicano and Chicano Film Practices*, University of Minnesota Press, is forthcoming.

John Hess is Assistant Professor of Communication at Ithaca College. He is a founding editor of *JumpCut: A Review of Contemporary Media*, and has published extensively on Latin American film and media.

Randal Johnson is Professor of Brazilian Literature and Culture in the Department of Romance Languages at the University of Florida. He is the author of *Cinema Novo x Five* (1984), *The Film Industry in Brazil: Culture and the State* (1987), and *Brazilian Cinema* (1982) with Robert Stam. Currently he is working on the question of authority in the Brazilian literary field and is editing a book of essays on art and literature by Pierre Bourdieu.

John King is Senior Lecturer in Latin American Cultural History at the University of Warwick. He has written several books on Argentine culture and is the author of *Magical Reels: A History of Cinema in Latin America* (1990).

Paul Lenti is a freelance journalist specialising in Latin American cinema. In addition to working for eight years as a film critic for the *Mexico City News* and eight years with the trade publication *Variety*, he more recently co-ordinated the film section of the 1990 and 1991 New York Festival Latino. He is currently translating *Buñuel on Buñuel*, a book of interviews with Spanish film-maker Luis Buñuel for the University of Texas Press.

Marvin D'Lugo directs the Screen Studies Program at Clark University. He has published widely on Spanish cinema and is the author of *The Films of Carlos Saura: The Practice of Seeing* (1991). He is currently working on a book-length study of the construction of national identity in Cuban cinema.

Ana M. López is Associate Professor of Communication at Tulane University where she teaches film and cultural studies with a Latin American focus.

In addition to numerous articles and book chapters on Latin American film, media and Latino/a representation, she has recently co-edited a special issue of *Quarterly Review of Film Studies*. Her book *The New Latin American Cinema* is forthcoming from the University of Illinois Press.

Carlos Monsiváis is perhaps Mexico's best-known and most prolific cultural critic. His essays and books on politics, history, literature and cinema have helped to reshape political and cultural debates in Mexico over the last thirty years. His works on film culture include *Amor perdido* (1977) and *Escenas de pudor y liviandad* (1988).

Kathleen Newman teaches Latin American and Chicano Cinema at the University of Iowa. She is one of the co-authors of *Women, Culture and Politics in Latin America* (1990), and is working on a book on state theory and cultural studies.

Chon A. Noriega is Assistant Professor in the UCLA Department of Film and Television, is editor of *Chicanos and Film: Essays on Chicano Representation and Resistance* (1992) and special issues of *The Spectator* and *JumpCut*. He has also curated numerous film series and served as a consultant on documentaries and media curriculum projects.

Margarita de Orellana is a Mexican historian who teaches in Mexico City and who is on the editorial board of the journal *Artes de México*. Her numerous publications on Mexican history and cinema include: *Imágenes del pasado: el cine y la historia* (1985) and *La mirada circular: el cine norteamericano de la revolución mexicana* (1991).

Laura Podalsky teaches in the Latin American Studies and Communication Departments of Tulane University and is completing a dissertation on Latin American film. Her essay on melodrama in the Mexican cinema is forthcoming in *Studies in Latin American Popular Culture*.

Beatriz Sarlo is Professor of Literature and Cultural Theory at the University of Buenos Aires. She has written a number of key works on Argentine cultural history and theory which explore the processes of modernity and modernisation in Argentina. Her most recent books are *Una modernidad periférica: Buenos Aires 1920 y 1930* (1988) and *La imaginación técnica* (1992). Her first work to appear in English, *Jorge Luis Borges: A Writer on the Edge*, is published by Verso in 1993. She is the editor of the cultural journal *Punto de Vista*.

Robert Stam is Professor of Cinema Studies at New York University. He has published widely on cinema studies, with a special focus on Brazilian film and Bakhtinian theory. With Randal Johnson, he co-edited *Brazilian Cinema* (1982), an important anthology in the field. He is the author of *The Interrupted Spectacle* (1981), *Reflexivity in Film and Literature* (1985) and *Subversive Pleasures: Bakhtin, Cultural Criticism and Film* (1989), and co-author of

New Vocabularies in Film Semiotics (1991) with Robert Burgoyne and Sandy Flitterman-Lewis and *Multiculturism* (forthcoming) with Ella Shohat.

Nissa Torrents died tragically in September 1992 just as this book was going to press. She was Senior Lecturer in Latin American Literature and Film Studies at University College, University of London, and the co-ordinator of Postgraduate Cultural Studies at the Institute of Latin American Studies. She wrote numerous articles on cinema and a book co-edited with John King, *The Garden of the Forking Paths: Argentine Cinema* (1987). This book is dedicated to her memory, in recognition of her contribution to the field.

Michael Wood is Professor of English at the University of Exeter. His books include *America in the Movies*, and works on Stendahl and Gabriel García Márquez. He is a regular contributor to the *New York Review of Books*.

Ismail Xavier teaches Cinema Studies at the University of São Paulo. He is the former director of Embrafilme's publishing department, a frequent collaborator with *Filme Cultura* and the author of numerous books. His most recent titles include *Sertão/Mar: Glauber Rocha e a estética da fome* (1983), *D W Griffith: o nasciemento de un cinema* (1984) and *O Desafio do Cinema* (co-authored, 1985).

GENERAL INTRODUCTION

JOHN KING, ANA M. LÓPEZ, MANUEL ALVARADO

Vivez, heureuse gent, sans peine et sans souci.
Vivez joyeusement, je voudrais vivre ainsi.
> Pierre de Ronsard in the 1530s on the Brazilian Indian[1]

Brazil plays a sort of giant chlorophyll role for the whole of humanity. It is the planetary accumulator of joy, elation, languor, physical animality and seduction, coupled with vital exuberance and political derision. If ever the human race should fall into depression, it is there that it would regain its vitality, just as if it should ever be near to suffocation, it is beside the Amazon that it would get its breath back.

> Jean Baudrillard[2]

So 1992 came and went. Spain hosted the Olympics and the World's Fair and marked five hundred years since its unification, the expulsion of the Moors and its role in the first encounter between Europe and the Americas.

It now seems likely that a Viking ship had visited North America hundreds of years before the Spanish expedition. Ivan Van Sertima has provided persuasive evidence that there were long-standing trading links between Africa and the more southerly parts of the Americas.[3] Nevertheless, it was the historic voyage of Cristóbal Colón which provided the initial impetus for the decisive transformation produced by the wholesale colonisation of the Americas by Europeans.

When Bernal Díaz del Castillo, a soldier in Cortés's conquering army, first saw Mexico City he compared it to the wonders explored in sixteenth-century chivalric romances:

When we saw all those cities and villages built in the water and other great towns on dry land, and that straight and level causeway leading to Mexico, we were astounded. These great towns and *cues* and buildings rising from the water, all made of stone, seemed like an enchanted vision from the tale of Amadis. Indeed, some of our soldiers asked whether it was not all a dream.[4]

From the very first encounters, the Americas excited in the European imagination a host of mythical and legendary images. In the crisis of representation caused by the experience of the new world, conquistadors and chroniclers turned to the language of medieval romance. Hernán Cortés himself would read these romances to his soldiers and figures from these fictions would then appear in their accounts of their travels. In 1510 the sixth volume of the Amadis cycle, *Sergas de Esplandián*, appeared and quickly went through a number of editions. In it there is mention of Calafia, queen of an Amazon race which lived on a rugged island celebrated for 'an abundance of gold and jewels'. Cortés's fourth letter to the King of Spain bears the exhilarating news of a sighting of this fabled kingdom:

> The lords of the province of Ciguatán ... affirm that there is an island inhabited only by women, without a single man, and that at certain times men go over from the mainland and have intercourse with them; the females born to those who conceive are kept, but the males are sent away. This island is ten days' journey from this province and many of those chiefs have been there and have seen it. They also told me that it was very rich in pearls and gold.[5]

When Cortés's men discovered this 'island' for themselves, they named it California, and it remained marked on the map as an island throughout the sixteenth century. The romances of chivalry thus named the location which, many years later, would provide the site for the dissemination of twentieth-century romance: Hollywood, an island similarly 'rich in pearls and gold', though without the radical sexual politics.

From Ronsard to Baudrillard, the European imagination has been fired by images of noble savages, luxuriant landscapes, and fantasies of the continent's hidden wealth. The sixteenth-century lust for gain that produced the image of El Dorado, a golden king whose body was spread with resin every morning and then sprinkled with gold, has been reworked over the centuries to symbolise the hope of new markets or civilisations or new fields for colonisation or the search for new frontiers.[6] But this regime of the marvellous was premised on the equation of the unknown distant lands with wealth and wonder, and the knowledge generated by the process of 'discovery' and colonisation eventually conquered the marvellous itself; the marvellous dreams would turn also into nightmares. Bernal Díaz was very conscious that the Aztecs, despite the scale of their buildings and the wealth of their markets, also committed human sacrifice and ingested part of their victims. And so alongside the golden kings and the cities of gold, wild men and cannibals also stalk the pages of the European chroniclers, as El Dorado turned dystopian. These conflicting images make up an 'imaginary of the other' which has been formed and reformed in the last five hundred years of unequal 'meetings' between the different worlds.

In the margins of European discourses of power, contemporary native records tell other stories of extremely complex cultures in hundreds of different languages.[7] One hundred million people lived in the great civilisations and cities of Tikal, Cuzco, Tenochtitlán, and in the plains and forests. A hundred years later some ten million remained. The accounts talk of a cultural death, but also of cultural resistance. After all, even amid a conquest – caught within the wheels of a resolutely uneven 'encounter' – the Amerindians also articulated their own vision of the unknown newcomers. They too had a 'marvellous', a prodigious 'new world' to think of, one based on their first encounters with radical difference, and which many of them could only imagine in terms of the artillery, weapons and ships of the Europeans – their technology – contributing directly to their own desires and fears.

The consequences of Columbus's voyages and those that followed him cannot be reversed. Anyone who lives in the Americas or Europe today has been shaped – consciously or unconsciously, as victim, conqueror, or both – by that five-hundred-year history of voyages, desires, and cross-fertilisations. Among other things, as Hobsbawm argues, 1492 signals the start of Eurocentric history, but it also marks the impossibility of conceiving of that history as a totalising project.[8] The very process of 'imagining' the Americas described above established the dialectic of the frontier and the 'other' – as lure (desire, profit, curiosity) and danger (death) – as the cornerstone of the post-encounter imagination and thus of its modes of representation. If (from a Eurocentric perspective) the conquest was a time when, as Guillermo Giucci argues, 'to have seen was less important than to have heard someone's tale',[9] then the cinema marks the apogee of the historical trajectory that dispelled the discourse of the encounter's marvellous-unknown (based on the word and the tale) and demanded the centrality of vision and the ability to see.

Albeit a late addition, the cinema has participated fully in this logic of the encounter. Both colonising – used to appropriate and tame others, to make them 'marvellous', to ravage and pillage – and an essential addition to the technological repertoire of 'marvels' imported from abroad, the cinema has always functioned as a mediator between different worlds. Irredeemably flawed by the unequal distribution of wealth, power and technology, the mediation has not been balanced, but its existence is nowhere more visible than in the relationship among the cinemas of Latin America, Europe and the USA.

Mediating Two Worlds is addressed precisely to the exploration of the echoes of this cinematic 'encounter'. When the cinema arrived in Latin America, about six months after the Lumière premiere at the Grand Café in Paris, the former colonies were already peripheric yet an essential part of the nascent capitalist world system. The cinema's appeal in this Latin American context was manifold and would develop gradually: from technological wonder and curiosity and the desire for self-representation, to the potential for profit and the seeming ability to generate a classless 'mass' audience and thus, symbolically, the nation itself. Although the essays we have gathered here cannot possibly offer a complete historical chronology of the 'encounter' between the technologies and cinemas of Europe, the USA and Latin America, we have attempted to chart some of the complex mediations that have determined the nature and development of that history. *Mediating Two Worlds* is best thought of as a 'map' of different ways of seeing and being seen; as an attempt to off-centre contemporary essentialist debates about multiculturalism and 'otherness' by exploring, in depth, the consequences of

xix

difference for the theory, practice and criticism of the cinema of and about Latin America.

However, the book's organisation – unlike that of most maps – is designed to throw into relief the sites where vision and knowledge are produced. The first part looks at the North American and European visions of Latin America, from the Western to Werner Herzog, and attempts to present a number of vantage points from which to consider questions of difference and its representation. Thus, for example, a group of essays traces the trajectory of Hollywood's 'imagined' relationship to Latin America; from the appropriation of foreign 'otherness' (Margarita de Orellana's piece on Hollywood's treatment of the Mexican revolution in the silent cinema) and the generic play involved in the creation of ethnic differences (Ed Buscombe's essay on *The Magnificent Seven*), to the historical forces impinging on the creation of places for 'others' both by classic Hollywood cinema (Chon Noriega's analysis of the place of Chicano citizenship and Ana López's exploration of Latina representation during the years of the Good Neighbor policy), and by contemporary US films (James Dunkerley's assessment of Hollywood's treatment of Central America). Another group deals directly with the 'European' look: Michael Wood's essay on Buñuel's productive sojourn in Mexico, Laura Podalsky's analysis of Eisenstein's reconfiguration of Mexico as the primitive, Thomas Elsaesser's reading of the work of Francesco Rosi and Werner Herzog. Yet a third group looks from other sites: Jean Franco crosses the US/Europe border by analysing the representation of indigenous peoples in *The Emerald Forest*, *The Mission* and *Fitzcarraldo*, while John Hess traces the influence of Italian neo-realism on the development of a New Latin American Cinema. However, we could also group these essays from a non-geographical perspective according to how they approach the question of difference/influence, ranging from appropriation to (re)creation and transformation. We hope that the brief contextualising notes that precede each essay help to further establish the theoretical and geographical connections among them.

The second half of the book offers a number of essays which provide new scholarship on almost one hundred years of Latin American cinema. Some essays deal specifically with the theme of conquest or metaphorical encounters (Ismail Xavier's analysis of the Brazilian Cinema Novo's appropriation of the idea of the conquest, Robert Stam's multicultural study of the representation of race). Others explore, in various fashions, the way in which boundaries are constantly traversed in the process of transculturation,[10] and the paradoxical centrality of nationalist discourses in the Latin American cinema. Thus Carlos Monsiváis, Ana López and Nissa Torrents, from different perspectives and focusing on different eras, address the relationship between the cinema and the nation in Mexico; Randal Johnson and Paul Lenti analyse the role of the state/nation dichotomy in film production in Brazil and Colombia; Tim Barnard and Kathleen Newman focus, respectively, on Cuba and Argentina to unpack questions of the national; and, finally, Julianne Burton-Carvajal, Rosa Linda Fregoso and Marvin D'Lugo problematise their discussions of the 'nation' (real or imagined) by questioning the gendering of nationalist discourses in the Chicano, Mexican and Cuban cinemas.

We pass by in silence the attempts of the international film industry to mark the quincentenary of the encounter. Predictably enough, they scarcely rose above the customary banalities of the Hollywood biopic. (In *Christopher Columbus: The Discovery*, the hero remarks to his wife about his ship the *Santa Maria*: 'She's a fine vessel, a bit top-heavy and too narrow in the beam. Not unlike someone I know.')[11] This book is not, after all, about 1492, or even 1992. It has a more diffused focus. It attempts to look beyond anniversaries, and across borders, across hemispheres, at a process which promises even more dynamic encounters in the years ahead.

Notes

1. Quoted in John Hemming, *Red Gold: The Conquest of the Brazilian Indians* (London: Macmillan 1978).
2. Jean Baudrillard, *Cool Memories* (London: Verso 1990).
3. Ivan Van Sertima, *They Came Before Columbus* (New York: Random House, 1976).
4. Bernal Díaz in 1580, commenting on the Cortés conquest of Mexico City in 1519. See Bernal Díaz, *The Conquest of New Spain* (Harmondsworth: Penguin, 1963), p. 214.
5. Hernán Cortés's *Letters from Mexico* (New Haven and London: Yale University Press, 1986), pp. 298, 300.
6. See John Silver, 'The Myth of El Dorado', *History Workshop Journal*, No. 34, Autumn 1992, pp. 1–16.
7. Gordon Brotherston, *Book of the Fourth World: Reading the Native Americans through their Literature* (Cambridge: Cambridge University Press, 1993).
8. Eric Hobsbawm, 'Goodbye Columbus', *London Review of Books*, 9 July 1992, pp. 14–15.
9. Guillermo Giucci, *Viajantes do Maravilhoso: O Novo Mundo* (São Paulo: Companhia das Letras, 1992), p. 110.
10. As Rowe and Schelling usefully define it, transculturation is the opposite of acculturation, or the one-way process of conversion and substitution of native cultures by European ones. It 'is used to counter critically the assumption that acculturation is the only long-term possibility for Latin America: it is concerned with the mutual transformation of cultures, in particular of European by the native'. William Rowe and Vivian Schelling, *Memory and Modernity: Popular Culture in Latin America* (London: Verso, 1991), p. 18.
11. There were three Columbus films during the year: *Christopher Columbus: The Discovery* (dir. John Glen, USA); *1492: Conquest of Paradise* (dir. Ridley Scott, USA); *Carry On Columbus* (dir. Gerald Thomas, UK).

At Iguaçu Falls filming The Mission *(Roland Joffe, GB, 1986)*

PART I

THE CIRCULAR LOOK

The Incursion of North American Fictional Cinema 1911–1917 into the Mexican Revolution

MARGARITA DE ORELLANA

Editors' Introduction

Margarita de Orellana's essay is taken from her recently published book, *La mirada circular* (The Circular Look), which analyses North American documentary and fictional cinema about the Mexican revolution. The timespan of 1911–17 covers the armed phase of the revolution. In this period, Mexico (filtered through the lenses of the film-makers, whose ideas were also filtered through the stereotypes of the dime novels of the late nineteenth and early twentieth century) became a constant and extremely popular presence on North American screens. The United States followed events down south very closely and had ambiguous, inconsistent views of successive leaders. Taft supported Madero, but a year later Woodrow Wilson played an important part in the plot of General Huerta against him. Wilson later moved against Huerta and also against Pancho Villa, helping the Constitutionalist General Carranza to defeat the revolutionary leader. Wilson then moved against Carranza. The newsreel men, and even the fiction film-makers, cut their footage to suit the policy of the day. The main star of the show, a presence that beguiled all the journalists and movie-makers, from John Reed to Raoul Walsh, was Pancho Villa. Villa even signed a film contract with Mutual Film Corporation and, in return for $25,000, gave them exclusive rights to film 'his' war. Villa, after all, was the only military leader in the world who, since the war of 1812, had attacked the metropolitan territory or the United States and managed to escape, despite the attentions of a punitive expedition of more than ten thousand men sent out to capture him.

Margarita de Orellana reveals that, despite these official changes in US policy, a consistent range of stereotypes is used to describe the 'other', the Mexican people. She analyses these under the categories of the bandit/revolutionary, the greaser, the beautiful señorita and the frontier. Her work, developed in the late 70s and early 80s, draws on the pioneering work of Edward Said on orientalism and predates Tzvetan Todorov's idiosyncratic but suggestive study, *La Conquête de l'Amérique, la question de l'autre* (Paris: Editions du Seuil, 1982; translated as *The Conquest of*

3

America, New York: Harper and Row 1984). She reveals clearly in her study of the North American 'imaginary', that zone of conscious or unconscious collective images, how the history of this cinema is the 'history of a directed gaze and its transformations, the history of a circular look'.

□

MANIFEST DESTINY ON SCREEN

Between 1910 and 1919 the Mexican revolution was reported daily in the main US newspapers; it was also a central issue for newsreel companies. The continuous presence of this revolution in the public life of the United States for almost ten years also extended to feature film. Many love stories or adventure films were played out against the background of the 'Mexican War'.

The film producers could hardly fail to exploit the public interest in a war that was narrated in the press in daily episodes, as if it were a serial. Its central protagonists had many of the features of the typical heroes and villains of legend and adventure; the violence of their encounters was described in minute and often exaggerated detail against the background of an exotic nature populated by equally exotic Mexicans. Further, this was a story that involved North Americans in a number of ways; the US public were sensitive to the violence that threatened those of their compatriots who lived beyond the Rio Grande or near the border.

Apart from the specific interests of the US government in the Mexican revolution, public opinion often debated whether US forces should or should not invade their southern neighbour. It was even proposed that Theodore Roosevelt should become president of the country to bring an end to the prevailing chaos and anarchy. Indeed, Roosevelt's presidential address of 1904 had referred to the concept of 'manifest destiny' to which many advocates of US intervention in Mexico now returned. There was a kind of naïvety in the arguments of those who, like an editorial writer in the US newspaper *The Independent*, argued that the extension southwards of the US border 'would be, not for our own benefit, but for the good of the people in those troubled regions, in defence of the peace and good order of the Western hemisphere whose guardians we are in fact and by right'.[1] It was generally believed that it was thanks to the United States that those countries in the world whose governments were democratically elected would gradually evolve towards the kind of democratic society in which Americans believed themselves to be living.

These and other arguments about whether US intervention in the Mexican war was or was not necessary helped to maintain the interest of a potential public for films about the Mexican revolution. It is not surprising, therefore, that the central characters of many such feature films should be North Americans carrying democratic virtues to the Mexicans.

One of the best examples is John Emerson's film *The Americano*, starring

Spottiswoode Aitkin, Alma Rubens and Douglas Fairbanks Sr in The Americano *(John Emerson, USA, 1916)*

Douglas Fairbanks Sr and with a script by Anita Loos (writer of *Gentlemen Prefer Blondes*). In this film, as in many others concerned with Mexico, the names of the country and the political protagonists are replaced by parodies, primarily in order to avoid diplomatic problems. The characterisations and the political situations, however, are easily identifiable for a public that could recognise in them actual or very recent events. Fairbanks, the Americano of the title, represents the great white hope of a chaotic Latin American country called Paragonia. He is a seductive, ingenious, audacious and above all omnipotent hero.

An official representative of Paragonia arrives at the mine engineering company where Fairbanks works and asks him to intervene in a conflict with the miners. He explains that there is an atmosphere of tension in his country and that a threatened revolution has spread panic among its inhabitants. Fairbanks initially rejects the official's requests, but recants when he meets the daughter of the country's president, the weak and well-meaning Valdés (who clearly represents President Madero). Valdés explains that he is powerless since 'without American capital and American engineers the mines are useless'; a wink from his daughter Juana is then sufficient to persuade Fairbanks to help Paragonia.

When he arrives in the country Fairbanks discovers that Valdés has been overthrown by a General Gargaras, who now wishes to marry Juana. Fairbanks decides to participate in the revolution on the side of Valdés, who at that point is in prison. While he is rescuing him, the new rulers also seek Fairbanks's help in dealing with the miners, but he ignores them. The attempted rising against the generals fails, and it is only with the help of the

5

Americano that the counter-revolution is successfully carried through, Valdés restored and Gargaras (representing Huerta) overcome. The Americano marries Juana and also becomes armed forces minister in the Paragonian government; it is only through him that the light of reason, democracy and freedom can return to Paragonia.

The generals sport the long moustaches and suspicious glances typical of *mestizo* villains. The people of Mexico, for their part, appear in the final scene of the film all dressed in white and wearing wide sombreros, while the women are wrapped in shawls. With one voice they call for their saviour, the Americano, to appear on the balcony. When he does he announces, 'I am here to ensure that the mines keep working and the country is governed with justice and honour'.

A number of silent films dramatised the mission of the American nation. *The Aztec Treasure* (1914) portrays a rising led by an American, Dick Henshaw, against the oppressive governor of a Mexican province. Dick is captured but manages to escape, kill the cruel governor, marry the sensual Mexican woman and rediscover the Aztec treasure which provides the means to improve the lot of the people. They then 'call' him to govern them. *Captain King's Rescue* (1914) and *Captain Alvarez* (1914) repeat the formula with minor variations. But *The Americano* remains the best synthesis of the films of this type, as well as pointing ahead to the films produced after the revolution which repeat the same idea – that Mexicans are incapable of carrying out a struggle for democracy without the assistance of the United States.

Such films were shown exclusively to American audiences; the majority of them served, albeit unintentionally, as didactic material on 'manifest destiny'. A central theme was the heroism and superiority of the United States, whose citizens alone were portrayed as capable of bringing peace, order, justice and progress to a country like Mexico.

Many of these films offered commentaries on the most important events of the revolution. For example, from the beginning of the revolution the rebels bought arms from the United States. When Madero came to power in 1911 the US government prohibited the export of arms, though it sometimes turned a blind eye, especially when the recipients were the Constitutionalists, the enemies of General Huerta. President Wilson wanted the fall of Huerta (who had assassinated and replaced Madero) at all costs, and a tolerance of arms smuggling was an indirect form of support for the armies which later overthrew the dictator. This contraband in arms was also the topic of several films. *Mexican Filibusters* (1911) showed the smuggling of arms to those fighting the dictatorship of Porfirio Díaz as an act of patriotism, while condemning the treachery of some Mexicans. In subsequent films the same paradox recurred. In *The Gun Smugglers* (1912) the hero of the film is a loyal officer of the Mexican government who prevents the smuggling operations; but in the same year *The Colonel's Escape* represents the cross-border passage of arms to a group of rebels as an act of patriotism.

THE PERSHING EXPEDITION DRAMATISED

The year-long punitive expedition into Mexico led by General Pershing in retaliation for Pancho Villa's raid on the town of Columbus provided the cinema with another opportunity to intervene directly in events. The most important of these films, *Liberty, a Daughter of the USA* (1916), underlined the urgency of US intervention in Mexico. At one point, for example, one of the protagonists says, 'Mexico is a country infested by bandits who are threatening the security of the United States, of its citizens and its most elementary democratic principles'. Other films in the same series praised the patriotism of the US soldiers stationed along the frontier and insisted on the obligation of the US government to employ military means to 'protect the country'. In films like *Lieutenant Danny USA* and *The Patriot*, both made in 1916, the expedition provided an opportunity for further exhortations closely linked to the intense debate then arising around the need for the USA to prepare to enter the First World War.

In 1914 the US blockade of the Mexican port of Veracruz provoked films like *The Insurrection* (1915) and *The Mexican Sniper's Revenge* (1914), whose clear purpose was to justify US intervention. A third film on the same theme, *Uncle Sam in Mexico* (1914), provided the production company with the opportunity to underscore the marriage of high drama and historical truth which gave the film its particular quality:

> Díaz, Villa, Huerta and Madero are responsible for the situation which required the intervention of *Uncle Sam in Mexico*. The death of the first American hero at Veracruz has brought to the center of world attention the historic steps taken by Uncle Sam. The best literary minds have been employed to crystallize these events in the universal language of images.

All these historical fictions set in the Mexican revolution were at pains to stress their realism. On the other side, the newsreel-makers were also anxious to make films that would attract the public.

From the industry's point of view, it was logical that, having sent their cameramen to the front and used their material in newsreels, they should then use the same takes in longer documentary features about the same battles or in more dramatic montages. This was the case with the Mutual Film Corporation's *The Life of General Villa* (1914) – but with the difference that the best battle scenes were in fact studio re-creations. Producers soon realised that film shot on the actual field of battle was not particularly appealing to the public, and that reality seemed more convincing dressed up in the studio than photographed direct.

The Mexican revolution also offered training for cameramen who later filmed the battlefields of the First World War. Yet, as one of them (Louis Powell) observed,

> The actual field of battle bears no resemblance to the public conception of it. There is no glory, no banners waving in the air, no shouts of encouragement from the rank and file nor shouted orders from the officers – there is nothing even remotely spectacular about it.[2]

Homer Croy, historian of the war newsreel, has noted that 'the war front simply could not compete with the studio; the best war footage was made in Los Angeles, California'.[3]

The American fiction films of the early years of the revolution were mainly shorts of two to four reels (where each reel lasted around 10 minutes). Their relatively brief production time and the producers' wish to insert their films into the political reality meant that many of these films served as dramatic commentaries on the main events of the Mexican revolution. In fact, a significant number of them were made by two companies. The Lubin enterprise, which produced at least 20, made its first film in 1897 and was quite successful until 1914. Kalem, which produced around 10 such films, was based in Chicago and had to its credit the great box office success *Ben Hur* (1908). It was also responsible for a film set in Mexico which was notable for its differences from the eighty or so feature films set in the revolution and produced between 1911 and 1917. *The Mexican Joan of Arc* was made in July 1911, just two months after the departure of the ex-dictator Porfirio Díaz. It referred to the cruelty and injustice of his regime, and recounted the true story of a woman who took arms against it after the arbitrary killing of her husband and children. The film went beyond its melodramatic and exotic elements to achieve an exceptional epic power in its portrayal of the popular rising. Further, its publicity stressed the fact that it was filmed in Mexico using Mexican actors.

The many adventure stories created by North Americans to portray what was happening beyond their southern border were located in that area which might tentatively be described as the 'imaginary representation of the "other"'. It does have a geographical location, on the southern frontier, an area open to moral expansion just as the West had been in the previous century. This zone of the imaginary 'other' also had its inhabitants – the 'greasers', caught midway between love and war. The conquest of the 'other' begins with the seduction of their women who for the white man represent both a temptation and a challenge.

Mexico, with its chaotic revolution and its dark-skinned population, has always offered to Americans the exemplary expression of the 'other'. It is often the opposite, negative image to the positive perception that the United States has of itself. The feature films made during the Mexican revolution, as well as many made later, belong then in this imaginary zone in the encounter between the frontier, the greaser (bandit or revolutionary?), and the beautiful señorita.

THE FRONTIER

The Mexican side of the frontier, as it appears in North American films, has an air of anarchy and confusion. The frontier zone is a place of adventures and danger. From the North American point of view it became an even more dangerous place during the revolution, and to cross the line was to immediately enter an area of high risk. In *A Prisoner of Mexico* (1911), for example, Ethel is thrown into despair when she finds herself accidentally trapped on a train travelling across the frontier. She falls into the hands of Mexican federal soldiers and it is her American lover who rescues her from the consequent danger and returns her to her native land where peace and harmony reign.

Saved by the Flag (1911) follows a North American couple pursued by Mexican soldiers. They just manage to cross the border before they are caught and, tearing down the flag from the customs post flagpole, wrap themselves in it as a challenge to the Mexicans waiting on the other side. *Lieutenant Danny*, for his part, enters hostile Mexican territory twice to rescue two endangered Mexican women, one of whom he loves.

The frontier that divides Mexicans from Americans crosses many of the feature films concerned with the revolution; it is not always visible, but it is present in the narrative, in however diluted a form, emphasising the contrast. In the USA the population enjoys a security that stems from order and democracy. The other side of the Rio Grande is dark and confusing, a place of exile for all sorts of North American ruffians fleeing from the law of their own country, a land of bandits, arbitrary crimes and perpetrators who go unpunished. Over there it is evil, and it is those who provoke disorder and chaos who are protected.

When these films about the Mexican revolution began to appear it was already twenty years since the USA had officially ended its territorial expansion and frontiers had been fixed, for the United States had reached the Pacific seaboard. The Rio Grande thus became the definitive dividing line between the two countries. Yet despite the fact that the river was a fixed frontier, the separation was not made at all explicit in the feature films about the revolution. Suddenly the border dissolved into a North American conception of the frontier, that area of movement that separated the inhabited areas from those yet to be settled and which represented the outer limit of the civilised world. Implicit in F. J. Turner's famous frontier thesis[4] was a defence of forced expansion, a justification of the Americans' colonisation of the West in pursuit of the extension of territory to the Pacific ocean, during which they rode roughshod over Indians and Mexicans alike. This expansionism was justified with an arrogance that was particularly extreme in relation to the Mexicans. In 1829, for example, the editorialist of the *Nashville Republican* discovered that the Rio Grande divided the fertile lands destined for an industrious North American people from 'the unproductive lands where crops do not ripen for lack of irrigation; these are destined for a nation of miners, shepherds and idlers like the Mexicans'.[5]

In 1850 Minister Gadsden argued that the river was an inadequate border and urged the Mexicans to sell to the United States the six provinces north of the Sierra Madre. A decade later, Senator Nye suggested that Mexico should simply be entirely incorporated to 'ensure the symmetry of the Republic'. But none went quite as far as Thomas Green, who asserted that the isthmus of Panama was 'our natural frontier, because it comes at the point where the two great oceans of the world meet'.[6]

North American films invariably sympathised with this expansionism in one sense or another, and their arrogance was reflected in the characterisation of both Mexicans and North Americans and in scripts which always cast in the worst light those on the other side of the border. The land there was often presented as empty virgin desert full of snakes, scorpions, tarantulas and cactus. When a North American went into the wilderness he became a kind of animal at ease in such a landscape. It was as if the hostile environment he

9

faced gave him the same strength that the pioneers discovered in themselves when they were conquering the West. These strange lands thus came to represent the continuation of those other lands previously colonised.

Just as the Western evoked the history immediately prior to the conquest of the West, so the fiction films of the Mexican revolution may unwittingly have pointed to a new colonisation, the domination of a new frontier – an allegorical journey confirmed by the very way in which the landscape was portrayed.

The exploits of the North Americans in such terrain are represented in the individual heroes of films like *The American Insurrecto* (1911), *His Mexican Sweetheart* (1912) or *The Mexican Spy* (1913), where the North American lovers escape certain death at the hands of Mexican soldiers led by a spy. Yet despite the hostile environment, both continue their journey into the new lands. The Mexican inhabitants of these regions were part of nature; they were often presented as a collective, anonymous mass confronted by a single, individual, named North American.

THE 'GREASER' – BANDIT OR REVOLUTIONARY?
In *Bronco Billy's Redemption* (1910) a dying man needs medicines to save his life. A Mexican agrees to go and buy them but spends the money on the way and loses the prescription. In *The Cowboy's Baby* (1910) a Mexican throws the hero's small son into the river, while *Captured by Mexicans* (1914) shows a Mexican trying to murder a group of Americans who just a little earlier had saved his life.

Innate violence is the Mexican characteristic most often emphasised by North Americans; for them the Mexican is a villain capable of all kinds of criminal excess. From the beginning the North American cinema has portrayed the Mexican as irresponsible, treacherous, vengeful and prey to an uncontrolled sexuality. He is also represented physically in a specific way: his poncho and wide sombrero become a kind of uniform added to his dark skin and wide moustache. Silent-screen actors would often paint their faces when portraying their southern neighbours, and this served the extra purpose of distinguishing the good from the evil people. Indeed, in many films Mexicans were directly referred to contemptuously as 'greasers', as in *The Greaser's Revenge* (1911), *Tony the Greaser* (1911), *Bronco Billy and the Greaser* (1914), and D. W. Griffith's *The Greaser's Gauntlet* (1910). In these films these greasy characters are not just common villains; they actually enjoy carrying their violence to extremes. In describing the 'greasers', North Americans were not trying to suggest that all Mexicans were like those represented on the screen. Their object rather was to present the Mexican as a representative foreigner, to give the 'other' a shape and form in films directed principally to a North American audience. As they demeaned the 'other', the North Americans covered themselves in virtue. This formula was not born with the cinema, of course; many of the characteristics ascribed to the screen Mexicans were inherited from nineteenth-century North American literature where many of these stereotypes were born. Even a writer like W. H. Prescott, the great historian of the conquest of Mexico, saw in the Mexican a degenerate descendant of the Aztec inheritance, while Kate Chopin, in her excellent novel

10

The Awakening, has one of her characters articulate a common late-nineteenth-century view of Mexicans: 'Madame Ratignolle hoped that her friend Robert would exercise extreme caution in dealing with the Mexicans, who she considered were a treacherous people, unscrupulous and vengeful'.

North American cinema later extended, emphasised and deepened such conceptions of the Mexicans, for it was cinema that provided Americans with most of their ideas about Mexico and Latin America. As Walter Lippman put it, 'Americans would do anything for Latin America except read about it'.

When the Mexican revolution first appeared in films, the 'greaser' already had a history, having earlier played a particular role in various kinds of film, particularly in the Western. Despite the fact that most North American films about the revolution display an overt sympathy with the revolutionaries, especially between 1911 and 1914, it is difficult to distinguish between the typical 'greaser' and the revolutionary fighting for a cause, especially since that cause is rarely referred to in anything other than the most abstract ways. The 'revolutionaries' act exactly as the 'greasers' do in other films – with violence and cruelty – and even though they are sometimes capable of acts of heroism, like the cowboys of the Westerns, the fact that they are dressed as

Raoul Walsh, Miriam Cooper and Elmer Clifton in The Greaser *(Raoul Walsh, USA, 1915)*

11

Mexicans robs them of any heroic dimension they might otherwise have. The Mexican revolutionary thus automatically becomes a kind of sub-cowboy.

It is very rare for Mexicans to be described as people capable of struggle or heroism; on the contrary, vengeance and treachery are their more usual characteristics. *A Mexican Tragedy* (1913), for example, has as its central character a hotel proprietor who betrays his daughter's lover for money and ends by murdering his son in error. In *Blotted Out* (1914) a federal general sells the plans of the arsenal to the insurgents, betrays his brother in arms, and finally pays for his treachery with his own accidental death. There are times when sympathy for the revolution allows a film-maker to ascribe positive responses to the revolutionaries and to demonise the government. *The Mexican Revolutionist* (1912) shows a rebel saving the life of a threatened woman, while in *Mexico* (1914) López joins the revolution to avenge the cruelty of a federal officer. The differences between the opposing factions, however, are never explored; the battle is between good and evil. It is a different matter when it comes to conflicts between Mexicans and North Americans, in which the Mexican almost automatically becomes the bandit – *His Mexican Sweetheart* and *Uncle Sam in Mexico*, among others, are examples.

The North American is portrayed as having a superior intelligence and a high moral quality which ensures that he will emerge victorious whatever the forces at the Mexicans' disposal. The mere fact of being American ensures his mission to dominate and regenerate the other. Sometimes Mexicans do redeem themselves, usually when they accept the authority of their white superiors and betray their own people. In *The Bravery of Dora* (1914), for instance, a Mexican–American finds himself caught in a battle between Mexicans and North Americans. At first he refuses to fire on the people, but when Dora Miller, whom he loves, is wounded, he takes up a gun. Captured by the Mexicans and condemned to death, he is saved by North American soldiers. In fact, it is often Mexican women who most readily betray their own kind and submit themselves unreservedly to the 'superior race', for they invariably succumb to the gallant and 'refined' northerners.

THE BEAUTIFUL SEÑORITA

A US army lieutenant is the rival in love to a Mexican general in *Saved by the Flag* (1911). The two men have succumbed to the charms of a sensual Mexican girl who clearly prefers the North American. The Mexican, his pride hurt, decides to take revenge, but he fails when the couple take refuge in the United States, where the Mexican cannot act with the same freedom as in his own country.

In the majority of the films considered here Mexican women, faced with a choice between a Mexican and an American, invariably opt for the latter. In *Saved by the Flag* a Mexican general is worth less than a middle-ranking American officer. Other films draw the same comparison: *His Mexican Sweetheart*, for instance, or *Sealed Orders* (1914), in which a Mexican woman who accompanies her brother on a spying mission to the United States falls in love with the object of their espionage. The US officer is saved thanks to the woman's betrayal; she then marries him. In *Captain Alvarez* the heroine

Bonita is forced into marriage with a Mexican but falls in love with Captain Alvarez, who proves to be an American in disguise. *Across the Border* (1914) allows a Mexican woman to save an American officer imprisoned by Mexican arms smugglers – and it is she who brings the cavalry.

In these films the American is invariably sensitive, moral and chaste, while the Mexican is endowed with an uncontrolled sexuality which often expresses itself through rape. In *The Mexican's Faith* (1910), a labourer attempts to rape the rancher's wife, in *Mexico* a Mexican federal soldier assaults Villa's wife, while in *Lieutenant Danny USA* it is only the intervention of an American lieutenant that saves the Mexican girl from violation by a group of Mexican bandits.

At another level what is happening in the American imagination represented here is the appropriation of the 'other' through his women, in the hope of thus subjecting or taming the supposedly wild sexuality of the Mexican, of bringing under control an excess of passion. While they take over the Mexican women, however, there is never any question of a union between an American woman and a Mexican man (the only film in which an American woman marries a Mexican is *A Species of Mexican Man* (1914); but she then becomes president of the country). They guard their women against any contact with the rapist greasers. In the context of these films, the 'other' is thus doubly humiliated.

If the greaser or the bandit are representative Mexicans, why this fascination with Mexican women? Unlike their men, the women of Mexico are ascribed very different qualities, among them docility and sensuality. The representative of Mexican women is the 'beautiful señorita', a figure as picturesque as the greaser but not as deprecated. The model of the beautiful señorita is not the *mestiza* or the Indian but the white *criolla* or Spanish woman. Thus the Mexican woman appears superior to her male counterparts because she is Spanish. None the less, she is an exotic figure; the point is to make her attractive, and while she is more acceptable than the Mexican man represented on screen because she belongs to a higher social class, she remains culturally and racially inferior to the North American.

Generally speaking, the beautiful señorita sports long dark hair and long eyelashes which underscore her capacity for seduction with a look. Often in these films her shoulders are bare, and she wears Spanish folk costume with tight waist and raised breasts. Despite her disturbing appearance, the beautiful señorita is innocent and sweet, although full of passion. Surrounded by bandits, she nevertheless remains pure; it is her passion that matters. Thus, in *Sealed Orders*, passion and duty clash in the psychology of the beautiful Mexican woman. Love wins out, of course, but love for an American. Her docility in the face of the 'superior race' points to the central feature of the beautiful señorita: she is seductive, but obedient.

The character comes straight from the pages of the dime and romantic novels published in serial form in the USA in the 19th century. Many of the romantic plots in these and the Western films derive directly from those novels. The characterisation of the 'other', of the greaser, and the range of dramatic incidents on the frontier are already present in these writings and are later transferred to the screen where they are given a more immediate political reference. In this sense it can be argued that, given its characterisations and its imaginary universe, the fiction films about the Mexican revolution represent a meeting-point between the popular literature of the American South, the popular press reports of the revolution, the newsreel and the Western.

These films belong to the history of the representation of the 'other', the history of the imagination of a country thrown into turmoil by the closeness of someone different. There are a multiplicity of images, judgments and narratives about this neighbouring 'other', but rarely will it be given an opportunity to offer its own image of difference. This 'other' is a mirror on whose imperfect but sparkling surface the North Americans may glimpse the image of themselves they need to see. In any event, the American cinema about the Mexican revolution shows us that glance which invariably returns to itself confirmed and reaffirmed after its long journeys through the 'other'.

The history of the revolution through the fictional and newsreel films of North America is simply the history of the self-directed gaze and its transformations, the history of a circular look.

(Translated by Mike Gonzales)

Notes

For a more detailed discussion of the topic see Margarita de Orellana, *La mirada circular: el cine norteamericano de la revolución mexicana 1911–1917* (México: Joaquín Mortiz, 1991). See also Emilio García Riera, *México visto por el cine extranjero 1906–1940*, vols 1 and 2 (México: Ediciones Era y Universidad de Guadalajara, 1987).
1. 'No binding our hands', *The Independent*, LXXXVII, 1916.
2. Quoted by David Mould in *American Newsfilm 1914–1919: The Unexposed War* (Lawrence: University Press of Kansas, 1980), p. 146.
3. *Ibid.*, p. 146.
4. In 1893 Frederick James Turner presented an essay entitled 'The Significance of the Frontier in American History'. It argued that the frontier continually expanding into free land was the single most important factor in the make-up of the American character. The frontier experience differentiated American from European history; it developed a nation based on principles of individualism, democracy, hard work and a belief in self-help. It has also allowed the nation to constantly renew itself and its values. See Alistair Hennessy, *The Frontier in Latin American History* (London: Edward Arnold, 1978).
5. Quoted in Albert Weinberg, *Manifest Destiny: A Study of Nationalist Expansionism in American History* (Chicago: Quadrangle Books, 1935), p. 58.
6. *Ibid.*, p. 56.
7. Kate Chopin, *The Awakening* (London: Women's Press, 1980).

THE MAGNIFICENT SEVEN

EDWARD BUSCOMBE

Editors' Introduction

In the Western, Mexicans have traditionally received a press scarcely better than the indigenous peoples of the North American plains. Characterised in the movies by being shifty, unreliable and weak, their country nevertheless all too often provides gringo outlaws with a goal or haven outside the reach of the embryonic forces of law and order in the American West. As Christopher Frayling writes:

> ... ever since the earliest silent Westerns ... Hollywood has had a love–hate relationship with the people and the landscape 'south of the border, down Mexico way'. Mexico has been presented as a place of escape, a refuge; a noisy exotic alternative; a place for seeking lost ideals; and – its most characteristic role – as a breeding ground for vicious (and apparently unmotivated) bandits. (In Edward Buscombe (ed.), *The BFI Companion to the Western* (London: BFI/André Deutsch, 1988).)

In his account of *The Magnificent Seven*, Edward Buscombe contextualises the film in the liberal conjuncture of the early 1960s. He shows how a Hollywood movie using Hollywood stars and made for US audiences does not offer a Mexican view of the Seven, but also argues that the fundamental problem the film-makers were concerned to address was not representation but how to construct the difference between the Mexicans and the Seven within a narrative which does not make the former seem essentially inferior, that is to say, not worth saving.

It is interesting to note here that in the Japanese film *The Seven Samurai* (Akira Kurosawa, 1954), of which *The Magnificent Seven* is a remake, the difference between the peasants and the samurai is essentially one between different classes in a feudal society. Hollywood, in a not untypical shift, transforms this class relation into an ethnic one.

Having then outlined the liberal qualities of the movie (qualities which give rise to many patronising and sentimental moments) Buscombe concludes by indicating how, within four years, the genre was going to be

15

irrevocably shifted by the arrival of the Italian Western. Ironically, Sergio Leone's representations of Mexico and Mexicans are in many ways little better than their precedents, but they operate within a world view which is more politically aware albeit in a far more nihilist way.

□

I

Soon after the start of *The Magnificent Seven* (John Sturges, 1960) we are introduced to Chris and Vin (Yul Brynner and Steve McQueen), the foremost of the Seven, who are idling time away in a small American border town. Sam, an Indian, has died. The undertaker is reluctant to bury him; the townspeople do not want him in their cemetery. A travelling salesman in ladies' corsets, shocked by such intolerance, is willing to pay, but no one will drive the hearse. (The film is progressive in its sexual as well as its racial politics: you do not have to be macho to stand up and be counted.) Chris and Vin offer their services; not, ostensibly, out of any obvious desire to do their bit for racial equality, but because they are bored and it promises some action. But it is evident that even though they make no speeches about it, they are prepared to contest the townspeople's prejudice, or they would not make the offer. And so we know that when they meet the Mexican villagers we have already been introduced to, they will treat them with respect.

The Magnificent Seven is very much a film of its time: aware of the legacy of Hollywood's previous encounters with Latin America, determined, in the best traditions of 1960s liberalism, to atone for the prejudices of the past. It takes the past history of Mexicans in the Western for granted, as well enough known.[1] In early cinema a Mexican was almost invariably a villain, cowardly, treacherous and lascivious, explicitly vilified as a 'greaser'.[2] After vigorous Mexican protests in the 1920s the worst excesses were toned down, but Hollywood films, especially Westerns, remained unable to conceive of any Mexican characters other than malevolent bandits or their peasant victims.[3] It has been well remarked that Mexico is the Western's id. South of the border is to the body politic of the Western what below the belt is in popular physiology – a place where dark desires run riot, a land not just of wine, women and song, but of rape, treachery and death.

By the end of *The Magnificent Seven* the bandit leader Calvera lies dying in the dust of the Mexican village he has pillaged. He looks up at Chris, the leader of the American mercenaries who have, against his expectations, returned to defeat him, and asks: 'You came back, to a place like this. Why? A man like you. Why?'.

No answer is given. For Calvera none is possible. He is incapable of understanding the motives of his adversaries, and this is the cause of his defeat. For Calvera, only selfishness makes sense. The sensible thing for the Seven to do when Calvera gains the upper hand would be to cut their losses and go home. Instead, they return to battle against huge odds and, though

Calvera is overcome, most of them are killed. Calvera has no way of comprehending their action, which is based on the mix of a quasi-existential sense of their own identity, and human fellow-feeling reinforced by a dose of liberal ideology.

For the audience of the film, Calvera's question has already been answered. The entire picture has been devoted to uncovering the motives of each and every one of the eponymous heroes of the film, explaining just why seven hardened professional gunmen should risk their lives in defending a poor Mexican village against bandits. This is a film which parades its good intentions. It is not a radical break with previous representations: the Mexicans on view are, as usual, bandits and peasants. But the film promises at least a liberal rethink, an attempt to treat the 'good' Mexicans with respect. It is with the attitudes towards these Mexicans on the part of the Seven that the film is primarily concerned. (It goes without saying that, since this is an American film made for American audiences, we do not learn much of the attitudes of the Mexicans to their American visitors.)

As so often in the Western, the central drama turns on Calvera's question of why the hero helps those with whom he has no obvious ties. Shane is not a farmer; why, then, does he help the farmers against the landowner who is oppressing them? Why does Will Kane, the marshal in *High Noon*, help the townspeople against the bad guys? They certainly do not help *him*. And why should the Seven help a group of peasants whom they have never met and who cannot pay them properly for their services?

In order to pose the question in its most dramatic form, the film needs to establish a distance between the two groups, the needed and the needy. It must emphasise the difference, the gap across which ties are to be formed. The conundrum *The Magnificent Seven* sets itself, therefore, is how to achieve this without showing one side as inferior and therefore the object of prejudice. The problem is especially difficult because the entire plot turns on the inability of the peasants to help themselves. They are weak against Calvera; the Americans are strong. How, then, can the peasants not be inferior?

The film deploys a number of strategies in establishing a difference which is not necessarily an inferiority. At the very beginning we see the village raided by Calvera. (Significantly, perhaps, the village is not given a name. It stands for all villages; it is villageness.) The raids have been going on for years. But this time things have gone too far. The peasants decide something must be done. But what? 'I don't know,' says one. 'We'll ask the old man. He'll know.' The old man functions as a kind of father-figure to the village, a repository of ancient wisdom and a source of stern admonition. He tells them they must get guns and kill Calvera. The peasants reply that they do not know how to. 'Then learn – or die,' he retorts.

The peasants, then, are children. The old man treats them with the patronising but indulgent exasperation of a father. To the Seven he explains: 'You must excuse them. They're farmers here, they're afraid of everyone and everything. They're afraid of rain, and no rain, the summer may be too hot, the winter too cold. The sow has no pigs, the farmer is afraid he may starve. She has too many pigs, he's afraid *she* may starve.' When the Seven arrive in the village they set about organising the peasants, teaching them how to fight.

17

The peasants come, cap in hand, to plead for help from Chris (Yul Brynner) in The Magnificent
Seven *(John Sturges, USA, 1960)*

Taking their cue from the old man, they explain everything carefully and
slowly, in terms even a child would understand. One of the Seven, Bernardo,
despairs of his pupils' lack of manly skills with a gun: 'I tell you what, don't
shoot the gun, take the gun like this and you use it like a club.' After the first
battle with Calvera, three of the Seven set out after some bandits who have
remained behind as snipers. Each of the three has some of the inhabitants of
the village with him, in a relationship of tutelage. Vin has one of the men of
the village, who confesses to feeling fear. Vin counsels him. Bernardo has
been adopted by three boys, who are in search of substitute fathers. Chico has
found a girl. The term is exact: not a woman, but a child bride. In each case
the relationship is based on the kind of awe a small child feels for its parents.

Calvera and his bandits are a monstrous parody of this parent–child relationship. The bandit leader tells the peasants they should be grateful for
their lot. Hasn't he always left them enough food to carry on? 'What if you
had to carry my load, huh? The need to provide food like a good father to fill
the mouths of his hungry men. Guns, ammunition. You know how much
that costs?' When the Seven are betrayed by some of the peasants, Calvera
explains that the Seven have failed to understand that the peasants need
authority, a father-figure. The Seven have tried to make them take their own
decisions. This is a mistake. 'With me, only one decision. Do what I say.'

The film both advances and resists the notion of peasants as children. The
Seven do have to teach the villagers, as a father teaches a child, but the

ultimate objective is self-sufficiency, so that when the Seven have gone the village can be responsible for itself. In the case of Calvera, the father–child relationship is a mere pretext for exploitation. But it is the good intentions of the Seven, their refusal to assume complete authority, which allows Calvera back in. Ultimately the situation can only be redeemed by the Seven taking responsibility once more. The peasants are not able to stand up by themselves. They *are* children. And it is this which allows the film to save its conscience. Children are weak, they need help. But one should not therefore despise children as inferior.

Another way in which difference is established is by presenting the peasants as part of the natural world. As feminist analysis has shown, patriarchal ideology often identifies woman with nature: passive, without history, being not doing. So too the villagers are characterised in a series of metaphors derived from animals and inanimate forces. When they first arrive the Seven observe a fiesta in the village. The men dress up like animals, as a deer and a bull, and enact ritual hunting scenes (in a manner which one might also call child-like). Again, Calvera produces a cruel parody of such a view: 'If God didn't want them sheared he would not have made them sheep'. Chico, exasperated by the peasants' timidity, calls them 'chicken'. These slurs are not endorsed. The film identifies such views only to discredit them. And yet the old man, whose wisdom is not to be questioned, also thinks of the peasants as essentially part of the passive natural world. He tells the Seven:

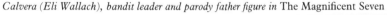

Calvera (Eli Wallach), bandit leader and parody father figure in The Magnificent Seven

19

'They are like the land itself. You helped rid them of Calvera, the way a strong wind helps rid them of locusts.'

The weakness of the peasants, then, can be presented as a function of their chief attributes. They are children. They are nature. In the classic phrase, they are children of nature. Their weakness is therefore no disgrace; they are not to be despised. But although the liberalism of the film can offer a critique of those who cruelly take advantage of the children of nature, it cannot address a more fundamental challenge to attitudes which have been structured by history. It cannot ultimately see the Mexicans as men, different but equal.

The film is a little more complicated than this suggests. Since it has seven protagonists, it can explore more than one position in this dialectic of difference. Chico is the youngest of the Seven. Eventually we discover that he is Mexican himself (a discovery the audience might have made rather earlier had the part been played by a Mexican, rather than by Horst Bucholtz, whose heavy German accent makes it hard to decode the ethnic origin of the character). Significantly, Chico too is shown to be both a child and close to the natural world, uniting in himself both positions which the film offers to the peasants. On the ride south we see him living off the land (tickling trout, for example). Later, he plays a little game of matador and toro with a cow he meets near the village, a piece of childish fun which instantly endears him to the extremely youthful village girl who observes his game and whom, at the end of the film, he returns to marry. Chico shows that differences can be effaced, an affinity discovered. He finds that he is what he had affected to despise. At this point assimilation becomes an option.

The other member of the Seven who proves to be not different after all is Bernardo. He tells the three boys who have adopted him that he is 'Mexican on one side, Irish on the other'. But Bernardo does not assimilate; instead, he idolises the peasants. Indeed, he goes so far as to claim their bravery exceeds that of the Seven. When the boys protest their fathers are cowards, Bernardo lectures them:

'You think I am brave because I carry a gun? Your fathers are much braver because they carry responsibility. For you, your brothers, your sisters and your mothers. And this responsibility is like a big rock that weighs a ton, it bends and it twists them and finally it buries them under the ground. And there's nobody says they have to do this, they do it because they love you and because they want to. I have never had this kind of courage. Running a farm, working like a mule every day with no guarantee anything will ever come of it – this is bravery. That's why I never started anything like that, that's why I never will.'

This speech, as patronising as it is self-pitying, would be unconvincing in any film, but singularly so when delivered by the hero of a Western. It shows how hard the film is prepared to try in order not to follow the equation different equals inferior equals contemptible.

In his book *The Conquest of America* Tzvetan Todorov identifies the twin poles between which the attitudes of Europeans to the indigenous inhabitants of America have oscillated:

> Columbus's attitude with regard to the Indians is based on his perception of them. We can distinguish here two component parts, which we shall find again in the following century and, in practice, down to our own day in every colonist in his relations to the colonized; we have already observed these two attitudes in germ in Columbus's report concerning the other's language. Either he conceives the Indians (though without using these words) as human beings altogether, having the same rights as himself; but then he sees them not only as equals but also as identical, and this behavior leads to assimilationism, the projection of his own values on to the others. Or else he starts from the difference, but the latter is immediately translated into terms of superiority and inferiority (in his case, obviously, it is the Indians who are inferior). What is denied is the existence of a human substance truly other, something capable of being not merely an imperfect state of oneself. These two elementary figures of the experience of alterity are both grounded in egocentrism, in the identification of our own values with values in general, of our *I* with the universe – in the conviction that the world is one.[4]

This seems to fit with uncanny accuracy the structure of attitudes in *The Magnificent Seven*. Five of the Seven, despite their liberalism, can only articulate the difference of the peasants as an inferiority. The liberalism of the film then consists in their responding to this perceived inferiority with kindness. For Bernardo, on the other hand, the peasants are superior, everything he has not the courage to be – this is the familiar noble savage syndrome. And Chico discovers that he is not different after all. He goes native, and performs the ultimate assimilation, marrying into the village.

At odds with the film's liberal intentions, then, is an attitude towards the Mexicans that does not differ in structure from the past history of Hollywood's dealings with south-of-the-border subjects. Yet *The Magnificent Seven* is more interesting than the liberal Westerns which had preceded it. There is a third force at work in the film, besides traditional attitudes and liberal intentions. Until about 1960, the Western conventionally espoused an agrarian ideology. Earlier heroes, like the characters played by James Stewart in the cycle directed by Anthony Mann, are powerfully drawn to the dream of a place of their own, a farm or a ranch. The hero may not ever achieve his goal, but what he most wants is to fulfil the Jeffersonian ideal, to be a free and independent farmer on his own plot of land. At face value, *The Magnificent Seven* attempts to perpetuate this view, that working the land is the most satisfying way of life. It idealises the villagers, who are seen to have in essence already achieved it. Unlike the Seven, they have roots. At the end of the film, the old man tells the three survivors of the Seven, rather in the manner of Ma Joad at the end of *The Grapes of Wrath*, that the people go on for ever, but that the gunfighters, who are as rootless as the wind, have lost. Chris appears to concur: 'The old man was right. Only the farmers won. We lost. We'll always lose.' In a sense, the Seven are structurally in a similar relation to the peasants as Calvera. That is precisely why their personal goodness, the individual liberalism of each of them, has to be insisted upon.

At times the plot anticipates in detail the American intervention in Vietnam – another foreign adventure begun by liberals with apparently impeccable motives. The military strategy of the Seven is to construct a fortified village and act as advisers, attempting to train a local army while still depending on their superior professionalism and fire-power. The ideological strategy is also familiar: to demonstrate that they are the good guys. While the villagers' fiesta is in full swing, Bernardo carves a little flute out of a piece of wood. He attracts the attention of a tiny girl, who is torn between the excitement of her own culture in the form of the rituals being enacted, and the gifts the Americans can offer. In an act of great symbolic (and indeed prophetic) force, she takes the proffered gift, but turns immediately back to the village pageant. In another sequence equally reminiscent of the 'hearts and minds' strategy, Vin discovers that while the Seven are eating well – chicken enchiladas, carne asada, Spanish rice – the villagers are existing on tortillas and beans. The Seven immediately organise a redistribution of food to the children of the village.

What the film thinks it is saying is that the Seven are no less deracinated than Calvera, that the peasants, rooted in the land, represent the unquestionable virtues of community and stability, and that the only redeeming virtue of the Seven is their liberalism, their desire to do good at whatever cost to themselves. But Chris's admission that the Seven 'lost' is unconvincing. Who can be in doubt that 'losing' in such a fashion is far more glorious than whatever it is that the peasants have won? Chico goes back to join his girl sitting on the ground engaged in the tedious labour of shucking corn. Chris and Vin ride off into the open landscape, to new adventures (which would be actually realised in the sequels to this very successful film). Much more convincing, much more appealing than the idealised but dull picture of peasant life, is the view of the gunfighter's existence advanced earlier in the film. In a quiet moment between fights, the Seven sit around ruminating on their chosen way of life. Vin sees the drawbacks: 'Home, none. Wife, none. Kids none. Prospects, zero.' Chris puts the other case: 'Places you are tied down to, none. People with a hold on you, none. Men you step aside for, none.' Lee agrees: 'Insults swallowed, none. Enemies, none.' 'No enemies?' questions Vin. 'Alive,' is the reply. Though later in a more introspective moment Lee is forced to admit, 'I have lost count of my enemies,' this is more an acknowledgment of his personal crisis of nerve than a damaging admission of the gunfighter's true condition. What comes across most powerfully in *The Magnificent Seven* is the self-confidence and self-sufficiency of the Seven, expressed visually in the litheness of their movements and aurally in the pithy terseness of their dialogue. By contrast, the peasants are shot in static groups, and their speech is earnest and plodding, devoid of jokes and repartee. They are, in the expressive old English vernacular, clods.

Near the beginning Chris is asked where he has come from; he points behind him. When asked where he is headed, he points in front. Sergio

Leone's Man With No Name could not be more tight-lipped. This quasi-existential philosophy of self-reliance, self-sufficiency, of deliberate disengagement, is quite at odds with the film's ostensibly liberal credentials. Ironically, it was Europe which was to see the next major development in this most American of genres, and which was to produce the most radical transformation of the Western's politics. The contradiction between liberal interventionism and the cool uninvolved code of the professional gunfighter is a slow-burning fuse which leads straight to the Italian Westerns of the later 60s; it will eventually detonate under the well-meaning pieties of the Hollywood Western.

Only four years separates *The Magnificent Seven* from *A Fistful of Dollars*, which set the spaghetti Western cycle on its way. *The Magnificent Seven* struck an instant chord in Europe. As Christopher Frayling has pointed out, *The Magnificent Seven* was three times as popular abroad as it was in America.[5] Audiences abroad may have been less burdened with the ideological weight of the myths of the genre, more willing to espouse the film's undermining of agrarianism. Italian film-makers, for their part, were heavily influenced by late-60s Marxism, predisposed to attack anything which smacked of imperialism, and eager to expose any sentimentality involved in the idea of the rich helping the poor. Nor, if they were correct Marxists (and urban Italians), did they subscribe to fantasies about the superior virtues of rural life.

Significantly, the French and Italian titles of the film translate as *The Seven Mercenaries*. The cat was out of the bag. Magnificent maybe, but mercenaries all the same. Once Leone got hold of the Western, he and his epigones set about systematically destroying the liberal credentials the Hollywood Western had been trying to construct for itself as a means of atoning for its 'guilty' past. By taking the figure of the self-sufficient gunfighter with no ties to place or person, and pushing this towards the total anaesthesia of the Man With No Name, the spaghetti Western cut itself loose from the ideological baggage of its Hollywood ancestor. The south-of-the-border Western is changed for ever. Mexico becomes the dominant setting for Italian Westerns not only because the locations available in Europe favoured it and Italians felt more at home in a Latin milieu: 'Mexico' offered the ideal space in which European film-makers could deploy their smart political cynicism, their third-worldist politics, their anti-clericalism and anti-liberalism. *The Magnificent Seven* provided, against its own intentions perhaps, the prototype for the late flowering of the genre which finally permitted the break with its compromised past. No more films about well-intentioned police actions south of the Rio Grande, no more missions to save the poor and oppressed in the name of civilisation and charity. From now on it is every man for himself, and we cannot even mutter God help the women and children, since in the Italian Western God is dead, and the priests are in the same racket as everyone else. Calvera, once again, has a wonderfully sardonic speech which anticipates the world which Leone was to construct:

'So much restlessness and change in the outside world. People no longer content with their station in life. Women's fashions – shameless. Religion –

you'd weep if you saw how true religion is now a thing of the past. Last month we were in San Juan. A rich town, much blessed by God. Big church. Not like here, little church, priest comes twice a year. Big one. You think we find gold candlesticks, poor-box filled to overflowing? You know what we find? Brass candlesticks, almost nothing in the poor-box.'
'We took it anyway.'
'I *know* we took it anyway. I'm trying to show him how little religion some people now have.'

Eli Wallach takes an almost sensual pleasure in performing Calvera's venality and cynicism. Not surprisingly, he was soon to find himself perfectly at home in the Italian Western, as 'the Ugly' in Leone's *The Good, the Bad and the Ugly* (1966).

Notes

1. See, for example, Christopher Frayling's entry on 'Mexico' in Edward Buscombe (ed.) *The BFI Companion to the Western* (London: BFI/André Deutsch, 1988), pp. 184–8.
2. See Peter Stanfield, 'The Western, 1909–1914: A Cast of Villains', *Film History*, vol. 1, no. 2 (1984).
3. See Allen Woll, 'Latin Images in American Films', *Journal of Mexican History* 4 (1974).
4. Tzvetan Todorov, *The Conquest of America* (New York: Harper & Row, 1984), pp. 42–3.
5. Christopher Frayling, *Spaghetti Westerns* (London: Routledge & Kegan Paul, 1981), p. 128.

PATTERNS OF THE PRIMITIVE

Sergei Eisenstein's Qué Viva México!

LAURA PODALSKY

Editors' Introduction

The question of influence has always been a thorny issue in film and literary criticism. From Harold Bloom's 'anxiety of influence' to more recent attempts to explain intertextual references and connections, the process whereby a film, film-maker or movement is influenced by others has given rise to debate and contention. Whereas studies that trace the effects of dominant practices upon its 'others' are commonplace, Podalsky's piece reverses this usual colonialist focus to explore the impact of Mexico on the work and theory of Sergei Eisenstein. That Eisenstein's presence in Mexico had an important impact on the Mexican cinema (especially apparent in the work of director Emilio Fernández and cinematographer Gabriel Figueroa) is a well-known and often acknowledged fact, but how Mexico and Mexican culture reverberated throughout Eisenstein's practice has been buried in chronicles and biographies and rarely linked to his theoretical work.

Podalsky carefully explores how Eisenstein's reading of Mexico as 'the primitive' is linked to specific gendered and nationalist tropes in *Qué Viva México!* and contemporaneous writings and given a prominent place in his later sublime aesthetics. Furthermore, Podalsky's essay also teases out the complex socio-historical cross-currents involved in the identification of Mexico with the primitive in the 20s and 30s, a practice indulged in by 'colonial' travellers as well as by Mexican intellectuals who linked the nation with the indigenous in their post-revolutionary search for national identity. Combining Mexican intellectual and cultural history, the history of ideas, post-colonial theories, and textual analyses, she offers us a fresh reading of Eisenstein's fascination with 'otherness'.

□

INTRODUCTION

In December 1920 the already world-famous Soviet director Sergei Eisenstein traveled to Mexico to make a film. Replying to reporters' questions as he boarded the train to Mexico, Eisenstein stated: 'Mexico is primitive. It is close to the soil.... To make a good picture, one must have a positive approach. This is possible in a country like Mexico, where the struggle of progress is still very real' (Seton, 1960, p. 190). Fascinated with the idea that Mexico contained both primitive cultures and a revolutionary government, he constructed *Qué Viva México!* to trace the dialectical movement of the forces of history from the origin of civilization to the triumph of the revolution.

Many film scholars have suggested that Eisenstein's trip to Mexico marked a turning-point in his work and, in doing so, often uncritically echo Eisenstein's vision of Mexico as primitive. In his introduction to *Eisenstein at Work*, for example, Ted Perry writes about the director's obsession with 'death and cruelty' and locates its origin in Mexico: 'the predominant source of inspiration was Eisenstein's encounter with a primitive world where even death was celebrated' (Leyda and Voynow, 1982, p. ix). Marie Seton, who published the definitive biography of Eisenstein in 1952, described Mexico as a place of self-realization for Eisenstein:

Sergei Mikhailovich, who had been too inhibited to express a hint of love or passion on the screen, or give expression to the gay, tender, and truly reverent elements of his innermost nature, was now released into a passionate love of the beautiful, of women, of the fulfillment of life itself, equally loving was he towards the deepest religious feeling (Seton, 1960, p. 196).

According to Seton, Mexico was a place of emotional and spiritual plenitude, an edenic location where repressive forces did not exist for Eisenstein. Yon Barna seconds Seton's explanation that Eisenstein experienced 'unprecedented peace and perfect internal harmony' in Mexico (Barna, 1973, p. 167). While it is hard to assess the effect of Mexico on Eisenstein, the incredible difficulties of the trip alone (including repeated sickness, bad weather, and bureaucratic complications) make these assertions questionable. The blithe acceptance of Eisenstein's designation of Mexico as primitive reflects an uncritical participation in the discursive practice of linking 'primitivism' and Mexico that had begun decades earlier, responding both to a widespread intellectual and artistic fascination with the primitive and to the appeal of a specific moment in Mexican history, the revolution.

That the primitive art object could serve as a source of renovation for Western art was already a commonplace in the early decades of the 20th century (from Gauguin and Picasso to Edgar Rice Burroughs's Tarzan series), but after the First World War the primitive also became important in debates about the restructuring of war-torn Europe (Clifford, 1988, p. 120). Influenced by the work of Charles Darwin and Sigmund Freud, anthropologists like Sir James Frazer and Lucien Lévy-Bruhl envisioned societal development according to an evolutionary model, suggesting that by studying 'primitive' societies they could understand 'our unformed selves, our id forces' (Torgovnick, 1990, pp. 7–9). Thus, as anthropologists created theories of societal development, artists like the surrealists, who delighted in 'cultural impurities and disturbing syncretisms', increasingly incorporated aspects of primitive cultures to rejuvenate European society (Clifford, 1988, p. 131). While early interest in the primitive centered on African and Oceanic societies, it soon turned to Mexico. For Georges Bataille, for example, 'the Aztecs were a locus of the "primitive" because of their "ritual of human sacrifice"' (Torgovnick, 1990, p. 277). However, it was not simply Mexico's past that drew international attention.

The Mexican revolution, the first of the 20th century, enticed foreigners to Mexico to capture it in print and film,[1] although, as Katherine Anne Porter commented in a 1921 essay called 'The Mexican Trinity', their efforts often failed to account for its complexities (*Collected Essays*, 1970, p. 399). As the interest in the African primitive responded to the needs of artistic circles in Europe, the representations of Mexico aimed at the US public reflected the needs of 'North American expansionism and racial and social prejudices' (King, p. 17) at a time when the frontier had closed and waves of European immigrants had altered the ethnic composition of the USA.

Within Mexico, the revolution also fostered ideological changes that parallelled those occurring in Europe. Most significantly, prominent Mexican intellectuals who supported the revolution proposed a return to indigenous values. Later, in the early to mid-20s, Minister of Culture José Vasconcelos fostered the pedagogical value of the visual arts and commissioned some of Mexico's leading artists (Diego Rivera, José Clemente Orozco, David Siqueiros) to paint the walls of public buildings. The particular vision of indigenous culture that emerged enabled successive post-1910 governments to reject the valorization of French culture perpetuated under Porfirio Díaz, and the indigenous became the locus of national identity.

The celebration of indigenous culture in revolutionary and post-revolutionary Mexico drew European artists and intellectuals looking for ways to break out of the stifling aesthetic and political structures of European society. Thus, among others, D. H. Lawrence, Aldous Huxley, Graham Greene, Malcolm Lowry and Stuart Chase explored Mexico 'as an alternative to Europe' (Torgovnick, 1990, p. 277), seeking answers to the European crisis in Mexico.

Like the writers mentioned above, Eisenstein shared a concern with the effects of the 'machine age' on man and saw the primitive as a source of renewal. Nevertheless, his particular vision of the primitive differed from that of his Western European contemporaries. As Marianna Torgovnick notes, the concept of the primitive is relative rather than absolute and exists in relation to a given formulation of the present (Torgovnick, 1990, p. 9). Eisenstein was the only one among these artists who came from a society that had experienced a recent revolutionary change as violent as Mexico's. For the Soviet film-maker, exploring the primitive in post-revolutionary Mexico implied tracing the process of an organic evolution toward a socialist state. In the following pages, I shall examine the tropes used by Eisenstein to articulate his vision of Mexico and, in particular, of the primitive in Mexico.

However, analysing Eisenstein's experience in Mexico and his representation of the country is problematic. First of all, the film he set out to make with Grigori Alexandrov and Eduard Tissé was never completed: after many

Sergei Eisenstein, Grigori Alexandrov and Edward Tissé dressed as revolutionaries in Mexico

delays and complications, the producers, Upton Sinclair and his wife Mary Claire, sold the footage to various groups.[2] The best available version of *Qué Viva México!*, compiled by Grigori Alexandrov, claims to be a faithful reconstruction of Eisenstein's intentions, but remains a sadly incomplete document. Furthermore, Eisenstein's written records about *Qué Viva México!* are equally scattered.[3] Given these spotty records, any examination of Eisenstein's work must be provisional, but the effort is, nevertheless, worthwhile. The Mexican trip marked Eisenstein profoundly: emotionally (in 1936, he claimed to be still 'slowly recovering from the blow of my Mexican experience' (Leyda and Voynow, 1982, p. 71), and aesthetically, for the expressionistic *mise en scène* of his later films can be traced to his exploration of primitive forms in Mexico. Furthermore, Eisenstein's visit to Mexico also greatly influenced Mexican cinema. According to various film historians, the determining influence behind the celebration of indigenous culture and landscape typical of Emilio Fernández and Gabriel Figueroa (which became emblematic of the national film industry and Mexican national identity) can be traced – through Paul Strand's *Redes* (1934) – to Eisenstein and Tissé. Finally, a close analysis of *Qué Viva México!* is necessary in order to outline the conventions which structure Eisenstein's representation of Mexico. By comparing Eisenstein's tropes for the primitive in Mexico with those of his contemporaries from Western Europe, we can begin to tease out the differences between capitalist and non-capitalist forms of colonial discourse.

In his autobiography, Eisenstein traces his preoccupation with the primitive to the editing of *October* during 1927–8. Under the influence of Soviet theories of perception, Eisenstein designed films to provoke a specific response from the audience. His theories of montage had, up to this point, relied on a vision of intellectual cinema which (ideally) forced the spectator to a given conclusion by juxtaposing two shots in a dialectical relationship. During the process of editing the gods sequence of *October*, Eisenstein theorized that the dialectical use of montage could be utilized to evoke an even more primal, less conscious response in the spectator. He postulated that the gods sequence, in which he juxtaposed shots of sculptures of deities from various cultures, was like

> ... *the reverse process* of that which takes place in the development of thinking from its primitive form to its conscious form. ... Thus, the 'method' of my intellectual cinema consists of a moving backward from a more developed form of expression of consciousness to an earlier form of consciousness; from the speech of our generally accepted logic to a structure of speech of another kind of logic (Eisenstein, *Immoral Memories*, p. 209).

Wondering whether 'this backward translation of today's level of our consciousness to forms of consciousness ... of an earlier kind is ... the secret – not only of my intellectual cinema but of art in general' (*Immoral Memories*, p. 209), Eisenstein was already placing the primitive, defined in terms of consciousness, at the center of revolutionary art.

It is significant that it is precisely at this time (November 1927), while he was reworking *October* to facilitate its release, that Eisenstein met the Mexican muralist Diego Rivera who was traveling through the Soviet Union (Helperin). At the very least, this meeting with one of the major figures in the artistic celebration of indigenous culture encouraged Eisenstein's interest in the primitive. His encounter with Rivera probably directed him to focus on Mexico as the embodiment of the primitive by rekindling the interest he had shown as early as 1920 when he staged his first theatrical production, an adaptation of Jack London's story, *The Mexican*.[4]

Eisenstein's interest in the primitive flourished under the influence of contemporary anthropology to which he was exposed in 1929 during his trip through Europe. In his autobiography, Eisenstein remembers picking up a copy of Lévy-Bruhl's *La Mentalité Primitive* (1922) shortly before his journey to America, and attempting to obtain Sir James Frazer's *The Golden Bough* (1915) (*Immoral Memories*, p. 210). In a letter to Maxim Strauch in May 1931, during his stay in Mexico, Eisenstein noted that he had finished reading Lévy-Bruhl's subsequent work, *Reasoning Among Primitive Peoples* (Michelson, 1980, p. 53). These readings served him as a guide. Speaking of a perilous flight he took over the volcano Popocatépetl, Eisenstein notes, 'I survived to sit at the foot of the volcano, surrounded by the representations of those very people whose system of thinking (for by that time I already knew that this kind of thinking is also called sensuous) seemed so fantastic and unreal in the pages of Lévy-Bruhl or Frazer' (*Immoral Memories*, p. 211).

While Eisenstein accepted certain aspects of Lévy-Bruhl's theories, he also expressed several reservations. He affirmed that 'not only does the process of development itself not proceed in a straight line, . . . but that it marches by continual shifts backwards and forwards' (*Film Form*, p. 142). Eisenstein declared that the 'so-called "early thought processes" ' were not limited to 'primitive' people; they existed in modern man as well and revealed themselves in states of extreme emotion (*Film Form*, p. 143). Furthermore, he criticized Lévy-Bruhl's theory for becoming an excuse for colonialism (*Film Form*, p. 141). Responding to a 1931 Edmund Wilson article about the Mexican project, Eisenstein rejected the suggestion that the Soviet filmmakers had escaped from the bleak Russian landscape to the 'complete liberty' and 'entrancing scenery of Mexico': 'We are no longer little boys who run away from home to see Indians stick feathers in their hair or cannibals pass rings through their noses.'[5]

Eisenstein saw Mexico as a complex society, as a place in which primitive and modern society coexisted. His film would represent:

> this history of the change of cultures, presented not vertically (in years and centuries), but horizontally (as the geographical coexistence of the most diverse stages of culture), for which Mexico is so amazing in that it has a province (Tehuantepec) that has a matriarchal society next to provinces that almost achieved Communism in the revolution of the first decade of this century (Yucatán, Zapata's program, etc.) (*Immoral Memories*, p. 260).

His original outline for the film expressed the difficulty of synthesizing all the different parts of Mexico into one narrative. In 1931, Eisenstein wrote to Upton Sinclair with a rough outline of the project in which he described his vision of Mexico as a serape:

> So striped and violently contrasting are the cultures in Mexico running next to each other and at the same time being centuries away. No plot, no whole story could run through this serape without being false or artificial. And we took the contrasting independent adjacence of its violent colors as the motif for constructing our film: 6 episodes . . . held together by the unity of the weave – a rhythmic and musical construction and an unrolling of the Mexican spirit (*Film Sense*, pp. 251–5).

According to Seton, Eisenstein was much influenced by Anita Brenner's 1929 book *Idols behind Altars*, a study of visual art in Mexico (Seton, 1960, p. 194). Eisenstein's words to Upton Sinclair echo the images expressed by Brenner: 'Without the need for translation or a story sequence, Mexico resolves itself harmoniously and powerfully as a great symphony or a great mural painting' (Brenner, 1929, p. 15). Brenner's vision of a syncretic Mexico provided an analog to Eisenstein's formulation of the different levels of awareness coexisting within 'modern man'.

Eisenstein envisioned the film divided into episodes.[6] Between the prologue and epilogue, four different sections or 'novellas' would represent the 'three historical steps of the conception of life from biological submission to death to the social surpassing of its principle by the immortal power of the collectivity of the people' (Eisenstein as cited in Seton, 1960, pp. 507–8).[7] While recognizing the complexity of Mexican society, Eisenstein focused on what he saw as the 'primitive' aspects. Recalling his trip in his autobiography, he noted:

It is here in *tierra caliente* [burning earth] that I come to know the fantastic structure of prelogical, sensuous thinking . . . from daily communion with those descendents of the Aztecs and Toltecs, Mayas, or Huichole who have managed to carry unharmed through the ages that meandering thought. It determined the astonishing traits of that miracle of Mexican primitive culture, as its tribes to this day stand beside the cradle of a cultural era that has not yet begun for them (*Immoral Memories.* p. 211).

Eisenstein saw Mexico as a bridge linking the age of biological submission (the primitive) to the triumph of the social collective (the revolution). Two of the episodes – 'Sandunga' and 'Soldadera' – focused on these ages and, for that reason, deserve special examination.

Eisenstein filmed 'Sandunga' (a term that refers to a local dance) in Tehuantepec, the isthmus which separates the Gulf of Mexico and the Pacific Ocean. He wanted the episode to express 'semi-animal, semi-vegetable and biologically unconscious existence' (Seton, 1960, p. 508). Because gendered constructions were central to Eisenstein's visualization of this primitive state (sketches from this period reflect the correlation that Eisenstein drew between the voluptuous body of a naked woman and earthly plenitude), various shots associate the Tehuantepec woman with nature: a close-up focuses on a woman's face encircled with white flowers, a cut from a medium close-up of a woman combing her hair to a long shot of a bird arranging its feathers.

Eisenstein was fascinated with Tehuantepec's tropical landscape and legendary matriarchal society. Contemporary writers like Ernest Gruening and Carleton Beals (whose works Eisenstein had read) referred to the independence and beauty of the Tehuantepec women and Eisenstein extended the characterization.[8] He described Tehuantepec with metaphors about the birth of mankind and postulated that 'Eden did not exist between the Tigris and Euphrates, but rather here, somewhere between the Gulf of Mexico and Tehuantepec' (Barna, 1973, p. 168). In the rough cutting notes he sent to Upton Sinclair in 1931, he described Sandunga as:

Life . . . the moist, muddy, sleepy tropics. Heavy branches of fruit. Dreamy waters. And the dreamy eyelids of girls. Of girls. Of future mothers. Of the fore-mother. Like the queen-bee, the mother rules in Tehuantepec. The female tribal system has been miraculously preserved here for hundreds of years until our time (*Film Sense*, p. 252).

When Eisenstein suggested that the descendents of ancient tribes stood beside 'the cradle of a cultural era that has not yet begun for them', he located the womb of the revolution in Tehuantepec. The name of the central character in the episode is, quite fittingly, Concepción.

Seton says that Eisenstein characterized 'Sandunga' as the 'harmonious security of the female tribal system' which would give way in the next episode to the cruelty of the male tribal system (*Film Sense*, p. 203). In many of the Tehuantepec shots, women appear naked from the waist up and their composition is reminiscent of Paul Gauguin's Tahitian paintings. Describing this series of shots, Leyda and Voynow commented:

> The matriarchal society in Tehuantepec required a change from all styles in use for the other novellas. The 'story' almost disappeared in the event shown. . . . The compositions became horizontal and passive, and Tissé's photography turned away from his well-known sharpness to a softening of all images (Leyda and Voynow, 1982, p. 67).

Leyda and Voynow identify and uncritically echo the way Eisenstein attached gender associations to form.

In his 1930 lecture to the Academy of Motion Picture Arts and Sciences (in a meeting devoted to the problems of the wide screen), Eisenstein suggested that the 'dynamic square' should replace the rectangle. His argument against 'horizontalism' invoked the anthropological studies he was immersed in at that point and foreshadow his use of women in the Mexico project:

> It is my desire to chant the hymn of the male, the strong, the virile, active, vertical composition. I am not anxious to enter into the dark phallic and sexual ancestry of the vertical shape as symbol of growth, strength and power. . . . But I do want to point out that the movement towards a vertical perception led our savage ancestors on their way to a higher level (*Film Essay*, p. 50).

Eisenstein illustrated the relation of vertical forms to progress using the following examples: man's ability to stand upright, the importance of the obelisk to Egyptian astrologers, and the importance of factory chimneys as symbols of industrialization. Furthermore, his sketches reflect how he envisioned the changes from the womanly, conical earth to the male, upright cactus, illustrating a variation of D. H. Lawrence's description of the maguey, a type of cactus, as a 'phallic bud' in *The Plumed Serpent* (p. 82). Eisenstein used gender associations to naturalize his theory about the horizontal and vertical forms and their relation to particular stages of civilization. His association of woman, the primitive, and horizontal form is successful to the degree that Leyda and Voynow identify the stylistic shift in Sandunga as natural; in order to represent a 'female space,' the style of the episode had to imitate the softness and passivity of a reclining woman.

Eisenstein was picking up on strategies for representing the primitive that were and are common. As Torgovnick points out, 'gender issues always inhabit Western versions of the primitive' (Torgovnick, 1990, p. 17). This association of woman with the primitive reappeared years later in one of Eisenstein's most important theoretical statements: the speech to the All-

32

Union Creative Conference of Soviet Cinematography in 1935. In that speech, Eisenstein spoke of the coexistence of early and later thought processes in one person and gave three curious examples: 1) a young girl who rips up a picture of her unfaithful lover, as if it were him; 2) Catherine de' Medici who, 'on the verge of an epoch that already knew minds like Leonardo and Galileo', stuck pins into effigies of her enemies; and 3) rural Mexicans who during droughts whip the statue of a particular Catholic saint because it corresponds to an ancient rain deity (*Film Form*, p. 143). Without saying so explicitly, these examples suggest that adolescents, females, and Mexicans have more than their fair share of early thought processes and that they tend to slip away from later, more scientific ones with greater ease.

For Eisenstein, woman was a construction equally useful for representing the biological basis of indigenous society and the achievements of the revolution. The 'Soldadera' episode was never filmed. However, as outlined, this central episode would have focused on the women who followed their husbands and partners during the revolution. In this episode, immediately before the epilogue, Eisenstein projected the possibility of national unification:

> historically, in the joint entry into Mexico's capital of the united forces of Pancho Villa the northerner and Emiliano Zapata the southerner; and in terms of the subject, the figure of the Mexican woman moving with the same care for her man from group to group of the Mexican troops, all fighting each other, torn with the contradictions of the civil war (*Immoral Memories*, p. 260).

The main character of the episode, Pancha, becomes the lover of a member of Zapata's army upon the death of her first lover, one of Villa's troops. Eisenstein centered the final episode of his film around the *soldadera* because to him 'she seems physically to personify the image of a single nationally united Mexico, opposing foreign intriguers who try to dismember the nation and set its separate parts against the other' (*Immoral Memories*, p. 260). Of course, writing the history of Mexico over the body of woman is a technique used by other contemporary writers. For example, in his 1931 book, *Mexico: A Study of Two Americas*, Stuart Chase noted that during the revolution 'Mexico turned from prostrating herself before white men from all parts of the compass, and regarded her own brown men, their impenetrable traditions, their authentic gifts, their gentleness and essential dignity' (Chase, 1931, p. 83). For Chase, the penetration of the national body by foreign forces represented a willful prostitution ('prostrates herself'). For Eisenstein, the union of Pancha with the two men follows the 'tradition of the ancient peoples [according to which] the widow of one brother should marry the surviving brother' (Seton, 1960, p. 507). In either example, the body of woman is the symbol for the integrity of the national family.

His use of the female body as a trope for the nation coincides with the Mexican myth about Doña Marina or La Malinche, the woman who supposedly facilitated the Spanish conquest of the Aztec civilization by acting as Hernando Cortés's translator. The myth associates the creation of Mexico

33

with the rape (willful prostitution) of the native woman, La Malinche. Eisenstein structured his middle episodes using a similar trope. 'Fiesta' occurs around a bullfight and traces the adulterous affair between a picador and the wife of an aristocratic landowner. His criticism of the decadence of the upper class continued in 'Maguey', where an hacienda owner rapes a young indigenous woman.[9] Like the Malinche myth, 'Fiesta' and 'Maguey' use the violation of the body of woman as a trope of societal breakdown. 'Sandunga' and 'Soldadera', however, construct woman as a force for regeneration. The matriarchal society of Tehuantepec represented the womb of civilization. The pure body of the *soldadera*, undefiled by foreign hands, represented modernity. The last shot of the film was to be a close-up on the face of a laughing 'little brown child'. Eisenstein posed the question, 'Will it be the child of Pancha?' (Seton, 1960, p. 511).

ECSTASY IN MEXICO

While the association between the primitive and the sensual present in the work of Lévy-Bruhl and elaborated by the surrealists influenced Eisenstein's vision of Mexico, we must also account for the impact of D. H. Lawrence's *The Plumed Serpent*, a work which transferred the themes of 'the erotic, the exotic, and the unconscious' so treasured by the surrealists (Clifford, 1988, p. 118) to a Mexican setting.[10] Kate, the protagonist, travels to Mexico on a spiritual quest because in Europe the '[white] men had had a soul, and lost it' (p. 85) and Lawrence characterized her encounter with the primitive as a cosmic union between femaleness and maleness (p. 140). Kate repeatedly experiences a feeling of being overwhelmed, trapped, and pulled down by Mexico (pp. 23–4, 145, 251) which is echoed in Eisenstein's descriptions of his experience of Mexico: 'Your head literally whirls when you see the treatment of the corner of Las Monjas Palace in Uxmal. . . . And . . . dizziness – is not simply a rhetorical phrase – it is what actually occurs' (*Nonindifferent Nature*, p. 142). Thus for Eisenstein, Mexico blocked off any possibility of conscious, analytical thought: 'The eye no longer sees at all, but perceives and feels things just as a blind man would perceive and feel them with his hands' (Barna, 1973, p. 167). As if viewing were automatically an intellectual activity, Eisenstein utilized a tactile metaphor to suggest the 'innate' sensuality of Mexico. Both Lawrence and Eisenstein envisioned Mexico as a place of release and renovation in which logical thought became subsumed to feeling. For Lawrence's Kate this meant losing her sterile individuality in a cosmic womanhood. For Eisenstein, this represented the possibility of freeing the individual spectator from the constraints of logical thought.

Eisenstein wanted to explain and control the chaos and vertigo of Mexico. In his letter to Maxim Strauch and Ilya Trauberg in 1931, the film-maker described himself as a:

. . . quiet, closet scientist with a microscope, searching out the mysteries of creative processes and phenomena, which submit only with difficulty . . . [and as a] respectable fellow . . . in a situation of high comedy: between earthquakes, drought-ridden tropics, tropical downpours . . . on carriages, airplanes, trucks, horseback, steamers.[11]

These experiences led Eisenstein to formulate his concept of the ecstatic (Michelson, 1980, p. 52) and among the many drawings he produced in Mexico is a figure of ecstasy. Barna affirms that in Mexico Eisenstein 'felt at one with nature and experienced a "most sublime sensation of ecstasy"'. That ecstasy, whose laws he had for so long tried to probe, became a 'living reality' (Barna, 1973, p. 167). The episode of the film entitled 'Fiesta' focused explicitly on religious ecstasy in the festival of a local patron saint. A series of shots shows a procession in which three indigenous men walk up a stiff incline to a church with cactus limbs tied on their backs and across their outstretched arms to form the shape of a cross. The way Eisenstein linked these shots to the ecstatic becomes even more explicit in shots of Catholic priests made during the same festival. A particularly magnificent shot placed a row of skulls in the immediate foreground and a line of four boys holding a cross between them in the background, and framed the boys by placing two priests on either side of them in the middle ground. Through deep focus and the extreme low angle of the camera, the film-maker paid tribute to the elongation characteristic of El Greco's compositions.

El Greco was important to Eisenstein because of his move from 'the representation of ecstatic characters to the ecstatic representation of characters'.[12] Eisenstein was looking for the mechanisms of early thinking which would allow an unmediated link between the emotional states of artist and spectator (*Nonindifferent Nature*, p. 141). Eisenstein felt he had located the patterns of ecstatic representation in Mexico.

Describing the vertigo he felt after viewing the ornamental heading adorning Maya ruins, Eisenstein noted that the dizziness 'is the result of a constant slipping from the prototypes' face, into this system of stretched-out details losing their human features, and again back to the face' (*Nonindifferent Nature*, p. 142). The movement from whole to part to whole is one of the processes he described in *Film Form: New Problems* (1935) upon which is based the effectiveness of the synecdoche or close-up. Eisenstein's description bears a curious resemblance to the experience of the protagonist of *The Plumed Serpent*. Kate recognizes in the features of her indigenous lover: 'symbols ... of another mystery, the mystery of the twilit, primitive world, where shapes that are small suddenly loom up huge, gigantic on the shadow, and a face like Cipriano's is the face at once of a god and a devil, the undying Pan face' (Lawrence, 1926, pp. 324–5).

Some of the shots of pre-Columbian ruins in *Qué Viva México!* repeat this formulation. Numerous close-ups frame ornamental heads of Quetzalcoatl, the plumed serpent god, while other long shots capture entire pyramids. Several shots place indigenous people next to the heads and frame the profile of one against the other. The way that Eisenstein might have ordered these shots is uncertain. However, the shots that juxtaposed the profile of the man and the stone head suggest the similarity, if not the unity, of the man with the people who built the pyramid and the unadulterated mystical link between the man and the godhead. If the gods sequence in *October* suffered for being too much of a conscious process, the depiction of gods in *Qué Viva México!* presented the possibility of cutting back to the origin in the most profound way:

35

'. . . the similarity, if not the unity, of the man with the people who built the pyramid . . .' – a shot of Chichén-Itzá in Qué Viva México! (Sergei Eisenstein, USA, 1931)

For in the attempt to 'enter' into the process of birth of these ecstatic – actually 'having become ecstatic' from the appearance given to them – images of the ornamental decomposing of faces and heads you enter a system of the norms of that process, which gave birth to these images of decomposed forms inaccessible to the normal state of consciousness. (*Nonindifferent Nature*, pp. 142–3)

According to Eisenstein, all art offers the possibility of returning to a primal state because the process of viewing mimes the process of creation; both processes function through the formulation and decomposition of structures. His theory functioned by eliding the complexities of Mexican culture.

CONCLUSION

Eisenstein's interest in other cultures began very early in his career. His early theories of montage were influenced by his fascination with Japanese writing and kabuki theatre. Speaking about the gods sequence in *October*, Eisenstein noted, 'I had already met with another structure of thought in studying the Japanese language' (*Immoral Memories*, p. 211). For Eisenstein, all 'other' cultures contained similar patterns. For example, he drew an explicit connection between Mexico and Japan when he compared the Mexican volcano Popocatépetl with the representations of Fujiyama by Japanese artists (*Immoral Memories*, p. 211). But Eisenstein was less interested in equating Mexico and Japan than he was in positing an 'other' in which latent structures became manifest.

36

Eisenstein linked 'otherness' to the idea of layered representation. In 1929 he used the ideogram, the fusion of two objects into a symbol that 'corresponds to a concept', as a linguistic model for his theory of montage (*Film Form*, p. 30). The syncretism he found in Mexico embodies the principles of layered representation that he had first teased out of the Japanese ideogram. Commenting on this study in his autobiography, Eisenstein says his interest in Japanese writing had been limited to 'the very mechanism of combination' (*Immoral Memories*, p. 209). But he developed these theories further on the basis of his work in Mexico, arguing that 'the development of consciousness goes step by step toward "condensation"' (*Immoral Memories*, p. 209). Thus Eisenstein invoked Freudian terminology to equate the function of the mind of the individual, modern man and the techniques by which modern culture represses latent primitive feeling.

His study of Japanese culture differed in many ways from his exploration of Mexico, for the latter was far more comprehensive. In *Qué Viva México!* he attempted to trace the development of civilization and, in so doing, moved away from what Clifford identifies as the 'ethnography of collage' and ultimately reduced rather than celebrated the aspects of Mexican culture which were incongruous to his model (Clifford, 1988, p. 147).

Notes

1. The fighting in northern Mexico (and Pancho Villa's troops, in particular) received special attention for several reasons. US-owned companies had invested heavily in the mines of northern Mexico, and the region was geographically accessible to US journalists and cameramen.
2. The history of Eisenstein's dealings with the Sinclairs is complicated and has been well chronicled by his various biographers.
3. See Geduld and Gottesman. See also Inga Katetnikova in collaboration with Leon Steinmetz, *Mexico According to Eisenstein* (Albuquerque: University of New Mexico Press, 1991).
4. The sources that inspired Eisenstein to explore Mexico are multiple. Yon Barna traces Eisenstein's interest to 'the stories of American writer Albert Rhys William, whom he had met in Moscow in 1928' and to his encounter with Robert Flaherty in Hollywood (p. 161). His desire to actually travel to Mexico can be traced to several people he met during his stay in Hollywood. Barna intimates that Eisenstein met again with Rivera, who arrived in San Francisco in November 1930. In his autobiography, Eisenstein mentions his encounter with Odo Stadé, a Hollywood bookstore owner who was writing a book on Mexico entitled *Viva Villa* (*Immoral Memories*, p. 192): 'Stadé told me a lot about Mexico. And the seeds of my interest in that country, once sown in me by photographs of 'The Day of Death' (in an issue of the *Kölnische Illustrierte*), nourished by the stories of Diego Rivera, when he visited the Soviet Union as a friend, grew into a burning desire to travel there' (p. 194).
5. See Seton, pp. 228–9, for a shortened version of Eisenstein's letter which appeared in *The New Republic* on 9 December 1931. Seton mistakenly claims that Wilson's article appeared in *The Nation*; it actually appeared on 4 November 1931 in *The New Republic*.
6. Even Eisenstein's vision of the overall structure of *Qué Viva México!* remains in doubt. All sources agree that the film would include a prologue, four episodes, and an epilogue. However, each proposes a different order: 1) the original plan

Eisenstein submitted to Sinclair on 2 October 1931: prologue, 'Sandunga', 'Maguey', 'Spanish *milagro*', 'Soldadera', epilogue (Geduld and Gottesman, pp. 149–50); 2) the original plan according to Seton and the one that appears in Leyda and Voynow: prologue, 'Fiesta/Conquest', 'Sandunga', 'Maguey', 'Soldadera', epilogue; and 3) the structure that Alexandrov used in *Qué Viva México!*: prologue, 'Sandunga', 'Fiesta', 'Maguey', 'Soldadera', epilogue.

7. Eisenstein placed a great deal of importance on establishing a biological basis for society. The epilogue to *Qué Viva México!* included a number of dancing skeletons. In his notes, Eisenstein wrote, 'choose skulls of primitives – more character and disproportion in the faces' (Leyda and Voynow, p. 72). Apparently Eisenstein did not reject the correlation made by certain contemporary anthropologists between the level of one's thought processes and one's physical form.

8. Post-Conquest Spaniards refer to reports of ruling women in Tehuantepec. See Rafael Carrasco Puente, *Bibliografía del Istmo de Tehuantepec* (México: Secretaría de Relaciones Exteriores, 1948), p. xix. However, writers in the early 20th century do not. See Miguel Covarrubias, *Mexico South: The Isthmus of Tehuantepec* (New York: Alfred Knopf, 1946) and Carlos Macías, 'Los Tehuantepecanos Actuales', *Boletín del Museo Nacional de México*, 2.2 (1912), pp. 18–29.

9. My analysis supports Judith Mayne's discussion of women in Eisenstein's earlier films, *Potemkin* and *October*. See 'Soviet Film Montage and the Woman Question', *Camera Obscura* 19 (1989), pp. 25–52.

10. On 28 February 1931 Upton Sinclair wrote to Eisenstein about Lawrence's *Plumed Serpent* (Geduld and Gottesman, p. 56). A year later, Eisenstein wrote to Kenneth McPherson, the editor of the film magazine *Close-up*, that he had read *The Plumed Serpent* (Seton, pp. 257–8; Leyda and Voynow, p. 77).

11. See Sergei Eisenstein 'Letters from Mexico to Maxim Strauch and Ilya Trauberg in *October*, n. 14, 1980, p. 56.

12. Michelson, p. 53, citing Eisenstein, 'El Greco y el Cine', in *Cinématisme: peinture et cinéma* in *October*, n. 14, 1980.

Works Cited

Barna, Yon. *Eisenstein*. Bloomington: Indiana University Press, 1973.

Brenner, Anita. *Idols behind Altars*. New York: Harcourt, Brace, 1929.

Chase, Stuart. *Mexico: A Study of Two Americas*. New York: n.p., 1931.

Clifford, James. 'On Ethnographic Surrealism', in *The Predicament of Culture: Twentieth-century Ethnography, Literature, and Art*. Cambridge, Mass.: Harvard University Press, 1988.

Eisenstein, Sergei. *Film Essay and a Lecture*. Ed. Jay Leyda. New York: Praeger, 1970.

– *Film Form*. Ed. Jay Leyda, 2nd edn. San Diego: Harcourt, Brace, Jovanovich, 1975.

Film Sense, Ed. Jay Leyda, 4th edn. San Diego: Harcourt, Brace, Jovanovich, 1975.

– *Immoral Memories: An Autobiography*. Trans. Herbert Marshall. Boston: Houghton Mifflin, 1983.

– *Nonindifferent Nature*. Trans. Herbert Marshall. Cambridge: Cambridge University Press, 1987.

Geduld, Harry M. and Gottesman, Ronald. *Sergei Eisenstein and Upton Sinclair: The Making and Unmaking of 'Qué Viva México!'*. London: Thames and Hudson, 1970.

Helperin, Morris. 'Eisenstein's New Film: Russian Director in Mexico at Work on *Qué Viva México!*', *New York Times*, 29 November 1931: 6.

King, John. *Magical Reels: A History of Cinema in Latin America*. London: Verso, 1990.

Lawrence, D. H., *The Plumed Serpent*. Harmondsworth: Penguin, 1926.

Leyda, Jay and Voynow, Zina. *Eisenstein at Work*. New York: Pantheon, 1982.

Michelson, Annette. 'On Reading Deren's Notebook,' *October* 14 (1980): 47–55.

Porter, Katherine Anne. *The Collected Stories of Katherine Anne Porter*. New York: Harcourt, Brace & World, 1965.

– *The Collected Essays and Occasional Writings of Katherine Anne Porter*. New York: Delacorte Press, 1970.

Seton, Marie. *Sergei Eisenstein*. New York: Grove Press, 1960.

Torgovnick, Marianna. *Gone Primitive: Savage Intellects, Modern Lives*. Chicago: University of Chicago Press, 1990.

BUÑUEL IN MEXICO

MICHAEL WOOD

Editors' Introduction
Luis Buñuel travelled to Mexico in the mid-40s on a brief visit from the
United States, where he had spent the war years working in the Museum of
Modern Art in New York. He arrived, he told the Mexican writer, Elena
Poniatowska, at the time of All Saints Day and the Day of the Dead and
was immediately fascinated by Mexico. He made Mexico City his
permanent residence, and he became naturalised in 1949. He made 18
'Mexican' films from 1946 until the mid-60s, yet the adjective 'Mexican',
for Michael Wood, cannot be used conventionally to refer to a nation or a
sense of place. Certainly Buñuel, even at his most neo-realist (*Los
olvidados*), disagreed with the fundamental tenets of neo-realism. Nor did
he have any truck with the dominant mode of Mexican lyrical nationalism.
Carlos Fuentes, his close friend, offers a revealing anecdote:

> While *Nazarín* was being filmed on location near Cuatal . . . Gabriel
> Figueroa carefully prepared an outdoor scene. . . . Figueroa set up the
> camera with the snow-capped volcano Popocatépetl in the background, a
> cactus at the right-angle of the composition, a circle of clouds crowning
> its peak and the open furrows of the valley in the foreground. Looking at
> the composition, Buñuel said, 'Fine, now let's turn the camera so that we
> can get those four goats and two crags on the barren hill.'

Nor was Mexican cinema capable of assimilating his radical lessons. Michael
Wood explores the imaginary world of this solitary wanderer, this
paradoxically sedentary *flâneur*.

Michael Wood met Buñuel in Mexico in 1978 and had many
conversations with him, discussing all of his films and much else. Buñuel
preferred technical talk to thematic talk, and was always surprised that
anyone should have a continuing interest in his old work. He had a number
of well-rehearsed anecdotes, most of which appear in *My Last Breath*, but
he also had an alert curiosity about the world, a great appetite for new
jokes, and an imagination which was always seeing possibilities, ways of

40

framing a situation or turning a story on its head. Asked about his one really turgid film, *Una mujer sin amor*, he nodded sadly and said that 'nothing occurred to him' during the filming: '*no se me ocurrió nada*'. He meant he had counted on the arrival of some idea, angle or gag to animate a dim and sentimental scenario, and counted, on this occasion, in vain. It says a lot about Buñuel's intelligence and openness as a film-maker that he should wait for ideas in this way; and a lot about the films themselves that the ideas should have shown up, almost always, in such profusion.

□

Luis Buñuel said more than once that his films were designed to show us that we do not live in the best of worlds. They certainly do that, but the formulation scarcely seems strong enough, or flexible enough. It suggests that those who know that they do not live in the best of worlds have nothing to learn from Buñuel, which I hope is not true. It also implies that those who think they do live in such a world can be persuaded to think otherwise by a movie, which is pretty unlikely. Buñuel's films display a world which *must* be changed, which is intolerable. But they offer no indication of how this world *can* be changed: indeed, they usually intimate that it cannot. 'I can't go on, I'll go on,' a voice says in Samuel Beckett's *The Unnameable*. Buñuel's films, in so far as they *say* anything at all, seem to mutter, 'This can't go on, how could it end?'

This essay is an attempt to place Buñuel's Mexican movies, and to explore some of their concerns and their relation to his other works. It also contains, as a continuing question, a doubt about whether these movies *can* be placed, whether placing is an activity we can actually perform in relation to them. What if Buñuel is a genuinely displaced movie-maker? More generally, we may want to wonder about place and nationality in movies, which are perhaps not quite the transparent ideas they seem.

Luis Buñuel was born in Spain in 1900; made his first films in France; lived in France (with a spell back in Spain in the early 30s) and then the USA until 1944. He arrived in Mexico in that year, hoping to make a film of Lorca's *La casa de Bernarda Alba* (*The House of Bernarda Alba*); stayed, was naturalised in 1949; lived there till his death in 1983. Buñuel speaks in his autobiography[1] of having made twenty films in Mexico, out of a total of 32. He must be counting the two French-speaking films he shot there – *La Mort en ce jardin* (*La muerte en este jardín*, *Evil Eden*) 1956, and *La Fièvre monte à El Pao* (*Los ambiciosos*, *Republic of Sin*), 1959. There are 18 Mexican films in the ordinary sense – that is, made in Mexico, with Mexican money, actors, producer and so on. For a while Buñuel made nothing but Mexican films (1946–55); from 1966 (the year of *Belle de Jour*), he lived in Mexico and made French films. His working career thus falls into three rather different major phases: the Surrealist years, 1928–32; the years of exile, 1936–61; the time of international fame, beginning in 1961 with *Viridiana*. Buñuel's last Mexican film was the short *Simón del desierto* (*Simon of the Desert*), 1965.

How are we to describe these Mexican films? The categories which follow are not arbitrarily chosen; but some will look more arbitrary than others, and none of them is meant to bear any great critical weight. I offer them only as a useful preliminary mapping, and indeed I shall need to scrap them well before the essay reaches its end. So: one musical *Gran Casino (En el viejo Tampico)*, 1946; one truly terrible version of a famous novel, *Una mujer sin amor (A Mother Without Love)*, 1951, based on Maupassant's *Pierre et Jean*; two very interesting versions of famous novels, *Las aventuras de Robinson Crusoe*, 1952; *Abismos de pasión (Cumbres borrascosas)*, 1953, a reworking of *Wuthering Heights*; one comedy (*El gran calavera*), 1949, one light melodrama, *La hija de engaño (Don Quintin el amargao)*, 1951, two melodramas with social ambitions, *Susana*, 1950, *El bruto (The Brute)*, 1952; two comedies set in closed, travelling worlds, *Subida al cielo*, 1951, *La ilusión viaja en tranvía*, 1953; two sermons, *El río y la muerte*, 1954, *La joven (The Young One – Island of Shame)*, 1960; one 'documentary' film, *Los olvidados (The Young and the Damned)*, 1950; two 'psychological' films, *El*, 1952, *Ensayo de un crimen (The Criminal Life of Archibaldo de la Cruz)*, 1955; two 'religious' films, *Nazarín*, 1958, *Simón del desierto (Simon of the Desert)*, 1965; one surrealist parable, *El ángel exterminador (The Exterminating Angel)*, 1962. Eighteen in all. The most memorable and durable films are probably the last six mentioned – *Los olvidados, El, Ensayo, Nazarín, El ángel, Simón* – but almost all have flickers of interest, flashes of Buñuel's cinematic signature.

It may be worth saying something about the lesser-known or more unlikely of these movies. Buñuel's musical, for example, *Gran Casino*. Here two glittering stars of the Latin American cinema, the motherly Libertad Lamarque and the portly Jorge Negrete, sing away at each other in an intricate story about skulduggeries over an oil well. Whenever Negrete performs a song, a trio with guitars, entirely unprovided for by the plot, joins him as his backing. Negrete shows only faint surprise when they show up in a jail, or in an adjoining room, but when he leaps on to a stage to escape the bad guys, sings a chorus of a song called 'La Norteña', 'The Girl from the North', and then catches sight of the trio grinning in the balcony, even he seems a little taken aback, and lifts his hat to them in a elegant acknowledgment of their unlikely but undeniable presence. There are other nice gags in this film: a love scene played straight by the principals while the camera lingers resolutely on a sickening-looking patch of oily mud; an insistence on showing Lamarque in extravagant close-ups and soft focus, so that she looks like a movie-star in a museum, a rehearsal for *Sunset Boulevard*.

The two closed-world comedies have interesting points of resemblance. The most striking sequence in *Subida al cielo* is a dream in which the hero sees his dumpy new wife replaced by the local vamp, who rises out of a river in a sort of Ophelia rig. Hero and vamp then find themselves in a rattling and shaking bus which has no driver but is full of tropical plants and trees, and carries a few assorted goats and sheep. A seemingly interminable apple peel leads out of the hero's mouth and out of the bus up to his mother on a pedestal, smiling as she shaves the spiralling skin off the fruit. *Viridiana*, some ten years later, peels an apple in the same way for Don Jaime. The plot of *Subida al cielo* is a pretext for an undreamed bus ride from and back to a small village on the Pacific, and the bus is a *world*. A child is born in it, a coffin transported; and the whole excursion is framed by marriage and death. In spite of wobbly back projection, cardboard mountains and awful acting, this film has quite a bit of charm, and is one of the most light-hearted of Buñuel's movies. Only the dream really stays in the mind, though, with its glimpse of a realm where contraries are cancelled, vamp and wife become one, mother approves of the vamp. Eve is Adam's mother, and Oedipus just holds his mum's hand. *La ilusión viaja en tranvía* contains a number of visual echoes of the earlier film, although this one is set in the city, not on a country route. The driver and conductor of a tram gets drunk and borrow their vehicle for a night. They then find they can't return it to the depot in broad daylight without getting caught, so they shunt it around all day, trying to look unobtrusive and running into various adventures. The film has more of the flavour of Mexico City than any of Buñuel's works except *Los olvidados*. We see an empty, darkening street, for example, hear the shrill, plaintive whistle of a vendor of fried bananas, and we are *placed* as we rarely are in Buñuel's films. The movie's most striking sequence is when the tram on its illicit run stops at the abattoir, and a crew of slaughterers and their assistants get on, carrying hunks and sides of meat, which they hang up inside the car. A pig's head sways with the movement of the vehicle, tilting the top hat of a bewildered, drunken toff, who has also somehow come aboard. The tram stops for a couple of women who are carrying a clumsily wrapped bundle, and the deep joke of this episode comes to the surface. The bundle turns out to be a carving of a bloodstained Christ; meat too, in its way, tortured flesh, lamb of God.

I call *El río y la muerte* a sermon because it carries an unusually heavy and conventional message – Buñuel himself said in an interview that he hated its 'educative pretensions'.[1] The film is a Mexican Western, full of shoot-outs and revenge, but lovelessly made, animated by a heartless liberalism which simply and flatly condemns all violence in the name of progress and science. Mexico City and our hero, who survives a spell in an iron lung to become a doctor himself, are set against the provinces and the feuding families to be found there: saving life against wasting it. The film makes no serious distinction between killing in self-defence and murder provoked by rancour; indeed, makes no distinction between a rancour which is generations old and constantly fed by new aggression, and the casual, apparently unmotivated violence of excitable people – the Montagues, Capulets and Gary Gilmore all thrown into one basket. Mexico: a country blurred by randomness, where they just bump each other off at the drop of a sombrero. This is Buñuel's most 'European' film; not 'clearly intended for the Mexicans', as Francisco Aranda says, but clearly aimed at the Mexicans. Of course Mexico is a violent place, in its rather introverted way, and the movie does have an eloquent sense of the horror of the feud, of the ugly stubbornness of all such narrow fidelities to hatred; but nothing substantial is opposed to this horror, and the hollowness and abstraction of the supposedly progressive world makes one hanker for the *humanity* of revenge, stunted and cruel as it is.

I run into more difficulties with the movies I have called 'documentary', 'psychological', 'religious', and 'surrealist'. In fact, most of Buñuel's movies are *all* those things. Or, more precisely, all his films are psychological, in an ample sense – even the religious films are psychological. And most of them are documentary in impulse – even (especially) when what is documented is a state of mind. And surrealist? I am tempted to say they are all surrealist too; but Buñuel himself used to speak of his surrealism in the past tense: 'When I was a Surrealist . . .' Well, it may be possible to say both things: the movement is over, but the impulse, the angle, the attitude may remain. If I call *El ángel exterminador* a surrealist parable, I am thinking of it as animated by certain surrealist principles – the war on settled meaning, for example, the assumption that ordinary bourgeois life may well be crazier than anyone's wildest dreams – but would agree that it does not look like a surrealist movie, or generally behave like one.

Buñuel's images, the material he places in front of the camera and frames, are usually both literal and metaphorical objects – or, if you like, both metonymies and metaphors. The cinema copes with both quite comfortably (with a leaning towards metonymy) but not often with both at once. In Buñuel's movies, the seen and the ordinarily unseen inhabit the same film space; he pictures the picturable, and strongly alludes to what cannot be pictured. Scorpions in Buñuel, for instance, are offered both as a natural history lesson and as a moral emblem. Natural history, for Buñuel, is social history with the mask off; but he is also interested in the natural history of dreams, the whole heraldic menagerie of the mind. Before turning finally to the question of place in these films, I should like to look a little more closely at this natural history, and also at its accompanying sociology. I shall leave Buñuel's more strictly psychological or religious concerns for another occasion.

A spider scuttles out of a cross-shaped shadow in *Susana*. A man's face is covered with flies in *L'Age d'or* (*The Golden Age*), 1930, a couple is consumed by insects at the end of *Un Chien Andalou* (*The Andalusian Dog*), 1928. A death's head moth in the latter film offers its spectacular, all too obviously codified meaning – what is baffling is not the code but the absence of a context for it, the sense of the symbol escaped from its zoo. Marcel Martin suggests that this is what we expect from Buñuel: the beasts are a sort of signature, or self-quotation, an espoused cliché. 'There is the bestiary,' Martin says of *Le Journal d'une Femme de Chambre* (*Diary of a Chambermaid*), 1964: 'butterflies which are shot at, persecuted mice, slowly slaughtered geese, a wild-boar hunting . . . and snails on a spree up the legs of a little girl who has been killed'[2]. Some of Martin's plurals are rhetorical licence, just getting into the spirit of things. There is only one slaughtered goose, only one exploded butterfly. Still, the suggestion is interesting. We see the scorpions in *L'Age d'or*, the ants swarming out of a man's hand in *Un Chien Andalou*, and we know we are in Buñuel's world. Do we? And if we do, what do we know about this world?

Let us pursue the bestiary a little further, and especially those of its creatures which seem most telling in the Mexican context. The bear belongs to a joke in *El ángel exterminador*, a prank a society hostess is planning; but as disorder descends on her house, the bear becomes both more natural and more allegorical. It makes strange noises and it swings from a chandelier. It is

Nature itself, the unknown and the untameable escaped from its cosy script. Buñuel and his cameraman Gabriel Figueroa teased each other about this bear for a long time afterwards, each insisting it was the other's duty to stay and face the beast if it turned nasty. Buñuel said Figueroa was, after all, the cameraman; Figueroa said Buñuel was, after all, the man who had a gun, and the director. Sheep appear with the bear in the hostess's planned joke in *El ángel exterminador*, but they just bleat and get in the way. At the end of the movie they are frankly allegorical: woolly analogues of people trapped in a fold of unconsidered and unshakeable assumptions.

Cocks and hens are more threatening than threatened, oddly on the side of our tormentors. A woman wreaks a terrible vengeance in *El bruto*, destroying everything she cares about, and as she stares around crazily, appalled at her achievement, her gaze meets a jaunty rooster perched on a wall, a mocking emblem of the male she has betrayed, the Brute himself, and also, I think, of something more diffuse: something like a persistent meaningless or mindlessness in human passions. A white hen stands on the chest of a dead boy in *Los olvidados*, and earlier in the same film a black cockerel (a hen, according to the Spanish version of the script) figures in one of Buñuel's most famous and most eerie shots. A group of thugs stone and knock over a blind man, and destroy his musical instruments. The camera follows one thug disappearing in long shot, then returns to a close-up of the blind man lying on the ground. Then it tracks sideways to find the cockerel peering at the man, inches from his mud-covered face. The music in the soundtrack shrieks as if it had uncovered an instance of witchcraft. Why is this image so disturbing? The movement of the camera matters, the finding of the bird which waits just outside the frame without our knowing – Buñuel's films are full, so to speak, of what is outside the frame. We also see what the blind man cannot see, the inquisitive, indiscreet rooster. More, we see him *not seeing*, and for a moment his blindness seems impossible, unimaginable. How could he not see what is so black and so close? Not that the sight would console him. The cockerel is whatever there is in life that jeers at our bewilderment, makes it trivial. It is also a cockerel.

The 'beast with five fingers' is one of the oldest inhabitants of Buñuel's menagerie. Visually a man's hand is cut off by a door which traps it in *Un Chien Andalou*, thus prolonging the image of a more literally severed hand – which lies in a roadway while a boyish young woman pokes at it with a stick. Later the hand is put in a box, and the young woman is run down by a car and killed. There are really too many meanings here for manageable interpretation. What interests me most is the sense of the hand as a creature, a form of crab or spider, or scorpion perhaps. It recurs in this shape in *El ángel exterminador*, where it slides across the floor of a dream and tries to throttle a woman, and also in the Hollywood movie called *The Beast with Five Fingers* (Robert Florey, 1946) where it has the title role, no less. It suggests wishes that get away, desire not rotting or repressed but on the loose, beyond recall or even recognition. The hand in this film scampers about on its own, is nailed to a desk, and is finally burned – this is fairly ordinary horror movie nastiness. But there is one sequence (the one said to have been directed by Buñuel) where the hand comes to beg for the ring its late owner used to take

45

off when he played the piano. The hand is now a genuinely longing, needy, beseeching creature, and when Peter Lorre puts the ring on the uplifted middle finger, there is the uncanny impression of a marriage. It is the independent life of the hand that matters, and this is surely what these hands must mean in Buñuel: life after castration, so to speak, a castration which serves not to end your sexual activity but to alienate it, to set it so free from you that you must either disavow it or formally marry it.

This is strange natural history; and Buñuel also works with a strange sociology, which we can glimpse through the treatment of children in his films. Children, throughout Buñuel's work, are associated with interruption and neglect, with failures of concentration and acts of violence. *Los olvidados* is built up of wrecked family relations: absent or drunken fathers, a bewildered, unloving mother, various cruel or hollow substitutes in parental roles. It ends with a mother belatedly looking for a son who is already dead, wrapped in a sack and tipped into a rubbish dump. Indeed, there are an extraordinary number of children in Buñuel's films: raped, wounded, killed, lost, orphaned, teased, exploited, mistaught, dead. They are what might have been: broken history.

One of the most curious, and elaborate, of Buñuel's scenes involving children occurs in *La ilusión viaja en tranvía*. A group of schoolboys pile into a tram for an excursion. One boy is being tormented by his fellows because he is illegitimate, and the teacher is equally cruel on the same subject. The other boys suddenly shout, 'Look, there's your mother!'. The boy peers anxiously out of the window, and sees a large whorish-looking woman hitching up a stocking. A second or two later, all the kids having piled out of the tram, we see that a film is being made, that the woman is not a whore, or the boy's mother, but an actress. She still does not want an unsolicited son. The boy stands by her, tenderly looking up, caught in his companions' clumsy joke. The woman tells him to beat it. I am not sure what to make of this intricate set-up, but certainly the child's loneliness and neglect, his difference from the others, his lack of connection to any comfortable adult world, are clear. He is forgotten as a human being: *un olvidado*. That the schoolboy joke should be overtaken by a film in the making may say something about the games adults play. We cannot care for children, perhaps, because we are too busy making movies of our lives.

In *Abismos de pasión*, Ricardo (alias Hindley Earnshaw) is always chasing and beating his son, and the frightened fatalism of the boy is something a Mexican child is peculiarly, sadly suited to express. Any visitor to Mexico has seen those handsome, unsmiling Indian features. They haunt you like a withheld reproach. At one point Ricardo lies down and bawls at the boy, 'Well, what are you waiting for?'. The child sits down at Ricardo's head, and begins to give his drunken father a massage. The camera moves slowly up into a long close-up of the boy's solitary-looking, resigned face. It is a face which, strictly, says nothing, impassive. All the dark eyes tell us, if we keep looking, is that they know that suffering is their inheritance, that there is no running away. Rebellion belongs to another order of the imagination.

In *Nazarín*, a peasant child wearing a long dress comes towards the camera down a rocky, unpaved village street, bare Mexican mountains closing the

'. . . *what would happen if these forgotten children were* remembered?' Nazarín (*Luis Buñuel, Mexico, 1958*)

vista behind her. She is trailing a vast sheet, and she is crying, alone and presumably parentless, since we know her whole village has the plague. The shot, which as a still was to become a famous, prize-winning photograph, contains the whole desolation of the disease; its effect, the way it empties the world, rather than its showy, baroque horrors. The sheet is all the girl has left of her home, and there are other, more obscure suggestions in the shot: the child as diminutive, helpless washerwoman, women as mourners, sheets as shrouds.

But then what would happen if these forgotten children were *remembered*? Would that save or straighten out the children and a future society? It would help. There is much to do in this direction; more than we shall ever manage to do, no doubt. But this is only one aspect of Buñuel's theme. Another and perhaps more radical aspect is anger, and children again are the vehicle for his searching questions. A little girl sits astride a circling wooden horse, in an urban park. She is beaming, having the time of her life, all the fun of the fair. A small shift of the camera shows us two desperate-looking boys, only slightly older than the girl. They are pushing the merry-go-round, and they are sweating and weary and hungry. Her play is their work. What is more, her play and their work are someone else's profit, since the bullying owner of the ride now comes into view, and in answer to the boys' plea that they are tired, amiably says they can rest when they die. They can't go on, they'll go on.

Los olvidados is a documentary film, or a near-documentary; a translation of Italian neo-realism to Latin America. Buñuel says in his autobiography how much he admired de Sica's *Shoeshine*, 1946. There is the same attention to the urban poor, the same focus on children, the same condemnation of liberal capitalism, and the use of (some) non-professional actors. But Buñuel is also seeking to meet what he sees as one of the deficiencies of neo-realism:

> In a conversation with Zavattini [de Sica's scenarist, Buñuel was talking to a group of Mexican students in 1950], I explained to him . . . my disagreement with neo-realism. . . . For a neo-realist, I said to him, a glass is a glass and nothing more; you see it taken from the sideboard, filled with drink, taken to the kitchen where the maid washes it and perhaps breaks it. . . . But this same glass, contemplated by different beings, can be a thousand different things, because each one charges what he sees with *affectivity*; no one sees things as they are, but as his desires and his state of soul make him see. I fight for a cinema which will show me this kind of glass.[3]

This kind of glass and also de Sica's kind of glass. What Buñuel identifies here is not a problem of perception, of the sort that comes up in Antonioni, for example: have I really seen what I think I have seen, does my subjective world match anyone else's? It is a problem of interpretation. What Buñuel is asking us to face is the radical alteration of the world by desire; or fear, or need, or memory, or rage. Buñuel's more overtly 'psychological' films, like *El* and *Ensayo de un crimen*, his 'religious' films, like *Nazarín* and *Simón del desierto*, are versions of desire, but also of the world caught up in desire's transfigurations. No one sees things as they are, but there are plenty of things to see. Paranoia, magic, piety, sanctity are all ways of looking at the neo-realist glass.

How much of Mexico do we see in these films? I want to say not much, but I should be happy to be corrected. It certainly does not help to say that Buñuel was Spanish, first and last and always. He was as Spanish as Goya or Quevedo (to make what have become the obligatory references). But nationality, as I hinted at the beginning, is a capacious concept; a useful reminder at times, but not much of an analytical instrument. Buñuel's Spanishness is profound but also discreet, diffuse and tempered with a rootlessness which is less an accident of history than a feature of his mind. At the age of 24 he went to Paris to become a playboy and became a monk instead. But he remained a wanderer, a *flâneur* in a sense related to that proposed by Walter Benjamin – a largely sedentary wanderer, the oddness of the phrase hinting at the strangeness of the case. He did literally walk the streets of Mexico City, in the years before *Los olvidados*, but he did not travel, except to make movies, and then not much.

Yet the curious thing about Buñuel's later films is not only that they do not appear to have been made by a man in his 70s; they do not seem to belong to a man who lived in a cul-de-sac and rarely went out. They are *topical* films, full of drugs and terrorism and up-to-date chatter. But they are also curiously placeless. They are *somewhere*, of course, an individual spot has posed for the camera in France, or Spain, or Mexico. But it does not seem to matter much where that somewhere is, or what language is being spoken. The films slip easily into other times and other countries, as if the famed fixity of history and geography had been grossly exaggerated. When the word 'Buñuel' appears in Julio Cortázar's *Hopscotch* it is an adjective, meaning addicted to games with time and space.

Everything is specific in these movies, almost nothing is local. I have no word for this peculiar quality, but I want to suggest that Buñuel's Mexico is very much a part of it. These places which are not places *are* Mexico, or at least they are what Buñuel found there, having prophesied their possibility in his first films. This sense of things is clearest, perhaps, in *Los olvidados*.

The film opens with stock shots of New York, Paris and London, familiar, famous sights – New York Bay, the Eiffel Tower, Big Ben, the Thames – the tourist's world, but also signs of the modern city. We then see a park in the centre of Mexico City; then the main square; then a piece of waste ground. The soundtrack burbles on for a moment about the hidden miseries of urban life, and the whole sequence would be terribly banal, were it not for the drabness of the last Mexican shot, and for what Buñuel is about to show us about the place where he lived for so long.

It is a place of shanties and hovels, rickety structures that seem to be waiting for the wolf to blow them down; of deserted lots, empty patches of dust and grass; and of new constructions going up, large, ambitious, modern buildings. Like Godard's Paris, Buñuel's Mexico City is permanently being

'. . . *ragged children playing ancient games.*' Los olvidados (The Young and the Damned, *Luis Buñuel, Mexico, 1950*)

49

built. It *is* the Waste Land, in a sense far less figurative than T. S. Eliot's, and *Los olvidados*, which seems a little dated in other ways (slow motion for dream sequences, significant music at excessively appropriate moments, 'artistic' patterns of imagery) is extraordinary contemporary in this respect. The half-finished buildings seen in *Los olvidados* are finished now; they are even old. But their descendants are going up everywhere, scaffolding and reinforced concrete promising newer, better things. New waste lots spring up as the result of clearances and demolitions, and the shanties and hovels migrate from zone to zone but remain what they always were. It is still possible, any day in Mexico City, to turn a corner, to step off a fashionable street, and find yourself in the setting of *Los olvidados*, complete with ragged children playing ancient games. The fact that this experience is available in other cities too (is available in all large cities, no doubt, if not quite as readily as in Mexico) underscores the point started by the nondescript shot I mentioned a moment ago.

But the Mexico City which appears more often than any other in Buñuel's work (more often than any other place at all, perhaps) is slightly different. Neither shanty nor high-rise nor waste land, but the anonymous city which flourishes among them. Dull, spacious, impersonal, modern streets – that one of them should be called la Calle de la Providencia, Providence Street, is a sort of historical joke. How could Providence play a role here? The city is flattened out, emptied of its variety, of its parks and fountains and architectural interest, converted into a long suburb on film. These streets appear to be nowhere, faceless, nameless even when we see their names. But they appear to be nowhere not because they could be anywhere, but because they *are everywhere*. Their very facelessness reflects their ubiquity: the generalising tendency is not Buñuel's but our culture's; they are the streets of the century.

El ángel exterminador is a Mexican movie in the straightforward sense: shot by Gabriel Figueroa, in a Mexican studio, produced by Gustavo Alatriste; Mexican actors, Mexican technicians. The script is by Buñuel and Luis Alcoriza, another exiled Spaniard. But it is also one of two films Buñuel said he would have liked to remake – with, say, English actors, like Olivier and Irene Dunn – because the collapse of culture, the descent into barbarism, would have seemed more complete and poignant, he said. The target is the middle class, not particularly the Mexican middle class; the servants have the necessary intuitions, know they must leave, not because they are Mexicans but because they are servants. Class, not nation. The discreet charm of the bourgeoisie *is* international. But of course we hear Mexican accents, see well-known Mexican actors whom we can see in other Mexican films; the dialogue sounds Mexican (what would an international dialogue sound like?) The irremediable specificity of film as a medium anchors this movie in Mexico, it cannot be anywhere else. The paradox then is that the message is clearly international while the faces and the voices and the words are clearly Mexican.

Well, the paradox is even deeper than that. The film can be seen as a parable about meaning: not about the meaninglessness of the world or of social life, but about our rage for meaning in those areas. To speak of a 'message', national or international, and to ask whether the film is Mexican or not, is to resist, to seek to disperse, the very mystery this film articulates for us. The mystery is *there*, among these people who cannot tell the difference between joking and flipping out, between conspiracy and accident, between freemasonry and black magic; who do not know why they cannot leave this room in this house. The question is not what the mystery means, but how we are to put up with it. Do we not rush to moralise the story, allegorise it, rationalise it, place it? Could we really leave it alone? Should we leave it alone? 'No one sees things as they are ...' Perhaps we do see things as they are; their nudity is what is intolerable, and we hasten to cover it with words and explanations, theories, nationalities, contexts. There is no way out of this procedure, it seems; we cannot bear much reality. The real, Jacques Lacan says, is what *sticks* to us; we feel better when we have converted its mere stickiness into meaning. But we might be able to undeceive ourselves a little about what we are doing. And some meanings, Buñuel would no doubt agree, are more liberating than others; are liberating exactly in the measure that we have chosen them, not merely reached for them in a panic.

Notes

1. Luis Buñuel, *My Last Breath* (London: Faber, 1983).
2. Marcel Martin, *Le Journal d'une Femme de Chambre* (Paris: Le Seuil/L'Avart-Scéne; 1971, p. 9.)
3. Francisco Aranda, *Luis Buñuel* (Barcelona: Editorial Lumen, 1969).

INTERNAL 'OTHERS'

Hollywood Narratives 'about' Mexican–Americans[1]

CHON A. NORIEGA

Editors' Introduction
The Hollywood stereotypes for Mexican people in films about the revolution – the bandits, greasers and señoritas analysed in Margarita de Orellana's essay – were also used to represent the more problematic place of the 'Mexican' who lived north of the border and to provide a narrative resolution to the issues raised by the border conflict era (1848–1929). However, Hollywood actually produced few films that explicitly addressed the place of the Mexican–American in the United States. Focusing on the ten 'social problem' films about Mexican–Americans produced between 1935 and 1962, Noriega's essay explores how classic Hollywood dealt with the problems of Mexican–American representation and citizenship. Within the limits imposed by the Production Code Administration (especially during the Good Neighbor Policy years), the social problem films placed the Mexican–American in *his* appropriate place as an American citizen: in the *barrio*, or 'repatriated, segregated, and institutionalised in the name of assimilation'. Combining archival research with textual analysis, Noriega's piece outlines how Hollywood positioned the Mexican–American in relation to gender and sexual relations, social spaces, and institutions. Furthermore, he argues that the collective impact of these representations has been deeply felt by subsequent generations of Chicano artists and film-makers: the Chicano film movement of the 60s and 70s (analysed from a different perspective by Rosa Linda Fregoso's essay in Part II) syncretically 'signifies' upon the Hollywood social problem film to establish a counter discourse on Mexican–American citizenship.

☐

In hundreds of Hollywood feature films, 'Mexican' characters function as the exotic, criminal or sensual 'other' in narratives of national self-definition (Woll, 1977; Pettit, 1980; García Riera, 1987). The use of the term 'Mexican' to describe both Mexican and Mexican–American characters further elides or represses issues of citizenship. After all, even the 'classic' Western depicted the period *after* the Treaty of Guadalupe Hidalgo, when Mexicans in the conquered states of the south-west became United States citizens. But if Mexican–Americans have functioned as convenient villains in numerous films 'with' Mexican types (Lamb, 1975), few Hollywood films have been 'about' the Mexican–American. Between 1935 and 1962, however, at least ten social problem films addressed the issue of the place of the Mexican–American in the United States: *Bordertown* (1934), *A Medal for Benny* (1945), *The Lawless* (1950), *Right Cross* (1950), *My Man and I* (1952), *The Ring* (1952), *Salt of the Earth* (1954), *Trial* (1955), *Giant* (1956), and *Requiem for a Heavyweight* (1962). With the exception of two gang exploitations films – *Boulevard Nights* and *Walk Proud* (both 1979) – these remain the only feature-length films to be 'about' Mexican–Americans or Chicanos, until the emergence of Chicano-produced feature films in the late 70s.

These films were produced at a significant moment in the development of an American as well as an ethnic-American national identity. Chicano scholars have identified the period between the Depression and the election of John F. Kennedy as the 'Mexican–American generation', in which political interests shifted from those of conquest and immigration to 'uncompromising . . . demands for first-class citizenship' (García, 1989, pp. 17–19). These demands occurred within the context of a 'politics of denial' that included the deportation of Mexican–American political activists, labor leaders and citizens under 'repatriation' programs and Operation Wetback.

Within Chicano historiography, the Mexican–American generation is preceded by the border conflict era (1848–1929). In that period, as Anglo–Americans consolidated economic and political control over the conquered south-west territories, the 'greaser' emerges as a product of American thought and popular culture (De León, 1983). In numerous dime Westerns and silent films, from *Licking the Greasers* (1910) to *Guns and Greasers* (1918), the Mexican bandit threatened death and rape, while the Anglo–American hero often ended up with a 'greaser' wife, as in *Bronco Billy's Mexican Wife* (1915). These narratives represent an expression and resolution of border conflict, anticipating the more direct and 'enlightened' treatment of Mexican–American citizenship of the social problem films. While the 'greaser' was always Mexican, he often lived north of the border. And, in the treatment of the concurrent Mexican revolution, these films initiated, indirectly, the immigration narrative, with Mexican women as the sanctioned border crossers. In this manner, the 'greaser' genre resolved the south-west's 'political unconscious' (Jameson, 1981, pp. 79–83), which re-emerges under the impetus of increased Mexican immigration and, in 1912, statehood for Arizona and New Mexico (exceptional for its Mexican–American majority).

In the social problem films, however, the political, socio-economic and psychological issues related to race and ethnicity operate at the manifest level of the narrative, rather than as the 'political unconscious'. In the end, these films must still resolve these social contradictions and situate the Mexican–American within normative gender roles, sexual relations, social spaces, and institutional parameters.

Between 1934 and 1968 the Production Code Administration (PCA), or Hays Office, served as the self-regulatory, institutional mechanism between Holly-wood films and the moral and political *status quo* (Jacobs, 1989). While the PCA did not mandate film production, censorship did define and monitor the outer limits of ideological expression. Its evaluations of the social problem films about Mexican–Americans were often based on the anticipated reaction of the Mexican government and people. PCA Director Joseph Breen's letter to Dore Schary, producer of *My Man and I*, is typical: 'We would like to urge that you get proper technical advice from the Mexican angle to make certain that there are not details in the script that might be offensive to that nation.'[2] In all other films, phrases such as 'you Mexican jerk', 'damn' Mexicans; and 'greaser fighter' were flagged by the PCA and removed.[3] In April 1955, Breen's replacement, Geoffrey Shurlock, went so far as to question 'one aspect of *Giant* which has nothing to do with the Code': errors in the Spanish-language dialogue. In particular, he pointed to the phrases, '*Bien venudo*' and '*Perdonome*', and cited the film's 'rather touchy subject matter' as an impetus for correcting the errors.[4]

But despite the fact that these films depicted Mexican–Americans *cum* social problem, from the start the PCA positioned the central issue, or 'touchy subject matter', as a 'racial question' or 'race distinction' that existed on an international level, between Mexico and the United States. For example, in a letter to Jack Warner, Breen raised numerous objections to the script for *Bordertown*, including the fact that 'Mexicans [*sic*] are constantly referred to as "greasers" and other derogatory names.'[5] One month later, Breen acknowledged Warner's assurances that the final script would not elicit Mexican protest.[6] The concern was a legitimate one for the industry, in so far as international distribution generated profits, while Mexico and other Latin American countries had in the past banned studios which produced deroga-tory films (Woll, 1977, pp. 16–22; Delpar, 1984). But, in the repeated references to 'our neighbors to the south', the PCA also revealed the influence of FDR's Good Neighbor Policy, whose sentiments were expressed in one of the Code's twelve 'particular applications': 'The history, insti-tutions, prominent people and citizenry of other nations shall be represented fairly.'

The advent of the Second World War reinvigorated the Good Neighbor Policy, and its impact on film production. In April 1941 the PCA hired a bilingual Latin American affairs expert, Addison Durland, while the State Department Office for Coordination of Inter-American Affairs established a Motion Picture Section, charged with, according to Director John Hay Whit-ney, the 'basic job of spreading the gospel of the Americas' common stake in this struggle' (quoted in Woll, 1977, p. 54). Together, these two agencies monitored Hollywood films and provided 'technical assistance' in order to protect both international alliances and markets. In the process the represen-tation of Mexican–American – and concurrent civil rights activities – was measured against an 'external guiding intelligence' (Mazón, 1984, p. 27): Mexico, rather than the Mexican–American community.

Likewise, the censors invoked the Communist threat when the films' critique of domestic 'social problems' suggested that discrimination had either institutional or popular (hence, democratic) underpinnings. In a letter to Luigi Luraschi about *The Lawless*, Breen made these ideological limits clear:

> ... certain it is that the story itself is a shocking indictment of America and its people, and, indeed, is a sad commentary on 'democracy at work', which the enemies of our system of government like to point to. The shocking manner in which the several gross injustices are heaped upon the head of the confused, but innocent, young American of Mexican extraction, and the willingness of so many of the people in your story to be a part of, and to endorse, these injustices, is, we think, a damning portrayal of our American social system.
>
> The overall effect of a story of this kind made into a motion picture would be, we think, a very definite disservice to this country of ours, and to its institutions and its ideals. Our apprehensions about it is [sic] very deep.[7]

Responding to the script for *The Ring*, Breen warned that, 'We feel that it would not be good to infer that the police discriminate against these boys because of their nationality.'[8] In *The Ring*, Tomás 'Tommy Kansas' Cantanios (Lalo Rios) tries (and fails) to make it out of the East Los Angeles *barrio* as a professional boxer. While Tomás blames the 'Anglos' for the limited opportunities and discrimination that he faces, in the final film version it is a police officer who makes sure that 'the boys', including Tomás, are served at an all-white diner.[9]

The PCA based its censorship of material that criticized social institutions on the potential for 'public hue and cry', in this case an American rather than a Mexican one. As Shurlock made explicit, that the mere 'likelihood' of public protests would lead the PCA to withhold the Seal of Approval[10] suggests that the popular appeal, like the Communist threat, provided a convenient façade for the *status quo* upheld by the Code's 'General Principles'. Thus, the PCA diffused the challenge presented by the Mexican–American experience, bifurcating it into Mexican and American components. Mexican–Americans could not be called 'greasers' or portrayed in a negative or inauthentic manner. Nor could social institutions be ridiculed and 'natural' and human laws violated. The PCA's overall strategy, however, engaged the same politics of citizenship found in the state courts and federal immigration policies, a politics of denial. On the one hand, control over Mexican–American representation was 'repatriated' as a *Mexican* issue; while on the other hand, the 'racial question' or social problem was defined within institutional parameters as an *American* one.

THE BORDERS AND BARRIOS OF REPRESENTATION

The social problem films operated within these ideological limits, enforced by PCA censorship. Given the nature of the social problem (broadly speaking, American citizenship), however, the narratives had to define the internal–external paradigm as domestic rather than international. As Arthur Pettit argues, American popular fiction and, later, film function to 'localize' Mexican–Americans to a specific geographical space: the south-west (Pettit, 1980, p. xv). But, if we apply his concept more broadly, feature films 'about' and 'with' Mexican American characters also 'localize' or delimit them to certain genres: Western conquest, social problem and exploitation films. Filmic discourses on Mexican–Americans are 'localized' to violence (and sex) within narratives aimed toward a judgment that determines the appropriate place for the Mexican–American character. Thus the films reinforce, in the words of Homi K. Bhabha, the 'space of identification' or 'fixity' for the Mexican–American 'other' (Bhabha, 1983). Nevertheless, these films must also give expression to the social contradictions, ambiguities and contestations that are the historical basis for 'fixity' or 'localized' discourse.

I want to offer an initial elaboration on the schema presented above with respect to genre, action, judgment and social placement. In the first instance, the social problem films fall into three overlapping genres: romantic melodramas (*Right Cross*, *My Man and I*, *A Medal for Benny*); courtroom dramas/juvenile delinquent films (*The Lawless*, *Trial* and, as a precursor, *Bordertown*); and boxing films (*The Ring*, *Right Cross*, *Requiem for a Heavyweight*). In addition, *Giant* can be classified as a modern Western; while, in theme, *Giant* and *Salt of the Earth* combine if not conflate labor, racial and gender issues.

While these genres provide for diverse plot elements, the above films have an act of violence as the 'inciting incident' which the narrative attempts to resolve.[11] In the boxing films, of course, the 'inciting incident' has to do with the Mexican–American boxer's temper and anger, which are depicted as the result of ethnic paranoia about the 'gringo conspiracy'. In addition, fist fights also start at least two other films: *Bordertown* and *The Lawless*. In *A Medal for Benny*, the 'inciting incident' occurs off-camera, but frames the entire narrative: Benny Martin had been a violent and criminal youth 'run out of town' by the local judge, whereupon he enlisted in the services, killing 'more than one hundred Japs' before he himself is killed. Beyond violence between men (often between Mexican–American and Anglo–American), nearly half the films are based upon accusations of interracial rape or crimes of passion or both: *Bordertown*, *My Man and I*, *The Lawless* and *Trial*. Thus, as the narratives explore Mexican–American citizenship with good and earnest intent, they do so through the textual filter of the Mexican bandit stereotype, the 'greaser' who threatens to 'shoot the cowboy' and 'rape his woman'.

The social problem films did attempt to transcend the stereotypical representations of the 'greaser' genre. In particular, the films produced in the 50s constitute a significant liberal impulse from within Hollywood, one often poised against the House Un-American Activities Committee (HUAC) investigations. These include: King Brothers Productions (*The Ring*), which regularly hired blacklisted personnel under pseudonyms; MGM's Dore Schary, producer of *My Man and I*, *Right Cross* and *Trial*, who attempted to mediate or mitigate HUAC decrees; Herbert Biberman (*Salt of the Earth*), one of the 'Hollywood Ten'; and blacklisted director Joseph Losey (*The Lawless*) (see Navasky, 1980). The nature of the changes, however, was a matter of degree rather than of kind: rape and murder became false accu-

'. . . judgement is the result of . . . a fist fight . . .' Anthony Quinn in Requiem for a Heavyweight (Ralph Nelson, USA, 1962)

sations of rape and murder. While the false accusations allowed the films to play upon and expose racist expectations, they did little to expand the discourse on Mexican–Americans. Thus, the violent 'inciting incident' leads to a comparable climax: the judgment. In most films, judgment is the result of either a fist fight (*Right Cross*, *The Ring*, *Giant* and *Requiem for a Heavyweight*) or a court decision (*Bordertown*, *The Lawless*, *My Man and I* and *Trial*). In all cases, the Mexican–American protagonist loses the physical fight, but wins the legal battle.

In a broad sense, these two judgments or resolutions mark a crucial boundary within the domain of discourse on the Mexican–American, one that circulated within immigration, legal and censorship institutions: *Mexican* psychological deficiencies and *American* institutional activism. In *Right Cross* and *The Ring*, the fight ends the protagonist's career, causing his considerable anger at Anglo–American society to dissipate. These characters are revealed to have shadow-boxed, and destroyed, not a racist society, but the demons within themselves. Likewise, the young men in *Bordertown* and *A Medal for Benny* are shown to have misdirected their inherent violence toward 'making it' under American capitalism, and are redirected toward more acceptable and distant arenas: helping one's people in the *barrio*, or fighting for one's country overseas. While the films that are resolved in the courtroom affirm Mexican–American virtue, the fact that the narratives are predicated on Mexican–American violence, even if by false accusation, restricts the judgment. After all, it is the Mexican–American who is on trial, and not the racist individuals or society that put him there. At the same time, the trials reaffirm the activist role of the legal system and state (often with lynch mobs

57

as the alternative), so that racism must, in effect, be worked out through the passing of judgment upon the Mexican–American protagonist. In both instances, the judgment functions to situate the Mexican–American characters within a social matrix of ideological assimilation, within either *barrio* segregation or, in a few instances, racial integration.

For the most part, the social problem films return the protagonist to the *barrio*. The Mexican–American's efforts to enter the professional mainstream (*Bordertown*) or achieve economic parity (*A Medal for Benny*, *The Ring*, *Salt of the Earth*) are sanctioned only within the confines and reduced scale of the *barrio*. In *Bordertown* Johnny Ramirez (Paul Muni) fails both as a lawyer, having been disbarred for violent behavior, and as a bordertown casino manager. In the end, he returns to the *barrio*, 'Back where I belong . . . with my own people', framed between his *padre* and mother, between church and home, the *barrio*'s two more traditional (that is, conservative) institutions. Here, *padre* refers to a priest, but its other meaning, father, is also significant because of how the ending situates Ramirez within the *barrio* via a symbolic, institutional family. Even that, however, may not have been enough closure within the Mexican–American generation, as the *New York Times* reviewer made clear: 'The Mexican's [*sic*] feeble confessional . . . is an unconvincing and inconsistent denouement for the career of such a vigorous rebel against the *established order*' (Sennwald, 1935; emphasis mine). The reviewer may have also objected to the fact that Ramirez uses his ill-gotten wealth to endow a *barrio* law school. In any case, subsequent films would achieve closure through national, rather than *barrio*, institutions: the press, military, legal system, and labor unions.

In *A Medal for Benny* and *The Lawless*, discrimination is identified as the product of small-town provincialism. In particular, the films contrast the town's business leaders and police with more benevolent national institutions: the military in *A Medal for Benny*, and the free press in *The Lawless*. Ultimately, however, this conflict is a red herring, in so far as the towns' social hierarchies remain unchallenged. The conflict is not over federalism, but over the 'space of identification' for the Mexican–American. In *A Medal for Benny* – one of many wartime 'racial unity' films that were released as enlistment propaganda – Joe Morales (Arturo de Córdova) at first identifies himself with the economic opportunism of the town's chamber of commerce, which intends to exploit the national recognition of Benny Martin's heroism. When the general and military come to town, Martin's father, Charley (J. Carroll Nash), is given a nice house, rather than have him represent the town from his *barrio* shack. Likewise, earlier in the film Morales 'borrows' Charley's rent money in order to invest in a boat and, when it sinks, 'borrows' even more in order to purchase an expensive dress for Benny's girlfriend, Lolita Sierra (Dorothy Lamour). When Charley refuses to play along, the general, to the surprise of the town leaders, insists on going to the *barrio* to present the medal, since 'a lot of fine Americans come out of shacks'. Whereas the town leaders, with full police escort, had earlier descended upon the *barrio* in order to retrieve Charley, the general arrives with a full military parade in order to salute the contribution Charley made from within the *barrio*. At this point, Morales's identification shifts from economic opportun-

58

ism (business/town) to national service (military/*barrio*), and he enlists, a move that rewards him with Benny's girlfriend, when and if he returns to the *barrio*.

In *The Lawless* and *Trial*, each accused, 'fatherless' Mexican–American youth acquires an Anglo–American, institutional father-figure who defends him. The journalist in *The Lawless* saves Paul Rodriguez (Lalo Rios) from a lynch mob, and later uses the press to initiate a defense committee. Although Rodriguez's father is alive, his 'defeatist withdrawal' (Roffman and Purdy, 1981, p. 255) allows the journalist to assume a father-like role. In *Trial*, the paternal connection is made even more explicit, in the lawyer's half-hearted insistence that Angel Chavez (Rafael Campos) behave like his client and not his son. Throughout the trial, Chavez asks questions so that he, too, can become a lawyer. These questions provide a clever exposition device that allows the film to describe due process and guilt by association, with Chavez complicit, if not eager, in how these lead to his own conviction and death sentence.

Chavez is accused of murder when he is caught at an all-white beach with his white girlfriend dead at his feet. She had just recovered from rheumatic fever, and the excitement of 'making love' (kissing) resulted in a heart attack. In the course of the trial, Chavez's lawyer discovers that his own boss is a Communist, and is using the case to raise funds, stir up racial hatred, and martyr Chavez for the Party. In the end, the jury finds Chavez guilty of murder, punishable by death. Chavez's lawyer, however, exposes his boss's affiliations and intentions to the judge, and offers an alternative judgment, since Chavez is a minor. Rather than apply the letter of the Felony Murder Act, he suggests that the judge *also* apply the letter of the Juvenile Defenders Act (normally for trivial offenses), which allows for an indeterminant sentence. Thus, he argues, 'through its own technicalities', the law can correct its own errors. The prosecution agrees with the defense's 'most ingenious theory of law', and admits that he was 'sure that Angel Chavez was technically guilty . . . [but] . . . that his guilt was only technical'. In essence, the two lawyers agree that Chavez is, in fact, innocent of murder, but uphold the conviction and the harsh rules of law that secured it. In these two references to legal technicalities, *Trial* suggests that the law is an arbitrary construct, not rooted in a moral absolute. What does hold the legal system together, then, is the notion of 'guilt by association': that in his sexual and political mis-associations, Chavez merits some form of punishment. (Meanwhile, the racist townspeople 'have learned an awful lot' as mere spectators.) Thus, the judge sentences Chavez to the State Industrial School for an indeterminate period of time, 'until the principal determines that your release will serve your own best interests and those of society'. In perhaps the most visceral way, the law(yer) becomes Chavez's father, and metes out the 'justice' he claims the reformed townspeople now desire: his socialization by the state into the working class.

In an apparent (and isolated) shift in the above dynamic, two Ricardo Montalban films – *My Man and I* and *Right Cross* – end with his character's marriage to an Anglo–American blonde. For perhaps the first time in the American cinema, the sanctioned miscegenation between Mexican and

American involved a Mexican–American male. Upon closer examination, however, these films do not result in the Mexican–American's integration into the so-called 'dominant white culture', but nor do they punish and exile the Anglo–American woman to the *barrio*. While the Mexican–American was repeatedly identified in the United States as a racial minority, the PCA defined its prohibition on miscegenation as sex between the *black* and *white* races. If in cultural politics Mexican–Americans were represented as neither Mexican nor American, the same dynamic held with respect to race: neither black nor white. But even such an ambiguous position had to be constructed and maintained. Montalban's status as a second-generation Latin lover (of Spanish descent), itself a step removed from 'Mexican', and his light skin color allowed him to function within the color line's grey zone.

The Ricardo Montalban films, however, also reveal a class-based stratification of 'whiteness' in the decade after the Second World War. While the women in both films are blondes, neither represents the dominant culture. In *My Man and I*, Shelley Winters, Hollywood's 'bad girl', portrays a low-class alcoholic down on her luck; while in *Right Cross*, June Allyson, Hollywood's 'girl next door', portrays an ethnic-Catholic Irish–American. Thus, the Mex-

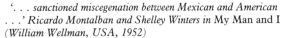

*'. . . sanctioned miscegenation between Mexican and American
. . .' Ricardo Montalban and Shelley Winters in* My Man and I
(William Wellman, USA, 1952)

60

ican–American character can, through assimilation and miscegenation, leave the *barrio* behind, but still be placed within class and ethnic boundaries. In *Right Cross*, the Irish are shown to be as short-tempered, devout, dispossessed, and nostalgically nationalist as the Mexican–Americans.

While the script for *My Man and I* led Breen to recommend to MGM producer Dore Schary that he 'get proper technical advice from the Mexican angle', the end product raises questions about the narrative function of Mexican–American representation in the social problem films. On a manifest level, the social contradictions about Mexican–American citizenship are resolved, with the Mexican–American generation repatriated, segregated and institutionalized in the name of assimilation, the same ideal the Mexican–American generation incorporated into its own, reformist political discourse. But in its representation of the Mexican–American, most social problem films were more concerned with not offending Mexico than with presenting an 'authentic' ethnic-American portrayal. In *My Man and I*, *A Medal for Benny*, and *Bordertown*, the Mexican–American characters speak a pidgin English devoid of articles and pronouns, even though the Spanish language makes even greater use of these determiners than does English. But perhaps the most telling sign is that every film presents Spanish-language dialogue *without* subtitles. In these respects, *Giant* is an exception. While Shurlock cites errors in the Spanish-language dialogue, *Giant* alone uses that dialogue, again un-subtitled, to establish two levels of signification. Bick Benedict speaks fluent Spanish to give orders to his 'Mexican' employees, while his new wife from the East Coast does the unthinkable, and asks for their names and about their health in English. When the characters speak Spanish in the other films, it functions as an empty code for ethnicity. In short, there is no need for subtitles, because nothing is said.

It is here that the narrative function of emplacement becomes visible, in the recognition of the *de facto* mainstream, English-monolingual audience for these films. These were not, after all, the equivalent of the Hollywood 'race' films. The oft-praised *Salt of the Earth* was no exception: it spoke more to the ex-Hollywood production team's blacklisting than to the New Mexico *hispano* community, which it portrays as *mexicano* with an even more improbable neo-indigenous nationalism. These internal distinctions, of course, are often overlooked in most films – whether exploitation, social problem or progressive parable – since the narratives are more concerned with the opposition between dominant culture and subculture. Thus, the social problem films situated the Mexican–American character for a largely Anglo–American audience. For a narrative articulation of this process, recall the townspeople in *Trial* who learn 'an awful lot' as courtroom spectators.

But the significance of the audience is perhaps most evident in the relationship between sanctioned miscegenation and genre. Briefly, the two films in which Ricardo Montalban marries a blonde woman are romantic melodramas; in other words, women's films. The print ads for both films feature a shirtless Montalban embracing the female lead. For *Right Cross*, one caption read: 'Girls!!! Would you do what June Allyson did? Have you ever loved a man so much that you'd pursue him no matter what?'[12] Perhaps more than anything, these ads construct a 'space of identification' for the post-Second

World War working-class woman. In fact, the role of women serves as the 'political unconscious' in these social problem films, so that the Anglo–American and Mexican–American female characters become complicit in the placement of the Mexican–American male protagonist within an appropriate class-defined, protestant work ethnic. In *A Medal for Benny* and *The Ring*, for example, it is the 'traditional' Mexican–American girlfriend who leads the protagonist back to the *barrio*, where – one way or another – he will support her. In this way, the female spectator, to the extent that she identifies with the female lead, unwittingly places herself alongside the Mexican–American male, becoming the mechanism that will keep him (and by extension, her) within a marginal social context.

That identification is constructed in opposition to other female characters who serve as the real evil or racist forces in these films: the married seductresses in *My Man and I* and *Bordertown* (classified at the time as a melodrama); and the 'overprotective mamá' in *Right Cross*, among other films (see Berg, 1992). Furthermore, in *Bordertown*, the single socialite who sexually taunts Ramirez, calling him 'savage', is also punished (with death) for her willful transgression of class *and* racial boundaries.

In *Giant*, the Anglo–American man marries the Mexican woman, for in the male-identified Western genre, the Anglo–American protagonist can cross racial *and* class boundaries. After all, in the 50s variant on American patriarchal society, it is the man who determines and provides economic and class status, as well as family name. *Giant*, however, provides a subtle turn on these conventions: the hero's effeminate son, Jordan (Dennis Hopper), is the one who marries the submissive *mestiza* Juana (Elsa Cárdenas). Furthermore, the nearly equitable relationship between Jordan and Juana produces the logical outcome that the 'greaser' films point toward, but can in no way envision: a *mestizo*–Anglo infant (and his Anglo cousin), depicted in widescreen close-up. This rare moment in the American cinema on ethnicity stops the 'epic' narrative cold, with both hope and uncertainty.

With the exception of *Salt of the Earth* and *Giant*, the social problem films 'about' Mexican–Americans center on a 'Mexican' male protagonist and his place or role within American society. In contrast, *Salt of the Earth* and *Giant* employ a feminist critique in order to reorient class and racial hierarchies. *Giant*, however, does so on both corporeal and symbolic levels, with 'miscegenation' between East (Leslie [Elizabeth Taylor]) and West (Bick), and, in the next generation, North (Jordan) and South (Juana). In this sense, the film embodies, or finds affinities with, the Latin American concept of *mestizaje*, which, in post-Second World War thought, offered *mestizo* racial mixture as the solution to Nazi (et al.) ideologies of racial purity.[13] In its familial construction of a new American culture – Eastern liberalism, Western capitalism and Mexican–Americanism – *Giant* also anticipates the cultural redefinition of *mestizaje* by Chicano and Anglo–American border artists.[14]

TOWARD AN ALTERNATIVE: 'CAN TWO FIGHTERS BRING OUT A THIRD?'

In the period before a Chicano counter-cinema offered the possibilities of self-representation, Mexican–American (and, later, Chicano) audiences were by no means passive viewers and engaged in a range of responses: editorials and boycotts since the 1910s (Limón, 1973; García, 1989, p. 216), behind-the-scenes negotiations by Mexican-born actors over character portrayal (Rios-Bustamante, 1988), and cultural syncretism (Monroy, 1988–90). The latter response can be seen in the use of cinematic tropes and themes in Chicano literature (for example in the novels of Ron Arias and Oscar Zeta Acosta) and poetry. In an unpublished collection of 20 poems, *Scene from the Movie 'Giant'*, Tino Villanueva explores the impact of the film's café scene in which the racist protagonist defends a Mexican–American family only to be beaten up by the café owner, Sarge. Villanueva had seen the film in 1956, when he was fourteen, and found himself 'awakened, transfigured in some/ Faint and inner way by rage' by that brief scene near the end of the film. In 'Fight Scene: Final Frames', he wonders, 'When may I learn strongly to act, who am caught/In this light like a still photograph? Can two fighters/Bring out a third?' If that scene marked the moment when the young Villanueva became self-conscious, it also set in motion the 'still photograph' or third fighter soon-to-be: 'Now I think: *the/Poem's the thing wherein I'll etch the semblance/Of the film.*' Villanueva's collection (begun as early as 1973) is in some sense a return-of-the-repressed of the impact of Hollywood and 'American' culture on the development of Chicano artistic expression in poetry, literature and film. In references from *Hamlet* to *Giant*, Villanueva makes dominant representations and traditions subordinate to the cultural syncretism of the so-called margins.

In the late 60s Chicano cinema developed as an alternative film practice within the overall project of the Chicano civil rights movement. In the post-movement period, but especially under the historical amnesia of the Reagan era, Chicano directors initiated a historical revisionism of the Mexican–American Generation. In feature films (*Zoot Suit* (1981), *La Bamba* (1987), *Break of Dawn* (1988)), documentaries (*Ballad of an Unsung Hero* (1985), *The Lemon Grove Incident* (1985)), and short dramas (*Distant Water* (1990)), film-makers researched and reclaimed the 'Chicano experience' within American history. Chicano film-makers also researched the unwritten history of Mexican–American and Chicano cinematic representation. For example, in his writings, Jesús Treviño criticized the café scene in *Giant* for its portrayal of the Chicano as passive: 'Despite countless historical incidences in which Texas Mexicans have stood up for their rights, in *Giant* they must once again await help from well-intentioned saviors of the dominant society' (Treviño, 1985, p. 15). For Treviño, Chicano and Latino film-makers were the 'third fighter' brought forth by these films. From the start, 'classical' and Chicano-themed films became part of the film-makers' self-conscious frame of reference, if not their *raison d'être*.

In their efforts to provide an alternative to Hollywood, the Chicano film-makers entered into an intertextual dialogue with previous representation. In fact, one can argue that the first two Chicano feature films 'signify' upon the Hollywood social problem film, thereby inverting the genre's usual ideological thrust (see Gates, Jr., 1988). Treviño's *Raíces de sangre* (Mexico, 1977), for example, retells *Bordertown*, shifting the moral point of view from the Anglo–American to the Chicano community, thereby transforming the earlier film's enlightened segregationism into a radical separatism. In both films the protagonist, a bordertown lawyer, reforms when he comes around the film's moral point of view, eschews violence and returns to the *barrio*. The independent feature *Only Once in a Lifetime* (1978, directed by Alejandro Grattan), on the other hand, uses the social problem 'drama-comedy', a hybrid used in *A Medal for Benny* and somewhat typical of American social problem films in the 70s. Again, the protagonist returns to the *barrio*, but, as in *Raíces de sangre*, with an activist intent designed to confront American society on a collective, rather than individual, level. The Chicano vernacular equivalent to 'signify' would be to render the Hollywood genre *al estilo chicano*, a discursive strategy attributed to Chicano cinema by both film-makers (Camplis, 1975) and critics (Barrios, 1985).

In that subtle yet significant shift, these two Chicano-produced feature films initiated a counter-discourse on Mexican–American citizenship, one that stressed a cultural nationalist, rather than assimilationist, identity, or found traces of it in historical dramas of resistance such as *Zoot Suit* and *Break of Dawn*. For its part, Hollywood responded as it had in the past, when Mexico protested the silent 'greaser' films: it simply stopped producing films 'about' Mexican–Americans or Chicanos when *Boulevard Nights* and *Walk Proud* encountered organized protests. Rather than 'reform' Chicano representation, Hollywood moved the 'convenient villains' to the margins of other narratives, especially the new, urban Western: the action or police drama.

Taken together, the silent 'greaser' films, the social problem films about Mexican–Americans, and the Chicano-produced feature films constitute the American cinema's explicit discourse on Chicano citizenship. Throughout the eighty years of that discourse, Hollywood has engaged – through outright stereotype, 'enlightened' segregationism and, now, silence – in a politics of denial. In the period between 1930 and 1960, often with the intervention of PCA censors, these films attempted to mediate Mexican–American demands for assimilation and the rights of citizenship, and resituate them around other issues related to national politics, juvenile delinquency and changes in class-based gender roles. It is little wonder, then, that the post-Mexican–American generation, or Chicanos, would reject political accommodation and assimilation, and stress instead a politics of cultural difference.

Notes

1. Portions of this essay appear in earlier versions in Noriega, 1991a, and Noriega, 1991b. Archival research into the production files and censorship correspondence at the Margaret Herrick Library (Beverly Hills) and the Warner Brothers Archives (University of Southern California) was made possible through a travel grant from the Stanford Center for Chicano Research, January 1990.
2. Joseph Breen, letter to Dory Schary, MGM, 9 July 1952. MPAA Production Code Administration (PCA) case files: *My Man and I* (1951). The Margaret Herrick Library (MHL).
3. These particular phrases are taken from an initial script of *The Ring*. See Joseph Breen, letter to Franklin King, King Bros. Productions, 19 November 1951. MPAA PCA case files: *The Ring* (1951). MHL.

4. As cited in Finlay McDermid, memo to George Stevens and Henry Ginsberg, 13 April 1955. Production Files: *Giant* (1956). Box #403. Warner Brothers Archive, University of Southern California (WBA).
5. Joseph Breen, letter to Jack Warner, Warner Brothers, 10 July 1934. Production Files: *Bordertown* (1935). B-29. WBA.
6. Joseph Breen, letter to Jack Warner, Warner Brothers, 10 August 1934. Production Files: *Bordertown* (1935). B-29. WBA.
7. Joseph Breen, letter to Luigi Luraschi, Paramount Pictures, 5 October 1949. MPAA PCA case files: *The Lawless* (1949). MHL.
8. Joseph Breen, letter to Franklin King, 19 November 1951. Cited above, n. 3.
9. One of the earliest uses of 'Anglo' in a Hollywood film that I have come across.
10. Geoffrey Shurlock, letter to Dore Schary, MGM, 30 March 1955. MPAA PCA case files: *Trial* (1955). MHL.
11. In my discussion, I rely upon the concepts of practitioner-oriented script analysts for 'classic' story structure. For an initial application of these concepts to recent Chicano-produced and -themed feature films, see Barrera, 1992.
12. MGM Press Book: *My Man and I* and *Right Cross*. School of Cinema–Television, University of Southern California.
13. For a historically important expression of this concept, see Vasconcelos, 1948.
14. In particular, I refer to writers such as Gloria Anzaldúa, and the Border Arts Workshop/Taller de Arte Fronterizo (BAW/TAF) in San Diego/Tijuana, whose members have included Isaac Artenstein, David Avalos, Phillip and Amy Brookman, Emily Hicks, and Guillermo Gómez-Peña.

Works Cited

Barrera, Mario. 'Story Structure in Latino Feature Films', in Noriega, 1992: 245–68.
Barrios, Gregg. 'A Cinema of Failure, A Cinema of Hunger: The Films of Efraín Gutiérrez', in Keller, 1985: 179–80.
Berg, Charles Ramírez. '*Bordertown*, the Assimilation Narrative and the Chicano Social Problem Film', in Noriega, 1992: 33–52.
Bhabha, Homi K. 'The Other Question . . .' *Screen* 24.6 (Nov./Dec. 1983): 18–36.
Camplis, Francisco X. 'Towards the Development of a Raza Cinema', in *Perspectives on Chicano Education*, Tobias and Sandra Gonzales (eds.). Stanford, Calif.: Chicano Fellows/Stanford University, 1975. 155–73. (Reprinted in Noriega, 1992: 317–36.)
De León, Arnoldo. *They Called Them Greasers: Anglo Attitudes Toward Mexicans in Texas, 1821–1900*. Austin: University of Texas Press, 1983.
Delpar, Helen. 'Goodbye to the "Greaser": Mexico, the MPPDA, and Derogatory Films, 1922–1926'. *Journal of Popular Film and Television* 12.1 (1984): 34–41.
García, Mario T. *Mexican Americans: Leadership, Ideology and Identity, 1930–1960*. New Haven: Yale University Press, 1989.
García Riera, Emilio. *México visto por el cine extranjero*. Vols. I–IV. México, D.F.: Ediciones ERA, 1987–90.
Gates, Jr., Henry Louis. *The Signifying Monkey: A Theory of African–American Literary Criticism*. Oxford: Oxford University Press, 1988.
Jacobs, Lea. 'Industry Self-Regulation and the Problem of Textual Determination'. *The Velvet Light Trap* 23 (Spring 1989): 4–15.
Jameson, Fredric. *The Political Unconscious: Narrative as Socially Symbolic Act*. Ithaca, NY: Cornell University Press, 1981.
Keller, Gary D. (ed.). *Chicano Cinema: Research, Reviews, and Resources*. Binghamton, NY: Bilingual Review/Press, 1985.
Lamb, Blaine P. 'The Convenient Villain: The Early Cinema Views the Mexican–American'. *Journal of the West* 14.4 (October 1975): 75–81.
Limón, José E. 'Stereotyping and Chicano Resistance: An Historical Dimension'.

Aztlán: International Journal of Chicano Studies Research 4.2 (Fall, 1973): 257–70. (Reprinted in Noriega, 1992: 3–20.)

Mazón, Mauricio. *The Zoot Suit Riots: The Psychology of Symbolic Annihilation*. Austin: University of Texas Press, 1984.

Monroy, Douglas. 'Our Children Get So Different Here': Film, Fashion, Popular Culture and the Process of Cultural Syncretization in Mexican Los Angeles, 1900–1935'. *Aztlán: A Journal of Chicano Studies* 19.1 (Spring, 1988): 79–108.

Navasky, Victor S. *Naming Names*. New York: Viking Press, 1980.

Noriega, Chon A. *Road to Aztlán: Chicanos and Narrative Cinema*. PhD dissertation. Stanford University, 1991a.

– . 'Citizen Chicano: The Trials and Titillations of Ethnicity in the American Cinema, 1935–1962'. *Social Research: An International Quarterly on the Social Sciences* 58.2 (Summer, 1991b): 413–38.

– (ed.). *Chicanos and Film: Essays on Chicano Representation and Resistance*. New York: Garland Publishing, 1992.

Pettit, Arthur G. *Images of the Mexican–American in Fiction and Film*. College Station: Texas A&M University Press, 1980.

Rios-Bustamante, Antonio. 'Latinos in the Hollywood Film Industry, 1920–1950s'. *Americas 2001*, January 1988: 6–12.

Roffman, Peter and Purdy, Jim. *The Hollywood Social Problem Film: Madness, Despair and Politics from the Depression to the Fifties*. Bloomington: Indiana University Press, 1981.

Sennwald, Andre. 'The Strand Reopens With *Bordertown*, a Picturesque Melodrama With Paul Muni and Bette Davis'. *New York Times*, 24 January 1935: 22.

Treviño, Jesús Salvador. 'Latino Portrayals in Film and Television', *JumpCut* 30 (March, 1985): 14–16.

Vasconcelos, José. *La raza cósmica*. México, D.F.: Espasa-Calpe Mexicana, 1948.

Villanueva, Tino. *Scene from the Movie 'Giant'*. Unpublished manuscript, quoted with permission of the author.

Woll, Allen L. *The Latin Image in American Film*. Los Angeles: UCLA Latin American Center Publications, 1977.

ARE ALL LATINS FROM MANHATTAN?

Hollywood, Ethnography and Cultural Colonialism

ANA M. LÓPEZ

Editors' Introduction

Irvin Cummings's *That Night in Rio*, filmed in the early 1940s, has Carmen Miranda at her most ebullient. Her co-star Don Ameche appears in an early cabaret act, dressed in a US naval uniform, and sings a precise 'Good Neighborly' message:

My friends I send felicitations
To our South American relations
May we never leave behind us
All those common ties that bind us
One hundred and thirty million people send regards to you.

We seem light years away from the brutal racism of *The Greaser's Revenge* outlined in de Orellana's essay. From the early 30s the Good Neighbor Policy – an attempt to restore production, employment and prosperity to the domestic US economy after the slump, by expanding exports to, and investment in, Latin America – had paid close attention to cultural diplomacy. This policy was given further shape at the outbreak of war by the founding of the office of the Coordinator of Inter-American Affairs in 1940 under Nelson Rockefeller, which orchestrated economic and cultural programmes in Latin America.

Ana López charts the shifts in Hollywood's 'ethnographic' view of Latin America by tracing the work of three emblematic 'cross-over' stars, Dolores del Río, Lupe Vélez and Carmen Miranda, all of whom represented different aspects of the exotic 'other' from the late 20s to the mid-40s: from sultry temptress, to aloof indifference, to Mexican spitfire, to carnivalesque excess. She argues that the work of these actresses, especially of Carmen Miranda, fissures the stability of their films, allowing no easily consumable stereotypes to be formed. Carmen Miranda, with tottering heels, tutti-frutti hats and linguistic anarchy takes a parodic revenge on the format that brought her notoriety and a world-wide reputation.

□

She's a Latin from Manhattan
I can tell by her mañana
She's a Latin from Manhattan
And not Havana.

AL JOLSON in *Go Into Your Dance* (1935)

HOLLYWOOD AS ETHNOGRAPHER OF THE AMERICAS

To presume that Hollywood has served as an ethnographer of American culture means, first of all, to conceive of ethnography, not as a positivist methodology that unearths truths about 'other' cultures,[1] but as a historically determined practice of cultural interpretation and representation from the standpoint of participant observation.[2] It also means to think of Hollywood not as a simple reproducer of fixed and homogeneous cultures or ideologies, but as a producer of some of the multiple discourses that intervene in, affirm and contest the socio-ideological struggles of a given moment. To think of a classic Hollywood film as ethnographic discourse is to affirm its status as an authored, yet collaborative, enterprise, akin in practice to the way contemporary ethnographers like James Clifford have redefined their discipline.[3]

When ethnographers posit their work as 'the mutual, dialogical production of a discourse' about culture that 'in its ideal form would result in a polyphonic text', we also approach a description of the operations of an ideal, albeit not of Hollywood's, cinema.[4] The difference lies in the deployment of power relations, what Edward Said calls the 'effect of domination', or the ethnographic, cinematic, and colonial process of designing an identity for the 'other' and, for the observer, a standpoint from which to see without being seen.[5] Obviously, neither ethnography nor the cinema have achieved that ideal state of perfect polyphony or perspectival relativity where the observer/ observed dichotomy can be transcended and no participant has 'the final word in the form of a framing story or encompassing synthesis'.[6] Power relations always interfere. However, both ethnographic and cinematic texts, as discourses, carry the traces of this dialogic process and of the power relations that structure it.

Thinking of Hollywood as ethnographer, as co-producer in power of cultural texts, allows us to reformulate its relationship to ethnicity. Hollywood does not represent ethnics and minorities: it creates them and provides its audience with an experience of them. Rather than an investigation of mimetic relationships, then, a critical reading of Hollywood's ethnographic discourse requires the analysis of the historical–political construction of self–'other' relations – the articulation of forms of difference, sexual and ethnic – as an inscription of, among other factors, Hollywood's power as ethnographer, creator and translator of 'otherness'.

The way the history of Hollywood's representations of Hispanics has been told privileges a near-golden moment when Hollywood apparently became temporarily more sensitive and produced less stereotypical, almost positive, images of Latin Americans. I shall focus upon this period – the 'Good Neighbor Policy' years (roughly 1939–47) – in order to analyze the moment's historical coherence and its function for Hollywood as an ethnographic institution, that is as creator, integrator, and translator of 'otherness'. What happens when Hollywood self-consciously and intentionally assumes the role of cultural ethnographer? My emphasis is on three stars whose ethnic 'otherness' was articulated according to parameters that shifted as Hollywood's ethnographic imperative became clear: Dolores del Río, Lupe Vélez, and Carmen Miranda. That these three figures are Latin American and female is, as will become apparent, much more than a simple coincidence, for the Latin American woman poses a double threat, sexual and racial, to Hollywood's ethnographic and colonial authority.

THE GOOD NEIGHBOR POLICY: HOLLYWOOD ZEROES IN ON LATIN AMERICA

After decades of portraying Latin Americans lackadaisically and sporadically as lazy peasants and wily señoritas who inhabited an undifferentiated backward land, Hollywood films between 1939 and 1947 featuring Latin American stars, music, locations and stories flooded US and international markets. By February 1943, for example, 30 films with Latin American themes or locales had been released and 25 more were in production. By April 1945, 84 films dealing with Latin American themes had been produced.[7] These films seemed to evidence a new-found sensibility, most notably a sudden respect for national and geographical boundaries. At the simplest level, for example, it seemed that Hollywood was exercising some care to differentiate between the cultural and geographic characteristics of different Latin American countries by incorporating general location shots, specific citations of iconographic sites (especially Rio de Janeiro's Corcovado Mountain), and some explanations of the cultural characteristics of the inhabitants.

Why did Hollywood suddenly become interested in Latin America? In economic terms, Latin America was the only foreign market available for exploitation during the Second World War. However, pan-Americanism was also an important key word for the Roosevelt administration, the Rockefeller Foundation, and the newly created (1940) State Department Office of the Coordinator for Inter-American Affairs (CIAA) headed by Nelson Rockefeller. Concerns about America's southern neighbors' dubious political allegiances and the safety of US investments in Latin America led to the resurrection of the long-dormant Good Neighbor Policy and to the official promotion of hemispheric unity, cooperation, and non-aggression (in part, to erase the memories of the not-so-distant military interventions in Cuba and Nicaragua). Charged with the responsibility of coordinating all efforts to promote inter-American understanding, the CIAA set up a Motion Picture Section and appointed John Hay Whitney, vice-president and director of the film library of the Museum of Modern Art (MOMA) in New York, as its director.[8]

The CIAA sponsored the production of newsreels and documentaries for Latin American distribution that showed 'the truth about the American way', contracted with Walt Disney in 1941 to produce a series of 24 shorts with Latin American themes that would 'carry the message of democracy and friendship below the Rio Grande', sponsored screenings of films that celebrated the 'democratic way' in what became known as the South American embassy circuit, and, together with the Hays Office's newly appointed Latin

American expert, began to pressure the studios to become more sensitive to Latin issues and portrayals.[9] This impetus, when coupled with the incentive of Latin America's eminently exploitable 4240 movie theaters, was sufficient to stimulate Hollywood to take on the project of educating Latin America about the democratic way of life and its American audience about its Latin American neighbors.

This self-appointed mission, however, needs to be questioned more closely. How does Hollywood position itself *and* Americans in relation to the southern neighbors? How is its friendliness constituted? How does it differ from Hollywood's prior circulation of so-called stereotypes and its negligent undifferentiation of the continent?

Three basic kinds of Good Neighbor Policy films were produced. First, there were a number of standard, classic Hollywood genre films, with American protagonists set in Latin America with some location shooting, for example, Irving Rapper's *Now Voyager* (1942), with extensive footage shot in Rio de Janeiro; Edward Dmytryk's *Cornered* (1945), shot totally on location in Buenos Aires; and Alfred Hitchcock's *Notorious* (1946), with second-unit location shots of Rio de Janeiro. Then there were B-productions set and often shot in Latin America that featured mediocre US actors and Latin entertainers in either musicals or pseudo-musical formats: for example, *Mexicana* (1945) starring Tito Guizar, Mexico's version of Frank Sinatra, and the 16-year-old Cuban torch singer Estelita Rodríguez; Gregory Ratoff's *Carnival in Costa Rica* (1947) starring Dick Haymes, Vera-Ellen, and Cesar Romero; and Edgar G. Ulmer's remake of *Grand Hotel*, *Club Havana* (1945), starring the starlet Isabelita, Tom Neil, and Margaret Lindsay. Finally, the most successful and most self-consciously 'good-neighborly' films were the mid-to-big-budget musical comedies set either in Latin America or in the USA but featuring, in addition to recognizable US stars, fairly well-known Latin American actors and entertainers.

Almost every studio produced its share of these films between 1939 and 1947, but 20th Century-Fox, RKO, and Republic specialized in 'good neighborliness' of the musical variety. Fox had Carmen Miranda under contract and produced nine films that featured her between 1940 and 1946; RKO followed the Rockefeller interest in Latin America by sending Orson Welles on a Good Neighbor tour of Brazil to make a film about Carnival, and with films such as *Pan-Americana* (1945); Republic exploited contract players – Tito Guizar and Estelita, for example – in a number of low-budget musicals such as *The Thrill of Brazil* (1946).

Notwithstanding the number of films produced, and the number of Latin American actors contracted, by the studios in this period, it is difficult to describe Hollywood's position with regard to these suddenly welcomed 'others' as respectful or reverent.[10] Hollywood (and the United States) needed to posit a complex 'otherness' as the flip side of wartime patriotism and nationalism and in order to assert and protect its economic interests. A special kind of 'other' was needed to reinforce the wartime national self, one that – unlike the German or Japanese 'other' – was non-threatening, potentially but not practically assimilable (that is, non-polluting to the purity of the race), friendly, fun-loving, and not deemed insulting to Latin American eyes and ears. Ultimately, Hollywood succeeded in all except, perhaps, the last category.

THE TRANSITION: FROM INDIFFERENCE TO 'DIFFERENCE' ACROSS THE BODIES OF WOMEN

Before the Good Neighbor Policy period, few Latin Americans had achieved star status in Hollywood. In fact, most of the 'vile' Latin Americans of the early Hollywood cinema were played by US actors. In the silent period, the Mexican actor Ramón Novarro, one of the few Latin American men to have had a consistent career in Hollywood, succeeded as a sensual yet feminized 'Latin lover' modeled on the Valentino icon,[11] but the appellation 'Latin' always connoted Mediterranean rather than Latin American. Ostensibly less threatening than men, Latin American women fared differently, particularly Dolores del Río and Lupe Vélez.

Del Río's Hollywood career spanned the silent and early sound eras. Although considered exotic, del Río appeared in a variety of films, working with directors as diverse as Raoul Walsh, King Vidor, and Orson Welles.[12] After a successful transition to talkies in Edwin Carewe's *Evangeline* (1929), her place in the Hollywood system was unquestionable and further legitimised by her marriage to the respected MGM art director Cedric Gibbons. Undeniably Latin American, del Río was not, however, identified exclusively with Latin roles. Hers was a vague upper-class exoticism articulated within a general category of 'foreign/other' tragic sensuality. This sensual 'other', an object of sexual fascination, transgression, fear, and capitulation not unlike Garbo or Dietrich, did not have a specific national or ethnic provenance, simply an aura of foreignness that accommodated her disruptive potential. Her 'otherness' was located and defined on a sexual rather than an ethnic register, and she portrayed, above all, ethnically vague characters with a weakness for American 'white/blond' men: Indian maidens, South Seas princesses, Mexican señoritas, and other aristocratic beauties. Although she often functioned as a repeatable stereotype, her undifferentiated sexuality was not easily tamed by the proto-colonial ethnographic imperatives of Hollywood's Good Neighbor period. In a precursor of the Good Neighbor films like *Flying Down to Rio* (1933), the explicit and irresistible sensuality of her aristocratic Carioca character (all she has to do is look at a man across a crowded nightclub and he is smitten for ever) could be articulated because it would be tamed by marriage to the American hero. However, in the films of the Good Neighbor cycle, that resolution and partial appeasement of the ethnically undifferentiated sexual threat of 'otherness' she unleashed was no longer available. As Carlos Fuentes has remarked, del Río was 'a goddess threatening to become a woman',[13] and neither category – goddess nor woman – was appropriate to Hollywood's self-appointed mission as goodwill imperialist ethnographer of the Americas. Del Río's persona and her articulation in Hollywood films, in fact, constitute a perfect cinematic example of what Homi K. Bhabba has described as the phenomenon of the colonial hybrid, a disavowed cultural differentiation necessary for the existence of colonial–imperialist authority, where 'what is disavowed [difference] is not repressed but repeated as something different – a mutation, a hybrid'.[14]

'*Carioca me back to old Rio de Janeiro*'. *Dolores del Río and Fred Astaire in* Flying Down to Rio (*Thornton Freeland, USA, 1933*)

Del Río chose to return to Mexico in 1943 and dedicated herself (with a few returns to Hollywood, most notably to appear in John Ford's *The Fugitive* (1947) and *Cheyenne Autumn* (1964)) to the Mexican cinema and stage, where she assumed a legendary fame inconceivable in Hollywood. The impossibility of her status for Hollywood in 1939–47 was, however, literally worked through the body of another Mexican actress, Lupe Vélez.

Like del Río's, Vélez's career began in the silent period, where she showed promise working with D. W. Griffith in *Lady of the Pavements* (1929) and other directors. But Vélez's position in Hollywood was defined not by her acting versatility, but by her smoldering ethnic identifiability. Although as striking as del Río's, Vélez's beauty and sexual appeal were aggressive, flamboyant, and stridently ethnic. Throughout the 30s she personified the hot-blooded, thickly accented, Latin temptress with insatiable sexual appetites, on screen – in films such as *Hot Pepper* (1933), *Strictly Dynamite* (1934), and *La Zandunga* (1938) – and with her star persona – by engaging in much-publicized simultaneous affairs with Gary Cooper, Ronald Colman, and Ricardo Cortez, and marrying Johnny Weismuller in 1933.[15] (Impossible to imagine a better match between screen and star biographies: Tarzan meets the beast of the Tropics.) Vélez was, in other words, outrageous, but her

72

sexual excessiveness, although clearly identified as specifically ethnic, was articulated as potentially subsumable. On and off screen, she, like del Río, was mated with and married American men.

The dangers of such explicit on-screen ethnic miscegenation became apparent in RKO's *Mexican Spitfire* eight-film series (1939–43), simultaneously Vélez's most successful films and an index of the inevitability of her failure. Vélez portrayed a Mexican entertainer, Carmelita, who falls in love and marries – after seducing him away from his legitimate Anglo fiancée – Dennis Lindsay, a nice New England man. Much to the dismay of his proper Puritan family, Dennis chooses to remain with Carmelita against all obstacles, including, as the series progressed, specific references to Carmelita's mixed blood, lack of breeding and social unacceptability, her refusal to put the entertainment business completely behind her to become a proper wife, her inability to help further his (floundering) advertising career, and her apparent lack of desire for offspring. Although the first couple of installments were very successful, the series was described as increasingly redundant, contrived, and patently 'absurd' by the press and was cancelled in 1943. Not only had it begun to lose money for RKO, but it also connoted a kind of Latin American 'otherness' anathema to the Good Neighbor mission. Summarily stated, the question that the series posed could no longer be tolerated because there were no 'good-neighborly' answers. The ethnic problematic of the series – intermarriage, miscegenation and integration – could not be explicitly addressed within the new, friendly climate. Ironically highlighting this fictional and ideological question, Vélez, out of wedlock and five months pregnant, committed suicide in 1944.

Neither del Río nor Vélez could be re-created as Good Neighbor ethnics, for their ethnic and sexual power were not assimilable within Hollywood's new, ostensibly friendly, and temperate regime. Del Río was not ethnic enough and too much of an actress; Vélez was too 'Latin' and untameable. Hollywood's new position was defined by a double ethnographic imperative, that is, by its self-appointed mission as translator of the ethnic and sexual threat of Latin American 'otherness' into peaceful good neighborliness *and* by its desire to use that translation to make further inroads into the resistant Latin American movie market without damaging its national box office. Therefore, it could not advantageously promote either a mythic, goddess-like actress with considerable institutional clout (del Río) or an ethnic volcano (Vélez) that was not even subdued by that most sacred of institutions, marriage to an American. What Hollywood's good neighbor regime demanded was the articulation of a different female star persona that could be readily identifiable as Latin American (with the sexual suggestiveness necessary to fit the prevailing stereotype) but whose sexuality was neither too attractive (to dispel the fear or attraction of miscegenation) nor so powerful as to demand its submission to a conquering American male.

THE PERFECT 'GOOD NEIGHBOR': FETISHISM, SELF AND 'OTHER(S)'

Hollywood's lust for Latin America as ally and market – and its self-conscious attempt to translate and tame the potentially disturbing radical (sexual

73

and ethnic) 'otherness' that the recognition of difference (or lack) entails – are clearest within the constraints of the musical comedy genre. Incorporated into the genre as exotic entertainers, Latin Americans were simultaneously marginalized and privileged. Although they were denied valid narrative functions, entertainment, rather than narrative coherence or complexity, is the locus of pleasure of the genre. Mapped on to the musical comedy form in both deprivative (the denial of a valid narrative function) and supplemental (the location of an excess pleasure) terms, this Hollywood version of Latin Americanness participates in the operations of fetishism and disavowal typical of the stereotype in colonial discourses.[16] This exercise of colonial or imperialist authority would peak, with a significant twist, in the Carmen Miranda films at 20th Century-Fox, a cycle which produced a public figure, Miranda, that lays bare, with surreal clarity, the scenario of Hollywood's own colonial fantasy and the problematics of ethnic representation in a colonial or imperialist context.[17]

In these films, Carmen Miranda functions, above all, as a fantastic or uncanny fetish. Everything about her is surreal, off-center, displaced on to a different regime: from her extravagant hats, midriff-baring multi-colored costumes, and five-inch platform shoes to her linguistic malapropisms, farcical sexuality, and high-pitched voice, she is an 'other', everyone's 'other'. Not even Brazilian-born (she was born in Portugal to parents who emmigrated to Brazil), she became synonymous with cinematic 'Latin Americanness', with an essence defined and mobilized by herself and Hollywood throughout the continent. As the *emcee* announces at the end of her first number in Busby Berkeley's *The Gang's All Here*, 'Well, there's your Good Neighbor Policy. Come on, honey, let's Good Neighbor it.'

Miranda was 'discovered' by Hollywood 'as is', that is, after her status as a top entertainer in Brazil (with more than 300 records, 5 films – including her first sound feature – and 9 Latin American tours) brought her to the New York stage, where her six-minute performance in *The Streets of Paris* (1939) transformed her into 'an overnight sensation'.[18] Her explicit Brazilianness (samba song-and-dance repertoire, Carnival-type costumes) was transformed into the epitome of *latinidad* by a series of films that 'placed' her in locales as varied as Lake Louise in the Canadian Rockies, Havana, or Buenos Aires.

Her validity as 'Latin American' was based on a rhetoric of visual and performative excess – of costume, sexuality, and musicality – that carried over on to the mode of address of the films themselves. Of course, since they were produced at Fox, a studio that depended on its superior Technicolor process to differentiate its product in the market-place,[19] these films are also almost painfully colorful, exploiting the technology to further inscribe Latin Americanness as tropicality. For example, although none of the Fox films were shot on location, *all* include markedly luscious travelogue-like sections justifying the authenticity of their locales. Even more interestingly, they also include the visual representation of travel, whether to the country in question or 'inland', as further proof of the validity of their ethno-presentation within a regime that privileges the visual as the only possible site of knowledge.

Weekend in Havana (1941) is a prototypical example. The film begins by introducing the lure of the exotic in a post-credit, narrative-establishment montage sequence that situates travel to Latin America as a desirable sight-seeing adventure: snow on the Brooklyn bridge dissolves to a brochure of leisure cruises to Havana, to a tourist guide to 'Cuba: The Holiday Isle of the Tropics', to a window display promoting 'Sail to Romance' cruises featuring life-sized cardboard cut-outs of Carmen Miranda and a band that come to life and sing the title song (which begins, 'How would you like to spend the weekend in Havana . . .'). Immediately after, the romantic plot of the musical is set up: Alice Faye plays a Macy's salesgirl whose much-scrimped-for Caribbean cruise is ruined when her ship runs aground. She refuses to sign the shipping company's release and is appeased only with the promise of 'romance' in an all-expenses-paid tour of Havana with shipping-company executive John Payne.

The trip from the marooned cruise ship to Havana is again represented by an exuberantly colorful montage of the typical tourist sights of Havana – el Morro Castle, the Malecón, the Hotel Nacional, Sloppy Joe's Bar – with a voice-over medley of 'Weekend in Havana' and typical Cuban songs. Finally, once ensconced in the most luxurious hotel in the city, Faye is taken to see the sights by John Payne. They travel by taxi to a sugar plantation, where Payne's lecture from a tourist book, although it bores Faye to yawns, does serve as a voice-over narration for the visual presentation of 'Cubans at work': 'Hundreds of thousands of Cubans are involved with the production of this important commodity . . .' These three sequences serve important narrative and legitimising functions, testifying to the authenticity of the film's ethno-graphic and documentary work, although the featured native entertainer, Rosita Rivas (Miranda), is neither Cuban nor speaks Spanish.

More complexly, all the Fox films depend upon Miranda's performative excess to validate their authority as 'good-neighborly' ethnographic dis-courses. The films' simple plots – often remakes of prior musical successes and most commonly involving some kind of mistaken identity or similar snafu – further highlight the importance of the Miranda-identified visual and musical regime rather than the legitimizing narrative order. The beginning of *The Gang's All Here*, for example, clearly underlines this operation by pre-senting a narrativized representation of travel, commerce, and ethnic ident-ity. After the credits, a half-lit floating head singing Ary Barroso's 'Brasil' in Portuguese suddenly shifts (in a classic Busby Berkeley syntactical move) to the hull of a ship emblazoned with the name *SS Brazil*, docking in New York and unloading typical Brazilian products: sugar, coffee, bananas, straw-berries, and Carmen Miranda. Wearing a hat featuring her native fruits, Miranda finishes the song, triumphantly strides into New York, switches to an English tune, and is handed the keys to the city by the mayor as the camera tracks back to reveal the stage of a nightclub, an Anglo audience to whom she is introduced *as* the Good Neighbor Policy and whom she instructs to dance the 'Uncle Sam-ba'.

The Fox films' most amazing characteristic is Miranda's immutability and the substitutability of the narratives. Miranda travels and is inserted into different landscapes, but she remains the same from film to film, purely Latin American. Whether the action of the film is set in Buenos Aires, Havana, the Canadian Rockies, Manhattan, or a Connecticut mansion, the on-screen

Miranda character – most often named Carmen or Rosita – is remarkably coherent: above all, and against all odds, an entertainer and the most entertaining element in all the films.[20] While the American characters work out the inevitable romance plot of the musical comedy, Miranda (always a thorn to the budding romance) puts on a show and dallies outrageously with the leading men. Normally not permanently mated with an American protagonist (with the notable exception of *That Night in Rio*, where she gets to keep Don Ameche, but only because his identical double gets the white girl played by Alice Faye), Miranda nevertheless gets to have her fun along the way and always entices and almost seduces with aggressive kisses and embraces at least one, but most often several, of the American men.

Miranda's sexuality is so aggressive, however, that it is diffused, spent in gesture, innuendo, and salacious commentary. Unlike Vélez, who can seduce and marry a nice WASP man, Miranda remains either contentedly single, attached to a Latin American Lothario (for example, the womanizing manager-cum-gigolo played by Cesar Romero in *Weekend in Havana*), or in the permanent never-never land of prolonged and unconsummated engagements to unlikely American types (for example, in *Copacabana* she has been

'. . . she is an "other", everyone's "other" '. *Carmen Miranda and Don Ameche in* That Night in Rio (*Irving Cummings, USA, 1941*)

76

engaged for ten years to Groucho Marx and, at the end of the film, they still have separate hotel rooms and no shared marriage vows).

Miranda, not unlike other on-screen female performers (Dietrich in the Sternberg films, for example), is meant to function narratively and discursively as a sexual fetish, freezing the narrative and the pleasures of the voyeuristic gaze and provoking a regime of spectacle and specularity. She acknowledges and openly participates in her fetishization, staring back at the camera, implicating the audience in her aggressive sexual display. But she is also an ethnic fetish. The look she returns is also that of the ethnographer and its colonial spectator stand-in. Her Latin Americanness is displaced in all its visual splendor for simultaneous colonial appopriation and denial.

Although Miranda is visually fetishized within filmic systems that locate her metaphorically as the emblem of knowledge of Latin Americanness, Miranda's voice, rife with cultural impurities and disturbing syncretisms, slips through the webs of Hollywood's colonial and ethnographic authority over the constitution and definition of 'otherness'. It is in fact within the aural register, constantly set against the legitimacy of the visual, that Hollywood's ethnographic good neighborliness breaks down in the Fox Miranda films. In addition to the psychosexual impact of her voice, Miranda's excessive manipulation of accents – the obviously shifting registers of tone and pitch between her spoken and sung English and between her English and Portuguese – inflates the fetish, cracking its surface while simultaneously aggrandizing it. Most obvious in the films where she sings consecutive numbers in each language (*Weekend in Havana* and *The Gang's All Here* are two examples), the tonal differences between her sung and spoken Portuguese and her English indicate the possibility that her excessive accent and her linguistic malapropisms are no more than a pretense, a nod to the requirements of a conception of foreignness and 'otherness' necessary to maintain the validity of the text in question as well as her persona as a gesture of good neighborliness. That the press and studio machinery constantly remarked upon her accent and problems with English further highlight their ambiguous status.[21] At once a sign of her 'otherness' as well as of the artificiality of all 'otherness', her accent ultimately became an efficient marketing device, exploited in advertisements and publicity campaigns.[22]

Throughout the Good Neighbor films, Miranda remains a fetish, but a surreal one that self-consciously underlines the difficult balance between knowledge and belief that sustains it and that lets us hear the edges of an unclassifiable difference, product of an almost indescribable *bricolage*, that rejects the totalizing search for truth of the good-neighborly Hollywood ethnographer while simultaneously submitting to its designs.

'ARE ALL LATINS FROM MANHATTAN?'
Miranda's Hollywood career was cut short both by the demise of Hollywood's good neighborliness in the post-war era as well as by her untimely death in 1955.[23] However, Hollywood's circulation and use of her persona as the emblem of the Good Neighbor clearly demonstrates the fissures of Hollywood's work as Latin American ethnographer in this period. With Miranda's acquiescence and active participation, Hollywood ensconced her as the

essence of Latin American 'otherness' in terms that, on the surface, were both non-derogatory and simultaneously non-threatening. First, as a female emblem, her position was always that of a less-threatening 'other'. In this context, the potential threat of her sexuality (that which was troubling in Vélez, for example) was dissipated by its sheer visual and performative narrative excess. Furthermore, her legitimizing ethnicity, exacerbated by an aura of the carnivalesque and the absurd, could be narratively relegated to the stage, to the illusory (and tameable) world of performance, theater, and movies. This is perhaps most conclusively illustrated by the frequency with which her persona is used as the emblem of Latin American 'otherness' and exoticism in Hollywood films of the period: in *House Across the Bay* (Archie Mayo, 1940), Joan Bennett appears in a Miranda-inspired *baiana* costume; in *Babes in Arms* (Busby Berkeley, 1939), Mickey Rooney does a number while dressed like her; in *In This Our Life* (John Huston, 1942), Bette Davis plays and hums along to a Miranda record; and, in *Mildred Pierce* (Michael Curtiz, 1945), Jo Ann Marlow does a fully costumed Miranda imitation.

At the same time, however, Miranda's textual persona escapes the narrow parameters of the Good Neighbor. As a willing participant in the production of these self-conscious ethnographic texts, Miranda literally asserted her own voice in the textual operations that defined her as *the* 'other'. Transforming, mixing, ridiculing, and redefining her own difference against the expected standards, Miranda's speaking voice, songs, and accents create an 'other' text that is in counterpoint to the principal textual operations. She does not burst the illusory bubble of the Good Neighbor, but by inflating it beyond recognition she highlights its status as a discursive construct, as a mimetic myth.

When we recognize that Hollywood's relationship to ethnic and minority groups is primarily ethnographic – that is, one that involves the co-production in power of cultural texts – rather than merely mimetic, it becomes possible to understand the supposed Good Neighbor break in Hollywood's history of (mis)representations of Latin Americans textually as well as in instrumental and ideological terms. It is particularly important to recognize that Hollywood (and, by extension, television) fulfills this ethnographic function, because we are in an era that, not unlike the Good Neighbor years, is praised for its 'Hispanization'. While the media crows about the successes of films like *La Bamba*, *Salsa: The Motion Picture*, and the lambada cycle, and a special issue of *Time* not too long ago proclaimed 'Magnifico! Hispanic Culture breaks out of the Barrio',[24] it might prove enlightening to analyze this particular translation, presentation, and assimilation of Latin American 'otherness' as yet another ethnographic textual creation that must be analyzed as a political co-production of representations of difference and not as a mimetic narrative challenge.

Notes

1. This is, for example, how Karl G. Heider describes it in *Ethnographic Film* (Austin: University of Texas Press, 1976), one of the few texts to express the relationship between ethnography and the cinema directly (see especially, pp. 5–12).

2. See James Clifford, *The Predicament of Culture: Twentieth-century Ethnography, Literature, and Art* (Cambridge, Mass: Harvard University Press, 1988).

3. James Clifford, 'On Ethnographic Authority', in *The Predicament of Culture: Twentieth-century Ethnography, Literature, and Art* (Cambridge, Mass: Harvard, 1988), p. 41.

4. Stephen A. Tyler, 'Post-modern Ethnography: From Document of the Occult to Occult Document', in James Clifford and George Marcus (eds), *Writing Culture: The Poetics and Politics of Ethnography* (Berkeley: University of California Press, 1986), p. 126.

5. Edward Said, *Orientalism* (New York: Random House, 1979).

6. Tyler, op. cit., p. 126.

7. Donald W. Rowland, *History of the Office of the Coordinator of Inter-American Affairs* (Washington: Government Printing Office, 1947), pp. 68, 74.

8. For a popular assessment of the power of the cinema as democratic propaganda for the American way of life in South America, see, from the many possible examples, Florence Horn, 'Formidavel, Fabulosissimo', *Harpers' Magazine*, no. 184 (December 1941), pp. 59–64. Horn glowingly describes how well a young Brazilian boy and her housewife 'friends' understand and recognize 'America' because of their constant exposure to US films. After reading the following sentence, one wonders whether Orson Welles might have also read this piece before setting off on his CIAA-sponsored Brazilian project in 1942: 'He [the Brazilian boy] returns home, almost without exception, to tell his friends that it's all true – and even more so' (p. 60). For self-assessments of the power and efficacy of the Good Neighbor Policy, see, in particular, Nelson Rockefeller, 'Fruits of the Good Neighbor Policy', *New York Times Magazine* (14 May 1944), p. 15, and 'Will we remain Good Neighbors after the War? Are we killing our own Markets by promoting Industrialization in Latin America?', *Saturday Evening Post*, vol. 216 (6 November 1943), pp. 16–17.

9. See Allen L. Woll, *The Latin Image in American Film* (Los Angeles: UCLA Latin American Center Publication, 1977) and Gaizka S. de Usabel, *The High Noon of American Films in Latin America* (Ann Arbor, Mich: UMI Research Press, (1982).

10. As does Allen Woll's analysis of this period in *The Latin Image in American Film* (and a number of other texts). In particular, he praises the 'unheard of' cultural sensitivity of RKO's 1933 *Flying Down to Rio*, a film that featured the Mexican actress Dolores del Río as a Carioca enchantress and Rio de Janeiro as a city defined by its infinite romantic possibilities and as the South American meeting-place of new US communication technologies and capital: airplanes for southern travel, telegraphs for speedy communication, records and movies for music and romance. See Sergio Augusto, 'Hollywood looks at Brazil: From Carmen Miranda to *Moonraker*', in Randal Johnson and Robert Stam (eds.) *Brazilian Cinema* (Austin: University of Texas Press, 1988), pp. 352–61.

11. See Miriam Hansen on the Valentino legend in 'Pleasure, Ambivalence, Identification: Valentino and Female Spectatorship', *Cinema Journal*, vol. 25, no. 4 (1986), pp. 6–32.

12. Del Río's Hollywood filmography includes, among other titles: *What Price Glory?* (1926, *d.* Raoul Walsh); *Loves of Carmen* (1927, *d.* Raoul Walsh); *Ramona* (1928, *d.* Edwin Carewe); *The Red Dance* (1928, *d.* Raoul Walsh); *The Trail of '98* (1929, *d.* Clarence Brown); *Evangeline* (1929, *d.* Edwin Carewe); *Bird of Paradise* (1932, *d.* King Vidor), *Flying Down to Rio* (1933, *d.* Thornton Freeland), *Wonder Bar* (1934, *d.* Lloyd Bacon); *Madame Du Barry* (1934, *d.* William Dieterle); *In Caliente* (1935, *d.* Lloyd Bacon); *Lancer Spy* (1937, *d.* Gregory Ratoff); *Journey into Fear* (1943, *d.* Norman Foster). In *Journey into Fear*, del Río worked closely with Orson Welles (the first director of the film), with whom she had previously collaborated in the Mercury Theater production *Father Hidalgo* (1940) and during the production of *Citizen Kane* (1941).

13. Carlos Fuentes, 'El Rostro de la Escondida', in Luis Gasca (ed.) *Dolores del Río* (San Sebastian, Spain: XXIV Festival Internacional de Cine, 1976), p. 10: my translation.
14. Homi K. Bhabha, 'Signs Taken for Wonders: Questions of Ambivalence and Authority under a Tree outside Delhi, May 1917', in Henry Louis Gates, Jr. (ed.), *Race, Writing, and Difference* (Chicago: University of Chicago Press, 1986), p. 172.
15. For the best summary and analysis of Vélez's career, see Gabriel Ramírez, *Lupe Vélez: la mexicana que escupía fuego* (Mexico City: Cineteca Nacional, 1986).
16. See Homi K. Bhabha's discussion of this process in his 'The Other Question . . .', *Screen*, vol. 24, no. 6 (1983), pp. 18–36.
17. Between 1940 and her death in 1955, Miranda made 14 films: 10 for 20th Century-Fox, one for UA, two for MGM, and one for Paramount. The Fox 'cycle', between 1940 and 1946, consisted of: *Down Argentine Way* (1940, d. Irving Cummings), *That Night in Rio* (1941, d. Irving Cummings), *Week-end in Havana* (1941, d. Walter Lang), *Springtime in the Rockies* (1942, d. Irving Cummings), *The Gang's All Here* (1943, d. Busby Berkeley), *Four Jills in a Jeep* (1944, d. William A. Seiter), *Greenwich Village* (1944, d. Walter Lang), *Something for the Boys* (1944, d. Lewis Seiler), *Doll Face* (1946, d. Lewis Seiler), and *If I'm Lucky* (1946, d. Lewis Seiler).
18. See Rodolfo Konder, 'The Carmen Miranda Museum: The Brazilian Bombshell is still Box Office in Rio', *Americas*, vol. 34, no. 5 (1982), pp. 17–21.
19. See Douglas Gomery, *The Hollywood Studio System* (New York: St Martin's Press, 1986), pp. 76–100.
20. Among others, see, for example, the *Variety* reviews of her Fox films – especially of *Down Argentine Way* (9 October 1940), *Springtime in the Rockies* (24 November 1937) and *That Night in Rio* (12 March 1941) – which specifically comment upon the weakness of the romance/narratives and the strength of her musical/comedic performances.
21. See *New York Post*, 30 November 1955; cited by Allen L. Woll, *The Hollywood Musical goes to War* (Chicago: Nelson Hall, 1983), pp. 114–15. According to Woll, Fox encouraged Miranda to learn English on a 'fiscal' basis: a fifty cents raise for each word she added to her vocabulary. Miranda's quoted response again subverts the intended effect of Fox's integrationist efforts: 'I know p'raps one hondred words – preety good for Sous American girl, no? Best I know ten English words: men, men, men, men, and monee, monee, monee, monee, monee, monee.'
22. See, for example the full-page advertisement for Piel's Light Beer in the New York *Daily Mirror*, 25 July 1947: 'A lightning flash along Broadway means Carmen Miranda! That luscious, well-peppered dish! She glitters like a sequin, with her droll accent and spirited dances. And Carmen goes for Piel's – with all its sparkle and tang! "I tell everyone I know to *DREENK* Piel's" she exclaims.'
23. Miranda died at the age of 44, of a heart attack, on 5 August 1955, after taping a TV program with Jimmy Durante. By 1955, Miranda's screen presence had waned considerably, and, although she was still a recognizable star, she had begun to work far more for television than for the cinema.
24. Special issue of *Time*, 11 July 1988.

HIGH-TECH PRIMITIVISM

The Representation of Tribal Societies in Feature Films

JEAN FRANCO

Editors' Introduction

Brazil has occupied a prominent place in the European imagination since Sir Thomas More placed his Utopia there in 1516 and the Amazons of Greek mythology were given a geographical location. In the 1540s Fray Pedro de Carvajal reported back to his order in Spain that he had witnessed a battle in which the Amazons appeared by a river bank to join in the fray. He had the misfortune, he writes, to be shot in the buttocks by an arrow from one of these warrior women. Brazilian geography and its indigenous population had been seen throughout history as both desire and threat. A desire for the noble savage, for a retreat from civilisation, for the promise of caste harmony; the threat of savagery, the barbarian, the cannibal. Jean Franco looks at three contemporary European accounts of these myths (in *The Mission*, *The Emerald Forest* and *Fitzcarraldo*) and contrasts them to debates within Latin America about the survival and transformations of indigenous cultures. Her arguments are further developed in Robert Stam's article on race and multi-culturalism in Brazil.

□

Maybe man will kill the beast
and look into the eyes of the other as his equal.
MILTON NASCIMENTO[1]

During the five hundred years since the conquest of America, the representation of the indigenous has been essential both to the imperial venture and to the formation of the new Latin American nations. The cannibal and the noble savage stood on the other side of the boundary that defined civilization, signifying both 'otherness' and origins.[2] At the present time, as tribal societies turn into 'endangered species', as interminable hours of television documentary inform us that we are watching the last remnants of tribal culture, a marked change can be detected which transforms the indigenous

81

from being 'others' and converts them into multicolored strands in a pluralistic weave. The 1984 MOMA exhibition, '"Primitivism" in Twentieth-century Art: Affinity of the Tribal and the Modern', can serve as one 'benevolent' example of this 'neo-indigenismo'; it juxtaposed 'anonymously' created
artefacts of non-Western culture with some of the most famous paintings of
Picasso, Braque and Matisse.[3] By arranging its exhibits under innocuous
headings such as 'affinities' and 'concepts' the exhibit managed to ignore the
wars and the colonization which brought the African mask into the orbit of
the 'collectible'.[4]

A similar innocence marked the exhibit of South American cultures in
New York's Natural History Museum where a diorama of painted warriors
has the caption, 'There is no such thing as art for art's sake among the
Amazonian Indians' – thus suggesting that 'difference' is largely a matter of
aesthetics.

Neo-indigenismo has, however, acquired another facet because of the global *angst* over the environment and the destruction of the Amazon rain
forests. All of a sudden, the tribal 'other' has become a model of survival, a
natural ecologist. The worldwide attention given to the murder of Chico
Mendes (the rubber-tapper whose union had formed alliances with the forest
tribes) and the struggle among film companies in Hollywood for movie rights
over the Chico Mendes story, and the 1989 space voyage of the Discovery,
part of whose mission was to study the erosion of the rain forest, are sympto-
matic of a shift which has made hitherto remote struggles over land rights in
Amazonia central to planetary survival.[5] The difficulty here is that 'ecology'
all too often conceals a complexity of political and economic factors, not the
least important of which is capitalist development. Nothing illustrates the
difficulty of separating the mode of production from the ethnical intent than a
series of feature films all of which in one way or another depict critically the
Western conquest of untamed nature and tribal societies, yet end up by
reproducing oppressive acculturation.

NEO-INDIGENISMO WITH AN ALL-STAR CAST
Films such as *The Mission*, *Fitzcarraldo*, and *The Emerald Forest* were
intended to be something more than entertainment; they were made by
directors with reputations for making 'serious' films and they are explicit in
their critique of Western ideas of progress. Roland Joffe (*The Mission*) had
directed *The Killing Fields*, Werner Herzog had already filmed the much
acclaimed *Aguirre, Wrath of God* in South America and would go on to shoot
Where the Green Ants Dream in Australia, and John Boorman (*The Emerald
Forest*), an expatriate Briton, had directed *Deliverance*.[6]

What is astonishing about these films is their ghostly recapitulation of the
history of Amazonia itself; thus, even though *The Mission* takes place on the
borders of modern Paraguay and Brazil far south of Amazonia, the material
on which it draws reflects the history of the Catholic missions and their long
march over the centuries into the remotest areas of the rain forest. *Fitzcarraldo* records the history of a later period, that of the rubber boom at the end
of the 19th century; and *The Emerald Forest* brings us into the present and the
construction of the Trans-Amazon highway and dams as part of contempor-

ary Brazil's economic expansion. It is, however, this last stage of Amazonian expansion which is really at issue in the films even though they transpose their concerns into the past or into fantasy. It is important to bear in mind, however, that modern development in the Amazon dates from the military government that came into power in the 60s, although US experts were advocating the exploitation of the rain forests long before.[7] The military's 'national integration' policy promoted a 'land frenzy' in an area where the frontier law of the survival of the strongest prevailed, and encouraged destruction and even genocide whose net result is now predicted by some to be global disaster. The 'holocaust' of the Amazonian forest would in this case be an event that would rival 'the massive extinctions of dinosaurs and other species in the Cretacious Period, which changed for ever the world and the path of evolution'.[8]

There are obvious reasons why feature films which depend on capitalist modes of production should encounter difficulties in representing ecological concerns whose solution depends on global change. *The Mission* and *Fitzcarraldo* transpose the problem into the historical past, thus avoiding the complexity and messiness of contemporary struggles. Yet the appropriation of historical narrative undermines their objective, and serves to freeze real problems in an anachronistic mode. Furthermore, the demands of narrative structures that belong to the continuing saga of the white man's search for identity make it difficult for the films to avoid underpinning the already secure foundations of paternalism. The inevitable dislocation between stated intent and narrative logic is obvious in all three films, for each film begins or ends with extra-diegetic explanatory captions whose connection to the narrative is tenuous. The caption is, in fact, a kind of tag that indicates the contemporary problem that the narrative evades.

Our knowledge of tribal societies in South America comes in the main from missionaries, explorers and ethnographers. The Jesuit missionaries who (long before Rousseau) propagated the myth of the noble savage regarded America as a Utopia, as a territory that had not yet felt the corrupting winds of Europe. Their mission was both to bring the indigenous into the harmonious choir of the Christian world and to preserve their innocence. In Jesuit mythology, music soars over differences of culture and brings about an almost magical understanding:

> The priests were unable to penetrate the forest on foot: there were too few of them and, in any case, the Indians persisted in fleeing in fear from the white man. But the Fathers noticed that when they sang melodies from their canoes, the Guaraní crept to the river banks and surreptitiously watched them pass.[9]

Chateaubriand retells this tale in his *Spirit of Christianity* but it remains a potent myth down to the present. 'Indians', according to one historian, 'came into the settlements drawn by the magnificence of divine worship.'[10] The myth, of course, represses mention of the many skirmishes that accompanied the founding of the missions or their political importance as frontier posts in as yet uncolonized areas.

Jeremy Irons as Father Gabriel with his recorder in The Mission *(Roland Joffe, GB, 1986)*

The Mission draws heavily on this Jesuit mythology. Father Gabriel (Jeremy Irons) plays his recorder in an apparently empty forest out of which the Indians begin to emerge to listen to the music. This indigenous music is used to accompany 'sublime' scenes of the rushing Iguaçú waterfalls. The choral singing of the *Ave Maria* and the *Agnus Dei* reinforce the Jesuit vision of a missionary Utopia in which all voices sing in harmony. The Utopian is also suggested by scenes of naked children playing in the river, shots of flourishing crops and sweeping panoramas of unspoiled nature. The Utopia is, however, threatened by *realpolitik*, for the film is set in 1750, seven years before the Jesuits were expelled from Latin America by the Spanish crown and at a moment when some of the mission territories were about to pass from Spanish to Portuguese control. The issue is whether the Jesuit Fathers will allow the missions (and the Indians) to fall to the Portuguese. Two opposing strategies of resistance are represented in the clashing personalities of the aggressive guilt-ridden Father Rodrigo (Robert de Niro) and the passive resister, Father Gabriel. Both oppose the reasons of state which ordain the transference of Indian territories to the slave-owning Portuguese; Father Rodrigo resorts to armed struggle to resist the closure and is killed; Father Gabriel is an advocate of passive resistance and is also killed. Thus neither armed resistance (read guerrilla warfare) nor passive resistance (read liberation theology) prevail against reasons of state. Joffe himself explicitly saw the film as reflecting a contemporary dilemma and likened the opposing

84

tactics of the two Jesuits to modern discussions within the left.[11] The point is, however, that resistance fails and the Indians are either slaughtered or flee back into the jungle. At the end of the film, a naked girl comes into the ruins of the mission and picks up a broken violin from the water. Armed with this fragment of civilization, she gets into a canoe with a group of children and they paddle up-river, fleeing from the army and the slave-traders. The film is framed by a narrative voice, that of Father Luis Altamirano, a representative of the State, who was historically a major enemy of the missions. It is he who improbably voices a pious lament for the bloodshed just before the final caption, which reads:

> The Indians of South America are still engaged in the struggle to define their land and culture. Many of the priests who, inspired by faith and love, continue to support the rights of the Indians for justice, do so with their lives. 'The light shines in the darkness; the darkness has not overcome it.' (from John I: 5)

The words sound particularly strange when they are put beside other kinds of calculation – for instance, the violent death of 100,000 Guatemalans, mostly Indians, in the past ten years. How many Indians does it take to make one Jesuit martyr? Is the Church the only force defending the Indians? By bringing the audience into the present, in the final caption, the film reveals only too clearly its own limitations, and especially the fact that the drama is played out not by the indigenous community but by different and conflicting branches of the imperial power. What history teaches, in the film, is the inevitable triumph of *realpolitik*. Resistance takes the form of martyrdom.

In its opening caption the film claims the authority of historical truth. This 'truth', however, is from the first unable to stand up to the demands of dramatic narrative. For instance, one of the missions is headed by a Guaraní Indian (played by a Cambodian actor), although the indigenous were excluded from the Jesuit Order. The spectacular opening sequence in which a Jesuit martyr is tied to a cross and sent tumbling down the Iguaçú falls achieves its shock effect at the expense of historical accuracy. There is no record of any Jesuit being martyred in this particular way, but from a narrative point of view the scene serves to identify the Indians with those who crucified Christ and thus positions itself in the same relation to Indian culture as did the Church in the colonial period. In other words, the Indians are too childlike to understand the significance of what they are doing.

The Indians in the film were not Guaraní but Colombian Indians, brought in by air to Santa Marta and Cartagena, where most of *The Mission* was filmed. Does it matter? After all, *Lawrence of Arabia* was filmed in Spain. What makes *The Mission* different is its claim to be representing the truth of history; this is not to mention the paradox of uprooting tribes in order to make a film whose explicit message is ostensibly to show how Indians were enslaved and forced to abandon their tribal lands.

This contradiction clearly concerned Daniel Berrigan, the anti-war activist and Jesuit who was one of five Jesuits brought in as advisors and as actors for the film. In his published diary of the filming (see fn. 6), Berrigan is unable to reconcile his need to defend Jesuit heroism and his scepticism of the film industry. Shaken by his confrontation with a colossal dream machine which not only re-presents but *is* a mode of production whose embryonic forms were already embedded in colonial society, he unsuccessfully attempts to justify the transportation of 'unspoiled' Onani Indians 350 miles by air to inhabit a film village by suggesting that the Indians have 'chosen' to be in the film.

In consenting to travel to Santa Marta, the Indians have landed in the world for the first time. A truly awesome thought. They have arrived in our world, which goes by the presumptive name of the real world. One can only glance at the radiant faces and breathe a prayer. God help them.

They also entered the economy when they came here, perhaps that says it all, 'real' and 'world' and more. The arrangement is that the families will be paid two-thirds of the stipulated salary; the remaining third goes into a communal fund for education and medical needs. (p. 64)

Again and again in his diary, Berrigan reveals himself to be conscious of being a participant in the colonization he condemns, of being a cog in a machine oiled by the same colonial fantasies (the civilizing mission) that had haunted the eighteenth-century Spaniards and Portuguese.

Yet Berrigan's diary is situated within the same labyrinth of mirrors as the film. Although he sees the irony of reproducing an eighteenth-century struggle in a zone of Colombia where army units in camouflage fatigues are engaged in counter-insurgency against guerrillas and where one of the stars in the film, De Niro, had to have armed guards to protect him from kidnappers, he also believes that in portraying the Jesuits the film will be able to capture 'a spontaneous generation occurring in Western culture itself' (p. 34). But this is precisely the problem of a historical film which is too faithful to history, for it cannot represent what has gone unrepresented.

Fitzcarraldo is an even more thoroughgoing attempt to repeat history than *The Mission*. As Les Blank (whose documentary *Burden of Dreams* is a critical commentary on the filming of *Fitzcarraldo*) said, 'It's damned weird to have people risking their lives to fulfill a mad Bavarian's impossible fantasies.'

Those fantasies are, however, not just individual but collective, and have their origins in German Romanticism. The opening caption reads: 'the Cuhuari Yaku, the jungle Indians, call this the land where God did not finish creation. Only after man has disappeared, they think, will he return to finish his work.' This is Herzog's version of the myth of the return of the culture hero; but it also sounds like an echo of late Romanticism.[12]

Though nature is a necessary element of Herzog's particular version of the sublime[13] his outburst during the filming, recorded in Les Blank's film, seems to come right out of Hugo's *La Légende des Siècles*:

I see fornication and asphyxiation and choking and fighting for survival growing and just rotting away ... the trees are in misery, the birds are in misery.... They screech in pain.... It's an unfinished country. It's pre-historical. The only thing missing is the dinosaur. It's cursed ... even the stars look like a mess.

Had he listened to the Machiguenga Indians he had brought into his camp he might have told another story.

The historical Fitzcarraldo was a rubber baron and Indian hunter who did in fact take a boat across the land between two Amazon tributaries – though he sensibly did so by breaking the boat into pieces before carrying it across land.[14] Herzog tried the same feat by using bulldozers and winching the entire boat over a 40-degree incline, a feat which put the lives of workers at risk. The Brazilian engineer withdrew from the project. The actor Klaus Kinski, who replaced Jason Robards after the latter contracted amoebic dysentery, risked drowning in the rapids. There was an air crash in which people died. The actors spent months trapped in the rain forest. Herzog in his interviews with Les Blank seems obsessed with the awesome logistics of his film, but just as *The Mission* created the illusion of the eighteenth-century real only to become trapped in colonialism, so Herzog is trapped in the glories and miseries of entrepreneurial capitalism of which the film is a product. Music, in this case the opera that Fitzcarraldo will bring to Iquitos, expresses the will to power in non-destructive form. The Jesuit myth of conquest through music is recycled once again when Fitzcarraldo puts a record of Caruso on the phonograph when his boat is stopped by warlike Jíbaros. The Jíbaro drums cease as Caruso's voice soars across the forest and the tribe is then peacefully recruited to execute Fitzcarraldo's mad dream – which they also sabotage by loosening the boat from its moorings in the belief that it must be sacrificed.

Les Blank's film and book *The Burden of Dreams* is far more of a deconstructive enterprise than Berrigan's diary partly because, unlike Berrigan, he is not a participant in the film project. However, he is not a detached observer, either. *Burden of Dreams* positions itself precisely as an ironic entrepreneurship which is linked to the destruction of the rain forest and the Amazon basin. What *Burden of Dreams* reveals is what it means to shoot a film about old-style capitalist enterprise in a zone that is on the verge of devastation because of that enterprise and where ecological issues are deeply implicated in local politics.

Blank's film shows the indigenous to be anything but silent actors in the process. For instance, Herzog had originally intended to make the film in Ecuador, apparently unaware of the tense politics of a border zone which was rapidly being colonized by new settlers, explored by oil interests and overrun by the Ecuadorian and Peruvian armies. He originally contracted Aguaruna Indians as extras, but a newly formed Aguaruna Council objected to the filming. The Aguaruna Council, who knew quite well what the historical Fitzcarraldo had represented, believed that Herzog was intending to do a film on the exploitation of rubber workers at the turn of the century and they objected to this on the grounds that it did not represent indigenous culture in the present. In other words, they did not want to be represented either as victims or as living in some timeless world. They were conscious of belonging to a political movement and knew how to defend their right to control their own representation. In 1979, they surrounded Herzog's camp and the film crew were forced to flee down-river. Fourteen months later, Herzog had managed to recruit Indians, mostly from the Campa and Machiguenga tribes (traditionally enemies). The Indians had been promised land rights – though at the end of the film these had not been acquired. In any case, Herzog does not seem to have known that land rights in the Amazon are something of a myth unless they can be protected by force. In Les Blank's film, Herzog says he does not want the Indians to be contaminated with Western civilization and speaks of the tragedy of their disappearance – the loss of 'cultures, languages and mythologies'. Yet he makes a film which is an intervention in the process he deplores. As in *The Mission*, the director's understanding of historical truth stands in the way of any ironies – this is left to Les Blank's 'extra-diegetic' material. In both films, the mode of production is a continuation of the colonization they purport to describe and there is no way, within the realist convention, that critical distance can be achieved.

John Boorman's *The Emerald Forest* is an attempt to escape these contradictions worthy of Eratostratus, the man who won fame by burning down the temple. Boorman is clearly conscious of the problems posed by a film such as *Fitzcarraldo* and even alludes to Herzog by including a fanatical Italian photographer in the film who is so intent on photographing 'the Fierce People' that he does not realize that they are about to club him to death. Boorman uses

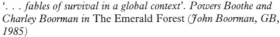

'. . . *fables of survival in a global context*'. *Powers Boothe and Charley Boorman in* The Emerald Forest (*John Boorman, GB, 1985*)

88

non-indigenous actors and gives the tribes fictitious names – 'the Fierce People', 'the Invisible People', 'the Bat People'. Yet his attempt to represent tribal culture from an ecological perspective is, if anything, even more problematic than the other two films.

The Emerald Forest is, however, more like *Crocodile Dundee* than *The Mission* or *Fitzcarraldo*. It belongs to a class of films described by Meaghan Morris as 'fables of survival in a global context'.[15] It is the story of an American dam builder working in the Brazilian Amazon whose son, Tommy, is kidnapped by the Invisible People. After twelve years of searching the father finds him, but Tommy now remembers his civilized life only as a dream. A neighboring tribe, the Fierce People, have been armed by Brazilians who are recruiting Indian girls for a jungle brothel, one of the inmates being Tommy's young bride. Tommy enlists his father's technological knowledge (and gun) as an ally in their struggle against the Brazilians and the Fierce People, and the brothel is destroyed. Tommy's father now realizes that the dam he is building threatens the survival of his son's tribe. While Tommy uses shamanistic knowledge to produce a downpour the father sabotages the dam, thus saving his son but presumably destroying his 'self'. The paradox of the film is that it tries to suggest the possibility of an ethic within capitalism by showing that we can learn ecology from the 'good' primitive and halt the unbridled conquest of nature – but only if we are prepared to destroy the products of our own technology. This sounds bolder than it really is. To begin with, the film remains within a masculinist ideology of the Oedipal narrative; secondly, the tribal peoples are simply a backcloth against which the father/son drama is played out. Thus *The Emerald Forest* can be read as the story of how capitalism (the father) can survive and save its own children. This is the significance of making a captive white boy its hero. What the white boy learns is not how to overcome nature but to survive. It marks the moment when there is no more nature to conquer so that the white male saga has to be recycled. Thus Boorman, like Joffe and Herzog, is trapped in his own story which turns opposition to capitalist development into the inner struggle of the failing hegemonic power which now needs to appropriate shamanistic knowledge for its own survival.

The Emerald Forest seems to illustrate Trin Minh Ha's comment that 'the part of the Savior has to be filled as long as the belief in the problem of "endangered species" lasts'.[16] The Father of the film not only plays the part of Savior but the explicit message that closes the film speaks on behalf of people who from the Western point of view are, indeed, 'invisible':

The rain forests of the Amazon basin are disappearing at the rate of 5000 acres a day. Four million Indians lived here; 120,000 remain. A few tribes have never been in contact with the outside world. They still know what we have forgotten.

The last phrase suggests that the film is in a position to understand what has been lost. Yet Boorman's own knowledge of tribal cultures can only come from Western discourse itself – for instance, an episode in which the boy is covered with stinging ants as an initiation ordeal is lifted straight out of Alain

Gheerbrant's *Journey to the Far Amazon*.[17] Nevertheless, there is a certain irony in Boorman's admission in his diary *Money Into Light*[18] that the father who built the dam must now destroy his own labor, an irony that is missing from *The Mission* and *Fitzcarraldo*.

WHAT CAN THE 'OTHER' SEE?

This post-modern indigenismo has developed in sublime ignorance of antecedents in Latin America where the conquest has remained such a haunting presence. Indeed, the fragments of indigenous civilization which are everywhere to be seen[19] were embedded in the walls of buildings, frozen in sculpture and stereotyped as actor in the constant recapitulation of the process of enslavement. In popular belief, the 'evil wind' of the conquest still blows, still infects society.[20]

The encounter of Western civilization with the New World tribal societies was without precedent; the mythic narrative of that encounter is as compelling as the myths of Moses, Oedipus, Antigone or Don Juan and, like these myths, it seems to have to be recast with each shift in history. The indigenous figured both in the Spanish Empire's self-legitimation as a universal monarchy and in the period of national formation in the 19th century as the mythic origin of nations. 'Indigenismo' was a literary mode that was closely connected to the consolidation of the state. It was not so much a confrontation with the 'other' as an argument about national identity and the problem of whether the Indian could be integrated into the nation. National institutions such as the Instituto Nacional Indigenista founded after the revolution of 1910–17 in Mexico were central to this project of acculturation. By the 60s, however, most Latin American writers were resisting any association with the primitive. Alejo Carpentier's *Los pasos perdidos* (*The Lost Steps*), which is indebted both to Lévi-Strauss's *Tristes tropiques* and Alain Gheerbrant's *Journey to the Far Amazon*, narrates a musicologist's journey (music, once again) into the primitive in order to reject its validity. The modern artist's task is not to retrace the passage from primitive to modern. His only place is in the contemporary world. Yet Carpentier exemplifies the modernism of writers such as Carlos Fuentes or Julio Cortázar, some of whose work is, nevertheless, strongly marked by the fantasy of a return of the primitive.

Just as in Europe, the 'discovery' of primitive art encouraged among some members of the avant-garde a mystical, reverential attitude to 'otherness', a desire for those shamanistic powers that had been excluded from Western science in Latin America, and inspired a re-evaluation of the indigenous civilizations.[21] Writers and poets such as José Maria Arguedas, Miguel Angel Asturias and Ernesto Cardenal turned to Maya and Inca civilizations as sources of cultural renewal and originality. This ethnographic indigenismo drew on a greatly increased repertoire of knowledge of indigenous cultures, including transcriptions of the orally transmitted literature of the Americas. The search for an authentic culture embodied in the indigenous was, however, questioned by many, particularly the Brazilian avant-garde who celebrated appropriation ('cannibalism') rather than originality and who recognized that, to paraphrase Meaghan Morris, 'predation' was 'the universal rule of cultural exchange'.[22] This 'cannibalism' would eventually find its expression in film, most explicitly in Nelson Pereira dos Santos's *How Tasty was my Little Frenchman*, which amusingly turned the tables on colonial myth by making a Frenchman who believes that he has found the treasures of El Dorado the unwitting victim of Tupinamba cannibalism.[23]

Appropriation is a characteristic of all levels of Latin American culture from salsa to the soap opera. The point I wish to make, however, is that appropriation always assumes the existence of a prior text to be used and 'cannibalized' – as Pereira dos Santos cannibalized the chronicles of discovery. This also permits the kind of ironic distancing that was absent from *The Mission* and *Fitzcarraldo*.

The intertextual irony acquires particular force when the prior text is central to the construction of hegemonic discourse. For instance, when he was in Mexico, the Spanish director Luis Buñuel made *Adventures of Robinson Crusoe*; this film turns the entrepreneurial Robinson of Defoe into a creature whom solitude makes mad. He is reduced to speaking to his own echo and libidinous women haunt his dreams. He is only saved by the arrival of another human being, Friday. For a time the two of them live as equals and together repel marauders who attempt to capture the island. Yet by the end of the film, Crusoe is dressed in the garments of a dead sea captain while Friday wears the clothes of a seaman, thus suggesting that the racial hierarchy will be restored.[24]

Appropriation thus takes on a different meaning when it is directed against the master discourse which has tended to be narcissistic. A recent catalog for an exhibition of a group of Venezuelan painters and artists who undertook the 'reverse journey' to Europe comments on this narcissism:

The seeker of dreams arrives finally at the gates of his [*sic*] city of desire, a fantastic city that has been revealed to him as a promised destiny. He discovers it and finds to his surprise that in place of the unknown gaze, is his own image, his own history.[25]

One member of this group, Diego Rísquez, made a series of films, one of which he called *Amerika Terra Incógnita*. This film is not merely a 'reverse journey' but a displacement of the ethnocentricity of Western discourse not only in the past but in the present.

The film opens with a citation from the now familiar repertoire of the sublime, a shot of virgin forest. A small group of Spaniards are loading treasure on to a boat. In a rustic cage they have entrapped a handsome young Indian warrior whom they are taking back as part of the plunder. The Indian is taken to the Spanish court where Velázquez is painting *Las Meninas*. Because the Indian is represented but has no voice within the dominant order, the film is without dialogue except for the words, 'Tierra, tierra' spoken when the Spaniards reach their own land on their return from the 'tierra incógnita'.

In Rísquez's film, the Indian peers through an aperture in the wall precisely as Velázquez prepares to paint *Las Meninas*, but the representation is thrown into disarray by this anomalous figure. In similar fashion, taking considerable poetic licence, Vivaldi, who is conducting at court, finds his music is disrupted by the calls of jungle animals and birds. Rísquez thus offers a counter-myth to that of the Jesuit conversion through harmony by showing that the New World introduced disharmony into the classical scheme of representation. What Rísquez suggests is that the scene of representation – the court and its painter and musician – perform for a spectator whose presence they cannot acknowledge, the subjugated Indian.

But though films like that of Rísquez foreground the problem of representation, they cannot themselves create an alternative discourse. Nor are they part of what Michel de Certeau calls 'the long march of the Indian peoples' who are concerned neither with irony nor inversion but rather, as de Certeau points out, with a *political* third way. In this third way:

> ... their specificity is no longer defined by a given, by their past, by a system of representations, an *object* of knowledge (and/or of exploitation) but finds its affirmation in a set of procedures – *a way of doing things* exercised within an encompassing economic situation which creates among the oppressed the foundations for revolutionary alliances. 'Cultural specificity' thus adopts the form of a *style of action* which can be deployed within the situations created by capitalist imperialism.[26]

Depredation has forced mobility on to once settled peoples, obliging them to resist and adapt in new ways. This is illustrated by Rigoberta Menchú's description of the resistance of Guatemalan Indians:

> In the jungle, the people are absolutely hidden beneath the mountains. They do not have specific spots to flee from and return to. Their huts are for fifteen days, for a month, for two months, depending on the climate, on the rain, on many things. The problem is that if they spend as much as two months in a community, because they travel to and fro to move their things, to collect their products, their trails begin to get big. When they get big it is easier for the army to follow them and attack a community. So the people are constantly mobile.[27]

Thus their problem is not simply 'preserving their culture', as we are often given to understand, but rather a political problem of how to achieve a social system that will permit their own – and our – survival.

Notes

1. From the album *Yahuarete* (Columbia Records, 1988).
2. I deliberately do not use the term Third World. For work on representation of the indigenous in the colonial period, see Peter Hulme, *Colonial Encounters: Europe and the Native Caribbean, 1492–1792* (London and New York: Methuen, 1986). See also volume I of Francis Baker et al. (eds), *Europe and its Others* (Colchester: University of Essex, 1984).
3. William Rubin (ed.), *'Primitivism' in 20th-century Art: Affinity of the Tribal and the Modern*, 2 vols (New York: The Museum of Modern Art, 1984).
4. James Clifford, 'Histories of the Tribal and the Modern', *The Predicament of*

Culture: Twentieth-century Ethnography, Literature, and Art (Cambridge, Mass.: Harvard University Press, 1988), pp. 196–7.

5. Susanna Hecht, 'Chico Mendes: Chronicle of a Death Foretold', *New Left Review*, no. 173, January/February 1989, pp. 57–68.

6. Two of these films, *The Mission* and *Fitzcarraldo*, generated a number of spin-offs. The filming of *The Mission* is recorded in Daniel Berrigan, SJ, *The Mission: A Film Journal* (New York: Harper and Row, 1986). The filming of *Fitzcarraldo* was recorded in the book, Les Blank and J. Bogan (eds), *Burden of Dreams: Screenplay, Journals, Photographs* (Berkeley: North Atlantic, 1984), as well as in the film, *Burden of Dreams*. See also the script *Fitzcarraldo*, trans. Martje Herzog and Alan Greenberg (San Francisco: Fjord Press, 1982), which differs considerably from the finished movie. *The Mission* also ran into trouble with the Indian extras who threatened to strike over non-fulfillment of the contract.

7. In the 40s, for instance, a well-known Latin Americanist, Carleton Beals, saw the Amazon as a 'storehouse for a super civilization' and described in Utopian terms a future of 'great air-cooled cities' that would arise 'on the banks of the Amazon and its tributaries'. See Carleton Beals, 'Future of the Amazon', in *Survey Graphic – Magazine of Social Interpretation*, vol. xxx, no. 3, March 1941.

8. Alexander Cockburn, 'Trees, Cows and Cocaine: an Interview with Susanna Hecht', *New Left Review*, no. 173, January/February 1989, p. 33.

9. Quoted by Philip Caraman, *The Lost Paradise: an Account of the Jesuits in Paraguay, 1607–1768* (London: Sidgewick and Jackson), p. 213.

10. Philip Caraman, op. cit., p. 213.

11. *Cahiers du Cinéma*, 1986, no. 66, p. 36.

12. Count Hermann Keyserling, *South American Meditations* (London: Jonathan Cape, 1932).

13. Alan Singer, 'Comprehending Appearances: Werner Herzog's Ironic Sublime', in Timothy Corrigan (ed.), *The Films of Werner Herzog: Between Mirage and History* (New York and London: Methuen, 1986), pp. 183–205.

14. See, for instance, the appendix (13) on Fitzcarraldo in P. Dionisio Ortiz, OFM, *El Pachitea y el alto Ucayali: Visión histórica de dos importantes regiones de la selva peruana*, vol. 2 (Lima: Imprenta San Antonio, 1974), pp. 894–6. According to this account Fitzcarraldo's father was North American, his mother Peruvian. The empire he built from rubber was destroyed by Indians when he died.

15. Meaghan Morris, 'Tooth and Claw: Tales of Survival and *Crocodile Dundee*', in *The Pirate's Fiancée: Feminism, Reading, Postmodernism* (London: Verso, 1988) pp. 241–69.

16. T. Trin Minh Ha, 'Difference: A Special Third World Woman Issue', *Discourse*, no. 8, Fall–Winter 1986–7, pp. 11–37.

17. Alain Gheerbrant, *Journey to the Far Amazon: An Expedition into Unknown Territory*, trans. Edward Fitzgerald (New York: Simon and Schuster, 1954).

18. John Boorman, *Money into Light – 'The Emerald Forest': A Diary* (London: Faber & Faber, 1985).

19. Oskar Negt and Alexander Kluge, 'The Public Sphere and Experience: Selections', *October*, vol. 46, Fall 1988, pp. 60–82.

20. Michael Taussig, *Shamanism, Colonialism: A Study in Terror and Healing and the Wild Man* (Chicago: University of Chicago Press, 1987).

21. See, for instance, Antoine Artaud, 'Concerning a Journey to the Land of the Tarahumaras', in Jack Hirschman (ed.), *Antoine Artaud Anthology* (San Francisco: City Lights Books, 1965), pp. 69–83.

22. Meaghan Morris, *The Pirate's Fiancée*, p. 267.

23. Richard Peña, 'How Tasty was my Little Frenchman', in Randal Johnson and Robert Stam (eds), *Brazilian Cinema* (Cranbury, New Jersey: Associated University Presses, 1982), pp. 191–9.

24. The film was made in Mexico and released in 1952 and was Buñuel's first color

93

film. See Francisco Aranda, *Luis Buñuel: A Critical Biography* (New York: Da Capo, 1976), pp. 156–9.

25. Flyer published by Museo de Arte Contemporáneo, Caracas, October 1984.

26. Michel de Certeau, 'The Politics of Silence. The Long March of the Indians', *Heterologies. Discourse on the Other*, trans. Brian Massumi (Minneapolis: University of Minnesota Press, 1985), pp. 225–33.

27. 'Rigoberta Menchú on the state of the opposition in Guatemala', *Central American Bulletin*, vol. 8, no. 1, December 1988, p. 8.

'ALL THAT TROUBLE DOWN THERE'

Hollywood and Central America

JAMES DUNKERLEY

Editors' Introduction
James Dunkerley's essay analyses Hollywood's interest in Central America over a ten-year period from 1979 to 1989. July 1979 saw the victory of the Frente Sandinista de Liberación Nacional (FSLN) in Nicaragua, 1989 the collapse of Communism and, by extension, the beginning of the end of the perceived 'Red peril' in the isthmus. The purported 'domino theory' threat to the isthmus came to dominate Washington's foreign policy actions in the 80s as the muddles of the Carter administration were replaced by the forthright hostility to social change embodied in the Reagan administration. The US government's interpretation of events in Nicaragua – Western democracy hijacked by totalitarian Marxist–Leninist regimes in the pay of the Soviet Union and Cuba, intent on spreading revolution to the rest of Central America – meant that Nicaragua spent the 80s embroiled in a devastatingly costly war against US-backed Contra insurgents. Other liberation movements, especially in El Salvador and Guatemala, had to fight against local oligarchies massively backed by US aid and armaments.

Dunkerley shows how Hollywood's reaction to these events did not follow unquestioningly Reagan's Cold War rhetoric. He traces the muddle and confusion of the film-makers' response by analysing well-known movies such as *Under Fire* and *Salvador*, but also a number of features rarely seen outside B-movie houses or the video circuit. He was documenting and personally experiencing Central America's struggles at the beginning of the Reagan regime and he therefore witnessed at first hand a number of the events later fictionalised by Oliver Stone and others.

□

Hollywood's response to the crisis in Central America following the Nicaraguan revolution of 1979 had been more muddled and interesting than might have been expected or, indeed, than some of the sharper critics are prepared

95

to allow. It may certainly appear a trifling achievement, but during the 80s relatively few feature films displayed the unquestioning codes of affinity and antipathy recycled from the first Cold War by a president whose political rhetoric was almost entirely couched in B-movie cadences and who was seemingly as obsessed by Central America as he was by anything else.

Here one should make proper allowance for the fact that the Sandinista overthrow of the Somoza dictatorship and the outbreak of civil war in both El Salvador and Guatemala raised the threat – diligently nurtured by Reagan and Haig during the 1980 US election campaign – of the deployment of US troops just as the first wave of post-Vietnam films, headed by *The Deer Hunter* (1978) and *Apocalypse Now* (1979), had made a major impact. Equally, it is worth noting that the tight 'bipartisan consensus' in Washington over Central American policy until the Iran–Contra scandal (November 1986) was never mirrored in California, where political and economic refugees from Mexico and Central America dominate the burgeoning Hispanic community, giving it a more progressive character than that, for example, in Florida. Given the success of a film such as *Stand and Deliver* (Ramón Menéndez, 1988), one suspects that consideration of their 'local constituency' by the moguls of Burbank may not have been completely tangential. In the event, it is safe to say that regional and conjunctural factors combined with more extensive political and cultural developments since the early 50s to ensure that the contested and often confused images of Central America that existed within the populace at large were also represented on film.

This does not, of course, mean that either Hollywood or the independents avoided producing a massive amount of rank tat, still less that the terrible conflicts of the isthmus engendered the making of outstanding movies. Indeed, while it is valid to insist on the contrast with the 50s with regard to formal political culture and base propaganda, in most other respects the record is very depressing. In the first place, although opinion polls throughout the 80s registered an alarmingly high ignorance about Central America and the Caribbean on the part of the US public, unprecedented coverage in the media heightened simple awareness of its existence as a site of conflict. This, allied with the long-standing manipulation of standard 'banana republic' motifs by Hollywood, made the region a natural successor to South-East Asia as an arena for the post-Rambo generation of killer-heroes.[1]

At one level this deserves little comment, since one set of steaming deciduous foliage is as good as another for the purposes of staging twig-snapping hunts and crashing chases or prompting glistening starlets to lose their shirts. But the replacement of the inscrutable oriental by the carelessly cruel Hispanic as the villain of the piece is not without some consequence. This is perhaps most notable in the predictably increasing attention to the drug trade in such films, which are primarily (often exclusively) aimed at the video market. If this audience is captive, it is still only on remand since the 'action and adventure' sections of the rental stores are as capacious as they are lurid, and 'actuality' is not an entirely redundant selling-point. Sometimes the directors have the temerity to assign their plots to an authentic country, *Blood Money* (Jerry Schatzberg, 1988) being set in Costa Rica because, like several other films, it involves gunrunning and the Contras. Sometimes they are content to settle for regional anonymity, as in Michael Kennedy's *Caribe* (1988), which approaches southern climes with scarcely greater specificity or sophistication than did the producers of *Dallas* who, it will be remembered, contrived to have Ewing *père* die in an aircrash that took place in a zone no smaller than 'South America'.

Sometimes also the new wave of violent exploitation pictures manifests a probably justified but nevertheless abusive attitude towards its audience by packaging its product in a manner almost entirely unconnected to the contents of the plot. Thus, *Sandinista. War is Hell* (1989), also directed by Michael Kennedy – who is acquiring quite some experience in this field – bears absolutely no correspondence to any recorded events in Nicaragua over the last decade. There is a dictatorial (and entirely fictional) General González, some drug smuggling by a run-of-the-mill bunch of murderous *mafiosi*, an unsurprisingly careworn mercenary, and a glamorous female journalist who is very stupid even by the formidable standards of the genre. But no effort is made even to identify the country in which the action takes place, still less to tie the FSLN to drug-running, as had been done several years earlier by US government agencies. In all probability nobody on the set had the slightest idea of the film's eventual title.

On these grounds it is tempting to bracket such stuff alongside the antics of sundry sorcerers, dragon-slayers, space-travellers and avenging Amazons. Yet what is most striking about the corpus is the total absence of either humour or history as elements to temper threadbare plots, poor production values and a reliance on violence that is impressive even in the post-Peckinpah age of gore. These are not smirking, camp spoofs made for the chattering classes but straight-faced offerings for the readership of *Guns and Ammo* that pillage Corman, Peckinpah and Sturges without intelligence as well as without shame.

It is more than Central America's bad luck to have attracted an unusually high proportion of such an inevitable output, which threatens to infect more mainstream production although it is, in truth, rather hard to distinguish the upper and lower ends of this market. Perhaps, drawing one's limits around the Caribbean as a whole, one could identify a superior example in Abel Ferrara's *Cat Chaser* (1989), which is not only derived from an Elmore Leonard novel but also pays more than fleeting and less than spurious reference to the 1965 invasion of the Dominican Republic by the US marines. At the other end of the spectrum, but with a rather superior cast, stands Tony Scott's *Revenge* (1989), which is set in Mexico. This, as soon becomes clear, represents the limit for Latin mores and conduct, a significant part of the movie involving passage to and from the US border, which obviously represents the margin of civilization.[2] Two aspects of this film attract attention. First, the use of Anthony Quinn to portray the jealous and vengeful *caudillo* betrayed by his beautiful young wife. Already the screen personification *sans pareil* of 'Latin' temper, Quinn effortlessly hams his way through a series of extravagantly brutal scenes; it is clear to the viewer that what we have here is an exceptionally mean and calculating Zorba. Second, and more telling, is the contrast in the role of the female lead, Madeleine Stowe, with that in her previous film, John Badham's well-received *Stakeout* (1987).

In both films Stowe plays an apparently resourceful but powerless object of desire sought, in different ways, by two men. In *Stakeout* she is an Irish–Mexican waitress under observation by two Seattle cops lying in wait for her ex-boyfriend, a cop-killer who has recently broken out of jail. This involves no small amount of voyeurism, but beyond the predictable male-bonding between the policemen (and an audience blessed with *a priori* exculpation) as one of them succumbs to Stowe's charms lies the disturbing possibility that her past (and blood) will force her to prefer the evil killer. Badham, though, does not lead us for long down this path; his denouement has the heroine unharmed (bar one casual backhander from the crook) and delivered into the arms of her new hero after a textbook finale fight.[3]

In *Revenge* we are south of a different border and, although Stowe is easily won away by a gringo (Kevin Costner) who is an old friend of Quinn's, we know that no quarter may be expected. The level of violence in this *ménage à trois* is not only much higher but also a significant amount of it is visited directly upon the woman. The stabbings, rape and intravenous administration of drugs undergone by Stowe's character are at the centre of both the images and the narrative of a film that is as small as its title. A bevy of worthless bit-parters expire as Costner battles to retrieve his love, yet she survives to recover in a convent, where he finds her having finally reached an *entente* with the resigned Quinn, who mumbles some cod philosophy and wanders off, presumably back to political fixing and generalised cow-raising activities. The point is not that it would be impossible to contrive a less veiled 'Madonna and whore' story. Rather, it is that what is merely imagined (in comic form) in Seattle can be openly practised (and hugely exceeded) in Sonora.

The part of the cop smitten by Stowe in *Stakeout* is played by Richard Dreyfuss, who the following year also took a leading role in a movie 'about' Latin America, albeit a comedy set in a fictional republic: *Moon over Parador* (Paul Mazursky, 1988). This spoof is entirely predictable but so amiably over the top that one is not completely convinced of the artlessness of its advertising copy: 'Where else in the world would a second-rate actor become president?' Yet whereas Reagan was elected fair and square (with all that this entails in terms of 'political culture') Dreyfuss is dragooned by Raúl Julia's police chief into impersonating a suddenly defunct dictator in a 'king for a day' romp that courts all sorts of dangers but eventually parodies itself – and its venerable genre – sufficiently to suggest that there is still space between PC (Political Correctness) piety and redneck philistinism in Hollywood's image of 'the south'.

Parador is saved both as a film and from the fictional clutches of Fascism in good measure by Sonia Braga's high-flying 'tart with a heart'. Even if the audiences for this film would only know Braga from *The Kiss of the Spiderwoman* (Héctor Babenco, 1985) or, at a pinch, *The Milagro Beanfield War* (Robert Redford, 1987), it is not difficult to grasp that her 'sultry temptress' part in *Parador* is so deftly played as to be typecast. In fact, Braga here offers a sanitised pastiche of her earlier roles in Brazilian cinema where on-camera fellatio and energetic couplings helped to raise a reputation that is exploited but could never be properly reproduced in *Parador*. While Dreyfuss plays an

Sonia Braga as Madonna in Moon Over Parador *(Paul Mazursky, USA, 1988)*

actor playing the *caudillo*, Braga simply mimics her own screen persona.[4] The question of identity is not fully triangulated, even courtesy of assistance from Raúl Julia and Fernando Rey. Yet neither is it so crassly handled as to give the impression that the latinos merely picked up Universal's cheque for lampooning their cultural birthright.

It is not simply the treatment of the core themes of sex and power that bracket the US vision of Central America, whether in comic or tragic voice. There is a wider sense of the relation between drama and the individual – one which, as Pauline Kael was quick to emphasise, is paradoxically but acutely evident in the progressive independent production *El Norte* (Gregorio Nava, 1983). Kael's criticism of this picture is that it reduces to simple emblems the Guatemalan couple who undergo the most bitter experiences in emigrating from their beloved homeland to an alien and aggressive USA; they lack discernible characteristics that might make them something more than the 'objects' of the rites of passage they are obliged to undergo.[5] Kael is also right to criticise the film's lack of attention as to why two young people should be forced to submit themselves to such indignity and severe risk. However, her criticism is sufficiently humane and informed to recognise that even if Nava's direction is wooden and derivative, the force of the movie lies precisely in its

99

veracity. The often unspeakable experiences of illegal immigrants are in reality conducive to *both* melodrama and anonymity – a contradiction for which it is as hard to find a filmic formula as it is a place in the American Way of Life. If may be that Nava's artisanal production stumbled clumsily upon this by dint of empathy rather than technique; certainly the film has received a far warmer reception than might be expected on the basis of its purely cinematic qualities. In some respects it stands as the polar opposite of *Stand and Deliver*, which is a fluent and pugnacious celebration of individual self-help and resolution within the Hispanic 'underclass'.[6]

El Norte does indeed fail to address either the role of the US in Guatemala since the CIA-backed counter-revolution of June 1954 or the bloody regression of the last decade that would have been the main cause for its protagonists to quit the largely spiritual protection of their sacred hills. Yet it will endure far longer as a commentary on the interface between North and Central America than two films – one of the right, the other firmly of the left – that treat the question of politics much more directly. It is perhaps stretching a point to include John Milius's *Red Dawn* (1984) in this context, but the fact that the 'Reds' who invade the USA in this risible reactionary piece include Nicaraguans as well as Cubans shows that Hollywood was by no means incapable of sharing Reagan's hyperventilated McCarthyite visions. The domino theory has always drawn its strength from the fact that it 'explains' why very distant events are far more dangerous than they seem to an American public that lacks experience of invasion or authentically dangerous neighbours. The unbending logic of the theory may be a grotesque distortion of events in post-war eastern Europe or Indo-China in the 60s, but it bears more than passing similarity to the wilful projections of populist biblical exegesis that prevail so formidably in the USA today with their positively baroque depictions of heaven and hell. Heaven, of course, is home, and hell has always been its invasion, rather than the holocaust. Here, then, Milius simply reheats the essence of Alberto Cavalcanti's *Went the Day Well?* (1942), but whereas that film was shot within weeks of the Battle of Britain and a tangible threat of enemy occupation, *Red Dawn* was being shown at the same time as US advisers were directing an undeclared war inside the national frontiers of El Salvador and CIA agents were blowing up neutral ships in Nicaraguan harbours. This conflict was so demonstrably unequal that it is surely most interesting to ask why it had to be masked in utterly implausible inversions of reality. The notion that 'we are doing this to them before they do it to us' incubates a desperately threadbare *realpolitik* but also a rich seam of fearfulness that need by no means be open only to the left – as in *Dr Strangelove* (Stanley Kubrick, 1963) – to exploit. Milius, though, is content to serve up a paltry action movie.

Haskell Wexler's *Latino* (1985) is shot with all the technical accomplishment that one would expect from this outstanding cameraman, but the film is a bitter disappointment for it simply mirrors *Red Dawn* from the other side of the ideological spectrum. The denunciation of US crimes in Central America – in the form of support for the Nicaraguan Contras – is so insistent and unproblematic that its worthiness is distilled into a sermon for the already converted. It may be argued that this at least comforted an embattled progressive constituency within the USA and represented a retort to the likes of Milius's film in a genuine propaganda exchange. However, one cannot escape the feeling that such tasks would have been better achieved more directly through documentary form, and that a fictional approach needs to incorporate a much greater quotient of ambivalence and doubt in order to gain purchase on the imagination of precisely those in whom agnosticism imbricates with ignorance.

This is perhaps the central vindication of the two films dealing with Central America that have proved to be at least modest box-office successes – *Under Fire* (Roger Spottiswoode, 1983) and *Salvador* (Oliver Stone, 1986). Both films share the device of telling a Central American story (respectively, Nicaragua between September 1978 and July 1979 and El Salvador between January 1980 and January 1981) through the eyes and actions of US photo-journalists. This is justifiable both as a means to reach a broad American audience and as an authentic story source. Moreover, although both pictures significantly inflate the role of US journalists in those brutal days, the issue of media representation is both legitimate and sufficiently self-referencing as to uphold doubt – but not disbelief – about the story. In fact, both films share the attribute of incorporating a single, major lapse into an otherwise remarkably faithful rendition of the actual passage of historical events (although *Salvador* is much more closely tied to the lived experiences of an individual protagonist – the notorious Richard Boyle, beautifully played by James

'. . . *telling a Central American story . . . through the eyes and actions of US photo-journalists.' Nick Nolte in* Under Fire *(Roger Spottiswoode, USA, 1983)*

Woods – than is *Under Fire*, where a compellingly reticent Nick Nolte is a fictional amalgam of altogether more modest people). At first sight it is Spottiswoode's taking of liberties with history that seems the more objectionable since he introduces into the Nicaraguan revolution an entirely fictional leader, known as Rafael, whose death Nolte's character eventually conspires to conceal in league with the rebels. In reality, as we know, the heroes of the Nicaraguan revolution – Sandino himself and Carlos Fonseca Amador – were already enshrined as martyrs for a movement that prided itself on its collective leadership and eschewing of personalism. By contrast, Oliver Stone appears to commit a minor infraction by depicting the uprising in El Salvador of January 1981 in the town of Santa Ana as a veritable cavalry charge by the FMLN guerrillas when, in fact, it began as a messy mutiny within the government garrison.

There is, however, some cause for reversing the importance of these 'tricks of the trade'. As Salman Rushdie has noted with respect to Sandino's hat, the politics of both pre- and post-revolutionary Nicaragua depended very heavily upon a pared-down symbolism; eventually, in the elections of February 1990, this was reduced to the two colours of two flags (red and black for the FSLN; turquoise and white for Violeta Chamorro's UNO).[7] Thus, although no Rafael ever existed, the use of this fictional motif does correspond to one critical feature of a lived experience. Moreover, it was precisely the issue of projection and concealment (particularly through the use of indigenous masks by the rebels) that caught the popular imagination within and outside Nicaragua in the first half of 1979. On the other hand, it is doubtful if this caused quite such a deep moral dilemma for the press as Spottiswoode would have us believe.

Stone ends *Salvador* with two twists. First he has the guerrillas ride on horseback into Santa Ana as heroic liberators in the true Western tradition, only – within a few frames – to begin executing government troops in cold blood once the revolt runs into difficulties. Then he has Boyle save his Salvadorean girlfriend by taking her to the USA, only for the immigration service to apprehend and expel her to an uncertain fate. This second twist explicitly draws a correspondence between the actions of the constitutional US and dictatorial Salvadorean states, most effectively exploding the liberal ambience created by the first. Yet Boyle is the only (and not hugely reliable) source for this denouement, and we know that the depiction of events in Santa Ana is a travesty of history. Thus, although these two Janus-like scenes provide both the dramatic apogee and political declension of the film, they rest on distinctly insecure foundations. Given that so much else in *Salvador* is scrupulously close to the record – the pacing of events is disarmingly accurate from the killing of Archbishop Romero to that of the US nuns – one wonders why such a final contrivance proved necessary.

Pauline Kael's answer to this question would almost certainly be that Stone's politics are too unbending to allow for anything but an absolute resolution. Indeed, it is interesting that Kael greatly prefers *Under Fire* to *Salvador* ('crude and profane'), not least because the former treats the female lead (Joanna Cassidy playing a gringa journalist) as an independent and authoritative figure whereas in *Salvador* Boyle's girlfriend María (played by the excellent Elpedia Carrillo, who takes a very similar role in *The Honorary Consul*) is passive and resigned.[8] Whatever Stone's intentions, this strikes me as an unusually superficial interpretation that corresponds to a wider misconception in 'the north' that caution, appreciation of the limited good and a reserved counsel are tantamount to fatalism. Nobody who has any experience of political terror would countenance such a brashly innocent reading. Stone's anger in *Salvador* may be disconcertingly direct but it is entirely justified. And while he and Spottiswoode predictably concentrate on the death of US citizens that took place in both countries, they, like Costa Gavras in *Missing* (1982), successfully impart the menace, fear and terror that so deeply pervaded these societies. At the end of the day it is the translation of that reality to audiences who have become so careworn in suspending their belief at the first sight of blood that constitutes the strongest achievement of these films.[9]

Notes

1. For an excellent synoptic treatment of this from the perspective of Latin America, see John King, *Magical Reels: A History of Cinema in Latin America* (London: Verso, 1990).
2. It is, though, rather a moot point as to whether Mexico 'stands for' the rest of Latin America. Perhaps its frequent projection as 'other' has, rather, given it the status of 'no-man's land', at least with respect to images of *political* culture. There is a real sense in which (for political as well as cultural reasons) Mexico 'is not political' in American eyes, at least not like Central America, even if it is also no longer just a place occupied by sleepy people on donkeys.
3. *Stakeout* is more than partially a road-movie, and it depends as much as did *Five Easy Pieces* (Bob Rafelson/Richard Wechsler, 1970) on the verdant chill of the landscape of Washington State. Yet Badham's film could not be more different in its treatment of the human condition: Stowe is the total opposite of the progressively disillusioned and jilted Karen Black, whose carping 'white trash' foibles are played off Jack Nicholson as they move north with a brilliance that Stowe is seemingly not required to (and maybe cannot) display.
4. However, what her part in *Parador* misses is the essential innocence of the sensuality projected by Braga in films such as *Doña Flor and Her Two Husbands* (*Dona Flor e seus dois maridos*, Bruno Barreto, 1976) and *Gabriela* (Bruno Barreto, 1983). In this sense she could not be more different from a European actress to whom she might otherwise be seen as very similar in her candid sexual activity – the knowing, and dangerous, Maruschka Detmers, given the lead by Godard in his *Prenom Carmen* (1983).
5. Pauline Kael, *State of the Art* (New York: Dutton, 1985).
6. It is, however, worth noting that the lead character in *Stand and Deliver* is based on the Los Angeles schoolteacher Jaime Escalante, who is Bolivian and manifests many of those traits of national character of his country that stand in stark contrast to those normally associated with the Caribbean region.
7. Salman Rushdie, *The Jaguar Smile: A Nicaraguan Journey* (London: Picador, 1987), pp. 15–22.
8. Pauline Kael, *Hooked* (New York: Dutton, 1989); *State of the Art*.
9. For further reading on Central America see James Dunkerley, *Power in the Isthmus: A Political History of Modern Central America* (London: Verso, 1988).

NEO-REALISM AND NEW LATIN AMERICAN CINEMA

Bicycle Thieves *and* Blood of the Condor

JOHN HESS

Editors' Introduction
Enamoured with radical alterity, critics and historians of the New Latin
American cinema have often failed to account for the transformative process
of influences or to account for similarities in the context of differences.
Most often, the influence of 'dominant' First World practices is read as a
damning lack of originality: the need to reject all aspects of the Hollywood
norm becomes a critical requirement for absolute 'otherness'. However, the
historical development of the New Latin American cinema makes such a
position untenable. Committed to a rejection of Hollywood, the film-makers
of what would later be known as the New Latin American cinema looked to
Europe for alternatives in the 50s and found in Italian neo-realism the only
viable cinematic model for a different kind of national cinema. Neo-realism
was a revelation to those struggling to create national cinemas in the face of
underdevelopment. Its theoretical and practical distance from existing
cinematic practices was, in the classical sense of the term, an
epistemological break: neo-realism represented the formerly unrepresented,
upheld, in Rossellini's words, 'a moral position from which to look at the
world', and explicitly rejected the dominant Hollywood cinema.

However, these film-makers and national cinemas did not simply 'import'
neo-realism wholesale into Latin America; rather, they transformed what
was an explicitly Italian aesthetic, linked to the moment and place of its
production, to the Latin American or national context. This complex
transformative process – a kind of *bricolage* or syncretic refashioning – is
what interests John Hess in the piece that follows. Hess, founder and co-
editor of *JumpCut* and a long-standing critic of Latin American cinema,
compares neo-realist theory and the work of *Rome: Open City (Roma Citta'
Aperta)*, 1945 and *Bicycle Thieves (Ladri di Biciclette)*, 1948, to the theory
of the New Latin American cinema movement and Jorge Sanjinés's *Blood of
the Condor (Yawar Mallku)*, 1969. He thus outlines how in Latin America,
'neo-realism' became an aesthetic primarily concerned with history,
memory, and political action and choice. Hess's formulations and analysis
should lead the way for even more extensive explorations of the complex

104

processes whereby existing practices undergo radical transformations in their border crossings.

□

In all ages and under all circumstances there will always exist abundant reasons not to fight, but that will be the only way not to obtain liberty.

FIDEL CASTRO

The point is that even 'stylistic' choices reflect not only individual 'taste' or inclination in matters of language, but something much deeper: the ethical (practical/operative) relationship which the artist – like everyone else – forms with reality, and which leads him [sic] to choose certain 'forms' of expression and not others.

MARIO CANNELLA

INTRODUCTION

Italian neo-realism had a tremendous influence on New Latin American cinema. Not only did many of the founding film-makers, such as Tomás Gutiérrez Alea, Julio García Espinosa and Fernando Birri, study at Rome's Centro Sperimentali in the 50s, but the neo-realist style and especially its artisanal mode of production greatly inspired film-makers in Latin America. Yet these film-makers significantly changed this style and mode of production to make them more suitable to the revolutionary movement that was sweeping their continent in the 60s.

After some introductory material about neo-realism and New Latin American cinema, I want to compare two films: *Bicycle Thieves* (Vittorio de Sica, 1948) and *Blood of the Condor* (Jorge Sanjinés, 1969). The first stands as one of the founding and most influential films of Italian neo-realism. The second reflects the profound influence Italian neo-realism has had on New Latin American cinema as well as the kind of changes film-makers had to make in that style to accommodate new political realities and possibilities. Each film in its own time and place greatly expanded the dialectical possibilities of realism. By first looking at the historical–political contexts in which each film was made and then carefully comparing the films themselves, we can learn a great deal about the possibilities and limits of neo-realism and the powerful tradition it initiated in world cinema.

At the beginning of his discussion of Italian neo-realism, Robert Kolker says that there are really two neo-realisms, the most obvious and discussed being a certain small group of films made in Italy between 1945 and about 1955. The other neo-realism is far more important and what I want to discuss here. It is, according to Kolker, 'a concept, an aesthetics, a politics, a radical reorientation of cinema that changed the perspective on what had gone before and made possible a great deal of what came after' (Kolker, 1983, p. 20). We can find this 'concept' most easily and clearly in the films themselves, in the

105

practice of neo-realism. But it also exists in theory. Neo-realism had its own ideology, one that helped it break through conventional film-making and gain the status Kolker and others give it, but that also limited it by preventing film-makers and contemporary neo-realist intellectual culture from carefully studying its own past or current context.

This ideology was that of the Popular Front, which the European socialist and Communist movements established in order to defend themselves against Fascism. Playing down traditional Marxist notions such as class struggle and internationalism, the Popular Front called for a cross-class alliance and nationalism and proposed a vague humanism that set good versus evil and freedom versus oppression (without further discussion). Thus contradictions disappeared in the face of an intense sympathy for the poor and the wretched. This ideology helps explain why so many neo-realist films represent life as viewed from the point of view of children and why none of the films examines the Fascist past.

The theoretical underpinnings for neo-realism, such as they are, came from the teacher, editor, and critic, Luigi Chiarini and the script-writer Cesare Zavattini. Chiarini directed the Centro Sperimentali from 1935 to 1950, founded *Bianco e nero*, and wrote extensively about film. Zavattini was the major neo-realist scriptwriter, working on all de Sica's neo-realist films, and the only one who actually claimed to be a neo-realist. The intellectual world and justification or explanation they create is rigidly bipolar in keeping with the Manichean conception of the Popular Front: good patriots against evil Fascists and traitors.

The clearest idea in their writings is that of renewal: the rhetoric, lies, and distortions of the Fascist period and the war had to be sloughed off. Chiarini carefully distinguishes the 'politics' of neo-realism from 'polemics', which would mean having some relation to or following the program of some party. Such an involvement would have ruined the 'expressive force of the films'. He goes on: 'Their position [the film-makers'] was determined in confrontation with the historical and social reality that they were discovering with the camera' (Chiarini, p. 142): that is to say, not through any political involvement with a party or any political theory. Their work is intuitive, not theoretical.

Yet, while not always very effective and often silenced by Mussolini's police, a resistance movement existed throughout the Fascist period and was in a position toward the end of the war to provide leadership to the armed resistance. Numerous artists were banished, put in jail, or killed for speaking out. It seems odd that Zavattini would ignore this history here. Chiarini defends neo-realism against criticisms that it wallows in crude presentations of cruelty and ugliness. Rather, neo-realism 'exposed – without pleasure, without exaggeration and without an evil taste for the picturesque – the human conditions which constituted *per se* both a condemnation of certain social systems and a warning against them' (Chiarini, p. 151). Why the vague plural 'certain social systems?' What is he talking about here? Fascism, capitalism, socialism? There is no way of knowing.

Finally, while the neo-realists put renewed emphasis on the audience, their concept of that relationship is surprisingly passive. The task of the film-maker, according to Zavattini, 'does not consist in bringing the audience to tears and indignation by means of transference but, on the contrary, it consists in bringing them to reflect (and *then*, if you will, to stir up emotions and indignation) upon what they are doing and upon what others are doing; that is to think about reality precisely as it is' (Zavattini, p. 68). While it is certainly true that the neo-realist films made much greater demands on an audience than the studio fictions they were reacting against, there is none of either the Eisensteinian or Brechtian sense of wanting to catapult the audience out of its present reality in order for them to make their own history. There is only the vague hope that the film experience will provide an opportunity to rethink or re-see one's reality. Zavattini pessimistically sees the world continuing a negative slide 'towards evil because we do not know the truth: we remain unaware of reality' (p. 72). Film seems to have only an informative role, not a catalytic one.

In his important critique of neo-realism Mario Cannella shows how the ideology of the anti-Fascist movement in Italy became the ideology of neo-realism itself. In examining the contemporary commentary on neo-realism, Cannella notes the overwhelming influence of idealism and how artistic imagination is seen as autonomous: 'The gravest weakness of these positions consists . . . in their having isolated the imaginative impulse from the intellective and active dimension, in their having relegated history to the status of a mere "environmental consideration" ' (Cannella, p. 8). For, while there is the sense of renewal, the interest in rebuilding, in finding concrete solutions to the problems of everyday life, there is also a strong sense of continuity, of Fascism as a momentary 'perversion', a parenthesis. Worse still is the notion that Italian culture was neutral during Fascism, a notion that Cannella sees as 'a case of unconscious psychological withdrawal on the part of a whole generation in order to justify their own responsibility as intellectuals for the ensuing events' (p. 12). From Cannella's point of view the enthusiasm for a renewal, for a new relationship between politics and culture, was undermined by the failure of the intellectuals to make a firm break with the past. This he blames on the ideology of the Popular Front.

ROME: OPEN CITY – POPULAR FRONT IDEOLOGY AT WORK

The first great neo-realist film, Rossellini's *Rome: Open City* (1945), reveals all the contradictions at work in neo-realist film-making more clearly than any other film because its subject is the resistance itself. The film pits a group of dignified and heroic Italian characters, representing the working class, petty bourgeois small business people, and bourgeois resistance leaders against a thoroughly corrupt and perverse group of German Nazis and a few weak Italian traitors. At the same time that the film sets out all the startling stylistic elements of neo-realism, it also performed an amazing evasion of truth and history.

Rossellini and his collaborators carefully chose the characters to represent the main forces in the resistance. Don Pietro, the parish priest, represents the church. Manfredi, the Communist resistance leader, is an educated middle-class professional. Francesco is a working-class printer who is about to marry his next-door-neighbor, the widow Pina who has a young son. Pina lives in a small apartment together with a crowded, vociferous extended family. This type of family, with its stock characters, exaggerated gestures, loud arguments, warmth and humor becomes a cliché in Italian films, as does Anna Magnani's loud, lusty, emotional, and sentimental working-class Roman woman.

The forces of evil against them are extremely corrupt and perverse. The effeminate German SS officer, Bergmann, and his lesbian counterpart, Ingrid, are the primary villains. (Rossellini begins here a long, viciously homophobic Italian cinematic tradition of associating Fascism and homosexuality.) The cynical officer, Hartmann, who realizes that the Germans are not a master race and are bound to lose the war, is also the officer who shoots Don Pietro at the end. However, Rossellini presents Rome's police chief as relatively neutral. He seems efficient in his job of discovering and hunting down resistance leaders, yet he is constantly insulted by his German boss. We never see him do anything bad and he does not participate in the torture of Manfredi. Basically, Rossellini lets him off the hook.

Particularly interesting are the two young women, Pina's sister Lauretta and Manfredi's former lover Marina. Several times they are referred to as *estupide* (stupid), a very harsh word in Italian (yet short of vicious or evil) for these young women who have been corrupted by the war (a topic which reappears in *Paisan*). The big fight in Pina and Lauretta's extended family about Lauretta's behavior shows what is at issue here: Lauretta and Marina have rejected family. They do not want to live in crowded apartments with squalling children and shouting relatives, eking out a living in some menial job or slaving away in the home. They are selfish, greedy, irresponsible, and they are trying to transcend their class background. They engage in casual prostitution (with German soldiers!) in order to finance their liberation from family life as well as to pay for fancy clothes and other luxuries. And Marina, corrupted by her lesbian relationship with the German Gestapo agent and by the drugs Ingrid gives her, turns in Manfredi, leading to his death by torture and to the death of Don Pietro.

Pina and Francesco's impending marriage and especially their conversation on the stairs outside their apartments set the other pole: the patriotic worker, his supportive wife, their family. That all this is idealized and extremely sexist is obvious. Women who do not want the traditional family life are *estupide*: greedy, selfish, unreliable, immoral, whores or lesbians or both, possible traitors. This is particularly painful to watch because Maria Michi, who plays Marina (and also the prostitute Francesca in the Rome section of *Paisan*), was a resistance activist herself. Rossellini has set up the primary antagonism in Italy in 1944 as that between patriotic Italians on the one hand, and nasty German occupiers and a few (female) traitors on the other. Certainly, Italian Fascism was less pernicious than German Nazism, but it did rule dictatorially over Italy for over two decades at the point of a gun. Rossellini, and the rest of the neo-realist film-makers, evade this history.

Rossellini's evasion leaves marks on the surface of the film, what some have alluded to as Rossellini's 'expressionism'. We can see two films in *Open City*, a neo-realist film about the Italian resistance and its helpers, and an expressionist film about the German oppressors of that resistance. Many of the scenes with Marina and especially those in the Gestapo headquarters look much more like German expressionism than Italian neo-realism. Peter Brunette finds the *mise en scène* of the Gestapo headquarters 'clearly symbolic, a stylized landscape and almost mathematical demonstration of the corruption of Nazi culture' (1985, p. 39). The scenes in Marina's dressing-room at the theater or night club where she performs and in her apartment clearly connote the same decadence and corruption.

While an expressionist *mise en scène* seems an appropriate way to connote German decadence, a 'realist' *mise en scène* could have done the same thing, perhaps even more effectively, without breaking the tone and style of the film. What, we must ask, does Rossellini gain by presenting the Germans as completely corrupt and decadent in a style that breaks with the dominant neo-realist style of the film? This characterization of the Germans and the stylistic break needed to present it save Rossellini from the necessity of examining recent Italian history – and perhaps even his own role in it. The Germans are monstrous, that is all we need to know. Rossellini does not have to explain why they are there, where their control comes from, how they got there, what their relation to Italian Fascism is.

I quoted Mario Cannella above to the effect that the Italian anti-Fascists tended to see Fascism as an aberration in their history, as something they really had nothing to do with and that needed no explanation because it was not part of the continuum of Italian history. In this film Rossellini is able to project his own guilt about participating in the Fascist culture industry on to the Germans and to exorcise it without having to deal with it in a conscious way. I agree with Cannella's contention that the Italian resistance and its Popular Front ideology provided the content and the intensity of neo-realist film-making at the same time that it undermined it intellectually and politically. Neo-realism was unable to deal with history and therefore was unable to cope with the rapid changes in post-war Italian society.

NEO-REALISM AND NEW LATIN AMERICAN CINEMA

Fernando Birri is a central figure in the continuation and further development of the neo-realist political aesthetic in Latin America. In the early 50s he studied in Rome's famous film school and, upon his return to Argentina in 1956, worked within the Institute of Sociology of the National University of the Littoral in Santa Fé. He went on to form the Documentary Film School of Santa Fé, where he made the sociological documentary *Tire dié* (*Throw us a Dime*, 1958) with his students. In 1961 he made a neo-realist style comedy called *Los inundados* (*The Flood Victims*).

To Birri, to be realist meant, as it did to the Italians, 'seeing things as they are', looking at aspects of the national reality that artists had not previously looked at. 'What I wanted', Birri has said, 'was to discover the face of an invisible Argentina – invisible not because it couldn't be seen, but because no one *wanted* to see it' (Barnard, p. 68), and: 'It is my belief that the first step to be taken by an aspiring national film industry is to document national reality' (p. 69). In both cases there is the desire to resist and overcome an imposed culture: the empty rhetoric of Fascism and the imposed forms and standards of imperialism. Birri has said:

109

Neo-realism is the cinema that discovers the Italy of underdevelopment, discovers in a country that apparently has the clothing, the tinsel, and what's more, the rhetoric of development, another reality, a hidden one, that of underdevelopment ... it was the cinema of the humble and offended. It was possible everywhere (*Cinema of the Humble*, Part 1).

Birri has told me in conversation that neo-realism's influence was not as much its style as the example it offered of making independent, highly artistic, nationalist, sociological films. And, in fact, this neo-realist declaration of independence for film-makers is perhaps its greatest contribution to post-Second World War film-making.

Cuban film-maker and theorist Julio García Espinosa also studied in Italy and his comments on neo-realism help us understand both its attraction and the need to go beyond it. In *The Cuban Image*, Michael Chanan says that the revolution pushed Cubans beyond neo-realism in search of more critical modes of film-making. In the 50s, Julio García Espinosa thought, according to Chanan, that

> ... [we] were preparing only for a multi-class government with the partici-pation of leftists alongside the bourgeoisie, and with a national programme [i.e., the Popular Front ideology of the Italian left]. Nobody thought at first the outcome would actually be a socialist government. ... Neo-realism they saw as the model for an appropriate cinema – a humanist and pro-gressive aesthetic that offered a real alternative to the dominant modes of Hollywood and Latin American commercial production. ... [I]t was a style that placed the people on the screen as historical actors, but without being too explicit about it (1985, p. 128).

In other words, because the Cuban revolution had gone beyond what the Italian left was able to achieve, or perhaps even conceive, Cuban film-makers, and by extension other film-makers in Latin America during these years, had also to go further.

SANJINÉS IN THE CONTEXT OF BOLIVIA
Bolivia was and remains an impoverished country with a very high illiteracy rate. Nearly 70 per cent of the population are indigenous people speaking Quechua and Aymara languages. The country's wealth depends on its famous tin mines, and its weak bourgeoisie has constantly needed military rule to control the well-organized tin miners. In 1941 the Revolutionary Nationalist Movement (MNR) was founded as a progressive coalition of the proletariat, petty bourgeoisie, and progressive elements of the bourgeoisie. It supported the government from 1943 to 1946 and led the nationalist revolution in 1952.

Backed (and encouraged) by armed workers, the new government pushed through basic reforms: nationalized the tin mines, initiated agrarian reform in the *altiplano*, dismembered the armed forces, implemented universal suf-frage, and created workers' control in the mines. The USA counter-attacked and finally, in 1964, the MNR government was overthrown by General René Barrientos. He opened the country to foreign investment which only heightened the contradictions that Che Guevara hoped to exploit when he went to Bolivia in the mid-60s (he was killed there in 1967).

In 1960, Sanjinés returned from studying film in Chile and began making sociological documentaries about the plight of Bolivia's poor with two friends, Oscar Soria and Ricardo Rada. General Barrientos put Sanjinés in charge of the Bolivian Film Institute in 1964, but then, because of the kind of documentaries they were making, he closed it in 1967. When Colonel Banzer came to power via a reactionary *coup d'état* in 1971, Sanjinés went into exile and has worked abroad for long periods ever since. The feature film *Roads to Death* (1969) was destroyed by the labs with some complicity by the Bolivian government. *Blood of the Condor* was banned and only screened in Bolivia after street demonstrations demanded it.

Whereas in Italy the film-makers only got a taste of the struggle for liberation after the long grayness of Fascism and then returned quickly to a relatively comfortable and democratic existence, Latin American film-makers like Jorge Sanjinés have for most of their lives participated in national and revolutionary struggle – in order simply to make films. They have seen their work banned, censored, destroyed; they have had to leave their countries and been thrown out of others. They have seen their work as directly participating in this struggle, as a direct intervention into social and historical reality. Metaphorically, one could say that they have seen the brief 1944–8 period in Italian history intensified and extended indefinitely. Their films, the forms and styles they have chosen, the content and relation to both subjects and to audience have been greatly shaped by these experiences.

BICYCLE THIEVES AND BLOOD OF THE CONDOR

Vittorio de Sica made *Bicycle Thieves* in 1948 with his own production company for about $140,000, mostly his own money, from a script by his close collaborator Cesare Zavattini and himself. He used non-professional actors and location shooting to reproduce the impoverished Roman working-class milieu of the immediate post-war period. The long-unemployed worker Antonio Ricci finally gets a job as a bill poster, a job for which he needs a bicycle. The family pawn their last remaining sheets to redeem the bicycle, but on the first day of work a young thief steals it. The rest of the film follows Ricci's and his young son's search for the bicycle. De Sica uses the quest motif to explore the poor districts of Rome and to look at the various alternatives open to his protagonist. At the center of the film is the relationship between Ricci and his son Bruno. The film carefully reveals, as Birri said, Italy's underdevelopment: the family's austere apartment and poverty, the working-class tenements on the outskirts of Rome. Many of the film's most beautiful scenes are practically silent: workers streaming into the city on foot, by bicycle and bus, the search through the narrow streets and ancient monuments of Rome's former glory, the huge Porto Portese flea market.

Jorge Sanjinés made *Blood of the Condor* in 1968–9 in Bolivia's *altiplano* with a small budget of mostly personally raised funds, a small crew and a community of Quechua Indians. He used non-professional actors and location shooting to reveal the social environment of the Quechua. As in *Bicycle Thieves*, some of the most beautiful scenes are quasi-documentary,

'*At the center of the film is the relationship between Ricci and his son Bruno.*' Lamberto Maggiorani and Enzo Staiola *in* Ladri di Biciclette (Bicycle Thieves, *Vittorio de Sica, Italy, 1948*)

especially the various Indian ceremonies. Sanjinés, however, has very specific political reasons for including this material beyond its documentary quality. He has written that, while the indigenous people of the Andes have no written culture, their lives are filled with artistic creation.

> They have no poetry either, but they create it daily, singing to life, creating with dance and with their crafts. We also see this in their language. The Quechuan peasants speak and communicate in metaphors and constantly use their language as a vehicle of artistic creation (Pick, p. 95).

In *Blood of the Condor* the Quechua attack a US-sponsored clinic that has been sterilizing their women. In reprisal, soldiers shoot two community leaders and wound a third, Ignacio. His wife, Paulina, takes him to La Paz to get medical help. His assimilated brother, Sixto, searches unsuccessfully through La Paz for the blood plasma the doctors need to operate on Ignacio, who ultimately dies. Sixto, now dressed as an Indian, returns to the community with Paulina to continue the struggle. A freeze frame of raised rifles ends the film.

Bicycle Thieves has the linear, 'accidental', elliptical, narrative style of many neo-realist films. By this I do not mean that it is haphazard; in fact, the film is very carefully crafted. As Roy Armes explains:

> De Sica has pointed out that six months were needed for the mere elaboration of the script and continually the dramatic contrasts are cunningly exploited: the opulent glamor of Rita Hayworth on a street poster is set against the grim poverty of Antonio, his anguished search for help is played against the background of the rehearsal of a cheerful, if drab, musical show, and the cheering crowd at the football match form a striking counterpoint for Antonio's desperate surrender to temptation (pp. 152–3).

Armes also points out how de Sica uses the two visits to the clairvoyant, Madame Sartona, to achieve 'a great deal of dramatic irony' (p. 152). He also uses a near continual swirl of bicycles around Antonio and his son to heighten their desperate plight. None the less, it is primarily at the level of *mise en scène* and the interaction of characters that the film achieves its effects.

Though employing a neo-realist photographic style, *Blood of the Condor* has a radically different narrative style. The film begins when Ignacio is wounded and taken to La Paz. Sanjinés then intercuts a series of flashbacks, explaining how this happened, with Sixto's search for plasma in La Paz. Sanjinés goes beyond the naturalist determinism of neo-realism to analyze the situation of his characters and show the possibility and source of change. He juxtaposes time to compare life in the city with life in the *altiplano*, the life of the Quechua with the life of the Spanish in the city. Like *Bicycle Thieves*, *Blood of the Condor* also has a quest motif, in fact two of them. In the *altiplano*, Ignacio undertakes a search for the cause of the women's infertility, which leads to his death. Juxtaposed with this is Sixto's search for plasma which leads to his reintegration into the Quechua community and into communal struggle. What do these various odysseys reveal?

In *Bicycle Thieves* the quest reveals that the institutions of post-war Italy are useless, they can offer no help at all. Further, we see no communal or collective alternative to individual despair – only the child offers Antonio any significant support once the bicycle is stolen. The police, the unions (by their absence), the Communist Party (they shush Antonio during a meeting in the tenement to discuss their efforts to help the working class), the church, other poor people, even the clairvoyant all fail to offer support, help and comfort. In his defense of the film, Bazin states its thesis as 'in the world where this workman lives, the poor must steal from each other in order to survive' (p. 51). While this seems true, it only partially explains the film's statement about Italian post-war society. In a world with a very high degree of unionization and the largest Communist party in Western Europe, de Sica can see no alternative for this or any other worker except spiritual communion with a child.

The double quests in *Blood of the Condor*, by contrast, perform a precise analysis of the world of these indigenous peasants. We see an incompetent, impoverished, and heartless medical establishment designed to serve only the rich. We see the contrast between Sixto's search and Nazi-style military finery. We see self-satisfied and ignorant US medical volunteers who feel perfectly justified in sterilizing Quechua women because, as they say, 'there are too many children'. We see the Quechua drawn together to investigate and confront this attack on their very existence as a people. We see the upper class teaching their children English at the same time that doctors cannot speak to their Quechua patients. We see rich Bolivians lounging around a swimming pool and playing tennis as a desperate Indian searches for the plasma to save his brother's life. Finally, rather than a sort of spiritual transcendence over a difficult material reality visioned at the end of *Bicycle Thieves*, we see a Quechua who had tried to assimilate into Spanish Bolivian society return to his Quechua identity – in a sense, we see the decolonization of a mind.

The early neo-realist films seem to have been primarily independent productions, that is independent of the Cinecittà, the studio system founded by Mussolini in the 30s which remained closed until the end of 1947. Small companies, some extant under Fascism and some newly created, produced single films with quite small budgets (with the exception of Produziona De Sica, which produced *Bicycle Thieves* and also produced *Miracle in Milan* two years later). However, I have seen little evidence of efforts to make the films *with* the working class or to work with the unions or political parties. And, although Luchino Visconti was partially funded by the Communist Party (and was apparently inspired by Gramsci's theses on the problems of Italy's impoverished south) for *La terra trema* (1947) and the Italian Partisan Organization produced two films – Vergano's *Il sole sorge ancora* (*The Sun Rises*

'. . . *life in the* altiplano . . .' Yawar Mallku (Blood of the Condor, *Jorge Sanjinés, Bolivia, 1969*)

114

Again, 1946) and de Santis's *Caccia tragica* (*Pursuit*, 1947)), I have seen no evidence that these film-makers participated in any effort toward popular education or cultural revolution. This area of relation to subjects and relation to audience in Italian neo-realism seems a glaring gap in film history.

Unlike the neo-realists and participating in a long-standing activist tradition, Sanjinés worked closely with the Quechua. In 1960, when he returned to Bolivia from Chile, he and his friends Oscar Soria and Ricardo Rada founded the film group Ukamau ('That's the Way it Is' in Quechua). They began with short documentaries about the poor and oppressed residents of La Paz and outlying areas. He described these early films thus:

> The first films made by the Ukamau Group documented the poverty and misery of certain strata of the population. These films . . . served no other purpose than to remind the bourgeois audience that another class of people existed. . . . We screened our early documentaries in the mines and marginal *barrios*, and these popular performances opened our eyes and led us on a different track (Burton, p. 37).

Thus Sanjinés and his friends followed that path so characteristic of Third World intellectuals: involvement with the previously unnoticed majority of common people of their countries, leading to greater understanding and participation, leading to the kind of discovery that Birri was talking about. In Italy this process seemed to have begun within the resistance, but to have ended abruptly once the war was over. The disarming of the partisans had powerful intellectual and artistic repercussions: unable to participate in effecting change in the real, material and social world, the neo-realist film-makers could only document reality and envision some future idealistic, spiritual transcendence.

HISTORY AND MEMORY
From Gutiérrez Alea's *Memories of Underdevelopment* (1968) to the Chilean Jorge Durán's *The Color of his Destiny* (made in Brazil, 1986) the vast majority of Latin American films I have seen are about history or memory or both, using flashbacks, multiple time layers, historical reconstruction, historical documentary inserts and many other devices to historicize the narrative. Italian neo-realism contains none of this: its films have no memory, no history. Film time is in the specific present (*Bicycle Thieves*, *Bitter Rice*), an indefinite present (*La terra trema*), or an immediate brief past leading up to the present (*Paisan*, *Rome: Open City*). There are no films about Italy under the Fascists, very few films about the partisan war, no flashbacks or multiple-time films, and no use of memory as an organizing device. They are about people in a specific present context and not about their evolving relation to that context.

There are many reasons for the prevalence of history and memory in Latin American film. In his critique of neo-realism, Mario Cannella says that while there was an ideology of renewal and rebuilding, there was also a strong sense of continuity. Fascism was seen as a momentary perversion or parenthesis, something other people did rather than something that needed to be explained. Clearly, Latin American intellectuals cannot do this. Colonialism and imperialism are not brief interludes that can be overlooked, but violent, foreign impositions that people have fought against for centuries. Cultural renewal involves, as Fanon has made very clear, a recovery of national culture and history. History, and its more personal form, memory, become necessary tools for this recovery.

If nothing else did, expressing history and memory necessitated going beyond neo-realism as a form, for it did not readily admit history, and many of the formal innovations of Latin American film attributed alternately to Brecht, Eisenstein, Vertov and Godard are just as likely innovations necessitated by the need to express history. The documentary inserts in films like *Memories of Underdevelopment* (*Memorias del subdesarrollo*, 1968) and *One Way or Another* (*De cierta manera*, 1977), for example, show the historical context in which the characters are operating. Solanas and Getino used clearly Brechtian and Godardian devices in *The Hour of the Furnaces* (*La hora de los hornos*, 1968) to examine the history of Argentina.

Ultimately, New Latin American cinema was created within a revolutionary context (actual or hoped for) and their makers actively participated in their various national movements as well as aiding other national movements (Cuba in the 60s, Allende's Popular Unity government in Chile in the early 70s). The films demonstrate the convergence and synthesis of art and politics so common in revolutionary situations and in Latin America in the last several decades. Thus these films, unlike the neo-realist films, focus on choice and on people who choose. When Sixto returns to the mountains from La Paz wearing traditional clothing in *Blood of the Condor*, he indicates his clear choice to give up the dream of assimilation, with its accompanying social mobility, and take up the gun to defend his people. By their own choice, three Lucías transcend their upbringing and circumstances to begin a new phase in the development of Cuban women in *Lucía* (Humberto Solás, Cuba, 1968). And Sergio, in *Memories of Underdevelopment*, is paralyzed by his inability to choose exile or participate in the revolution. All he can do is observe.

The characters in neo-realist films, on the contrary, have no choice. They can only act out their destinies within a determinist situation. Even in *Rome: Open City*, where this may seem less true, the characters have all made their decisions before the film begins. Their decision is part of their character and what defines them as heroic. These films show characters who fail in the material realm, but triumph at a spiritual level through their sacrifice, and is thus a cinema of defeatism. G. M. Carraniga, writing about nineteenth-century Italian *verismo*, makes a point often quoted in discussions of neo-realism: '"To be defeated by life" is a natural subject for bourgeois *verismo*...; unable to free himself from his class ideology and to understand and express reality, the *verista* can achieve nothing more significant than to celebrate consciously and conscientiously his own defeat by chronicling the defeat of his characters' (p. 349).

As Brecht argued in his famous debate with Lukács, the issue is not form alone, but the relation between form and content, between form and circumstance, between art and politics. As I hope I have demonstrated, the formal choices that film-makers make have a great deal to do with their political ideology and political and historical situation. The inability of the Italian neo-realists to go beyond a kind of nineteenth-century realism lay in the ideology of the Popular Front and their distance from continuing political struggle, whereas the formal innovation of many Latin American film-makers lies in their need to deal with and express history and memory in a period of revolutionary change.

Works Cited

Armes, Roy. *Patterns of Realism: A Study of Italian Neo-Realist Cinema*, New York: A. S. Barnes, 1971.

Armes, Roy. *Third World Film Making and the West*. Berkeley: University of California Press, 1987.

Barnard, Tim (ed.). *Argentine Cinema*. Toronto: Nightwood Editions, 1986.

Bazin, André. *What is Cinema* (2nd ed.). Trans. Hugh Gray. Berkeley: University of California Press, 1971.

Birri, Fernando. 'For a Nationalist, Realist, Critical and Popular Cinema.' Trans. Michael Chanan, in Barnard: 79–82.

Birri, Fernando. *La escuela documental de Santa Fé*. Santa Fé: Documento del Instituto de Cinematografía de la U.N.L., 1964.

Birri, Fernando. 'The Roots of Documentary Realism' (An interview with Julianne Burton, Havana, 1986). Trans. Julianne Burton, in Barnard: 64–77.

'Bolivia: The War Goes On'. A special issue of *Latin American and Empire Report* (NACLA), 8.2 (February, 1974).

Bondanella, Peter. *Italian Cinema: From Neorealism to the Present*. New York: Frederick Ungar, 1883.

Brunette, Peter. 'Rossellini and Cinematic Realism'. *Cinema Journal*, 254.1 (Fall, 1985): 34–49.

Brunette, Peter. *Roberto Rossellini*. New York: Oxford University Press, 1987.

Burton, Julianne (ed. and trans.). *Cinema and Social Change in Latin America: Conversations with Filmmakers*. Austin: University of Texas Press, 1986.

Cannella, Mario. 'Ideology and Aesthetic Hypotheses in the Criticism of Neo-Realism'. [Originally *Geovane Critica*, 11 (1966)]. Trans. John Matthews and Judith White. *Screen*, 14.4 (Winter, 1973–4): 5–60.

Carraniga, G. M. 'Realism in Italy', in Hemmings: 324–56.

Chanan, Michael. *The Cuban Image: Cinema and Cultural Politics in Cuba*. London: BFI, 1985.

Chiarini, Luigi. 'A Discourse on Neo-Realism', in Overbey: 139–68.

Cinema of the Humble (Part I of *New Cinema of Latin America*). d. Michael Chanan. Great Britain. 1985. Cinema Guild.

Dalton, Roque. '*Yawar Mallku*: Something More than Just a Film', in Pick: 97–113. [originally, *Cine Cubano*, No. 60–61–62].

Hovald, Patrice-G. *Le Néo-Réalisme italien et ses créateurs*. Collection '7 Art.' Paris: Editions du Cerf, 1959.

Kolker, Robert Phillip. *The Altering Eye*. London: Oxford University Press, 1983.

Kolker, Robert Phillip. *Bernardo Bertolucci*. New York: Oxford University Press, 1985.

López, Ana M. 'Towards a "Third" and "Imperfect" Cinema: A Theoretical and Historical Study of Filmmaking in Latin America.' Dissertation. The University of Iowa, 1986.

Marcus, Millicent. *Italian Film in the Light of Neorealism*. Princeton: Princeton University Press, 1986.

117

Overbey, David (ed. and trans.). *Springtime in Italy: A Reader on Neo-Realism*. Hamden, Conn.: Archon Books, 1978.

Pick, Zuzana M. (ed. and trans.). *Latin American Film Makers and the Third Cinema*. Ottawa: Carleton University Film Studies Program, 1978.

Rhode, Eric. 'Why Neo-Realism Failed'. *Sight and Sound*, 30 (Winter, 1960–61): 26–32.

Sanchez, H. José. *Neo-Realism in Contemporary Bolivian Cinema: A Case Study of Jorge Sanjinés' 'Blood of the Condor' and Antonio Equino's 'Chuquiago'*. Dissertation. The University of Michigan, 1983. Ann Arbor: UMI, 1985.

Sanjinés, Jorge. 'The Search for a Popular Cinema', in Pick: 88–96. [Originally, *Cine Cubano*, Nos 89–90].

Sanjinés, Jorge. 'Revolutionary Cinema: The Bolivian Experience', in Burton: 35–48. [Originally, *Cine Cubano*, Nos 77–78 (1977)].

Sanjinés, Jorge. 'A Militant Cinema', in Pick: 73–7. [Originally, *Cine Cubano*, No. 68].

Sanjinés, Jorge. 'Language and Popular Culture'. Trans. John King. *Framework*, 10 (Spring, 1979): 31–3.

Sanjinés, Jorge, y grupo ukamau. *Teoría práctica de un cine junto al pueblo* (2nd ed.). Mexico: Siglo Ventiuno editores, 1980.

'Sobre Ukamau' [An Interview with Jorge Sanjinés]. *Cine Cubano* 48 (1968): 28–33.

Stam, Robert. *'Hour of the Furnaces* and the Two Avant Gardes'. *Millennium Film Journal*, 7/8/9 (1980–1): 151–72.

'Ukamau and *Yawar Mallku*' [An Interview with Jorge Sanjinés]. *Afterimage* (London), 3 (Summer, 1971): 40–53.

Zavattini, Cesare. 'Some Ideas on the Cinema'. Trans. Pier Luigi Lanza, in *Film: A Montage of Theories*, Ed. Richard Dyer MacCann. New York: E. P. Dutton, 1966: 216–28.

Zavattini, Cesare. *Sequences from a Cinematic Life*. Trans. William Weaver. Englewood Cliffs, NJ: Prentice-Hall, 1970.

Zavattini, Cesare. 'A Thesis on Neo-Realism', in Overbey: 67–78.

HYPER-, RETRO- or COUNTER-CINEMA

European Cinema and Third Cinema between
Hollywood and Art Cinema [1]

THOMAS ELSAESSER

Editors' Introduction

Because Thomas Elsaesser opens this essay with a late 60s quotation from Jean-Luc Godard and invokes Glauber Rocha (*Le Vent d'Est*, 1969 being the obvious cinematic connecting-point here), and relates the post-war 'new' national cinemas of Europe to Latin American cinema, the reader might be forgiven for expecting Thomas Elsaesser to tread some well-worn critical and political paths. Instead, after some brief notes on crucial shifts in Hollywood movies over the last two decades and on the hegemonic position television has come to occupy, Elsaesser offers a deft and intriguing account of Latin America's significance to the politics of the work of two important European film-makers.

Francesco Rosi's and Werner Herzog's interests in, and relationship to, Latin America are seemingly very different. A Gabriel García Márquez novella enables Rosi to further investigate male machismo and the power of the mother in Latin culture. The result, argues Elsaesser, is that Rosi uses Latin mythology and the 'magic realism' of Márquez as a way of achieving a displaced understanding of – a way of looking back at – Europe and of the failure of left intellectuals to understand a history already lost, a history dismantled by the conservative right.

Werner Herzog, on the other hand, uses the locations, cultures and myths of the Third World – in this case Latin America – to examine more deeply his own obsessive problems and struggles as a film-maker. The multi-layered range of tensions surrounding and interrelating the actors, their personae, the realities and the myths which constitute Herzog's films, all contribute to making the complex machine which is the film-making process and become an allegorical statement about human history and existence.

Both film-makers, Elsaesser argues, elaborate an ultimately tragic vision. Godard and Rocha, like Brecht, would no doubt see such films as being non- or apolitical, films which play into the hands of the fatalists and the defeatists. However, Elsaesser presents a different view, arguing that instead of engaging historically with cinema generally, or reacting

119

antagonistically to Hollywood specifically, directors like Rosi and Herzog look laterally to other cultures, literatures, mythologies in order to avoid and rethink the audio-visual terrains as colonised and defined by Hollywood and television. As he writes towards the end of this essay:

> This issue may well touch the core of why European directors might not be drawn to making films in developing countries, but why they prefer countries which have an indigenous mythology that can be made to signify: not a reality, but an attitude to a reality which, like Rosi's and Herzog's characters, is presented as ultimately unknowable.

According to this line of reasoning film-makers like Rosi and Herzog might seem to be making neither political films nor making films politically in the activist sense of a Godard or a Rocha, but they are engaged in a politics of cinema which does not offer a comfortable or easy seat for the European spectator.

☐

A FLASHBACK TO THE SIXTIES

Fifty years after the Russian Revolution, the American cinema dominates everywhere in the world. There is not much to be added to this fact. None the less, we should, each according to his abilities, start two or three Vietnams at the heart of the immense Hollywood–Mosfilm–Cinecittà–Pinewood Empire. Economically and aesthetically, on two fronts, we must fight for national cinemas, free, brotherly, comradely and joined in friendship.

JEAN-LUC GODARD[2]

Even before Jean-Luc Godard urged film-makers in 1967 not to make political films but to make films politically, the question of an 'alternative cinema' was on the agenda of European directors. While some directors were looking to formal, experimental, non-narrative traditions, Godard's notion was that of a counter-cinema, implying a film-politics that would challenge the economic supremacy of Hollywood, its monopolistic distribution and exhibition system not only in the countries of Europe but also in the Third World.

The moment for a radical break was opportune: renewed interest in avant-garde film-making during the 60s and 70s coincided with a period of stagnation and structural change in Hollywood which led to large-scale mergers, take-over bids and board-room struggles for the control of the industry's assets, acquired by multinational companies like Gulf and Western or the Kinney Corporation, whose main interests were in oil, canned food or real estate.[3]

Not least because of a general decline in the cinema as a form of mass entertainment, but due also to lighter and cheaper film-making equipment,

120

post-war Europe had seen the emergence of a number of 'new' national cinemas with an art cinema orientation – Italian neo-realism, the French *nouvelle vague*, the New German cinema, for instance. By the mid-60s, the moment was also propitious for another kind of cinema in Latin America, partly modelled on European auteurism, but partly also poised to be a political cinema, influenced by Marxist or Maoist perspectives such as those voiced by Godard. As so often in the history of post-colonialism and the liberation struggles, a European-educated intellectual and artistic vanguard sought to forge links with indigenous sources, often a combination of folk culture and the classic nineteenth-century European novel.

For this independent cinema after 1968, as well as for the political avant-gardes, the relation between Hollywood and Europe, and between Hollywood and Latin American cinema, tended to be conceived as radically and absolutely antagonistic in both theory and practice. Film-makers borrowed their metaphors from the vocabulary of oppression and exploitation, and occasionally, as in the case of Godard, from the class war. In Europe, the revival of political and formalist avant-gardes corresponded to a desire to abandon the notion of a 'national' cinema in favour of an international(ist) radical modernism. But in the case of Glauber Rocha and the Cinema Novo in Brazil, or the Peronist cinema of Argentina, anti-Hollywood could also mean self-consciously nationalist cinema.

FROM ANTI-ILLUSIONISM TO HYPER-REALISM

But Hollywood, art cinema and Third World cinema are communicating vessels. By the mid-70s, most of the initiatives – to join forces with political movements on the ground, as in the case of Glauber Rocha in Brazil; to break out of the isolated cottage and craft manufacture typical of the avant-garde film-maker, as Godard had tried when he co-founded the Dziga Vertov Group; or to win a cinema-going audience to an alternative practice, as with the New German cinema – had all suffered setbacks with the remarkable recovery of commercial Hollywood. Indeed, the self-consciously national cinemas of Latin America saw themselves courted mostly at international festivals, where they became part of a European radical chic. Much the same happened to the New German cinema: a modestly successful export item on the art cinema circuit, it was massively supported by government funds and government agencies, but showed no signs of rallying domestic audiences to its own films. It was American movies, the package deal and big-business production methods which became more than ever the dominant model on both European and world markets. The new independent cinemas, whether national, politically internationalist or author-based, gradually found themselves forced into coexistence on the Americans' own terms, or all but vanish altogether.

In so far as spectators returned to the cinema, it was to watch Hollywood blockbusters. With enormous profits for the industry came capital investments in new technologies, notable computerisation, special effects, and the improved sound reproduction made possible with the Dolby system. Such technical innovations were themselves the consequence of new promotion and marketing strategies. By borrowing from related entertainment indus-

121

tries like the music business, Hollywood was able to attract a different generation of spectators, whose pleasures derived from the thrill of film technology itself: these were better served by hyper-realism and simulation than by 'Brechtian' anti-illusion or distanciation. Special effects, displayed in horror movies and sci-fi epics like *Star Wars*, *Close Encounters of the Third Kind*, *Aliens*, or *Blade Runner*, to a certain extent 'deconstruct' classical narrative cinema by shifting the pleasure of representation from verisimilitude and realism to fantasy and the self-referential play of illusionist codes. Eight-track stereo or Dolby are not innovations that create a greater realism for the ear; instead, they advertise the presence of a separate sound space dedicated to creating a highly charged, imaginary sound experience. Not a counter-cinema superceded Hollywood, but a New Hollywood whose development was neither governed by the modernist telos of the medium's self-realisation through self-reflexivity, nor by the political logic of opposition and confrontation. Instead, it followed the capitalist logic of penetrating new markets in the wake of the activity generated by the interplay between technological innovation, media advertising, and mass-produced, cheap consumer electronics. In this strategy, even avant-garde techniques could find profitable uses and, as a consequence, one critical dimension of film theory and film practice was thrown in crisis, overtaken by the dynamic of transformation and change that realised the agenda of self-reflexivity, but devoid of radical political potential or pretensions, and with sometimes immense popular success.

THE INTERNATIONAL MARKET

Given the extent of Hollywood's revival, it is clear that the balance of forces between Hollywood and European independent, art or avant-garde cinema could not continue to be represented as pure opposition. If the term 'international market' draws attention to the economic realities of film production in competition for the world's spectators, the term 'national cinema' disguises another term: an auteur cinema will often be more opposed to its own national commercial cinema than it is to Hollywood film. The *'politique des auteurs'* or 'cinephilia' are based on such preferment. But in other respects, films are commodities like any other: while the Hollywood product dominates most countries' domestic markets, as well as leading internationally, each national cinema is both national and international, though in different areas of its sphere of influence. Nationally, it participates in the popular or literary culture at large (the New German cinema's predilection for filmed literature, the intellectual cult status of French film directors, the acceptance of Fellini, Antonioni, or Francesco Rosi as 'artists' and Italy's sacred monsters). Internationally, national cinemas used to have a generic function: a French, Swedish or Italian film set horizons of expectations for the general audience which are negative mirror images to that of a Western, a science fiction film or a horror movie, as essential a prerequisite for brand-name identity as the Hollywood generic classifications or star vehicles.

From the perspective of Hollywood, on the other hand, it makes little difference whether one is talking about the Indian cinema or Argentinian cinema, the French cinema or the Chilean cinema: none is a serious competitor for America's domestic output, but each national cinema is a 'market' for American films, with Hollywood practices and norms having major repercussions on the national production sector. In most countries this has led to different forms of protectionism, bringing into play state intervention and government legislation, but usually to very little avail, especially since the different national cinemas, however equal they seem before Hollywood, are of course emphatically unequal among themselves, and locked into yet another form of competition when they enter an international market.

The situation has often been described as a form of cultural and economic colonisation, whose dialectics have been analysed either in Hegelian terms of master and slave (by, among others, Frantz Fanon,[4] Amilcar Cabral[5]), in terms of a national 'imaginary' (Anthony Wilden,[6] Benedict Anderson[7]), in terms of 'otherness' (Edward Said[8]), or as a particular form of miscognition, as in Fredric Jameson's Lacanian formulation of 'the politics of otherness'.[9] It can even be figured as an unsuccessful Oedipal challenge, where identification and antagonism are two sides of the same coin, competition with Hollywood leading to an emulation of the American model, as with the many Latin films ironically or lovingly quoting mainstream cinema (Héctor Babenco's *Kiss of the Spider Woman* or Ruy Guerra's 'adaptation' of Brecht's *Threepenny Opera*).

THE HEGEMONIC FORCE OF TELEVISION
In the debates of the avant-garde around hegemonic Hollywood and a counter-cinema, the oppositional tactics elided another crucial term, namely television, which during the period in question had itself become the dominant cultural form of visual representation, in relation to which both Hollywood as well as the avant-garde had to reorient themselves. While Hollywood did so, re-emerging as one of television's major attractions (the recycling of 'movie classics', of stars and cult figures: in short the start of a whole new film culture), the avant-garde was unable to mount an effective challenge to television. Video art has had to retreat to the museums and galleries in order to find any public space at all. The national cinemas of developing or post-colonial countries – despite theorists and film-makers successfully giving them a new identity as 'Third Cinema'[10] – have had to struggle even on the festival circuits. In so far as some film-makers who had been identified with political, avant-garde or independent cinema were able to secure state funding or the co-production of television, they continued to make films, but perhaps at a price. Sharing a segment of the general movie-going audience, at least in Europe, these film-makers became international 'auteurs', which is to say, double agents for a cinema which knowingly pastiched or cleverly inverted movie mythology. Under contract to Britain's Channel Four, Italy's RAI, France's Antenne 2 or Germany's WDR, directors could upgrade their television co-productions via film festivals to the status of (art) cinema.

The relative failure of the various avant-garde movements to give roots to an 'alternative cinema' thus cannot simply be explained in political terms. The demand for a 'different depiction of reality' has, for most audiences, been met by television and its documentaries, its soap operas, its serious dramas and sit-coms. But the relation of television to the cinema is precisely the one least accepted by the avant-garde, since it is not based on opposition or struggle, not even on competition, but more like 'the same as different'. Thus, on the face of it, it cannot be seen in categorical terms, but only as shifts, as intertextuality or *mise en abîme* in an expanding, constantly self-differentiating field of representations.

In this field, Hollywood retains its pre-eminent position because of the totalising effect which its stories, myths and stereotypes have on national as well as international cultural production: Hollywood dominates trade in both film and television, with classical feature film-making being a sort of medieval Latin, in relation to which television represents the vernaculars: feeding off the classical, but also treating it as merely one more specialised language among many others. Such a role is particularly striking in developing countries. US, Italian or Brazilian soap operas watched in the slums of Rio de Janeiro or Bogotá by people who have neither jobs nor homes, can give the illusion of unity, of belonging, cohesion and participation to a social body that in any other sense is utterly atomised, antagonistically divided and segregated: in such a situation, media spectacles become political, by their very negation of the political, while the political is demoted to a mere variant of televisual forms of participation (game shows, talk shows, quizzes, phone-ins).

One of the consequences might therefore be that the relation of national cinemas to Hollywood, of television to national cinema, and of national cinema to counter-cinema should be thought of as a series of palimpsests, a sequence of texts, each rewriting other cinematic and pre-cinematic spectacles in the form of intertextual narratives, each restaging the 'primal scenes' of specularity and self-alienation itself. I want to explore this a little further around what seem to me two exemplary encounters of the European art cinema with Latin America, encounters across which a whole history of the image as political may be reconstructed. Francesco Rosi's *Cronaca di una Morte Annunciata* (*Chronicle of a Death Foretold*, 1987), after a Gabriel García Márquez story, and Werner Herzog's *Fitzcarraldo* and *Cobra Verde* (after *The Viceroy of Ouidah* by Bruce Chatwin) illuminate this particular complex, not least because the directors rewrite in these films their own national and personal film history.

FRANCESCO ROSI AND THE DEATH OF A HERO
Chronicle of a Death Foretold, the story of a vendetta killing in a Colombian town, is, according to Rosi, 'about a crime that is atrocious and unacceptable. Not because of destiny, but because a whole town abdicated the responsibility to prevent it'. On the face of it, this is a good description of the genre Rosi has made his own: political thrillers from *Salvatore Giuliano* and *Hands over the City* to *Lucky Luciano* and *Exquisite Corpses*, inexorably revealing beneath the individual case the conspiracy of silence, the cover-up of crimes and corruption by state bureaucracies or even whole communities. But by the same token, it is an odd summary of Gabriel García Márquez's short novel, and even more so of Rosi's own film based on it: there is no sense of moral outrage towards the characters, and no enlightened distance separates the camera's view from the social mores that make their behaviour possible. On

'. . . *a crime that is atrocious and unacceptable . . . because a whole town abdicated the responsibility to prevent it.*' Cronaca di una Morte Annunciata (Chronicle of a Death Foretold, *Francesco Rosi, Italy/France, 1987*)

the contrary, the code of honour which demands an eye for an eye and a life for a hymen becomes, in the course of the film, the language of a deeper wisdom, not so long ago regarded as politically reactionary: the necessity to preserve a tragic sense of life.

The twin supports of Latin culture, in Márquez as in Rosi, are male machismo and the power of mothers. Both are in secret collusion with each other, energising a field of force that, whatever its cruelty and barbarism, appears ennobling because it raises the stakes in the battle of the sexes to the point of giving the illusion of two beings evenly matched. This is the case in Rosi's *Carmen* (where the heroine shouts at her suitor, 'I tell you, once I love you, José, you're a dead man') and in *Chronicle*, where the fiancée of one of the unwilling avengers declares, 'If you fail in your duty as a man, I shall never marry you.' Such a predilection for the double binds of (hetero)sexuality make one wonder whether Rosi's earlier social commitment has mellowed into melodrama. *Christ Stopped at Eboli* and *Three Brothers* were investigations in which a sense of history emphatically endowed the tales of private passion unfulfilled, of personal memory and inner struggles, with a political place as well as a geography. In *Chronicle*, by contrast, the investigation into the murder (which could have opened up to history and politics) soon peters out, even if auspiciously inaugurated by the heavy-lidded Gian Maria Volonte scanning the faded colonial follies lining the embankment under a grey-blue sky.

There is firstly the fact that Volonte's presence fades before the flashbacks, the reminiscences and images crowding in on the witnesses still willing to talk: the old housekeeper, the priest, or the retired mayor rescuing the court records after a flood and hanging the pages on a clothes-line to dry. Secondly, the luxuriant vegetation with strange birds breaking cover as a boat drifts past their nesting places seem to turn the characters themselves into exotic creatures whose present is a time of auguries and premonitions, their past the timelessness of myth or the fatality of an ancestral curse. What is enigmatic about the chief protagonists Nasar, Angela or Bayardo is not some secret they harbour, but their beauty: it makes them mere surface, deflecting any mystery of motive or intent into pure being, at once out of time and doomed, as the clichés about youth, love and death (to which they owe their existence) have it.

Thus disarmed, the investigation hands over to the chronicle, with its different temporality and different causality, and no presiding consciousness pretends to put the events into an orderly procession. So why, even though only a *fait-divers*, does the story assume an epic sweep? Thanks to a very complicated chronology, an interweaving of fragments, tableau-like scenes and oneiric set-pieces (like Bayardo's overgrown house with his sports car rusted down to the wheel hubs, where Angela and Bedoya finally meet face to face), *Chronicle of a Death Foretold* becomes a Faulknerian 'tale told by an idiot', almost a sort of *Citizen Kane* or *Rashomon* set in the swamps of Colombia. A dense forest of symbols linking white birds, white pages and dead letters, a repetition of motifs around the arrival of a stranger, the return of the prodigal son, and the blessings of a bishop, create the impression of messages only half-deciphered and allegorical depths never quite plumbed. Equally plausible, though, is the realisation that the complex narrative may have craftily constructed an echo chamber for a single note: that passion has to be utterly spent before it becomes liveable, that youth and beauty have to be sacrificed before they become a thing of value, and that the present has to be the past before its sound and fury become significant.

In some respects, this means that *Chronicle* is an old man's film, its moral anger appeased, its traditional truths and fundamentally tragic stance legitimised by the simplicity of its lyricism, and the naturalness and generality of its symbolic conflicts. But the starkness of the folk epic is also deceptive: if, on the one hand, the film depicts the power of honour (archaic, implacable, senseless and therefore impervious to either enlightenment or religion) and, on the other, the power of women (represented as confined to the cunning of biology and reproduction, and therefore strong because capable of crushing both conscience and individuality), the real threat to this world is the power of money, especially new money.

As embodied in the figure of Bayardo, money kills, not so much because it brings corruption, violence and greed to a community, and therefore upsets what one might call the ecological (or feudal) balance between servitude and security in 'primitive' economies (a favourite theme of the spaghetti Western), but because it devalues everything it touches: the lottery and its prize, the rituals of courtship and love, the old man's house and his memories. With this, a deliberate displacement of the political seems to have occurred in Rosi's film. Colonialism and its moral economy are an issue not because an alternative (political) economy can be their judge, but because a

126

First World metaphysics of value implicitly proposes a kind of ironic counter-ecology to the economics of post-colonialism. How else make a film about virginity in Colombia, a country notorious for its export of cocaine, the white substance from the Third World dominating the black economy of the Second World?

THE DEATH OF A HERO

One of the more puzzling things about *Chronicle of a Death Foretold* is no doubt the presence of Rupert Everett. As a character in a fictional story, he is barely present. Even by the end, we do not know who he is, where he is from, or what he wants. With so passive a part, it is difficult to accept him as the star of a major international production. But as a screen icon, he is almost too present, his image telescoping several generations of Hollywood masculinity. He wears his stetson and lounges in his rocker like Henry Fonda in *My Darling Clementine*, the camera lingers on his figure as it does on James Dean in *Giant*, or it frames him with the obsessive symmetry reserved for Alan Ladd in *Shane*. At times he contemplates his doomed splendour as if he were the Great Gatsby himself. The role dissolves into poses, narcissistic and non-functional in the narrative. Is this a flaw in the acting, the consequence of a production with an eye to the market, using up a face while it is still in the news, or is it the sign of a mutation in the concept of the European anti-hero who has become the clone-hero of jeans ads and beer commercials? In other words, are we watching a European art film, a Hollywood movie, or a Third Cinema post-modernist co-production? In either case, Rupert Everett is an interference, the element that troubles the codes: which is of course what, in a sense, Rosi's film is all about.

For even though Rosi is not Wim Wenders indulging in cinephile citations, or Martin Scorsese exorcising the ghost of Jerry Lewis or *The Hustler* by an elaborate mirror game of fictional projections and Oedipal moves (as in films like *King of Comedy* and *The Color of Money*), there is a sense in which the older generation of European directors like Resnais or Rosi look into the same mirror of movie myths, but from the other side: nostalgia rather than cinephilia, the myths affirmed because they are irrecoverable, where the young directors reanimate them by clever pastiche, by ironies and cross-references. When Rosi ends his film with the dead man spreadeagled on the ground in exactly the pose familiar from his own *Salvatore Giuliano* he seems neither ironic nor playful, merely advertising that a certain language of cinema, as a commitment to, say, critical or investigative realism, has definitively entered into myth. Opting for the 'magic realism' of Márquez thus becomes for a European director of Rosi's generation neither a commitment to a political counter-cinema nor a Latin American director's pastiche of folk-elements, European modernism and Hollywood kitsch, but a complex displacement: revisiting his own (European, Italian) belief in realism and the structure of investigation, he encounters a Latin American mythology across which he hopes to reconcile the fact that the left in Europe since 1945 has been nostalgic for a past that the conservative right had already dismantled. Comparable to Visconti in *The Leopard* more than two decades earlier, and Bertolucci in *1900*, Rosi, like them a man of the left, discovered that he understood the values of feudalist regionalism better than those of the bourgeoisie making common cause with international capital.

WERNER HERZOG: TARZAN OR PARSIFAL OF THE ART CINEMA?

Werner Herzog is one of those film-makers who with rather fewer films than Rosi has created exemplary heroes, even icons, not least because here, too, there is a blurring of the boundaries between actor and role in his films, though apparently quite different from the decal pin-up Rupert Everett. Klaus Kinski, an old professional and a trained actor, and Bruno S, the 'natural', have both become permanently identified with the parts they play in Herzog's films, a fact that suggests that there is a deeper bond between the meaning of their archetypes. At first sight worlds apart as the eternal underdog and eternal overreacher, Bruno S and Klaus Kinski are brothers underneath the blundering and blustering egos: they are the two sides of Kaspar Hauser: one, the child abandoned by the father, the other the child abandoning the father to pre-empt being abandoned. Where Rosi pastiches machismo and matriarchy, Herzog focuses on two complementary aspects of the same crisis of patriarchal values: the failed submission to, but also the failed rebellion against, the symbolic order. Whether supermen or victims, however, Herzog's protagonists are always extreme, marginal and outside, in relation to the centre which is the social world, the world of history, that of ordinary beings. Thus, the existential dimension of his characters seems to take precedence over any social ill against which they might revolt or from which they might suffer.

Behind Herzog's heroes stands the figure of Hercules, doing other people's dirty work, as well as Prometheus, who tried to steal from the Gods, bringing fire down from the heavens to the benefit of mankind. The role of scapegoats, of self-tormented egomaniacs, can thus easily be related to the basic Western myths and their derivations. One of his first films, a ten-minute short called, characteristically, *Herakles* (*Hercules*) sums up this ambivalence succinctly. A body-building contest is intercut with scenes from a scrap metal yard where a huge machine is crushing automobile wrecks into handy parcels. Around this surreal collage, Herzog has packed the basic configuration of practically all his subsequent films: heroic effort and endeavour in a mockingly futile situation. This asymmetry might also be what attracts Herzog to Latin American locations and figures, for emerging from the image of his superman fighting a losing battle with a world dominated by technology is the very possibility or impossibility of revolution, where the choice often seems to be between degeneration into anarchic revolt, or operatic self-display and exhibitionism.

Pauline Kael once called Herzog a 'metaphysical Tarzan'.[11] Yet if the figure refers to Herzog, it is not the man but the manner of his film-making that is targeted. Although he never stated it as openly as Rainer Werner Fassbinder, Herzog always wanted to be an international director. Yet at a time when the cost of the average Hollywood movie reaches figures that make up the entire production volume of most other countries, an independent director practically shoulders with each film the burden of reinventing not, as Herzog is fond of saying, film history but the film industry. His seriousness makes up his capital, and his naivety is his key production value. The poet Erich Fried, seeing Herzog in action at a New German directors' press conference, once called him 'a Parsifal among the Tuis' (Brecht's word for mandarin intellectuals).[12] But also a Siegfried: the preparations for a Herzog film resemble a military campaign, and for them he casts himself as victor and vanquished.

Thus, it is the very real anachronism of independent film-making in the age of global media wars that is one of the buried themes of Herzog's work: not the least of the many ironies of championing individuals or groups who eke out their existence on the margins of the capitalist world is that the symbolic opposition between the weak and the strong, the underdogs and the overreachers, splits Herzog himself. The film-maker has a foot in either camp, and often David is difficult to tell from Goliath.

Two of his increasingly rarely screened feature films from the 80s are no exception: behind the Aborigines' resistance to the mining company determined to drill for minerals in *Where the Green Ants Dream* (1984) stood Herzog's determination to make a film about this resistance. And in *Cobra Verde* (1988), Kinski's ambiguous pact with Brazilian slave traders and a mad African monarch is like Herzog's wily but also nervous deals with the US major studios. Herzog, in a sense, is doing battle on his characters' backs, and they are inevitably also the foot-soldiers thanks to whom the machinery of his own film-making can fight it out with the juggernauts of the commercial film industry.

'The idea of pulling a full-size river boat across a jungle mountain was entirely in keeping with the excessive bravado associated with Herzog's public persona.' Klaus Kinski in Fitzcarraldo *(Werner Herzog, West Germany, 1982)*

The extent to which Herzog's film-making is both an act of allegorising and of literalising a particular situation could already be seen in *Fitzcarraldo* (1982). The film, it will be recalled, tells the story of an Irish rubber planter in South America, whose enthusiasm for Caruso makes him want to build an opera house in the jungle, if necessary by hauling a boat across a mountain and opening up a waterway that will generate the cash needed to finance such a scheme. The idea of pulling a full-size river boat across a jungle mountain was entirely in keeping with the excessive bravado associated with Herzog's public persona.

The filming itself was accompanied by an unusual amount of pre-publicity, although in the context of Herzog's habitual self-promotion this was perhaps to be expected. No less than two films were in fact made about Herzog making *Fitzcarraldo*. The circumstances of the production itself provided ample copy for the newspapers: there was Hollywood-type show-business gossip about difficulties with the leading actors, the replacement of Mick Jagger by Jason Robards, and of Jason Robards by (inevitably) Klaus Kinski. This made the film crystallise around Kinski and Herzog's obviously privileged relationship with this preferred actor, since he had already used him in *Aguirre, Wrath of God*, *Nosferatu, Phantom der Nacht* and *Woyzeck* to portray the Herzog persona *par excellence*. However, more publicity was generated by Herzog coming face to face with global concerns about rain forests, land politics and genocide. *Fitzcarraldo* was political news because it started a minor civil war in Peru, in a scenario only half written by Herzog himself, touching issues about the debt crisis, the situation of the Amazon Indians, all of which exposed the dilemma of European liberalism when faced with the problems of population explosion, and the extinction of tribal cultures for the sake of 'modernisation' and economic development in Latin America. That the production and its difficulties somehow became the real event of which the film when it finally appeared seemed merely the record seemed peculiarly apt for a cinema that is infatuated with the reality of its own making.

While *Fitzcarraldo* was thus the object of considerable controversy, Herzog himself seemed to think of it as a German *Heimatfilm* transposed to the jungle, a film about his own homeland, Bavaria in other words, with a figure not unlike Mad King Ludwig who had built fantasy castles and had funded lavishly extravagant productions of Wagner's operas. Certainly Fitzcarraldo can be seen as an anti-hero, who, frustrated in his desire for social progress, turns to art and music, on a scale symmetrically inverse to his lack of social standing and the degree of professional failure.

But this underlines the ambiguity of Herzog's recourse to Latin American locations: metaphoric constructions of a cultural 'other' in order to say something about the 'self' cannot be easily distinguished from a genuine concern and sympathy for the world's victims of the West, while beneath it all there is always an allegory of the director himself. Having hundreds of Amazon Indians move a tugboat over a mountain is not only Herzog's idea of a perfect image for his own film-making, but maybe even of the cinema altogether: an obsolete technology with a (sweaty) human face. The slaver is always also a slave. In many of Herzog's films the poorest of the poor, the most deprived of Western civilisation, possess strength of resistance directly proportional to

130

the degree to which they are dispossessed. Is the spiritual freedom that Herzog seems to grant them a mere consolation prize for material rights that no one is prepared to concede, perhaps not even Herzog himself, who moves the Aborigines in *Where the Green Ants Dream* before his camera in much the same way the mining company has them moved by the police?

DOCUMENTING A FICTION OR FICTIONALISING A DOCUMENTARY?

Herzog has been called a visionary film-maker, mainly because he contrives so often to suggest the possibility of a radically non-communicating, *stupid* relation between people and between things. Sometimes it is the encounter of a solitary character and an object or scenery that touches off the pathos inherent in a 'land of silence and darkness' even under a blazing sun: Aguirre and the jungle, for instance, Kaspar Hauser in the market square, or the woodcarver Steiner alone at the bottom of his ski piste. *Cobra Verde* resumes many of these moments from other films, not least because Kinski is so evidently the amalgam of the underdog and the overreacher, even more so than he had been in *Nosferatu* or *Woyzeck*. One does not require a hunchback telling the spectator that he and the bandit are alike in their contempt for the normal and their capacity to dream the extraordinary, or a cripple on the beach shadowing Kinski's futile efforts to launch his boat, in order to recognise in *Cobra Verde* all the twists and turns of the master and slave dialectic. Kinski is the clown of power, a creature in whom we are meant to identify magic realism as the fever symptom of a colonised imagination, and because there can be no narrative development in Herzog's nightmares of real exploitation and imaginary identifications, the heroic–pathetic characters he has created are usually more lasting than the stories in which they figure. Yet here, too, we glimpse complex palimpsests: what would Herzog be without Kinski, who is always Kinski, which is to say, the living embodiment of the contradictions and collusions between the Italian spaghetti Western, the Brazilian Cinema Novo, the Hollywood sexploitation picture, and the New German cinema?

In so far as Herzog's films are often associated with landscapes, the director does not always escape the charge of celluloid tourism. Many of his early documentaries came out of his own experiences of travel which he undertook, as much a child of the 60s as Wim Wenders, to have a vantage point on his own country and its history: Germany is the subject he has conspicuously avoided treating head-on. He has travelled to the Sudan and West Africa, to Greece and the United States, to Ireland and the Canary Islands, to Latin America and Australia. There is thus, in Herzog's choice locations, a curious and altogether typical mixture of uncivilised, primitive places, and some of the by now traditional holiday spots of affluent Europeans. His landscapes are of an ambiguous other(worldli)ness, most offensive to political internationalists, but Herzog is probably subject to the same pressures and constraints as other film-makers scouring the continents for natural production values at unnaturally low production costs.

CINEMA OF PAIN AND TOIL, OR A NEW THEATRE OF CRUELTY

In a *Guardian* lecture promoting *Cobra Verde* at London's National Film

131

Theatre,[13] Herzog confessed to a new passion for opera, hinting that he might follow the track beaten by other German directors to Bayreuth and Bologna, putting on *Lohengrin* for Wolfgang Wagner and Bussoni's *Faust*. He also told his audience that he makes no difference between a jungle or desert setting for his films and the stage of an opera house. Both oblige a director to think big, and both allow the spectator to step out of reality. *Cobra Verde* – being more deadly serious than Fitzcarraldo's rather harmless obsession with Caruso and an opera house in the jungle – provides a rationale for Herzog's startling assertion, in so far as the effort, enthusiasm and resistance of the early heroes has become a theatre of cruelty and humiliation. The court rituals on the Brazilian *haciendas*, the military regime in the fort, the customs and rites of the royal house in Dahomey: so many ways of taking account of politics as spectacle, and the spectacle as politics. Opera perhaps allows for the self-display of subjectivity, even when the stakes are thus raised.

In an effort to close off one kind of transparency (that which classical narrative gives), a structure of meaning imposes itself on Herzog's images that can only be called Manichean: if the level on which his films are meant to work is cosmic, then the issues he chooses are too politically urgent, and the cases too specific, for the metaphysical fiction to become convincing. If, on the other hand, Herzog documents in *Cobra Verde*, even in reconstructed form, an actual case, then the fantastic anthropology of the African kingdom seems something of an intrusion. This issue may well touch the core not of why European directors might be drawn to making films in developing countries, but why they prefer countries which have an indigenous mythology that can be made to signify: not a reality, but an attitude to a reality which, like Rosi's and Herzog's characters, is presented as ultimately unknowable. Herzog, for instance, surrounds himself with people – primitive, innocent, or slightly mad – whose behaviour, use of language, reactions and gestures can indicate, unconsciously and by default, a certain kind of reification, making visible the pressures of a deformed life. Through them the director represents in action the very processes of alienation, dehumanisation and exclusion which society imposes. But what is this society? Sometimes it seems that, for the sake of his films, Herzog turns himself into the instrument of this society, its terrible jester, in order to simulate the conditions he sets out to document. There is, in other words, a poetry of social anomy and alienation which Herzog's cinema cannot but recognise as an aesthetic value and with which it colludes.

Against a background of temporal decay, Herzog's view of history is, like Rosi's in *Chronicle of a Death Foretold*, essentially tragic: he sees the flawed nature of his characters' rebellion, the radical innocence of their deformation, the resilience and perseverance they oppose to their situation. But to what extent can these African settings, Latin mythologies, and Third World subjects serve as allegories? The tension between the documentary attention to detail on the one hand, and the exhibitionist spectacle on the other, is perhaps Herzog's special contribution to contemporary cinema which should not be underestimated. Yet it is a fragile tension, and the sensibility it manifests is not in fashion. The play of insufficiency and overexplicitness between image and commentary in his early films like *Fata Morgana* has in

Cobra Verde made way for the many incongruities and incompatibilities between the natives and their sympathetic exploiter.

At times, *Cobra Verde* appears to want to say something about Idi Amin or Pol Pot and the Khmer Rouge, about the madness of regional politics under the pressure of the super-powers' global strategies. But Herzog might also pursue his own counter-strategy, detecting in the Third World politics of the European left an abused and vulgarised fascination with the imaginary 'other' at too little cost to its comfort and moral security. As a specialist in cultural and social 'others', Herzog has always insisted on the risks involved, and so he is more interested in dramatising the act of self-representation as one which escapes the speaking subject's control than in passing judgment. What is politically more ambiguous in the figure of Cobra Verde than the peacock-strutting of ceremonial power is the extent to which Herzog seems prepared to read as a resistance to the regime of signs, and thus as a resistance to social deformation, precisely those signs that speak most clearly of the hold that Western civilisation has even on the bodies of those it marginalises and rejects. The chorus of young women at the end of *Cobra Verde*, functioning as a carnivalesque mockery of the male world of both Kinski and his real or imagined adversaries, and as such a very new element in Herzog's world: are they not performing for a camera still hungry for exotic spectacle? Yet in Herzog's documentaries from the 60s and early 70s the distrust of significa-tion was always a matter of refusing to have the handicapped, the blind or the sick become subsumed under the discourses of institutionalised medicine, charitable religion or the welfare worker; instead, he intended them to have a chance to appear first and foremost as human beings. The pieties of liberal politics were rejected by Herzog in the name of human dignity, viewed beyond sentimentality or pathos with an almost Buñuelian, surrealist cruelty. But when his Kinski heroes play devil's advocate and the wrath of power politics, such a perception of dignity without histrionics is difficult to main-tain, and Herzog's cinema appears increasingly to freeze the image, to create a kind of frame which makes icons out of Europe's cultural 'others'.

THE SPIDER'S STRATAGEM OR THE KISS OF THE SPIDER WOMAN?
How did Italian critical realism or the New German cinema come to this apparent impasse: academic and metaphysical, cultivating the hero as icon, escaping into myth, music and opera? The flashback to the 60s with which I started, where Europe saw its 'new' national cinemas give rise to auteurs, each creating an individual *oeuvre* but sustained by the nation's literary and political culture, must be one answer: as Hollywood languished, the art cinema flourished, some of it by playing off the Hollywood of the 40s and 50s against the Hollywood of the 60s. But while a Wenders or Fassbinder tried to cast a cinephile and necrophile eye on the maverick Hollywood of Sam Fuller, Douglas Sirk or Nicholas Ray, film-makers like Rosi and Herzog in their very different ways did not look backwards but sideways, to the Latin traditions of literature and folk mythology, to the travellers' tales, the bad conscience of a Joseph Conrad about white colonialism mitigated by their own principled dissent from the political orthodoxies of their own countries. The Latin settings and subjects become the subtext not only for a non-

antagonistic relation to Hollywood (which distinguishes them from Godard or Glauber Rocha), but they also prevent too easy a play with Hollywood's own icons (as in the work of European cinephile directors): displacing but also refocusing through palimpsest texts that are difficult to read, politically ambiguous and morally radical, their own 'coming to terms' not with the old Hollywood of the 50s but the new Hollywood of the 70s.

For it seems that the literature (and, in a wider sense, the visual imagination) of Latin American authors becomes attractive to European film-makers wherever they feel in competition with Hollywood over the truth of the image, but also whenever film-makers – independents or auteurs – find it difficult to envisage a terrain not colonised by television. One can see the same problem in film-makers from Latin America who work in Europe, such as Ruy Guerra's adaptation of a Márquez story, *Erendira*, for a French production company, or Raoul Ruíz, the Chilean director who, along with a number of Argentinian film-makers (Edgardo Cozarinsky, Eduardo de Gregorio), works in Paris. Common to the latter group is an awareness of a literary culture which, in contrast to European writers who distrust spectacle, has always been closer to the carnival and spectacle as political, and yet has a very precise historical experience of 'colonisation' as it permeates the vernacular idiom. European directors, on the other hand, seem to tread a warier path between Latin America as a set of clichés already replete with meaning, and a political reality opaque enough to resist meaning.

Hence the sense of an uncomfortable and paradoxical literalness one takes away from both Rosi and Herzog. Rosi's adaptation of Márquez may be a collages of clichés, but they are hardly folkloristic: if the clichés are all on show, it is because they are accompanied by strong feelings, clear outlines, bold colours, simple motifs, archaic spaces. The distance is not in a critical irony, nor a political allegory, but in a literalism that marks the gap between the (European) spectator and the (non-European) 'other'. This, as in the case of Herzog, may leave the sophisticated spectator with the task of trying to become naive: a difficult and fraught task, whose dangers are signalled by the fact that not the romantic, heroic or sentimental cliché speaks the truth, but its repetition: obstinate, desperate, Utopian. But what price naivety, in our dealings with Europe's 'others'?

Notes

1. This essay incorporates passages from three articles which were first published in the *Monthly Film Bulletin*: 'Eréndira' (*MFB*, July 1986); 'Chronicle of a Death Foretold/Chronicle of a Death Retold' (*MFB*, June 1987), and 'Werner Herzog: Tarzan or Parsifal' (*MFB*, May 1988). I am grateful to the editor, Richard Combs, for his permission to use this material. It is dedicated to the memory of Klaus Kinski.
2. Jean-Luc Godard. *Godard on Godard*, Ed. and trans. Tom Milne. New York: Da Capo Press, 1986, p. 243 (from the press book of *La Chinoise*, August 1967).
3. See 'Appendix: Who owns the Media' in James Monaco (ed.). *Media Culture*. New York: Delta Books, 1978, pp. 305–16.
4. Frantz Fanon, 'National Culture', in *The Wretched of the Earth*. Harmondsworth: Penguin Books, 1967.

5. Amilcar Cabral. *Unity and Struggle*. London: Heinemann, 1980.
6. Anthony Wilden. 'The Canadian Question, Why?' *Cine-tracts*, vol. 2, no. 2, Spring 1979, pp. 1–27.
7. Benedict Anderson. *Imagined Communities*. London: Verso, 1983.
8. Edward Said. *Orientalism*. London: Routledge & Kegan Paul, 1978.
9. Fredric Jameson. 'Imaginary and Symbolic in Lacan'. *Yale French Studies*, 55–6 (1977): pp. 378–9.
10. Fernando Solanas and Octavio Getino. 'Towards a Third Cinema'. *Afterimage*, no. 3 (Summer, 1971): pp. 16–35.
11. Pauline Kael, 'Metaphysical Tarzan'. *New Yorker*, 20 October 1975.
12. Quoted in *Filmkritik*, June 1977, p. 277.
13. *The Guardian Lecture*, 7 April 1988.

Cabeza de Vaca (*Nicolás Echeverría, Mexico, 1990*)

PART II

MEXICAN CINEMA

Of Myths and Demystifications

CARLOS MONSIVÁIS

Editors' Introduction
Over the last 30 years, Carlos Monsiváis has become Mexico's most engaging and acerbic critic of popular culture. He has written a number of books on culture and politics, which contain many essays on Mexican cinema, its industrial base, its impact on society and its emblematic stars, from Dolores del Río to Cantinflas. Mexico has a tradition of serious film history and criticism and Monsiváis is at the cutting edge of this work, combining an encyclopaedic knowledge with an uncompromising humour. Monsiváis has always avoided the clutches of the 'philanthropic ogre', Octavio Paz's evocative description of the Mexican State, and remains a critic of state power and the culture industry and a historian of new social movements and the possibilities for alternative cultural practices.

This essay gives an exhilarating panorama of six decades of Mexican cinema, concentrating on the 'Golden Age' of Mexican cinema from 1935 to 1955. This period offered a chorus of singing *charros* from Tito Guízar to Jorge Negrete; the brothel as a space of exalted passions and sensibilities, captured in the lyrics of the famous singer–composer Agustín Lara or in the later rumbustious tones of the Cuban sex-symbol Ninón Sevilla; the lyrical nationalism of director Emilio Fernández and the great cinematographer Gabriel Figueroa who created, with the Edenic couple Dolores del Río and Pedro Armendáriz, lofty visions of courage, machismo and feminine endurance set against an elemental, expressive landscape; the wilful, passionate María Félix, the Doña Bárbara of numerous movies; the extraordinary comedian Cantinflas; the numerous family melodramas and some hard-boiled film noir. All these films were eagerly appreciated by a Mexican public who know that what they were watching was not Mexico, but maybe only what it could or should have been. Monsiváis's work has rarely been translated, and it is hoped that a wide range of his work will shortly be available to English-language readers.

☐

MARRIAGE AND DIVORCE ON THE SCREEN AND IN THE STALLS

Between 1932, when the first talking film *Más fuerte que el deber* (*Stronger than Duty*) was produced, and today, the Mexican national film industry has produced a few masterpieces and hundreds of worthwhile films; it has created its own myth of origin (The Golden Age of Mexican Cinema); it has lost its family audience and then recovered it (though on very different terms) through television; it has affirmed its nationalism, then so blurred its image that only a caricature remained; it has gone from morality plays to immoral tales, and from the machismo of the screen to the machismo of the city slums; it has accumulated a valuable body of information on the values of an epoch, its ways of life and forms of expression, its ideas of the beautiful and the vulgar, its development of an image for tourists, its highest and its most degraded forms of popular culture, the integration and disintegration of its sense of humour, its ratifications and rectifications of traditional morality and, above all, its vision of a world experienced through misfortune, the privileged locus of melodrama. The achievements of Mexican cinema have been sociological rather than artistic. In its six decades it has passed through several stages:

– excitement at the powers of technology (submission to the 'magic' of the new medium).
– the conquest of credibility with its credulous audience, gained by idealising provincial life and the rural world, demonising and consecrating the urban environment, exalting machismo, transforming social defects into virtues, defending conservative values to the bitter end (verbally at least) and putting on a pretence of attacking the 'heterodox' attitudes assumed in the attempt to win back audiences to the box office;
– the unification of 'public morality', the product of censorship exercised jointly by the State, the Church and the official representatives of The Family;
– the elaboration of images of community which, despite their glaring falsity, are both effective and lasting – the 'cinema of the poor', 'the culture of the slums', the 'dramatisation of machismo';
– spectacular success in the Spanish-speaking world for more than two decades combined with an indifference in the international sphere hardly mitigated by the exceptions like the early work of Emilio Fernández, El Indio, the films of Buñuel from *Los olvidados* on, and features like *Macario*;
– the indifference of the State to a cinema it saw as mere 'mass entertainment'. The State's preoccupation was to maintain a rigid censorship (there shall be no criticism of the institutions of the State, no attacks on the morality of family life), combining this disdain with generous support for private producers through the Banco Cinematográfico (Film Bank). During the six-year regime of Luís Echeverría, the policy of official indifference was modified, with a whole series of consequences;
– the desertion of the middle-class cinema audience which, from the 60s onwards, for reasons both good and bad, rejected the image of the 'typical Mexican', expressing its growing distance from popular sentimentality and belligerent nationalism;

– the activities of new film-makers, advocates of an artistic cinema and rebels against 'a cinema without meaning';
– the devaluing of the industry, manifest above all in the proliferation of 'throwaway', short-life films – the cinema of the bargain basement;
– the evaporation of a *Mexican cinema* (as a meaningful body of representative work), and its replacement by a series of exceptions whose impact was to confirm the dismal quality of the rest.

HOLLYWOOD: THE APPRENTICESHIP OF DREAMS

In Mexico, as everywhere else, the Hollywood model was inescapable. While trying to establish a star system, with its cult of exceptional faces and personalities, its 'deification' of the stars, the Hollywood formulas were carefully adhered to: entertainment for its own sake, the cultivation of genres, the repetitions that become habit-forming. Drawn to the new centre of world power, with or without a plan, the future creators of Mexican cinema go to Los Angeles. They settle there and receive a kind of education; later, the scene shifters will become directors, the extras will turn into producers, and ten years on the vagabonds will be considered stars. Among those who spent whatever time they could in Hollywood were Dolores del Río, Pedro Armendáriz, Arturo de Córdova, Jorge Negrete, Andrea Palma, Delia Magana, Lupe Vélez. There, working against the stream, the directors Emilio Fernández, Ismael Rodríguez and Roberto Gavaldón, and the cameramen Gabriel Figueroa and Agustín Jiménez, learned their trade.

In the opposite direction the cameramen Paul Strand, Jack Draper and Alex Phillips, and the directors Fred Zimmermann and Norman Foster, went to Mexico for a time or to settle for good.

From Hollywood came the genres, the stylistic conventions, the formal skills, the hypocritical and servile games with the censors, the favoured tricks: contradicting the explicit message with the flow of images, making mileage out of minor scandals while offsetting them by including in the film scenes in which someone, preferably a priest, delivers sermons in mechanical tones. Wherever they could, they copied Hollywood's publicity techniques, its use of suspense and of music to manipulate and startle, its disdain for logical continuities, its improvisation of directors and stars.

The founding enterprise of Mexican Cinema (the capitals reflect its institutionalisation) is the 'nationalisation' of Hollywood. Some genres are untranslateable: the screwball comedy, for example, which requires something that does not exist in Mexico – a culture of humour and reliable scriptwriters; the thriller, blocked by a censorship that does not recognise the basis of its plots – the combination of official corruption, sex and violence; the Western, which requires more skilful directors – in Mexico it only appears in the form of parody. All the others do lend themselves to full assimilation, and soon appear as original visions – for example, the singing cowboy films of Gene Autry or Roy Rogers. In 1936 Fernando de Fuentes directed *Allá en el Rancho Grande* (*Out on the Rancho Grande*), a comedy which added a pastoral fantasy to the Autry/Rogers formula. The success of the film both in Mexico and in the rest of Latin America was so extraordinary that the national film industry changed direction; if the provincialism that recognises itself in local

141

For her first Mexican feature, Flor silvestre (Wild Flower), *Hollywood star Dolores del Río is given a kitchen to run.* (*Emilio Fernández, Mexico, 1943*)

faces, landscapes, plots, speech and customs is so widespread, then it is best to aspire to becoming a 'national cinema'. Recognising the background and the sound, the audience happily accepted the mechanics of emotional black-mail, of a lack of resources turned into a pride in poverty (in Mexico, the luxury of epic productions tended to belong to those who were happy to accept cardboard castles and crowds of fifteen people).

'THE GOLDEN AGE OF MEXICAN CINEMA': GIVE THE PUBLIC WHAT IT WANTS SINCE IT ALWAYS WANTS THE SAME THING
The so-called Golden Age, between 1935 and 1955 more or less, was in reality the period of an alliance between the film industry and the audiences of the faithful, between the films and the communities that saw themselves represented there. During those years, in many parts of Latin America, those communities watched those films and saw themselves in them, distinct and recognisable. What today is described as an exasperating naivety in the majority of these films had more to do with the technical ineptitude of directors and 'stars' in particular, and with the lack of any critical response on the part of the audience. For a long period they considered films to be neither art nor spectacle but rather the continuation of everyday life, the believable explanation of the meaning of their lives.

In the 30s and 40s the cinemas, or the shacks that often took their place, fulfilled a double role: they were the social clubs of the town or the district (where the city could let its sentimentality float free), and they were the

142

classrooms of an *alternative education*, accessible to the collective guffaw, to theatrical solidarity, or to a pre-coitus or post-masturbation sexual activity. In shabby halls or spaces the audience recognised wit, enjoyed complicity in the darkness, legalised fucking; the spectators become the faithful followers of the new religion.

In the cinema, they learned some of the keys to modern life. The modernisation presented in films was superficial, but what was seen helped the audience to understand the changes that affected them; the destruction or abandonment of agricultural life, the decline of customs once considered eternal, the oppressions that come with industrialisation. Imagine a worker from Celaya, a peasant in the Oaxaca Hills, a waitress in Chihuahua, a woman worker in Mexico City. Repressed in every sense, they never identified their daily life with emotion. In the urban conglomeration, in the solitude of the rural world, in the weariness of the endless hours of work, people did not live out 'the intimate life' day in and day out; but it was what they would have liked to live, the flow of dreams that are more personal the more collective they are. Each melodrama was an encounter with identity, each comedy the proof that we do not live our lives in vain.

WHERE EVERYTHING IS POPULAR CULTURE
From the beginning the film industry set out to mirror popular culture, to reflect its achievements, its myths, its prejudices, its tastes, its attitudes to fiestas, to the search for Mexican national identity, and so on. Thus Mexican popular culture, both rural and urban, was drastically transformed and re-

Mexico's most famous comedian Cantinflas doing his bit for the Revolution in ¡Asi es mi tierra! (That's My Land!, *Arcady Boytler, Mexico, 1937*)

143

shaped through the cinema. However you choose to define popular culture (community practices, the catalogue of rituals and tastes, the methods of resistance against the powers that be, the transformation into folklore of the realities of class, race and gender, the assimilation and re-elaboration of the messages of the culture industry, or simply something directed at a large number of people), what is clear is that in the invention or preservation of customs, the cinema is the most powerful influence.

If all over the world cinema dazzles its audiences, there are Latin American variants that complement a deterministic view of cinema: the very high proportion of total and functional illiterates, the cult of the abstract woman in the land of the macho, the depths of poverty which move people to see in the cinema the only desirable reality. In this context, the catalogue that lists everything as 'of the people' (because 'Mexico is a popular nation') is built on the foundation of a certainty: that 'That is how the public is and it cannot and should not be any other way because we, the directors, actors, scriptwriters, we are the public too.' So that the photography and the sets should do them justice, let them all come – the mothers bathed in the tears of self-pity, the prostitutes redeemed at the point of death, the priests who direct lives like traffic cops, the severe heads of the family who are God's messengers at the after-dinner conversation, the policemen who are as good as gold, the gangsters who were once foremen, the families who suffer because they were not informed in time of the separation of body and soul, the leading men and comic actors whose attraction comes from their similarities to their audience, the dancers who set the clubs a-tremble with the sensual whirling of their bodies, the haughty horsemen from the big ranch, the revolutionaries who dig their own graves without realising that they are the ideal fit. . . . Involuntarily satirical, wilfully funny and sentimental, occasionally epic, unexpectedly tragic, the repertoire of three decades of Mexican cinema presents the central myths and their neighbouring legends and paints a generous, bigoted public, all the more emotional for its lack of thought, racist towards its own and towards outsiders, pious and holier than thou, hostile to bigots and more liberal than it is willing to admit, inhibited when it comes face to face with The Boss or The Law, simple and honest, rebellious where it can be, a great believer in the joke committed to memory and always alive to the joy that is to be found in the simple presence of the comics.

'DREAMS, THE SOURCE OF THE IMAGES; THEY DRESS UP SHADOWS IN BEAUTIFUL CLOTHES'
Between 1935 and 1955 (approximately, of course), it was the cinema more than any other cultural instrument that brought pleasures and prejudices up to date, and reshaped the notion of Mexican national identity by turning nationalism into a great show. There the farewells were said with ringing rhetoric and false sorrow to the traditions that no longer had a place, and there the new ones demanded by the selective and partial modernisation of the country were greeted with laughter and verbal abuse.

What were the mythic atmospheres and ritual manias (the box office formulas, the limits of imagination) of this 'Golden Age'? For me, the main ones were these:

The Mexican fiesta, with its torrent of *charros* (skilled horsemen) and beautiful girls in folk costume, *mariachis* and folk trios, defiant women and cockfights.

The Broadway-style fantasy: here, for example, the Aztec past, seized by the exaggerations that leave historical truth far behind, is Americanised and becomes the choreographic future of the folk-dance companies.

The cabaret: moral hell and heaven of the senses, at the cabaret all that is forbidden is normal; here slightly *risqué* songs become hymns to dissipation, while the tropical orchestras pump out the lustful sounds that later become popular music.

The dance hall: the 'Classical town square of Tenochtitlán', where dance is the discourse of social relevance *par excellence* among those who have no aspiration to it.

The cantina or (preferably rural) bar: the outer limit of experience, one of the three great scenarios for pain (the other two are dark churches and the bedrooms of abandon). In the cantina men build up their virility and prepare their physical decline, fatal decisions are taken and the ballads (*rancheras*) ring out like hymns to self-destruction.

Patriotic history: a kind of masked ball interwoven with school recitations.

The countryside (the pastoral idyll, the bivouac, the serenade): the background to the primitive and to the purity of the race.

The red light district: where noble souls are sullied while they long for virginity again.

Xochimilco Lake and the Isthmus of Tehuantepec: paradise lost; *Jalisco* the little farm defending its identity with manly eloquence.

The 'Mexican gothic' hacienda: the secular 'beyond' expressed through vampires, Aztec mummies, wolf-men, priests of the cult of Huitzilopochtli, the Aztec god of war, women vampires.

The boxing ring: a metaphor for the struggle for life (or rather the reverse).

The chapel, the priesthood, the confessional: spirituality expressed in an undertone; the absolutely forbidden as the privilege of those whose eyes are cast down.

ON THE MANY WAYS TO CREATE A TRADITION

To government and religious censorship is added the submission of a collectivity that compulsively memorises its own repressions and eliminates moral and political dissidence. No one need concern themselves about ethical questions. After all, everything is resolved beforehand; everyone has his place on the ladder of command and everyone knows how to react to sex, food, drink, death. Producers, directors, scriptwriters and actors take as their starting-point traditional morality, in its most defensive version, and have the right wing in the forefront of their mind.

Everything is premeditated – realism and fantasy, doubts and certainties. The main concern is the box office, where success is assured by issuing films like orders; weep, repent, enjoy the beautiful unity of the family, swear never to break the rules, depart this valley of tears with an indulgent smile, get drunk as if you were leading a mob to the town hall, serenade the whole town, kiss the hand of the little old mother, go directly to the nearest *happy ending*.

145

This *costumbrismo*, this folklore cinema, is so false it becomes genuine, an advertiser's nationalism designed to reach the provincial in every member of the audience, a certainty that films, let's be honest, are entertainment, and *entertainment* means removing whatever might complicate matters for this audience of '8 to 80', in which all are one. Only a handful of directors and cameramen dream of creating works of art; for most people cinema is an agreeable job, big business born out of technology and authenticity. Improvisation is the measure of consciousness, and once the economic achievements of the institution have been clarified the search for new forms stops or is proscribed.

In the rest of Latin America Mexican cinema brought others to their knees, forced peoples and villages into submission. For three decades it gave form to the moral law. It was voracious and cynical, and it influenced society and urban culture. At its best (and there was more of it than is usually recognized), these were films distinguished by their sincerity, which I would define in this context as the inability to keep themselves at a distance, physically or culturally, from their audience. And if run-of-the-mill actors, stars, set designers, directors and cameramen invented a country also called Mexico, they did it in collaboration with those who, in the stalls of theatres or the hard seats of rural cinemas, recuperated and remade the events they saw on the screen and transformed them into myths, enjoyment, family culture and, on more than a few occasions, into artistic emotion.

(*Translated by Mike Gonzalez*)

TEARS AND DESIRE

Women and Melodrama in the 'Old' Mexican Cinema

ANA M. LÓPEZ

Editors' Introduction
This article marks the beginning of a much-needed revision, in English-language scholarship, of what Ana López calls the 'old' cinema of Latin America. Until now critics have been in the main drawn to an analysis of the 'new' cinemas, of the last thirty to forty years, often dismissing earlier work as the traditional prehistory before the dawn of innovative, revolutionary, socially aware cinema. The critics Enrique Colina and Daniel Díaz Torres made the point bluntly in 1972:

> Commercial [Argentine] cinema, impregnated with the prevailing pessimism, translated a collective sense of hopelessness into an explosion of sentiment, thus becoming a hindrance to the development of the people's consciousness. . . . This cinema is the refuse, the excrescence of a reactionary populism. . . . God, Fatherland and Home make up the inseparable trinity of social equilibrium in these films.

Criticism has moved away from such bombastic statements into a more careful consideration of the dominant mode of melodrama. Ana López argues convincingly that the urgent task 'is not to salvage this golden age for some critical pantheon of progressive texts, but to relocate it . . . as an integral part of Latin American and Mexican social formations'. Her work draws on recent studies of melodrama, but with a particular Latin American inflection. She debates with Octavio Paz and in particular with Carlos Monsiváis, whose works on film and popular culture in the first half of the century open so many avenues for further scholarship.

□

INTRODUCTION
Since the 60s the 'old' Latin American cinema – produced in the 30s, 40s and

147

50s – has been the 'other' against which the 'new' cinemas struggled to define themselves. Vehemently criticized, the old cinema was rejected as imitative of Hollywood, unrealistic, alienating and sentimental. Over the years, it became little else than a clichéd straw man in all arguments for cinematic and cultural renovation and change. Although the accomplishments of the new cinemas are enormous (and have been well chronicled elsewhere[1]), the characterization of the 'old' cinema as ideologically complicit and servile to the interests of the dominant classes, albeit in many ways justified, was too broad, ignoring the subtleties and differences of cinematic practices, their audiences, and this cinema's tremendous popular appeal.

The old cinema was an easy victim: the studio systems which produced it were by the late 50s to early 60s ideologically and commercially bankrupt. From Vera Cruz in Brazil to Argentina Sono Films, the failed attempts to establish film production on an industrial basis demonstrated the problematic nature of the Latin American market for national films: without control of distribution and exhibition, producers could not sustain production or compete on equal terms with Hollywood imports. Latin America was a 'natural' market only for Hollywood. However, awareness of the market limitations for national films (which led to a search for other, non-industrial modes of production) was not the immediate cause behind the rejection of the old cinema. The old cinema's principal sin was (as the Cuban critics Enrique Colina and Daniel Díaz Torres argued in 1972 in the pages of *Cine Cubano*) its melodramatic proclivities. Making the melodrama synonymous with the Hollywood cinema, they argued that the Latin American films of the 30s, 40s and 50s were little else than a poor imitation 'which opened the floodgates to a manifold process of cultural colonization' in Latin America.[2] However, Colina and Díaz Torres did not take into account that this was the first indigenous cinema to dent the Hollywood industry's pervasive presence in Latin America; the first to consistently circulate Latin American images, voices, songs and history; the first to capture and sustain the interest of multinational audiences throughout the continent for several decades.

The melodramatic was so easily identified with cultural colonization because of its popularity. Although Colina and Díaz argued that the melodrama was popular simply because it was the only readily available dramatic form, what most worried these and other critics was the melodrama's privileged access to popular consciousness.[3] On the one hand, the excesses and sentimentality typical of the melodrama rankled the sensibilities of Europeanized critics, who could not understand or explain popularity as anything other than bad taste. On the other, later politicized critics simplistically reproduced an élitist mistrust of mass communication and popular culture and were unable to see in the popularity of the melodrama anything but the alienation of a mass audience controlled by the dominant classes' capitalist interests. With little differentiation or attention to the processes of reception and identification, they rejected the melodrama as 'false' communication.[4] It is ironic, however, that the new cinema's efforts to establish so-called 'real' communication – as important as they have been – have rarely attained the levels of popular acceptance of the old cinemas. And when that popular success has been achieved, as in *La historia oficial* (*The Official Version*, Luis

Carlos Puenzo, 1986, Argentina), for example, it has been precisely by recourse to the melodramatic.[5]

Assuming that, even in underdeveloped societies, mass culture serves as an instrument of hegemony and not one of simple mass domination, my goal in this essay is to situate the melodrama of the most prolific of the 'old' Latin American cinemas, the classic Mexican cinema, in some of its textual, industrial and socio-cultural contexts. The point here is not to salvage this golden age for some critical pantheon of progressive texts, but to relocate it, by highlighting its contradictory discourses, as an integral part of the Latin American and Mexican social formation of the 30s–50s. Emphasizing the different articulations of gender and subjectivity in a society formed by colonization and with a history marked by violence and discontinuity, this essay makes an effort to link the history of the classical Mexican cinema melodrama with Mexican society, tracing the inscription of the melodramatic alongside gendered social positioning and highlighting those moments when conflicting voices and needs visibly erupt into the cinematic and social sphere. Aware of the dangers of imposing upon the Latin American cinema critical modes that do not reflect its socio-historical conditions, I shall not be proposing an argument based on the melodrama's ability to put into question the patriarchal codes of classic cinematic realism.[6] It is undoubtedly true, as John King argues, that Latin American cinema and literature do not participate in the strong realist tradition of their European or US counterparts and that the terms of Latin American realism are still to be defined.[7] On the contrary, by emphasizing the complex lines of historical and cultural affiliations that link and differentiate the social functions of the melodramatic in Mexico, my goal will be to confront conflicting, historically-specific claims of national, ethnic and gendered identity that have often gone unchallenged in Latin American film studies.[8]

THE MELODRAMA AND THE LATIN AMERICAN CINEMA

As has been extensively detailed elsewhere, the melodrama, along with music and comedy, became synonymous with the cinema in Latin America after the introduction of sound.[9] Taking advantage of Hollywood's temporary inability to satisfy the linguistic needs of the Latin American market, local producers used the new technology to exploit national characteristics. Argentina took on the tango and its melodramatic lyrics and developed the tango melodrama genre in the early 30s. Similarly, in Mexico, the melodrama became a central genre of the sound cinema after the success of the early sound feature *Santa* (Antonio Moreno, 1931), an adaptation of a well-known melodramatic novel by Federico Gamboa about an innocent girl from the provinces who is forced into prostitution in the big city and finds redemption only in death.[10]

Furthermore, the rapid establishment of a specific Latin American star system heavily dependent on radio and popular musical entertainers gave rise to melodramas which always included at least one or two musical performances to heighten a film's 'entertainment value'. Starring singers-turned-actors, narratives about entertainers sprinkled with performances became *de rigueur*. Thus Libertad Lamarque's suffering mothers always also sang,

149

Pedro Infante could weep over his little black child with the popular song 'Angelitos Negros' ('Little Black Angels') in the film of the same title, and Ninón Sevilla could vent her sexual anger and frustration dancing wild rumbas in the *cabaretera* (brothel) films of the 50s. In these and other films the narrative stoppage usually generated by performances was reinvested with emotion, so that melodramatic pathos emerged in the moment of performance itself (through gesture, sentiment, interactions with the audience within the film, or simply music choice). In a film like *Amor en las sombras* (*Love in the Shadows*, Tito Davison, 1959), which featured ten complete performances in less than two hours' screen time, music and song rather than dramatic action propel the narrative.

Despite this diversity, however, two basic melodramatic tendencies developed between 1930 and 1960: family melodramas focused on the problems of love, sexuality, and parenting, and epic melodramas that reworked national history, especially the events of the Mexican revolution. Although the two categories are somewhat fluid, with some family melodramas taking place in the context of the revolution and its aftermath, I shall be concerned primarily with the operations of the former. The revolutionary melodramas are perhaps as significant for the development of a gendered 'Mexican' consciousness as the family ones, but I am interested in analyzing the cinematic positioning of women within the Mexican domestic sphere, and the ideological operations of the family melodramas provide us with privileged access to that realm. Set in quintessential domestic spaces (homes or similar places) that, as Laura Mulvey says, 'can hold a drama in claustrophobic intensity and represent . . . the passions and antagonisms that lie behind it',[11] the family melodramas map the repressions and contradictions of interiority and interior spaces – the home and unconscious – with more urgency than is possible within the cathartic large-scale action of revolutionary dramas.

THE MELODRAMA, WOMEN AND MEXICO

The melodramatic is deeply embedded in Mexican and Hispanic culture and intersects with the three master narratives of Mexican society: religion, nationalism, and modernization. First of all, Hispanic culture carries the burden of its Christianity which, as Susan Sontag argues, is already melodramatic (rather than tragic) in structure and intention. In Christianity, as Sontag says, 'every crucifixion must be topped by a resurrection', an optimism inimical to the pessimism of tragedy.[12] Furthermore, the staples of the family melodrama – sin and suffering abnegation – are essential components of the Christian tradition: sin allows for passion and, although it must always be punished, passion, after all, justifies life.

Second, and perhaps most significantly, the melodrama always addresses questions of individual (gendered) identity within patriarchal culture and at the heart of the definition of Mexico as a nation. In Mexico, questions of individual identity are complicated by a colonial heritage that defines woman and her alleged instability and unreliability as the origin of *national* identity. The Mexican nation is defined, on the one hand, by Catholicism and the Virgin of Guadalupe, the Virgin Mother and patron saint, and, on the other, by the *chingada*, the national betrayal of Doña Marina (also known as La

Malinche or Malintzin Tenepal), the Aztec princess who submitted to Cortés and handed her people over to the conquistadores.[13] As Cherrie Moraga succinctly puts it, 'Malinche fucked the white man who conquered the Indian peoples of Mexico and destroyed their culture. Ever since, brown men have been accusing her of betraying her race, and over the centuries continue to blame her entire sex for this "transgression".'[14]

Raped, defiled and abused, Malintzin/Malinche is the violated mother of modern Mexico, *la chingada* (the fucked one) or *la vendida* (the sell-out). As Octavio Paz explains, Malinche's 'sons' (*sic*), the Mexican people, are 'the sons of *la chingada*, the fruits of a rape, a farce'.[15] Thus the origins of the nation are located at a site – the violated mother – which is simultaneously an altar of veneration and the place of an original shame. The victim of a rape, Malinche/*la chingada*, mother of the nation, carries the guilt of her victimization. Deeply marked by this 'otherness', Mexican national identity rejects and celebrates its feminine origins while gender identity, in general, is problematized even further, as the popular saying, 'Viva México, hijos de la Chingada' so vividly illustrates. To be Malinche – a woman – is to be a traitor, the great whore mother of a bastard race. In fact, Mexican consciousness and gender definitions have been so intertwined and scarred by the Spanish conquest that the belief that all things of a foreign or European nature are superior to their Mexican equivalents is deprecatingly called *Malinchismo*. The melodramatic became the privileged place for the symbolic reenactment of this drama of identification and the only place where female desire (and the Utopian dream of its realization) could be glimpsed.

Mexico's colonial heritage, first Spanish and most recently American, also affects the social functions of the melodrama. Colonialism always implies a crisis of identity for the colonial subject, caught between the impulse to imitate the colonizer and the desire for an always displaced autonomy. Like Caliban in *The Tempest*, the colonized must use the colonizer's 'words' – the imported cinematic apparatus – and learn the colonizer's language before he or she can even think of articulating his or her own speech: 'You taught me language; and my profit on't/Is, I know how to curse'. Just as in Brazil the development of the parodic *chanchada* genre can be seen as a response to the impossibility of thinking of a national cinema without considering the Hollywood cinema as well as Brazil's own underdevelopment, in Mexico, melodrama's excess explicitly defies the Hollywood dominant:

> Since there can be no nostalgic return to pre-colonial purity, no unproblematic recovery of national origins undefiled by alien influences, the artist in the dominated culture cannot ignore the foreign presence but must rather swallow it and recycle it to national ends.[16]

As Carlos Monsiváis has said, 'If competition with North America is impossible artistically or technically, the only defense is excess, the absence of limits of the melodrama.'[17] Thus the melodrama's exaggerated signification and hyperbole – its emphasis on anaphoric events pointing to other implied, absent meanings or origins – become, in the Mexican case, a way of cinematically working through the problematic of an underdeveloped national cinema.

151

The melodrama is also formally and practically linked with the specific trajectory of Mexican national identity and the significance of the revolution for the nation-building project. If we agree with Peter Brooks that the melodrama is 'a fictional system for making sense of experience as a semantic field of force' that 'comes into being in a world where the traditional imperatives of truth and ethics have been violently thrown into question',[18] then we should not be surprised by the cultural currency of the melodrama in post-revolutionary Mexico. In the midst of the great social upheavals of the post-revolutionary period, the country seemed ungovernable and the city an unruly Mecca: the revolution changed the nature of public life, mobilized the masses, shook up the structures of the family without changing its roots and, as Carlos Monsiváis says, 'served as the inevitable mirror where the country recognized its physiognomy'. The revolution may not have 'invented' the Mexican nation, but 'its vigor, for the first time, lent legendary character-istics to the masses that sustained it'.[19] In other words, the revolution created a new class (the new urban poor soon to be a working class) whose will-power, roughness, and illiteracy became insistently visible in the formerly feudal national landscape.

The revolution also further problematized the position of women in Mex-ico. Women had fought alongside the men and had followed the troops cooking, healing, and providing emotional and physical solace, either as legitimate wives, lovers, or paid companions. Known generally as *soldaderas*, these women formed the backbone of an incipient feminist movement that emerged after the revolution. Yet as Jean Franco argues,

... the revolution with its promise of social transformation encouraged a Messianic spirit that transformed mere human beings into supermen and constituted a discourse that associated virility with social transformation in a way that marginalized women at the very moment when they were, supposedly, liberated.[20]

Precisely when the nation created itself anew under the aegis of revolutionary mythology and its male superhero redeemers, women were once again rele-gated to the background, and in cultural production (especially in national epic allegories) represented as a terrain to be traversed in quest for male identity. Simultaneously, while the new secular state ostensibly promoted women's emancipation to combat Catholicism and its alleged counter-revolutionary ideology,[21] Mexico also found itself caught in the wheels of capitalist modernization.

The new class thus created by the revolution – an increasingly mobile, urban, migratory class of male and female workers – was entertained by the popular theater (*teatro frívolo* or *género chico*) before it found the cinema, but after the coming of sound, Spanish-language movies became the principal discursive tool for social mapping. While the *género chico* and its carnival-esque ribaldry[22] attracted a socially but not sexually mixed audience, the cinema was family entertainment[23] – by design and by commercial impera-tives, broader-based. By the late 30s and through the 40s and 50s, the national cinema manifested itself as an efficient way of life, granting access not only to entertainment but to vital behaviors and attitudes: 'One didn't go to the cinema to dream, but to learn.'[24] There was not much room here for the carnivalesque celebration that continued to take place in the *teatro frívolo*: the cinema helped transmit new habits and reiterated codes of behavior, providing the new nation with the common bases and collective ties necessary for national unity. In fact, the cinema helped make a new post-revolutionary middle class viable.

If it is indeed true, as Monsiváis says, that film melodramas served this kind of socializing function, what exactly were the lessons they taught women? How did the melodrama mediate the post-revolutionary crisis of national and gendered identity and its subsequent institutionalization? Rather than blindly enforce or teach uncontradictory high moral values, stable codes of behavior, or obedience to the patriarchal order, the family melodramas staged specific dramas of identity which often complicated straightforward ideological identification for men *and* women without precluding accommodation. However, the melodrama's contradictory play of identifications constituted neither false communication nor a simple lesson imposed upon the people from above. On the contrary, these films addressed pressing contradictions and desires within Mexican society. And even when their narrative work suggests utter complicity with the work of the law, the emotional excesses set loose and the multiple desires detonated are not easily recuperated.

The narratives of the Mexican family melodrama deal with three principal conflicts: the clash between old (feudal, Porfirian) values and modern (industrialized, urban) life, the crisis of male identity that emerges as a result of this clash, and the instability of female identity that at once guarantees and threatens the passage from the old to the new. These conflicts are played out in two distinct physical and psychic spaces: the home, a private sphere valorized and sanctified by the law, and the nightclub, a barely tolerated social space as liminal as the home is central. Only marginally acceptable, the nightclub is nevertheless the part of the patriarchal public sphere where the personal (and issues of female subjectivity, emotion, identity, and desire) finds its most complex articulation in the Mexican melodrama.

THE HOME: MOTHERS, FAMILIES, AND THEIR 'OTHERS'

Although Mexican patriarchal values insist on the sanctity of the traditional home (as an extension of the 'fatherland' blessed by God), the extended families growing in them are rarely well adjusted precisely because of the rigidity of the fathers' law and in spite of the saintliness of the mothers. In Mexico, the family as an institution has a contradictory symbolic status as a site for the crystallization of tensions between traditional patriarchal values (especially the cult of machismo) and modernizing tendencies and as a source of maternal support and nurturing that the secular state could not replace.[25] This ambivalence is clearly evidenced in the deployment of the Mexican cinema's so-called mother obsession. Although it is undoubtedly true that the Mexican melodrama's fascination with saintly mother figures can be traced to the deeply conservative social impulses of the post-revolutionary middle classes, who countered their insecurity over the legitimacy of their status with aggressive nationalism and an obsessive attachment to traditional values, how this mother obsession is worked out in the melodrama complicates any straightforward assessment of the politics and social mapping of such representations.

Director Juan Oro and the actress Sara García created the archetypal mother of the Mexican melodrama in *Madre querida* (*Dear Mother*, 1935), the heart-wrenching story of a young boy who goes to a reformatory for arson and whose mother dies of grief precisely on 10 May (Mothers' Day in Mexico). Over the next decades, García played suffering, self-sacrificing mothers in countless films such as *No basta ser madre* (*It's Not Enough to Be a Mother*, 1937), *Mi madrecita* (*My Little Mother*, 1940), and *Madre adorada* (*Beloved Mother*, 1948). However, despite their self-acknowledged narrative focus on mothers and their positioning of the mother as the central ideological tool for social and moral cohesion, these and other films ostensibly glorifying mothers as repositories of conservative family values were clearly maternal melodramas rather than women's films. This distinction, invoked by E. Ann Kaplan in her discussion of Hollywood 20s and 30s melodramas,[26] is significant for the Mexican case, because it helps to distinguish between those films that focus on male Oedipal dramas and films that more self-consciously address female spectators and concerns.[27] Indeed, one could argue that, despite their focus on mothers, these family melodramas are patriarchal rather than maternal because they attempt to preserve patriarchal values rather than the sanctity of the mother. In attempting to reinforce the patriarchy their narrative logic breaks down: the moral crisis created in these films revolves around the fathers' identity and not the mothers', whose position is never put into question.

In *Cuando los hijos se van* (*When the Children Go Away*, Juan Bustillo Oro, 1941), for example, a rigid provincial family is torn asunder by the father's (Fernando Soler) inability to see the true characters of his sons or to recognize their mother's (Sara García) more sensitive assessment of their characters. Influenced by the 'bad' son, the father banishes the 'good' son to the city, while the mother, with her unerring maternal instinct, never doubts his integrity and is ultimately proven right by the narrative: the banished son returns a popular radio star and saves the family from a bankruptcy engineered by his sibling. Despite the narrative's obvious privileging of the mother's sight, the film attempts to shore up a patriarchal family structure threatened not only by the patriarch's inability to see, but by the other world lying outside the patriarch's control: Mexico City, emblem of modernization and progress, and the modern and highly pleasurable world outside the family. The film attempts to idealize the family as a unit whose preservation is worth all sacrifices, even death, but its suggestion that the familial crisis is caused by the father's blindness and irrational rigidity, especially when compared with the mother's unerring instinct, puts in question the very patriarchal principle it seeks to assert.

Mothers may have a guaranteed place in the home as pillars of strength, tolerance and self-abnegation, in other words, as Oedipal illusions, but outside the home they are prey to the male desires that the Mexican home and family disavow. As a foil to the mother's righteous suffering and masochistic

'. . . *the* mala mujer, *the haughty independent woman . . . passionate and devilish'. María Félix in* Doña Diabla (The Devil is a Woman, *Tito Davison, Mexico, 1949*)

respect for the law, men, especially father-figures, are self-indulgent and unable to obey the moral order. It is their desire, unleashed because of maternal asexuality, that most threatens and disturbs the stability of the family and its women. While denying desire within the family, it is a compelling and at times controlling force outside it. Thus a variant of the family melodrama focuses on the impossible attraction of 'other' women: the 'bad' mothers (*las malas*), the vamps, the mistresses.

While Sara García portrayed the archetype of the good mother, María Félix depicted her opposite, the *mala mujer* (bad woman), the haughty independent woman, as passionate and devilish as the mothers are asexual and saintly. The titles of Félix's films clearly reveal her star persona: *Doña Bárbara* (Fernando de Fuentes, 1943), *La mujer de todos* (*Everyone's Woman*, Julio Bracho, 1946), *La devoradora* (*The Devourer*, Fernando de Fuentes, 1946), *Doña Diabla* (Tito Davison, 1949). *Doña Bárbara*, her third film, most clearly defined this persona.[28] After being brutally raped as a young girl, Bárbara becomes a rich, independent landowner – la Doña – who enjoys despoiling and humiliating other human beings, especially men. She exults in her power and discards lovers and even her own daughter easily, exhibiting neither pity nor shame and relishing her hatred. Despite her power, Bárbara, like most of Félix's characters, is simply the vampiresque flip-side of the saintly mothers of the family melodramas. Easily classified as anti-family melodramas in so far as they reject the surface accoutrements of the patriarchal family, her films do so simply in order to re-inscribe the need for the standard family with great force. Despite titles which call attention to the female character, Félix's films are male-centered narratives, where the spectacular pleasure lies with the woman (and her masquerades of masculinity), but the narrative remains in the hands of the male protagonist. Even in *Doña Bárbara*, the principal narrative agent is Santos Luzardo, a young man (Julián Soler) who challenges la Doña's power when he refuses her seduction. The film is more concerned with how he defeats Bárbara than with Bárbara's point of view or her downfall. Bárbara remains unknowable, an enigma given a sociological *raison d'être* (the rape) and the face of a goddess, but whose subjectivity and desires the audience has no access to. As a star, Félix could not embody female desire, for she was an ambivalent icon, as unknowable, cold and pitiless as the mother figure was full of abnegation and tears.[29] Her presence is simply an echo of the dangers of desire for men rather than its realization for women.

WOMAN'S DESIRE ON THE MARGINS OF THE HOME

In general, only two kinds of Mexican melodramas were structured around the issue of woman's identity and presented from a female point of view: the fallen-but-redeemed-by-motherhood women's films and the *cabaretera* subgenre. Each type of film also had its prototypical female 'star': whereas the former films most often starred Dolores del Río or, somewhat later, Libertad Lamarque (two stars who specialized in characters who suffered copiously for their meager sins and relished child obsessions without equal) the latter films were epitomized by the sexy *rumberas* portrayed by the Cuban actress Ninón Sevilla. Since neither Lamarque nor Sevilla are Mexican, the relative independence achieved by Lamarque's characters and the sexual wantonness of Sevilla's could always be distanced as foreign 'otherness', even when the actresses portrayed Mexican women. However, del Río, albeit Mexican-born, began her career in Hollywood, and, unlike the other two, was always considered a great actress, the *grande dame* of the Mexican cinema whose face would acquire mythical status as *the* archetype of the moral and physical perfection of the indigenous woman.

Lamarque, singer and Argentine stage and movie star, acquired a tango-inspired star persona after successfully competing for screen time with singing idol Jorge Negrete in Luis Buñuel's *Gran Casino* (1946): the young woman betrayed by weak men who nevertheless succeeds professionally as a high-class entertainer and manages to confront and conquer the ghost of the ideal family she could have had. Neither matriarchal mother, vampish 'other', nor a symbol of indigenous purity, Lamarque was most often a prototypically innocent fallen woman. In *Soledad* (*Solitude*, Tito Davison, 1948), for example, Lamarque plays a young orphaned servant (Argentine!) girl who is tricked into a false marriage, made pregnant, and abandoned by the willful family heir whom she loves.

Despite their innocence, however, Lamarque's characters fall uneasily into the prevailing stereotypes of the Mexican cinema. In her best films, where she portrays entertainers with tragic pasts or fates, the need to position her simultaneously in relation to family life and to public life as a performer complicates the affirmation of standard social structures and woman's position vis-à-vis the private and public spheres. Her status as a respectable performer (and the incumbent independence of a salary, relationships outside the domestic sphere, and the adoring gaze of diegetic audiences) destabilizes the apparent rigidity of her identity as a hopeless mother. Thus *Soledad* is unable to sustain the figurative melodramatic signification of its initial scenes (for example, prefiguring the falsity of the wedding ceremony via ominous *mise en scène* and the *coup de théâtre* of a candle blown out by violent wind when the couple first embrace) and depends increasingly on Soledad's performativity – on her voice rather than her silence – to unravel its melodrama. Told from her point of view and, by the film's end, literally dependent on her voice, the melodrama of *Soledad* ends appropriately with her long-lost daughter's anguished cry of recognition: 'Mother!' But the Soledad that greets it is far more than 'just a mother' and remains an outstanding model of self-sufficiency.

THE CABARET: *RUMBERAS* AND FEMALE DESIRE

Whereas Lamarque's characters are usually tricked or forced by circumstances into successful careers as singers while all they really want to be is wives and mothers, Ninón Sevilla and other *cabareteras* (María Antonieta

Ninón Sevilla struts her stuff in Señora Tentación (The Temptress, *José Díaz Morales, Mexico, 1947*)

157

Pons, Leticia Palma, and Meche Barba) present a different problematic. Much more sordid, their fates and entertainment activities project a virulent form of desire on to the screen. Nowhere else have screen women been so sexual, so willful, so excessive, so able to express their anger at their fate through vengeance. As François Truffaut (under the pseudonym Robert Lacheney) wrote in 1954,

> From now on we must take note of Ninón Sevilla, no matter how little we may be concerned with feminine gestures on the screen or elsewhere. From her inflamed look to her fiery mouth, everything is heightened in Ninón (her forehead, her lashes, her nose, her upper lip, her throat, her voice). ... Like so many missed arrows, [she is an] oblique challenge to bourgeois, Catholic, and all other moralities.[30]

Albeit uneasily, Lamarque's sophisticated performers could be narratively recuperated within an expanded domestic sphere, but Sevilla's excessively gendered gestures engaged melodramatic tropes beyond the point of hyperbole. Thus with Sevilla, the performative excess of the 'musical/performance melodrama' reaches its zenith and the boundary between performance and melodrama disappears entirely.

The most virulent of Sevilla's *cabaretera* films was Alberto Gout's 1952 *Aventurera* (*Adventuress*). The plot is extraordinarily complicated and evidence of the excess associated with such films. Elena (Ninón Sevilla), a happy bourgeois girl, is left destitute when her mother runs away with a lover and her father commits suicide. Unable to find a job, she is tricked into a Juárez brothel where she is drugged and gang raped. Eventually, Elena becomes the star/prostitute of the nightclub, but she is so unruly that the madam (Andrea Palma) hires a thug to scar her in punishment. She runs away, becomes a nightclub star again, and meets and seduces Mario (Rubén Rojo), only to discover that his high-society mother is the madam of the Juárez brothel. After many other melodramatic twists and murders, the film finally ends with Mario and Elena supposedly free of their family traumas and about to enjoy a normal family life. The film's resolution imposes an end to the story, but it cannot contain the excess of signification – the malevolence of Andrea Palma's icy glance as she watches Elena's first tastes of champagne through an ominously barred lookout, Sevilla's haughty cigarette-swinging walk around the cabaret, her lascivious drunken revelry during her own wedding party, the seven-fold multiplication of her image while she sings 'Arrímate cariñito' ('Come closer little love') in a Juárez nightclub – circulated by the film. This excess is narrative and visual, for the plot is only as excessive as Elena's own physical presence, the sum of Sevilla's exaggeratedly sexual glance, overabundant figure, extraordinarily tight dresses, rolling hips, excessive laughter, and menacing smoking. This excessive performance functions not so much as a parody of a mimetic performative ideal, but as an oblique affirmation of the gender identity that a mimetic repetition elides. Unlike the asexual mother-figures of García, the suffering mothers of Lamarque or the frozen sculptural beauty of María Félix's temptresses, Sevilla is made of flesh and blood, a bundle of unrepressed instinctive desires. If, as Judith Butler argues, the performative gesture 'as a certain frozen stylization of the body' is the constitutive moment of feminine gender identity, [31] Sevilla, like a drag queen, melts the style. This melt-down, her moral provocation, is much greater than the admonitions provided by the narrative.

This provocation is not, however, as straightforward as it might seem. In Mexico, the prostitute as emblem of desire, necessary evil, and mother of the nation (Malinche/Malintzin) has a prominent place in national cultural history. Prostitution might indeed be the oldest profession everywhere, but rarely have prostitutes been the preferred subject of so many popular culture texts as in Mexico. What we see in the *cabaretera* films of the late 40s and the 50s is the culmination of a complex process in which the figure of the prostitute (albeit cloaked with the shameful aura of Malinche) became the site of a serious challenge to the *Porfirian* moral order and an emblem of modernity.

Officially regulated and socially shunned, the post-revolutionary prostitute and her spaces – the brothel, assignation house, and cabaret – had a distinct social function: they offered men a place to escape from the burdens of home, saintly wives and *sábanas santas*,[32] and to engage in uninhibited conversations and the ambivalent pleasures of the flesh. Mexican culture always celebrated the myth of the prostitute, but in the 20s the prostitute also assumed a different iconic status in the wildly popular romantic visions of singer–composer Agustín Lara. Idealized and simultaneously romantic and perverse, the prostitute of Lara's songs was not pitied for falling from grace. Lara's popular songs embodied a fatalistic worship of the 'fallen woman' as the only possible source of pleasure for modern man.[33] Though at first considered scandalous (and prohibited in schools by the Mexican Ministry of Public Education), Lara's audacious songs were quickly absorbed as a new popular culture idiom: the exaltation of the Lost Woman.[34]

By the late 40s[35] the cinema had completely assumed Lara's vision of the prostitute as an object of self-serving worship, and his songs were the central dramatic impulse propelling the action of many *cabaretera* films. Thus, for example, *Aventurera* is clearly inspired by a song of the same title (sung by Pedro Vargas in the film):[36]

> *Sell your love expensively, adventuress,*
> *Put the price of grief on your past;*
> *And he who wants the honey from your mouth*
> *Must pay with diamonds for your sin.*
> *Since the infamy of your destiny*
> *Withered your admirable spring,*
> *Make your road less difficult,*
> *Sell your love dearly, adventuress.*

Lara's songs idealized woman as a purchasable receptacle for man's physical needs (the ultimate commodity for modern Mexican society) but also invested her with the power of her sexuality: to sell at will, to name her price, to choose her victim. Nevertheless, as Monsiváis says, his songs also made the object of pleasure, once used, abstract: 'The deified prostitute protects

159

the familiar one, exalts the patriarchy, and even moves the real prostitute herself to tears, granting a homey warmth to its evocation of exploited lives.'[37]

In literature, in Agustín Lara's and others' songs and, finally, in the cinema, the prostitute and the nightlife of which she is an emblem became an anti-Utopian paradigm for modern life. The exaltation of female desire and sin and of the nightlife of clubs and cabarets clearly symbolized Mexico's new (post-Second World War) cosmopolitanism and the first waves of developmentalism. The *cabaretera* films were the first decisive cinematic break with Porfirian morality. Idealized, independent, and extravagantly sexual, the exotic *rumbera* was a social fantasy, but one through which *other* subjectivities could be envisioned, other psychosexual and social identities forged.

But the *rumbera* is not a simple model of resistance. When analyzed as part of a specific process, a neurotic knot of determinations[38] – and, in the context of its flip-side, the suffering mother – the image of female subjectivity that emerges is deeply contradictory and without an easy resolution. In fact, it is a fantasy. As Ninón Sevilla with much self-awareness explains to her lover in *Mulata* (Gilberto Martínez Solares, 1953), another *cabaretera* film, the impossible challenge of female identity is summarized by the insecurity of 'never knowing whether a man has loved me or desired me'. It is not that one is necessarily preferable to the other – she can be either the wife *or* the sexual object – but that Mexican society nevertheless still insists that they are mutually exclusive social categories.

Notes

Research for this essay was made possible, in part, by grants from the Mellon Foundation and the Roger Thayer Stone Center for Latin American Studies at Tulane University.

1. For an assessment of the last decades of Latin American film scholarship, see my 'Setting Up the Stage: Latin American Film Scholarship, 1970–80s' in *Quarterly Review of Film and Video*, 13 (1–3), pp. 239–60. See also my *The New Latin American Cinema*, forthcoming, University of Illinois Press.
2. E. Colina and D. Díaz Torres, 'Ideología del Melodrama en el Viejo Cine Latinoamericano, *Cine Cubano*, no. 73–74–75 (1971), p. 15. Unless otherwise stated, all translations from foreign-language sources are my own.
3. D. Díaz Torres and E. Colina (1972), 'El Melodrama en la Obra de Luis Buñuel', *Cine Cubano*, no. 78–80 (1972), pp. 156–64.
4. Typical of this approach is Reynaldo González's recent study of the deployment of the melodramatic in radio serials, *telenovelas* and films, *Llorar es un Placer* (Havana: Editorial Letras Cubanas, 1988). The papers presented at the seminar on the 'Old' Latin American Cinema held during the 1989 Havana Film Festival also indicated that this resistance to the popularity and appeal of the melodrama is still quite alive. It was obvious, from the defensive inaugural speech by Julio García Espinosa ('this is, after all, the cinema we have been fighting against all these years') to the apologetic tone of most of the papers, that the melodramatic is still a difficult issue to sort through for Latin American critics. The papers presented at the seminar were reprinted as individual pamphlets by the Cinemateca Cubana.
5. Ismail Xavier, 'The Question of Melodrama and Politics', work in progress, Universidade de São Paulo.

6. This has been one of the principal tendencies of recent investigations of Hollywood film melodrama. See Christine Gledhill, 'The Melodramatic Field: An Investigation', pp. 5–39, and the other essays collected in Christine Gledhill (ed.), *Home is Where the Heart is: Melodrama and the Woman's Film* (London: British Film Institute, 1987).

7. John King, *Magical Reels: A History of Cinema in Latin America* (London: Verso 1990), p. 38.

8. Thus this essay needs to be situated in the context of recent work analyzing the historical and international inscription of the melodramatic in different Western and non-Western societies. See, for example, P. Petro, *Joyless Streets: Women and Melodramatic Representation in Weimar Germany* (Princeton: Princeton University Press, 1989); Ginette Vincendeau, 'Melodramatic Realism: On Some French Women's Films of the 1930s', *Screen*. vol. 30, no. 3 (1989), pp. 51–65; Ella Shohat, *Israeli Cinema: East/West and the Politics of Representation* (Austin: University of Texas Press, 1989); and R. Vasudevan, 'The Melodramatic Mode and the Commercial Hindi Cinema', *Screen*, vol. 30, no. 3 (1989), pp. 29–50.

9. This period of the Latin American cinema has generated much solid historical and archival research. For Mexico, see especially Emilio García Riera, *Historia Documental del Cine Mexicano*, 10 vols to date (Mexico City: Ediciones Era, 1969) and Moisés Viñas (ed.), *Historia del Cine Mexicano* (Mexico City: UNAM/ UNESCO, 1987). In English, see Carl J. Mora, *Mexican Cinema: Reflections of a Society, 1896–1980* (Berkeley: University of California Press, 1982). For a succinct and well-informed comparative historical analysis of this period in English, see John King, *Magical Reels: A History of Cinema in Latin America* (London: Verso, 1990).

10. Although the Mexican cinema did not take off on an industrial scale until the 1936 international success of the *comedia ranchera* (ranch comedy), *Allá en el Rancho Grande* (*Out on the Big Ranch*, Fernando de Fuentes), melodramatic films were a basic staple from the 30s through the 60s. Aided by US war-time policies (and US resentment of Argentina's neutrality), the Mexican cinema thrived during the war and immediate post-war periods, producing as many as 124 films in 1950, the majority of which were melodramas. I am using melodrama here loosely, for the Mexican cinema (and other Latin American cinemas, especially Brazil's and its *chanchadas*) proved extraordinarily adept at generic mixing. Thus I use the melodramatic, in its broadest sense, as a structuring principle of expectations and conventions against which individual films establish their uniqueness as singular products, while recognizing that the term has a different currency in the Latin American context than in the USA or Europe.

11. Laura Mulvey, 'Melodrama In and Out of the Home', in Colin McCabe (ed.), *High Theory/Low Culture* (New York: St Martin's Press, 1986), p. 95.

12. Susan Sontag, 'Death of Tragedy', *Against Interpretation* (New York: Dell, 1966), pp. 132–9.

13. An Aztec legend claimed that Quetzalcoatl, a feathered serpent god, would come from the East to redeem his people on a given day of the Aztec calendar which, coincidentally, was the same day (21 April 1519) that Cortés and his men (fitting the description of Quetzalcoatl) landed in Vera Cruz. Thus Malintzin Tenepal became Cortés's translator, strategic advisor and eventually mistress, believing that she was saving her people. This is how recent scholarship has reinterpreted the 400-year-old legacy of female betrayal which is the founding moment of the Mexican nation. See, for example, Nancy Alarcón, 'Chicana's Feminist Literature: A Re-Vision Through Malintzin, or, Malintzin: Putting Flesh Back on the Object', in Cherrie Moraga and Gloria Anzaldúa (eds.), *This Bridge Called My Back: Writings By Radical Women of Color* (Watertown, Mass: Persephone Press, 1981); Aleida R. del Castillo, 'Malintzin Tenepal: A Preliminary Look into a New Perspective', in Rosaura Sánchez and Rosa Martínez Cruz (eds), *Essays on La*

Mujer (Los Angeles: University of California Chicano Studies Center, 1977); and Rachel Phillips, 'Marina/Malinche: Masks and Shadows', in Beth Miller, (ed), *Women in Hispanic Literature: Icons and Fallen Idols* (Berkeley: University of California Press, 1983).

14. Cherrie Moraga, 'From a Long Line of Vendidas: Chicanas and Feminism', in Teresa de Lauretis (ed.), *Feminist Studies/Critical Studies* (Bloomington: Indiana University Press, 1986), pp. 174–5.
15. Octavio Paz, *The Labyrinths of Solitude: Life and Thought in Mexico* (New York: Grove Press, 1961), p. 85.
16. João Luiz Vieira and Robert Stam, 'Parody and Marginality: The Case of Brazilian Cinema', *Framework*, no. 28 (1985), reprinted in Manuel Alvarado and John O. Thompson (eds), *The Media Reader* (London: British Film Institute, 1990), p. 96.
17. Carlos Monsiváis, 'Reir Llorando (Notas Sobre la Cultura Popular Urbana)', in Moisés Ladrón de Guevara (ed.), *Politica Cultural del Estado Mexicano* (Mexico: Ed. GEFE/SEP, 1982), p. 70.
18. Peter Brooks, *The Melodramatic Imagination* (New Haven: Yale University Press, 1976), pp. xiii, 14–15.
19. Monsiváis, op. cit., p. 27.
20. Jean Franco, *Plotting Women: Gender and Representation in Mexico* (New York: Columbia University Press, l989), p. 102.
21. However, women did not win the right to vote in national elections until 1953.
22. The *género chico* or *teatro frívolo* was a vaudeville-like theatrical genre that developed in neighborhood playhouses and tents. While the bourgeois theater staged classical melodramas from Spain and France which outlined the parameters of decent behavior and exalted heightened sensibilities in perfect academic Spanish, the *género chico* thrived with popular characters and satire. The *género chico* was carnivalesque in the Bakhtinian sense, including in its repertory taboo words and gestures and popular speech while exaltating the grotesque and demanding a constant interaction between players and audience. Benefitting from the brief lapse of traditional morals that followed the revolution, the *género chico* made the sexual body verbally visible for the first time and gave the masses who had fought in the revolution a presence and a voice. See Ruth S. Lamb, *Mexican Theater of the Twentieth Century* (Claremont: Ocelot Press, 1975) and Manuel Manón, *Historia del Teatro Popular de México* (México: Editorial Cultura, 1932).
23. Each spectacle addressed and interacted with a specific sector of the population. The *teatro frívolo* attracted a socially hybrid audience – the homeless mixed with intellectuals, artists, politicians, and military men, according to the eye-witness description of muralist José Clemente Orozco in his *An Autobiography* (Austin: University of Texas Press, 1962) – but this audience was not sexually mixed. The only women mentioned in accounts of *género chico* spectatorship are prostitutes. Not only was the biting satire of the spectacle not considered morally appropriate, but women were also hardly represented on the stage. The cinema, however, was always a respectable entertainment option, appealing to men, women and children of all classes.
24. Carlos Monsiváis, 'El Cine Nacional', in *Historia General de México*, vol. IV (Mexico: El Colegio de México, 1976), p. 446.
25. See Jean Franco, 'The Incorporation of Women: A Comparison of North American and Mexican Popular Narrative', in Tania Modleski (ed.), *Studies in Entertainment: Critical Approaches to Mass Culture* (Bloomington: Indiana University Press, 1986).
26. E. Ann Kaplan, 'Mothering, Feminism, and Representation: The Maternal in Melodrama and the Woman's Film, 1910–40', in Gledhill (ed.), *Home is Where the Heart Is*, pp. 123–9.
27. Unlike Robert Lang, who argues in *American Film Melodrama* (Princeton: Prin-

ceton University Press, 1989) that 'in the end we learn everything about male desire from the melodrama and nothing about female desire', I maintain the distinction between those narratives explicitly motivated by female desires and organized according to a female point of view and those narratives which, despite their female 'content', function according to standard male patterns of desire and identification.

28. For an extensive analysis of María Félix's career and star persona, see Paco Ignacio Taíbo, *María Félix: 47 Pasos por el Cine* (Mexico City: Joaquín Mortiz/ Planeta, 1985).
29. See Carlos Monsiváis, 'Crónica de Sociales: María Félix en dos tiempos', in *Escenas de Pudor y Liviandad* (Mexico: Grijalbo, 1988), pp. 161–8.
30. Robert Lacheney, *Cahiers du Cinéma*, no. 30 (1954); cited by Emilio García Riera, *Historia Documental del Cine Mexicano* (Mexico: Ediciones Era, 1969, vol. IV, pp. 132–4, and Jorge Ayala Blanco, *La Aventura del Cine Méxicano* (Mexico: Ediciones Era, 1968), pp. 144–5.
31. Judith Butler, *Gender Trouble* (New York: Routledge, 1990), p. 140.
32. The *sábana santa*, or holy sheet, which continued to be used well into the 30s, was a special sheet with a round cut-out used to cover the wife's body during intercourse. Guaranteeing a minimum of pleasure, the holy sheet sustained the Catholic insistence that intercourse was sinful unless intended exclusively to procreate the race.
33. 'The Perverted One'
    To you, life of my soul, perverted woman whom I love,
    To you, ungrateful woman,
    To you, who makes me suffer and makes me cry,
    I consecrate my life to you, product of evil and innocence.
    All of my life is yours, woman.
    I want you, even if they call you perverted.
    'Sinner'
    Why did fate make you a sinner
    If you do not know how to sell your heart?
    Why do those who love you pretend to hate you?
    Why does he who hated you return to love you again?
    If each of your nights is a dawn,
    If each new tear is a sun,
    Why did fate make you a sinner
    If you do not know how to sell your heart?
34. As Eduardo Galeano summarizes it in *Century of the Wind* (New York: Pantheon, 1988), 'Lara exalts the Lost Woman, in whose eyes are seen sun-drunk palm trees; he beseeches Love from the Decadent One, in whose pupils boredom spreads like a peacock's tail; he dreams of the sumptuous bed of the silky-skinned Courtesan; with sublime ecstasy he deposits roses at the feet of the Sinful One and covers the Shameful Whore with incense and jewels in exchange for the honey of her mouth' (p. 110).
35. As Jorge Ayala Blanco indicates, in a few months between 1947 and 1948 alone, precisely coinciding with the Mario Rodríguez Alemán *sexenio*, over twelve *cabaretera* films were produced. See *La Aventura del Cine Mexicano*, p. 137.
36. The Lara song 'Aventurera' had already been featured in the 1946 María Félix film *La Devoradora* (Fernando de Fuentes). At the time, Lara and Félix were enjoying a much-publicized, albeit short-lived, marriage, and he ostensibly wrote the song explicitly for her.
37. Monsiváis, *Amor Perdido*, México: Ediciones Era, 1977, p. 60.
38. John Hill, *Sex, Class and Realism: British Cinema, 1956–1963* (London: British Film Institute, 1986).

MODERNITY AND CULTURAL MIXTURE

The Case of Buenos Aires

BEATRIZ SARLO

Editors' Introduction

The City of Dreams was the title of a popular Argentine film of 1922 by Argentina's most tenacious and prolific early film-maker, José Agustín 'El Negro' Ferreyra. He referred, of course, to Buenos Aires. A year later Jorge Luis Borges wrote of the 'mythical foundation of Buenos Aires': 'Hard to imagine that Buenos Aires had any beginning/I think of it as eternal as air and water'. The city acquired a privileged space in the imaginary of its artists and writers. Small wonder: Buenos Aires held 20 per cent of Argentina's population by 1930, a percentage that would increase every year due to internal migration. At the turn of the century, Argentina was one of the richest countries in the world, supplying beef and cereals to the world market. The wide boulevards and elegant town houses in Buenos Aires proclaimed that here was a city that aspired to be the Paris of the southern hemisphere, a metropolis positioned ambiguously on the periphery of the world. To this bustling, commercial, bureaucratic city flocked immigrants mainly from Spain and Italy. The nation's population grew from around 1,200,000 in 1852 to roughly eight million by 1914 as a result of immigration. In 1910, three out of every four adults in the central district of the city of Buenos Aires were born in Europe.

Argentina developed a highly sophisticated élite culture early in the 20th century. There was also a strong popular culture expressed in popular melodrama, farces, music hall, tango, cinema, serialised novels, women's magazines and political newsletters. Beatriz Sarlo explores the urban culture of Buenos Aires as it was propelled headlong into modernity from the 20s. She defines the very different nuances of the term 'modernity' and explains how Buenos Aires developed its own 'peripheral' modernity – to be located on the periphery might cause nostalgia for a centre, but it also offers the heterodox freedom of distance, allowing very distinctive cultural blendings, between Europe and America, 'high' and 'low' art, the city and the countryside. Studies on Latin American film culture, with very few exceptions, have failed to give any sense of the dynamism of cultural debates before the 50s. Most critics ignore these years as the 'sentimental' prehistory before the dawn of 'new cinema' in the 50s and 60s. Beatriz Sarlo paints a much more vivid and complex picture and points the way to future work in the field. Her essay is a product of that blending of theories and practices that she describes for the 20s: it combines European theorists of modernity and modernism, with a verve and dynamism reminiscent of Marshall Berman's brilliant *All That is Solid Melts into Air: The Experience of Modernity* (London: Verso, 1983) with a careful reconstruction and evocation of 'structures of feeling' that draws from the best work of Raymond Williams. All is grounded in very specific Argentine historiography and literary debates.

□

Buenos Aires in the 20s and 30s: although every attempt at periodisation is controversial, these decades, perhaps as no other, witness change in a spectacular manner. What is in play is not only the aesthetic avant-gardes, or economic modernisation, but rather modernity as a cultural style which permeates the fabric of a society which offers little resistance, whether in the projects of its political élites or in its density of life. The impact of the socio-economic processes, initiated in the second half of the 19th century, altered not only the urban landscape and ecology but also the lived experiences of its inhabitants. Thus, Buenos Aires is interesting as a physical space and as a cultural myth: city and modernity presuppose one another because the city is the stage for those changes brought on by modernity, it exhibits them in an ostensible and sometimes brutal fashion, it disseminates and generalises them.

It is not surprising, therefore, that modernity, modernisation and the city should appear intertwined with descriptive notions and categories that enable us to describe new physical spaces and material and ideological processes. In the degree to which Buenos Aires is altered, before the eyes of its inhabitants, with speed attuned to the rhythm of the new technologies of production and transport, the city is perceived as a symbolic and material condensation of change. As such, it is celebrated and from this perspective as well it is judged.

The idea of the city is inseparable from the changes caused by the processes of modernisation and it is inseparable also from another idea. The point has been reached, finally, where Buenos Aires may be placed in the perspective which had shaped the institutional projects of the 19th century drafted by Domingo Sarmiento and Juan Bautista Alberdi: the city has defeated the rural world, for immigration from Europe and local migrations (important from the mid-30s) offer a new demographic base. Economic progress super-imposes its model on reality (specially since the slump and the Depression of the 30s did not hinder for any extended period the process of Argentinian development). The illusion prevails that the peripheral character of this South American nation can now be read as a fluke of its history and not as a feature of its present.

At the same time, the idea of the periphery and of a tributary cultural area

– a formation that appears monstrous or inadequate when compared with a European model – persists, in a contradictory yet not inexplicable fashion.[1] Opposing sentiments – celebration, nostalgia or criticism – are scattered through the different tonalities of the period's culture. In the 20s and 30s, moreover, some vigorously political myths were constructed around Buenos Aires: the metaphor of the port-city, for example, emptying, like a voracious centripetal machine, the rest of the country which did not yet consider itself urban, even though urbanisation was spreading rapidly.[2] In the 20s and 30s, the desire and the fear of the city occupied a central space in Argentinian society and culture.

The *desire for the city* is as strong, in the Argentinian tradition, as the rural Utopias. In this sense, the intellectuals of the 20th century adhere to the urban paradigm of Sarmiento rather than the rural paradigm of José Hernández, the author of *Martín Fierro* and champion of the rights of the gaucho, with the exception of Ricardo Güiraldes, a cosmopolitan ruralist (to use an oxymoron), and Jorge Luis Borges who invented an image both of Buenos Aires and of Argentina's rural past.

The city as an ideal space has been not only a political theme, as may be seen in various chapters of Sarmiento's famous works *Facundo* or *Argirópolis*, nor just a stage on which the intellectuals discovered the mixture which defines Argentine culture, but also an imaginary space which literature invents and occupies, in the work of Roberto Arlt, Leopoldo Marechal, and Jorge Luis Borges. The city organises historical debates, social Utopias, dreams beyond reach, landscapes of art. To touch the city is equivalent to reaching a territory which has sustained many of our inventions. But, perhaps most important, the city is the stage *par excellence* for the intellectual, and both the writers and their public are urban actors.[3]

As Carl Schorske demonstrated,[4] the city is a problem, an inevitable landscape, a Utopia and a hell for the moderns. The city is also a form of approaching that other cluster of notions which at present dominate current theory: in the modernity–post-modernity debate, the city is a theme, as it was for the avant-garde.

MODERNITY AND RUPTURE

In his *Aesthetic Theory*, Theodor Adorno describes the authority of the new as something which is 'historically ineluctable',[5] and therefore defines the movement and the form of sensibility at least since Romanticism. Hans-Robert Jauss has traced the itineraries of this concept from the first disputes between Ancients and Moderns, considering it not only as a motor of aesthetic and cultural change, but also as one of the ways in which the present debates with and differentiates itself, in its projects, from the past.[6]

In Europe, the process of modernity is characterised by a position of relative independence with respect to the past, which Carl Schorske describes as a growing indifference: the past is no longer seen in terms of functional continuity. Schorske refers to a 'death of history', the precondition for the establishment of modernity as a global discourse and as a hegemonic practice in the literary and cultural spheres: the victory of Friedrich Nietzsche.

But it is also possible to think of the ways in which the past is re-functionalised, especially in the case of the Argentinian avant-gardes. It is the case that the extent of the break with cultural traditions is related to the force that these traditions exert. The break is more radical in a society where the modern forms of intellectual relations are already firmly rooted, where aesthetic and ideological factions and parties have been formed and where there are clear disputes over the canon, over symbols and authorities. When faced with a strong consolidated tradition, confrontation appears as a necessary strategy from the point of view of new artists and new poetics. In Argentinian culture, this general relationship with the past is given particular forms in the reading and the imaginary recuperation of a culture which seemed to have been affected by immigration and urbanisation.

Furthermore, in Argentina as in other Latin American countries, there is a difference between the forms of artistic modernity, which stress the vindication of autonomy, and the forms of avant-garde break, which are defined in the public legitimation of conflict. On the other hand, the process of cultural modernisation, carried out in the 20th century, includes at its centre the programmes of humanism and the left. If for the avant-garde 'the new' offers the basis for establishing aesthetic value, for the intellectual left this basis must be found in revolution or any other form of Utopian transformation. What highlights modernity are the processes of change in the basic foundations of cultural practices.

Walter Benjamim, Theodor Adorno and Peter Berger, in opposition to or in dialogue with the major avant-gardes of the 20th century, have explored the relations between the avante-garde and modernity, debating particularly the concept of autonomy, which desacralises art and produces the conditions to which the Surrealists responded with their Utopia of art and life reunited. The 'destruction of the aura', the aesthetic of the fragment, the modification of the concept of the 'work of art' (*oeuvre*) point to inflections in the problematic of the modern and the avant-gardes. In that context, new systems of relationships (and of conflict) between art and the public, art and politics, art and industrial society, art and technology, are opened.

The modern is also a form of feeling and a mode of experiencing the social, technological and spatial change brought about by capitalism. The artists represent and challenge, virtually at the same time, a body of new, often traumatic, experiences: the man of letters cast into the *tourbillon social* of the transformed city; the dandy and his inseparable counterpart, the *desperado*, who seek refuge in transgression or in flight; optimism in the face of a world in the process of transformation, and melancholy in the face of an irretrievable past. Different structures of feeling, to use Raymond Williams's phase, underlie a profound reconditioning of subjectivities and the emergence of new politics and new morals. Poetics of instability and of transience are linked to the instability and transience of the work of art itself, producing gestures, projects, events, one of whose distinguishing features is to join aesthetic discourse with public practices: from Dadaist or Expressionist cabaret to the parties and celebrations of the aesthetic Buenos Aires avant-garde, the *martinfierristas*.[7]

The space of the great modern city (a model to which Buenos Aires approximated in the 20s and consolidated in the 30s) proposes itself as a stage for cultural crossings where, hypothetically, all meetings and loans are possible. What is present here is, therefore, a culture marked by the principle of heterogeneity. A stage where we pursue the phantoms of modernity, the city is the most powerful symbolic machine of the modern world. The heterogeneity of the urban space makes difference extremely visible: there the limits between private and public are incessantly constructed and reconstructed; there the social sets out the conditions for mixture and produces the illusion or the effective possibility of dizzying rises and falls. And if the quick road to fortune makes the city the site for a Utopia of upward mobility, the possibility of anonymity converts it, as Benjamin indicated, into the preferred, indeed the only possible, place for the *flâneur*, for the conspirator (who lives his solitude in the midst of other men), for the erotic *voyeur* who is electrified by the gaze of the unknown woman who passes by; vice and the rupture of established moral limits are celebrated as the glory or the stigma of the city. The public space loses sacredness; all invade it, all consider the street as a common place, where offers are multiplied and at the same time differentiated, where merchandises are displayed, setting up desires which no longer recognise the limits of hierarchy.

Technology is the new machinery of the urban stage: it produces new experiences of space and time: futurist Utopias linked to the speed of transport, to the electric light which produces a profound break with the rhythms of nature, to the great enclosed precincts which are another form of street, of market and of *agora* (meeting place).

The Benjamin 'illumination' which discovers new forms of analysis in the modern city (his texts on Baudelaire are inextricably bound with the *Passagen Arbeit*, arcades project), places the urban stage as the axis around which the culture of the European 19th century is organised. The urban network, forcefully marked by what Marshall Berman considers the wounds but also the achievements of modernity,[8] offers places for the transaction of different values and the conflict of interests considered in the widest sense: aesthetic disputes, political confrontations, cultural mixture provoked by immigration or population displacements: the grand theatre of a complex culture.

This new type of aesthetic–ideological formation is seen, in the first place, in the crossing of discourses and practices, in so far as the modern city is always heterogeneous because it is defined as a public space: the street is the place, among others, where different social groups wage a war of symbolism. Architecture, urbanism and painting reject the past, correct the present and imagine a new city. The painter Xul Solar,[9] companion of the avant-garde groups of the 20s, deconstructs plastic figurative space, making it at once abstract and technological, geometric and inhabited by the symbols of a specific magical-scientific fiction. The aviators drawn by Xul float in planes where flags and insignia mix: here is an extremely elaborate image which may be seen as summarising the technical modernisation and national diversity which Buenos Aires represented.

The architectural Utopias are also a complex response to the process of

Mysterious millionaire Arturo de Córdova, dons beggar's clothes to explore the meaning of life on the streets of Buenos Aires in Dios se lo pague (God Will Reward You, *Luis César Amadori, Argentina, 1948)*

transformation. Wladimir Acosta imagined, between 1927 and 1935, an architectural fiction, the 'city-block' as an alternative to the truly chaotic growth of Buenos Aires. From another point of view, Victoria Ocampo (an intellectual aristocrat) became a patroness and Maecenas of architectural modernism and promoted it through her magazine, *Sur*,[10] which first began publication in 1931, as an instrument for the purification of taste, indispensable, in Ocampo's judgment, in a city where immigration had come to leave material traces, producing stylistic anarchy with diverse national origins. Modernism would propose a programme of homogenisation in face of the stylistic *volapuk* (heterogeneity) of immigrant origin: its volumes and façades would discipline the street.

But there exists another street, a symbolic space, which appears in almost all the Argentinian writers of the 20s and 30s, from Oliverio Girondo to Raúl González Tuñón, via Arlt and Borges.[11] In the street, time is perceived as history and as the present; if, on the one hand, the street is proof of change, on the other it may become the site on which this transformation is converted into a literary myth. Yet the street, criss-crossed by electricity cables and the rails of the street-cars, could be denied in order to look behind it for the remains of a street which might not yet have been touched by modernisation, that imaginary corner of the suburb invented by Borges in the image of '*las orillas*', an indeterminate place between the city and the countryside. On the one hand is the fascination with the down-town street where aristocrats are as

169

tangible as prostitutes, where the newspaper-vendor slips the envelope with cocaine to his clients, where journalists and poets frequent the same bars and restaurants as criminals and Bohemians. On the other hand there is the nostalgia for the neighbourhood street, where the city resists the stigmas of modernity, although the neighbourhood itself may have been a product of urban modernisation.

The neighbourhood street furnishes one of the central scenarios for tango lyrics in the 30s and 40s. In these streets are acted out the sentimental stories that the films of José 'El Negro' Ferreyra will make into classics, with the actress Libertad Lamarque: where the music of the tango and the *ingénue* heroine become a phenomenal success with the public and help sustain the growth of a vigorous cultural industry which attracts screen-writers from the ranks of the best tango poets (such as Homero Manzi) or writers who had, in earlier times, been part of the movements for literary renovation (such as Ulises Petit de Murat).

On the other hand, the heterogeneity of this public space (which is accentuated in the Argentinian case by the new cultural and social interstices provoked by demographic change) puts different levels of literary production in contact, establishing an extremely fluid system of aesthetic circulation and borrowing. There is an already vigorous and well-defined presence of a middlebrow and popular public, stratified socially, ideologically and politically, for which mass circulation books, serial novels and magazines covering a range of tastes from literature for 'pleasure and consolation' to explicit didactic and social propaganda were produced.

A reformist and eclectic left establishes institutions for cultural dissemination (popular libraries, conference centres, publishing houses, magazines) aimed at those sectors which remained on the edge of high culture. The questions of internationalism and social reform are posed, in terms of a process of education for the labouring masses who are gradually becoming incorporated into democratic and secular culture. In literary terms, this implies a system of translations (from Russian and French realism) and a poetic of humanitarianism.

The magazines in the style of *Caras y Caretas* (which first appeared towards the end of the 19th century) became modernised, articulating discourses and information of a different sort which tended to present a relatively integrated symbolic world in which cinema, literature, popular music, articles on daily life, fashion and comic strips began to find a place. The sentimental *feuilletons* and the magazines mapped out a horizon of desire, offered models of pleasure, and worked for and on a public which was beginning to consume literature (a public which had emerged from a successful movement for widespread literacy). Partially through this medium and also under the powerful spell of silent films, this public could dream the modern dreams of cinema, fashion, cosmopolitan comforts, the universe of the large department stores, shopping displays, the fashionable restaurants, and the dance halls. Pleasure was the motor of this news-stand literature, which legitimated both erotic enjoyment as well as sentimentalism and daydreaming. Those who produced this culture also intermixed and contributed both to the expansion of the system and to its instability: cultural borrowings, influences, a move-

170

ment between cultural levels, were all offered to a public which was also culturally diverse.

But this very heterogeneity is disturbing. The large modern newspapers such as *Crítica* and *El Mundo* (founded in 1913 and 1927 respectively), cinema, variety shows and theatres are addressed to different publics, demonstrating in the cultural sphere the social differences between old *criollos*, immigrants and children of immigrants. This coexistence and these superimpositions awaken nationalisms and zenophobia, and endorse the feeling of nostalgia for a city which was no longer the same after 1920, if it is measured against the images of the most recent past.

Buenos Aires may be seen with a retrospective gaze which puts into focus a past that is more imaginary than real (as is the case with the early Borges) or may be discovered in the emergence of a working-class and popular culture, formed under the influence of cinema and radio organised by a rapidly developing cultural industry. Capitalism has profoundly transformed the urban space and made the cultural system more complex. This system begins to be lived not only as a problem but also as an aesthetic theme, rife with the conflict of programmes and poetics which feed the battles of modernity: humanitarian realism opposes the avant-garde, but discourses with different functions are also opposed to one another (journalism against fiction, politics versus the general essay, the written word as against the cinematographic image).

The debates concerning cultural legitimation span the literary magazines: the old *criollos* are not easily prepared to admit that a language for literature might also be produced by writers whose parents had not been born in Argentina, whose accent betrayed a neighbourhood, a marginal tone, and who bear the marks of an immigrant origin. The cultural and ideological density of the period is the product of these different webs and of the intersection of discourses with a different origin and matrix (from Cubist painting or avant-garde poetry to tango, cinema, modern music or the jazz band).

The heterogeneity of discourses (from advertising to journalism, from poetry to *Trivialliteratur*, from radio soap operas to filmic melodrama) obliges literature itself to no longer appear as a singular entity, but rather as a system which includes, in its textual policies and strategies, these different actors.

Roberto Arlt is a case in point. Criticism has discussed at length the link between his novels and the *feuilleton*, represented in a direct fashion or figuratively in *El juguete rabioso* (*The Rabid Toy*, 1926). But, at the same time, and not only in this book, Arlt shows his relationship not just with 'high' literature but also with the new texts and practices of science and technical skill, of chemistry, physics and of those simulacra of popular science which then circulated in Buenos Aires, such as hypnotism, mesmerism, telepathic transmission and the like. Arlt's writing cannot be conceived of, nor the desires of his characters, if some reference is not made to this 'lore of the poor', learned in cheap manuals, in the popular libraries which operated in all the neighbourhoods, in the workshops of hair-brained inventors who had suffered the blinding illumination of electricity, of the fusion of metals, of galvanisation, of magnetism.

171

On the other hand, his futuristic vision of the city could not have been written without the impact of new forms of representing the urban stage, especially through films. The Buenos Aires that Arlt puts forward seems to share the nightmarish quality of the cinematic city as described in the Expressionist films that were shown in Buenos Aires in the 30s.

This referential universe becomes still more complex in *El amor brujo* (*Love, the Magician*, 1932), a novel written as a critique of sentimental mythology and of middle-class morality. Arlt uses precisely the resources and artifices of the literature of the *roman feuilleton* (which circulated in tens of thousands in weekly serial form), and of filmic melodrama in order to criticise them. In fact, one could affirm that Arlt takes and destroys their model of happiness, their romantic ideology and sexist positions, their idea of society, matrimony, money and the psychology of love.

Arlt's attitude towards sentimental film and literature, which he both used and rejected, may also be found in the '*Aguafuertes porteñas*' ('Buenos Aires Sketches'), which he published in the newspaper *El Mundo* from 1928 to 1942. In these brief texts, what had been learned in the practice of journalism is combined with the narrative structures of fiction. In truth, Arlt invented micro-structures which contain miniaturised plots and sketches of characters, from the lower urban middle class, presented and simultaneously criticised from a cynical vantage point. But there is much more: Arlt visited the city as no one had yet done. He went to the prisons and hospitals, he criticised the sexual habits of lower middle-class women and the institution of marriage, he denounced the selfishness of the *petit bourgeoisie* and the ambition which corrupts the rising middle class, he stigmatised the stupidity which he uncovered in the bourgeois family.

The operations of delimitation, mixing and transformation carried out by Arlt deal also with the processes by which a writer and his discourses are formed in a more general perspective: the formation of the writer through non-traditional modes which include, at their centre, journalism and different forms of popular culture. Both influences, which originate in the new industrial culture, presuppose the emergence of non-traditional publics and, in consequence, of new pacts of reading and of genre. With these elements, the subjectivity of the writer passes through contradictory processes: he is fascinated and horrified by the power of films and film mythology; he despises and courts his readers; he envies and refutes the values legitimated by 'high' culture.

The success of sentimental literature, which Arlt criticises, is repeated in the cinema and the most famous weekly serial *La vendedora de Harrods* (*The Harrods Salesgirl*) is brought to the screen. It is not merely a case of filming a successful plot: the new public finds in the cinema themes and values already enshrined in these hugely popular written narrations. On this relatively stable ground, cinema plants new myths that emerge from an original iconography and form new forms of collective identification. At the same time it contributes to the differentiation and stratification of the public although no one, not even élite intellectuals, can completely escape from the fascination of the movies. On the one hand, Borges often writes short film reviews, mainly on American and European cinema. On the other hand, dozens of magazines appear, with varying degrees of success, from the pioneering *Hogar y Cine* and *Cinema Chat* of 1920 or *Héroes del Cine*, 1923, to those produced by the publishing emporium of Julio Korn in the 40s and 50s. The cinema public grows and becomes differentiated from the 'literary' public, and in the area of cinema itself we also find very different positions being adopted. In 1931 a successful left-wing poet and journalist advised his readers not to miss two films that were being screened briefly in Buenos Aires, one by Pabst, the other by Murnau. At the same time, the advertisements page in the newspaper *El Mundo* announced the programme of more than thirty cinemas in Buenos Aires: almost all these cinemas were showing exclusively American films. Figures from this period reveal that there were more than six hundred cinemas spread throughout the country.

Hollywood offered the ideal of feminine beauty, but it also, in the style of its sets and costumes, provided a tone of elegance for the urban middle classes. The comedies of the Legrand twins in the 40s are perfectly aware that their public has been formed by American comedies, and an Argentine film like *La vendedora de fantasías* (*The Dream Seller*, 1950) shows that the director, in this case Daniel Tinayre, understood very clearly an aesthetic that harks back to Lubitsch melodrama (a genre prevalent in both Argentine and Mexican cinema) and displays the richness of its passions against an exuberant background made up of art deco, modern style and kitsch.

THE DEBATE AND THE QUESTION

Political aesthetic and cultural ideologies confront one another in this debate which has Buenos Aires as its stage and, frequently, its protagonist. The modern city is a privileged space where the concrete and symbolic forms of a culture in process of transformation are organised in the dense web of a stratified society. The social differences were represented or distorted in the intellectual field and were present in the institutional and aesthetic conflicts. Intellectuals moved in the area of culture as though the confrontations produced there were important chapters of a process in which, somehow, the future was at stake. In the face of that heterogeneity different reactions were displayed: the defence of a spiritual élite which might purify or, at least, denounce the artificial and corrupt nature of Argentinian society; a resort to myths and figures of the past which might restructure present relationships, something which often implied the invention of a past; the recognition of the present as diverse and the hope that it would be possible to construct a culture out of this diversity.

Affected by change, immersed in a city which was no longer that of their childhood, obliged to recognise the presence of men and women who, by being different, destroyed any notions of an original unity, and considering themselves to be different to the cultured élites of Spanish *criollo* origin, the intellectuals of Buenos Aires attempted to respond to, in a figurative or a direct manner, the main question of the day: how to accept or to annihilate the differences in lived experiences, in values and in practices. How could they construct a hegemony for the process in which they all participated, amidst the conflicts and uncertainties of a society in transformation? How could they redefine the place of the writer and the intellectual in a society in which the culture of letters now competed openly with a symbolic mass production which included the radio, recorded music and the cinema?

Notes

1. The discourse of the essay in the following decade will have as one of its focal points this 'monstrosity' which emerged from modernisation and which, for its authors, would not have been, in the European experience, a necessary companion to modernity. Ezequiel Martínez Estrada sets out in *Radiografía de la Pampa* (*Radiography of the Pampa*, 1933) his criticisms of a nation which has not responded to the promises and dreams of its 'founding fathers': massive immigration left in Argentina only a degraded image of Europe (which had already been anticipated by the Spanish conquest conceived of as rape). Buenos Aires is a mask which merely succeeds in showing in an overly evident manner the failure of civilisation in America. With a less pessimist inflection, Eduardo Mallea, in *Historia de una pasión argentina* (*History of an Argentine Passion*, 1937), shows astonishment in the face of the great city but, at the same time, imagines that the visible and material city covers another invisible reality on whose values Argentinian culture should be founded.
2. Raúl Scalabrini Ortiz, in the 30s, began his task of denouncing the economic destruction of Argentina by British imperialism which, by setting out the pattern of the railway network, was alleged to have deformed the national territory and to have converted Buenos Aires into the area where all the riches produced by the relegated provinces unjustly flowed. The works of Scalabrini Ortiz had a powerful impact on the constitution of nationalist ideologies and myths which, decades later, would come together in Peronism.
3. For José Luis Romero this productivity of the urban (and of the urban élites) is one of the main features of the cultural and institutional tradition of Latin America. See *Latinoamérica: las ciudades y las ideas* (México, Siglo XXI, 1976).
4. See Carl Schorske, 'The Idea of the City in European Thought: Voltaire to Spengler', in Oscar Handlin and John Burchard (eds), *The Historian and the City* (Cambridge, Mass.: MIT and Harvard University Press, 1963).
5. Theodor Adorno, *Teoría estética* (Madrid: Taurus, 1971), p. 36.
6. Hans-Robert Jauss, *Esthétique de la réception* (Paris: Gallimard, 1978); see particularly, 'La modernité dans la tradition littéraire et la conscience d'aujourd'hui'.
7. The *martinfierristas* were a group of artists and intellectuals who proclaimed these new sensibilities in the little magazines of the 20s, particularly in the magazine *Martín Fierro*.
8. Marshall Berman, *All that is Solid Melts into Air* (London: Verso, 1983).
9. See: *Xul Solar; 1887–1953* (Paris: Musée d'Art Moderne de la Ville de Paris, 1977), prologue by Aldo Pellegrini.
10. See John King, *Sur: a Study of the Argentine Literary Journal and its Role in the Development of a Culture, 1931–1970* (Cambridge: Cambridge University Press, 1986).
11. Oliverio Girondo, *Veinte poemas para ser leídos en el tranvía*, in *Obras Completas* (Buenos Aires: Losada, 1990, 2nd ed.); Raúl González Tuñón, *El violín del diablo* (Buenos Aires: Gleizer, 1926) and *Miércoles de ceniza* (Buenos Aires: Gleizer, 1928); Jorge Luis Borges, *Poemas (1922–1943)* (Buenos Aires: Losada, 1943); Roberto Arlt, *El juguete rabioso*, *Los siete locos*, *Los lanzallamas*, and *El amor brujo*, in *Obras completas* (Buenos Aires: Carlos Lohlé, 1981).

CROSS-CULTURAL DIALOGISMS

Race and Multiculturalism in Brazilian Cinema

ROBERT STAM

Editors' Introduction

Beatriz Sarlo's analysis of the cultural blendings characteristic of Buenos Aires in the 20s is curiously echoed, in a different context, in the essay by Robert Stam that follows. Like Sarlo's detailed cultural history, his call for a *multi*cultural, comparative understanding of the cultures and cinemas of the Americas and the Caribbean stresses precisely the need to reorganise standard critical categories such as high/low art, popular/élite culture, and centre/periphery. Stam's essay is, however, broader in scope. First of all, his stress on the need for pan-American and cross-cultural analyses is coupled with a rejection of canonical periodisations that cut off each nation's (and the continent's) cinematic and cultural past from discussions of post-60s cinemas. Furthermore, these arguments are the foundation upon which Stam develops a dialogic analysis of representations of race and ethnicity. Drawing on the work of Mikhail Bakhtin, he juxtaposes 'constellations of representational practices' of race and ethnicity in the USA and Brazil, making them 'susceptible to what Bakhtin calls "mutual illumination"'. How does the juxtaposition of the histories and cultures of each nation help us understand the place of race and ethnicity in the cinema? For example, how does our understanding of race and ethnicity change when we compare the treatment of indigenous people in Brazil as opposed to the US Western in relation to the representation of blacks in both nations? Stam's analysis discloses a series of analogies and disanalogies that, grounded in each nation's cultural, political, and economic history, enrich our understanding of both. This essay presents us with a potential working model for dialogic, 'mutually illuminating' discussions of the cinema of the Americas.

☐

The year of the quincentenary of what is euphemistically called Columbus's 'encounter' with the 'New World', 1992, provides an ideal conjuncture to

175

reflect on the representations of the racial and ethnic situation generated by the conquest, and on the commonalities and differences among the diverse societies of the Americas. The question of ethnic and racial representation in the cinema, I would argue, can be profitably studied in the larger context of the racial ideologies and cinematic representations offered by the other racially plural societies of the Americas, with their shared history of colonialism, conquest, slavery and immigration.

COMPARATIVE POLYPHONIES

Throughout the Americas and the Caribbean, we find variations on the same racial theme – the shifting relationships between the fundamental triad of indigenous 'reds', African 'blacks', and European 'whites'.[1] The nature of the mix may vary – in Mexico indigenous and European (with an admixture of black), in Jamaica and Haiti a black-dominated mix, in Brazil an indigenous–black–European *mélange* – but the fact of racial heterogeneity obtains almost everywhere, including the United States. One of the consequences of Eurocentrism, however, is that Americans tend to look to Europe for self-definition rather than to the multiracial societies of their own hemisphere. While Latin Americans know their continent to be *mestizo*, many Americans have been slow to recognize that its culture is also *mestizo*, mixed, hybrid. While the syncretic nature of other societies is 'visible', the syncretic nature of one's own society remains hidden.

While the American vision of national identity has generally been premised on an unstated yet none the less normative 'whiteness', the Latin American and Caribbean discussion of national identity – for thinkers such as Justo Sierra, José Vasconcelos, Carlos Fuentes and Octavio Paz in Mexico, for Edouard Glissant and Aimé Césaire in the Caribbean, and for Mario de Andrade, Paulo Prado and Gilberto Freyre in Brazil – has generally been premised on racial multiplicity. While the American national character has been explained as a function of the puritanical religious character of the country's founders (Perry Miller), or of the impact of the frontier experience on the national personality (Frederick Jackson Turner, R. B. Lewis), or of the shaping power of egalitarian political institutions (de Toqueville), theorists of national identity have tended to downplay its specifically racial dimension.

Latin American intellectuals, in contrast, have tended, at least since the beginning of the last century, to conceive national identity in racially plural terms. I am not suggesting that Latin American theorists were less racist (indeed, many excoriated racial mixing as a source of 'inferiority' and 'degeneracy'), only that they were more conscious of the primordial role of racial determinants informing national character. The Brazilian poet Olavo Bilac in the 20s saw Brazilian art as the 'loving flower of three sad races', while anthropologist Gilberto Freyre in the 30s saw Brazil's racial diversity as the key to its creativity and originality.[2] What Freyre was fond of calling a 'New World in the Tropics' was for him made possible by the cultural fusion of three genetically equal races, the Portuguese, the Indian and the African, each of which made an invaluable contribution (even if Freyre tended to romanticize slavery and 'folklorize' the black and indigenous contributions).

Brazilian film-maker Joaquim Pedro de Andrade's planned adaptation of Freyre's *Casa Grande e Senzala*, never finished because of the director's untimely death, would have dramatically staged (and critically updated) Freyre's theories.[3] An examination of the script reveals that the film would have orchestrated a kind of polyphonic encounter of Brazil's various source cultures, offering diverse racial perspectives – indigenous, Afro–Brazilian, Portuguese – on the national experience. There was to be a place for indigenous resistance (warfare and anthropophagy)[4], black resistance (the film refers to the *quilombos* or fugitive slave republics) and even for Sephardic Jews fleeing the inquisition.

A cross-cultural dialogical approach makes entire cultures and film traditions susceptible to what Bakhtin calls 'mutual illumination'. (The metaphor of *mutual* illumination assumes that the 'light' is generated from both sides of the cultural divide; it is not a question of a unilateral Promethean flame.) As a vast New World country, similar to the United States in both historical formation and ethnic diversity, Brazil constitutes a kind of southern twin whose strong affinities have been obscured by Eurocentric assumptions. Both countries began as European colonies, one of Portugal, the other of Great Britain. In both, colonization was followed by the conquest of vast territories and the near-genocidal subjugation of indigenous peoples. In the United States, the conquerors were called pioneers; in Brazil they were called *bandeirantes* (flag-bearers). Both countries massively imported blacks from Africa to form the two largest slave societies of modern times, until slavery was abolished with the Emancipation Proclamation of 1863 in the United States and the 'Golden Law' of 1888 in Brazil. Both countries received waves of immigration, often the same waves of immigration, from all over the world, ultimately forming pluri-ethnic societies with substantial Indian, black, Italian, German, Japanese, Slavic, Arab and Jewish communities.

Comparative analysis stresses the analogies not only within specific national film traditions, such as analogies between the representation of African–Americans and Native Americans within Hollywood cinema, for example, but also the analogies and disanalogies between the representations of both groups in relation to their representation within the other multi-ethnic film cultures of the Americas. Such a comparative approach juxtaposes whole constellations of representational practices. It is revelatory, for example, to compare the cinematic treatment of the indigenous peoples in Brazil as opposed to the United States, and the relation of that treatment to the representation of blacks. While blacks were a frequently (if much abused) presence in North American silent cinema, they form a kind of 'structuring absence' within silent Brazilian cinema, the exceptions being an adaptation of *Uncle Tom's Cabin* (1910), of Azevedo's *Mulato* (1917), and of *A Escrava Isaura* (The Slave Isaura, 1919). The film histories of both countries feature scores of silent films, on the other hand, devoted to the 'Native American' or the 'Native Brazilian'. Both cinemas offer numerous adaptations of nineteenth-century 'Indianist' novels, for example of José de Alencar's *Iracema* in Brazil, or of James Fenimore Cooper's *The Last of the Mohicans* in the United States. (In Brazil, there were four filmic adaptations of *O Guaraní* and three of *Iracema* in the silent period alone). The tradition of 'Indianist' works, in a broader sense, continues up to the present in both countries, as is evidenced by Guerra's *Quarup* (1989) in Brazil and Costner's *Dances with Wolves* (1990) in the United States.[5]

Brazilian cinema, however, lacks the Western's racist depiction of Native Americans as dangerous war-whooping savages; there is no 'imagery of encirclement' (Tom Engelhardt) pitting threatened whites against screaming hordes.[6] Instead, the early Brazilian films recapitulate the values of the romantic 'Indianist' movement whereby the indigenous populace is portrayed as healthy, pure and heroic, a nostalgic exemplar of a vanished golden age. The Brazilian films celebrate the '*bravo guerreiro*' (brave warrior). The myths purveyed in these works, moreover, are myths of racial syncretism and fusion. They constitute what Doris Sommer calls 'foundational fictions', in which 'star-crossed lovers . . . represent particular regions, races, parties, or economic interests which should naturally come together'.[7] Like the 'Indianist' novelists, the film-makers saw Brazil as the product of the fusion of the indigenous peoples with the European element into a new entity called 'the Brazilian', a fusion figured forth in the marriage of the Indian Iracema and the Frenchman Martins in *Iracema*, or the love of the indigenous Peri and the European Ceci in the same novelist's *O Guaraní*. *O Guaraní* concludes with the symbolic merging of two rivers, a figure for the melding of the indigenous peoples with those of Europe. American novelistic and filmic treatments of the Native American, in contrast, are more likely to emphasize the doomed nature of love between European and Native American. The idea of racial miscegenation, then, is celebrated, if ambiguously, in Brazilian culture, while the very idea of miscegenation has tended to generate fear and paranoia in the United States, a paranoia encapsulated in an intertitle from William S. Hart's 1916 film *The Aryan*: 'Oft written in letters of blood, deep carved in the face of destiny, that all men may read, runs the code of the Aryan race: our women shall be guarded.'[8]

But this difference in the representation of racial relations does not, ultimately, indicate that Brazilian cinema is more 'progressive' toward the Native Brazilian. First, the celebration, in Brazilian films, of the Indian as 'brave warrior', the spiritual source and symbol of Brazil's nationhood, the mark of its difference from Europe, involved an element of bad faith toward Indians themselves. Since the behavior of white Europeans, in Brazil as in the United States, was fundamentally murderous, this exaltation of the disappearing Indian, dedicated as it was to the very group being victimized by literal and cultural genocide, involved a strong element of hypocrisy. Second, the ambiguous 'compliment' to the Indians was a means of avoiding the vexed question of blacks and slavery. The proud history of black rebellion in Brazil was ignored; the brave Indian, it was subtly insinuated, resisted slavery, while blacks did not. The white literary and film-making élite in Brazil, in sum, chose the safely distant and mythically connoted Indian, symbol of the national difference from the detested Portuguese, over the more problematically present black, victim of a slavery abolished just a decade before the inauguration of the cinema in Brazil.

A third intermediate group, European immigrants, also enters into this complex and shifting set of relationships. In both Brazil and the United

178

States the cinema was profoundly inflected by the presence of immigrants, largely Italian in the case of Brazil and largely European Jewish in the case of the United States.[9] In Brazil this relationship meant that, while immigrants were not responsible for the institution of slavery, and while they were often themselves the objects of exploitation by the Portuguese-based élite, collectively they were the winners, and blacks the losers, of this period of Brazilian history. Immigrant film-makers, as a consequence, were not likely to filmically explore the oppressive situation of the very group that they themselves had economically displaced. (This displacement was quite literal, since the Brazilian élite consciously opted to recruit European immigrants as workers rather than employ the newly freed slaves.)[10] In the United States, in contrast, the wave of immigration that contributed to the formation of Hollywood cinema came many decades after the abolition of slavery, not just one decade later as in Brazil. Blacks, furthermore, were numerically a clear minority in the United Sates, rather than the marginalized majority as in Brazil. That the Hollywood immigrants were Jewish, furthermore, a group which was not simply European but also the victim of Europe, its 'internal others', in Todorov's apt phrase, meant that there operated a complex play of analogy and identification between Jews and blacks – seen in the black identification with the images and myths of the Hebrew Bible, and in the Jewish appropriation of black voices and musicality (Gershwin, Jolson) – an intricate dynamic of identification and appropriation more or less absent from the relation between Italian immigrants and blacks in Brazil. While some American films have thematized the black/Jewish encounter (from *The Jazz Singer* through *Angel Levine* to *Mo' Better Blues*) virtually no Brazilian films have focalized the black/Italian relationship. Tizuka Yamasaki's *Gaijin* posits a broad communality of interest between blacks and immigrants (be they Italian, Japanese or Spanish), but no specific ethnic dialogue structures the film. (Few Brazilian films, by the same token, focalize the black/Jewish relationship, although Carlos Diegues's *Quilombo*, as we shall see, constitutes a partial exception in this regard.)

THE MULTIRACIAL PROTAGONIST

A comparative approach also turns up surprising affinities and parallels between specific films. Both the Brazilian film *Macunaíma* (1969) and Woody Allen's parody documentary *Zelig* (1983), for example, feature multiracial protagonists. *Macunaíma*, an adaptation and updating of Mario de Andrade's classic modernist novel (1928), concerns the racial and social transformations of a Brazilian anti-hero, while *Zelig* revolves around a chameleon man's uncanny ability to take on the ethnicity of his interlocutors. The protagonists of both films undergo racial metamorphoses. Born white and Jewish, Zelig subsequently becomes Indian, black, Irish, Italian, Mexican and Chinese. Macunaíma is born Indian and black, but subsequently transforms himself into a white Portuguese prince and even into a French divorcée. These metamorphoses are diversely handled in cinematic terms, of course: *Macunaíma* relies on the use of two actors and 'magical' editing substitutions, while *Zelig* deploys a rich panoply of devices such as make-up, manipulated photographs, ironic 'anchorage', and trick cinematography. The theme, in any case, is the same. Both Macunaíma and Zelig are oxymoronic protagonists, larger-than-life composite characters who epitomize ethnic interaction and hybridization. Macunaíma, the 'hero without any character', as the novel's subtitle has it, lacks character not only in the conventional moral sense but also in that he is ethnically plural, simultaneously black, Indian and white European. Zelig too might be called a 'hero without any character', again both in a personal and in an ethnic sense. Both protagonists demonstrate the potentialities of chameleonism; both 'try on' ethnic selves like the carnival revellers evoked in Mario de Andrade's poem 'Carnival in Rio', who move from one identity to another simply by changing costume.

Both the novel and the film *Macunaíma* play on the same ethnic triad of 'red', 'black' and 'white'. In the first sequence, an improbably old white woman (actually a man in drag) stands and grunts until she/he deposits a wailing 50-year-old black 'baby' on the ground. The names of the family members – Macunaíma, Jigue, Manaape – are Indian, but the family is at once black, Indian and European. Both protagonists personify the cultural 'heteroglossia' or 'many-languagedness' of the cultures from which they emerge. They resemble their cities, New York and São Paulo, which are like them the sites of constant metamorphosis, maelstroms of perpetual tension, disintegration, assimilation, and renewal. Roughly equivalent in population, New York and São Paulo share common features in terms both of historical origins and present-day ethnic composition. In both cities indigenous populations preceded the European arrival, and in both cases the indigenous

Brazil's most distinguished black actor Grande Otelo as the child trickster Macunaíma in Macunaíma *(Joaquim Pedro de Andrade, Brazil, 1968)*

180

presence left traces in place names: Manhattan and Montauk in New York, Ipiranga and Pacaembu in São Paulo. The Brazilian city was founded on the site of an Indian village in 1554; its founder, Padre José de Anchieta, was versed in the local Indian idioms and even wrote a grammar and a dictionary of the Tupi language. New York was presumably 'purchased' from its indigenous inhabitants some 74 years later, although the indigenous tradition of communually-held territory makes it unlikely that they thought of themselves as 'selling' the land.

Historian Warren Dean points out that the historical destinies of New York and Brazil were linked from the beginning. In the 17th century, Dutch settlers brought Afro–Brazilian slaves with them from Brazil to what was then called New Amsterdam, and even granted them a measure of freedom in order to make them allies in the fight against the British.[11] The first Jews to arrive in New York were Sephardim who came from Recife, Brazil, in 1636 and founded the synagogue which still stands on West 70th Street in Manhattan. In the 19th and 20th centuries, New York and São Paulo received some of the same waves of immigrants from the same countries: Germans, Italians, Jews from Poland and Russia, Arabs from Lebanon and Syria, Chinese, Japanese and so forth. Both also received 'internal immigrants' such as blacks from the South, in the case of New York, and blacks from Bahia and Minas, in the case of São Paulo. Both cities have their Italian neighborhoods (Little Italy in New York, Brás and Bexiga in São Paulo), their turn-of-the-century Jewish communities (the lower east side in New York, Bom Retiro in São Paulo), and their Asiatic communities (Chinatown in New York and the Japanese district called 'Liberdade' in São Paulo).

In a description that might equally apply to New York, Mario de Andrade speaks in a 1929 letter of what he calls one of the 'most human aspects' of São Paulo: the sight of its diverse ethnic groups mingling in the street on a Saturday night. 'I feel happy,' he tells us, 'among all the Hungarians, the Czechs, the Bulgarians, the Syrians, the Austrians and the north-easterners who go out to have a good time.' It is a significant coincidence, perhaps, that both Mario de Andrade and Mikhail Bakhtin were elaborating theories of artistic 'polyphony' in the 20s. For Bakhtin, polyphony refers to the co-existence, in any textual or extra-textual situation, of a plurality of voices which do not fuse into a single consciousness but rather generate dialogical dynamism among themselves.[12] De Andrade, for his part, defined polyphony as the 'simultaneous artistic union of two or more melodies whose temporary effects of sonorous conflict collaborate to create a total final effect', a definition in some ways not terribly distant from Bakhtin's.[13] Although neither author was thinking specifically of a polyphony of ethnic voices per se, an ethnic interpretation is in no way excluded by the term.[14] Mario de Andrade, significantly, was himself of mixed race; he somatically embodied the indigenous, African and European inheritance, and multiplicity of identity was one of the leitmotifs of his work. Echoing Walt Whitman, Mario proclaimed that he contained multitudes: 'I am three hundred, three hundred and fifty.'[15] His identity was 'harlequinate', simultaneously red, black and white, but also French, through his schooling, and Italian, because of his love of music.[16] The concept of multiple and simultaneous racial identities, at once personal and national, then, made it possible for Mario de Andrade to imagine the self as a polyphony of racial and cultural identities.

TWO CINEMAS OF SLAVERY

While historians such as Eugene Genovese, Stanley Elkins and Frank Tannebaum have seen the necessity of understanding the history of slavery within a comparative perspective, and while black theorists like Paul Gilroy have insisted on an 'Atlanticist' and 'diasporic' perspective, historians of the cinema have rarely thought in such broad transcultural terms. Historians have pointed out that slavery in Brazil and the United States was hardly identical.[17] First, in Brazil, slavery existed across the entire national territory, while in the United States slavery existed only in the South, although it clearly implicated the entire national territory. Second, while the United States abolished slavery with a swift legislative stroke in 1863, Brazil abolished the institution only gradually, first freeing children born of slaves in 1871, then freeing slaves over 60 years of age (in 1885) before unconditional abolition in 1888. As a result there were a large number of free blacks whose status, both before and after abolition, was not very different from that of lower-class whites. Thus a film like *Chico Rei* (1982) can treat a historical freed black entrepreneur in 18th-century Minas Gerais, while *Xica da Silva* (1976) can explore the historical case of a black woman who became a kind of power behind the throne through her liaison with a Portuguese politician. Third, racial classification in Brazil as early as the 19th century was pluralistic, involving not an epidermic black–white dichotomy based on ascendancy, but rather a subtle (if none the less racist) schema involving a complex interplay of color, facial features, and social status. Fourth, in ideological terms, Brazilians rejected what they saw as a retrograde segregationist racism in favor of a paternalistic 'ideology of whitening' which 'allowed' a decidedly mixed population to gradually 'cleanse' itself through intermarriage. Faith in the likelihood of whitening, in other words, led Brazilian élites to encourage miscegenation, rather than proscribe it in the phobic American manner. Fifth, mixed-race Brazilians, meanwhile, were encouraged to take advantage of what Carl Degler calls the 'mulatto escape hatch', to abandon their darker brothers and sisters in the name of their own social ascension.[18] Sixth, while American racial segregation ironically favored the development of parallel institutions – the black Church, an independent black press, sports organizations – the Brazilian situation encouraged a paternalistic dependency on élite (that is to say white) institutions. On the other hand, while African–Americans largely adopted the Christian religion (even if read in a subversive and millenarian manner), Afro–Brazilians managed to maintain purely African religions such as *candomblé* (the subject of films such as *Barravento* (1962) and *A Força de Xangô* (1979)), or develop syncretic religions such as *umbanda* (the subject of *Amuleto de Ogum* (1975) and *A Prova de Fogo* (1981)).

An important demographic difference distinguishes American from Brazilian racial patterns. While blacks in the United States have always formed a minority both in terms of numbers and in terms of power, black and mulatto Brazilians form part of a marginalized majority of Brazilian citizens. It is a Eurocentric misnomer, Abdias de Nascimento points out, to call Brazil a

'Latin' country; it might better be called an Amerindian, Afro–Iberian country. The very definition of blackness, furthermore, is quite different in the two countries. The American vision inclines towards binarism: a person is either black or white, there is no intermediate position. Even partial African ancestry defines a person as black. (The sexual exploitation of black women in America led to a huge population of persons of mixed ancestry, and thus to Byzantine racial classifications, in the post-bellum period, involving quadroons, octoroons and so forth.) The 1980 Brazilian census, in contrast, lists four basic racial groups: *brancos* (whites, forming 54.9 per cent of the population); *pardos* (browns, mulattoes, 38.6 per cent); *pretos* (black, 5.9 per cent) and *amarelos* (yellows, asiatics, 0.67 per cent).[19] The combined figures for blacks and mulattoes give us a total of 45 per cent of people who would be considered black within an American spectrum – a conservative number, given the Brazilian tendency to 'whiten' one's self-definition. The Brazilian system, then, is less concerned with ancestry than the American: its racial spectrum nuances shade from *preto retinto* (dark black) through *escuro* (dark) and *mulato escuro* (dark mulatto) to *mulato claro* (light mulatto, *moreno* and *branco de Bahia* (Bahia-style white). These differences in racial perception are linked to the distinct modalities of Brazilian racism, which consists less in a binary, supremacist white-over-black than in the superimposition of an official integrationist ideology ('racial democracy') on a power structure that subtly enforces and promotes the idea that 'white' is 'better'. Rather than a strident racism, Brazil's white élite favors a kind of 'cordial' paternalism which is in some ways even more difficult to 'name' and thus to combat.

In both Brazilian and US society, the dumb historical inertia of slavery structures current oppression. In Brazil, the structural mechanisms of the Brazilian social formation largely deprive blacks of economic, social, and political power. Blacks are vastly under-represented in positions of prestige and projection; they are virtually non-existent in the higher echelons of the military, the diplomatic corps, and the government. There were only a dozen black representatives, out of 559, to the 1990 Constitutional Assembly, and among those few were some who did not identify with black causes. Roughly 40 per cent of the non-white population is illiterate, while white illiteracy rates are 20 per cent. Only 1 per cent of black Brazilians define themselves as *patrões* (bosses, owners) while 79 per cent of whites so define themselves.[20] While under-represented in the universities and the diplomatic corps, blacks are over-represented in the *favelas* (shanty towns or slums), the prisons, and in the ranks of the unemployed. Two documentaries by Afro–Brazilian directors register the oppression of blacks in Brazil. Zozimo Balbul's *Abolicão* (*Abolition*, 1988) exposes the limits of 'racial democracy' a century after the abolition of slavery, and Silvana Afram's *Mulheres Negras* (*Black Women of Brazil*, 1986) examines the ways that black Brazilian women have coped with both racism and sexism while exploring collective identity through African-derived religion and music.

Blacks are also under-represented in the mass-media, especially in television and in advertising.[21] In terms of the cinema, blacks have had only a minimal role in scripting, directing and producing Brazilian films. While there are many black actors and actresses (Grande Otelo, Tony Tornado,

Milton Gonçalves, Zezé Motta, Antônio Sampaio), there are only a handful of black directors (Haroldo Costa, Antônio Pitanga, Waldyr Onofre, Odilon Lopes, Zozimo Balbul) and few of them have managed to make second features. Their films, furthermore, unlike those of Spike Lee, Charles Burnett and Julie Dash in the United States, do not necessarily foreground racial themes.

Certain features of Brazilian life and society give a superficially humane face to what remains, in structural terms, a racist society. Brazilian history since abolition has not been marked, for example, by the virulent racism of the Ku Klux Klan. Unlike the United States and South Africa, there is no tradition of ghettoes or racial segregation, nor has there been a history of racially-motivated lynching or murder. Brazilian film history features no white supremacist films like *Birth of a Nation*. (On the other hand, it also features no independent black producer/directors like Oscar Micheaux or Spencer Williams, no *Do the Right Thing* or *Sweet Sweetback's Baadasssss Song*.) Because of the wide racial mixing, partially as a result of slave-owner rape of slave-women, but also as a result of voluntary unions going back to the earliest periods of Brazilian history, Brazil is a deeply *mestizo* country. Unlike the United States of slavery days, where white exploitation of black women was masked by a neurotic obsession with racial purity and a hypocritical phobia about sexual mixing, in Brazil no special onus has been attached to interracial sex or marriage. The carnivalesque festivities which greet the sexual liaison of the ex-slave Xica and the powerful Portuguese official on the Minas diamond frontier in *Xica da Silva* would be quite simply unthinkable in an American context. Indeed, the legendary power which Xica temporarily gathered in eighteenth-century Brazil would be inconceivable in the United States of the same period.

The causal relation between oppression and skin color is also obscured in Brazil by the lack of apparent racial tension and by the fact that blacks and mulattoes often share similar living conditions with many lower-class whites and near-white *mestizos*. This sharing of life conditions means that many blacks and whites occupy similar positions in the class structure. (Poverty is also at times shared by blacks and poor whites in the United States, but in a situation of segregation where divisions have been exploited by the power structure.) This neighboring of blacks, mulattoes and poor whites also implies a wide range of social intercourse between the two groups – evidenced in films such as *Rio 40°* (1954) or *Cinco Vezes Favela* (*Five Times Favela*, 1962) or even *Pixote* (1980) – ranging from friendly and superficial contacts on the job and in racially mixed neighborhoods to more intimate friendships and marriages. Nevertheless, the fact that Brazilian capitalism oppresses poor whites as well as blacks does not mean that this oppression is not also racial. Race, in this sense, is both a kind of salt rubbed into the wounds of class, and a wound in itself. A 1962 film, *Assalto ao Trem Pagador* (*Attack on the Pay Train*, 1962), a film about a multiracial gang of thieves, insists on this point by having a white member of the band tell a black member that he, the black, will never be able to spend his stolen loot since everyone would be suspicious of a black man with money. In a scene somewhat exceptional for its naked racial hostility, the white tells the black: 'I'm the one who looks like a guy

The dominant colonial order about to be turned upside down. Xica da Silva (*Carlos Diegues, Brazil, 1976*)

with money, not you. I have blond hair and blue eyes, while you – look like a monkey!' The black then shoots him and orders the other gang members to throw him in the river, so 'the fish can feed on his blue eyes'.

Many of the questions pursued in this essay have to do with the representation of the racial history of Brazil. To what extent are historical events in which 'the subaltern' played a major role portrayed on the screen? Which events are omitted or distorted? How are the films inflected by contemporaneous debates among historians, sociologists and anthropologists? In the United States, at least until the 40s, blacks were generally depicted in American films within the context of the southern plantation tradition, usually as subservient types such as faithful servants or comic slave figures. These films often presented southern plantations as idyllic places peopled by charming aristocrats and contented slaves. The ante-bellum South was idealized in films such as *Birth of a Nation* (1915), *The Littlest Rebel* (1935) and *Gone with the Wind* (1939). Brazilian films almost never idealize slavery. Such an idealization was rendered unlikely both by the fact of the high proportion of black and mulatto citizens and the relatively recent abolition of slavery, with the result that the Brazilian industry could not have 'gotten away with' such a representation even if it had wanted to. Films such as Tom Payne/Oswaldo Sampaio's *Sinhá Moça* (1953), a costume drama set around the time of abolition, show the institution of slavery as morally repugnant and even provide glimpses of black anger and concrete rebellion (flight from slavery, mass escapes, arson, people's trial of a slave-driver), something that would

185

have been quite inconceivable in a Hollywood film of the same period. The revolt in the film, interestingly, comes not from the blacks in the 'Big House' (who need to have abolition explained to them by whites!) but from the field laborers from the *senzala* (slave quarters).

Like *Gone with the Wind*, *Sinhá Moça* is based on a sentimental novel by a woman (Maria Dezonne Pacheco Fernandes), but while *Gone with the Wind* is about how the Civil War brought tragedy to the South, *Sinhá Moça* concerns the happiness brought to Brazilians by the abolition of slavery as the result of struggle by both blacks and whites. The credits of *Sinhá Moça* are superimposed, significantly, on shots of a slave on the run; thus the spectator is immediately confronted with black hostility to slavery. *Gone with the Wind*, in contrast, offers images of slaves who seem reconciled to their condition and even somewhat anxious about the outside threat to tranquility. The blacks pray for Confederate victory and cheerlead as the Confederate troops parade and march off to fight in the defense of 'the spirit of the south' and indirectly for the perpetuation of human bondage. *Sinhá Moça*, for its part, suggests a parallel between the heroine's personal revolt against what we now call patriarchy and the black and white abolitionist struggle against slavery. Unfortunately, the film systematically privileges its white stars (as is obvious from a look at the publicity stills) and idealizes the abolitionist movement. Unlike the Cuban film *El otro Francisco* (*The Other Francisco*), *Sinhá Moça* elides the economic forces and motivations shaping the abolitionist movement.[22]

CELEBRATING BLACK INSURRECTION

The history of both the United States and Brazil was marked by incandescent moments of black rebellion: Nat Turner, Denmark Vesey, Harriet Tubman in the United States; Palmares, the Hausa revolt, and the Sabinada of Bahia in Brazil. Mainstream American cinema, if one excepts the TV series *Roots* and Herbert Biberman's film *Slaves* (1969), has rarely touched this theme. Brazilian cinema has done considerably more with this tradition, partially because the revolts were more frequent and more significant and partially because a multiracial audience was more ready to hear about them. *Sinhá Moça*, as we have seen, treats the historical collaboration between abolitionists and rebel slaves. Oswaldo Sampaio's *A Marcha* (*The March*, 1977) features the soccer star Pelé as a black freedman who liberates slaves on the eve of abolition. Two films, Carlos Diegues's *Ganga Zumba* (1963) and *Quilombo* (1984), memorialize the 17th-century fugitive slave republic Palmares, a republic which lasted almost a century in the face of repeated assaults from both the Dutch and the Portuguese. At its height, Palmares counted 20,000 inhabitants spread over numerous villages in the north-eastern interior, covering an area roughly one-third the size of Portugal. Palmares bears witness not only to the capacity of Afro–Brazilians to revolt against slavery but also to mobilize an alternative life. Economically self-sufficient, Palmares practiced the diversified agriculture the slaves remembered from Africa rather than the monoculture characteristic of colonial Brazil, planting corn, beans, manioc, potatoes and sugar cane on communally shared land (as had been the pattern in much of Africa). There kings were kings in the

186

African rather than the European sense, not absolute monarchs but rather custodians of the common wealth. Although the penal code, especially in the later period, was harsh, the Palmarinos enjoyed basic civic and political equality. Along with the black majority, Palmares welcomed Indians, *mestiços* and renegade whites, ultimately becoming a refuge for the persecuted of Brazilian society.

Based on a historical novel by João Felício dos Santos, *Ganga Zumba* (1963) focuses on a black slave who discovers that he is the grandson of the king of Palmares. The film's portrait of slavery highlights forced labor, cruel slave-drivers, whippings, rape and murder, undercutting the idealized tableau of a benign Lusitanian servitude portrayed by some of the more euphoric historians. *Ganga Zumba* assumes a black perspective throughout, showing blacks not as mere victims but as active agents. A Fanonian ode to insurrectional violence, the film applauds the slaves' gesture as necessary and even laudatory. One scene, in which a male slave has his lover entice a slave-driver so they can kill him, would have been quite simply unthinkable in an equivalent Hollywood film of the period.

In *Quilombo* (1984), Diegues returns to the same theme, taking advantage of a bigger budget as well as of recent historical research by Décio Freitas.[23] Here Diegues pays homage to a historical act of the black political imagination, an ode to what the director calls the 'first truly democratic society in the western hemisphere'. The narrative of *Quilombo* sweeps over a historical period from 1650 to 1695, moving through three distinct phases. In the first, a group of slaves, led by Ganga Zumba, flees from a sugar plantation and makes its way to Palmares. In the second phase, Palmares, under Ganga Zumba, has become a prosperous and independent community. In the third phase, another leader, Zumbi, is forced to lead the struggle in an atmosphere dominated by internal tensions and external aggressions. The Palmarinos are ultimately massacred and Zumbi himself is killed, but outbreaks of resistance, as the final intertitles inform us, go on for another century. The overall movement of the film, then, is from spontaneous revolt to the construction of a community, to the violent destruction of that community, and a final coda pointing to continuing struggle.

Quilombo's fascinating gallery of characters includes Ganga Zumba (Toni Tornado), the African prince who leads the slaves out of bondage into the promised land of Palmares; Acotirene, a symbolic figure associated with African strength and spirituality; Dandara (Zezé Motta), associated with the African spirit Iansa, whose performance of religious rituals saves Ganga Zumba. The Jewish immigrant Samuel (Jonas Bloch), meanwhile, represents the many Jews and *marranos* who fled the Inquisition and took refuge in Brazil; his dialogue in the film brings to the flight of the slaves Biblical echoes of the Exodus, the parting of the Red Sea and the Promised Land. The film valorizes black culture by associating its characters with the *orixás* of *candomblé*: Ganga Zumba is linked to Xangô; Zumbi to Ogum (the *orixá* of metal, agriculture and war). At one point, a venerable slave refuses last rites in Latin and insists on singing in Yoruba. After his death, Ganga Zumba appears magically with Xangô's axe in hand. Thus Diegues foregrounds the symbolic value of African culture, while also insisting on the need for struggle.

A didactic saga based on fact, legend, and imaginative extrapolation, *Quilombo* is part historical reconstruction and part musical, one partially drawing its style from the carnival pageants of Rio's 'samba schools', whose spectacles also involve the fanciful re-creation of historic events. Diegues aims at poetic synthesis rather than naturalistic reproduction, constructing a 'historical hypothesis, anthropologically plausible but above all *poetically* correct'. The challenge of conveying the historical grandeur of Palmares while retaining a sense of magic and surreality is not, unfortunately, always successfully met. The ritual costumes, the turbans, body paint and hairstyles, along with the quasi-theatrical lighting, at times suggest a kind of Afro–Brazilian Disneyworld. At its best moments, however, the film, with the help of Gilberto Gil's indispensible soundtrack music (electronic Afro-derived samba-rock) not only evokes a historical Utopia but also communicates a sense of what that Utopia might have felt like.

In its affirmation of Afro–Brazilian culture, *Quilombo* reflects a broader tendency within Brazilian cinema. While the Cinema Novo directors tended to see Afro–Brazilian culture (and especially Afro–Brazilian religion) as alienated and marginal, the 70s and 80s films tend to see blackness as the vital source of the powerful originality of Brazilian culture as a whole. In their celebration of black rebellion, they continue the tradition of Lambertini's docu-fiction *A Vida do Cabo João Cândido (The Life of Commander João Cândido*, 1910), which celebrated the historical episode known as 'A Revolta do Chibata' (The Revolt of the Whip), in which the black sailor João Cândido led a multiracial revolt against corporal punishment in the Brazilian navy. (Lambertini's film was the first to receive the ambiguous compliment of official censorship.) The 70s and 80s films celebrate a variety of black historical heroes and heroines. Walter Lima Jr's *Chico Rei* (1982) presents a slave protagonist who buys his freedom through his work in the mines, and then purchases the freedom of all those who work with him. The protagonist of *Xica da Silva*, while in many ways not a model heroine, is celebrated as an exslave who gained a kind of power through the only means available to her in 18th-century Brazil – sexual prowess and cultural imagination. Nelson Pereira dos Santos's *Tenda dos Milagres (Tent of Miracles*, 1976), meanwhile, celebrates a turn-of-the-century black culture hero Pedro Arcanjo, a composite figure based on a number of self-taught black intellectuals from Bahia who defended the Afro–Brazilian cultural inheritance against racist theoreticians and repressive police. Unfortunately, the film also advances the notion, common to Gilberto Freyre and Jorge Amado, of miscegenation as social panacea, through a generational progression from the black protagonist Pedro through his 'mulatto' son Tadeu and his white bride Lou, suggesting a parable of whitening as 'progress', an idea whose implicit racism has been denounced by progressive Brazilian intellectuals.

AN AGENDA FOR THE 90S

This essay has hardly exhausted the 'comparabilities' opened up by a cross-cultural, pan-American approach. My discussion has privileged Brazil and the United States, eliding other major cinematic traditions such as the Cuban, the Argentinian, the Canadian, the Chilean. I have not discussed the peculiarities of the Mexican situation, where national identity is traumatically rent, as Octavio Paz has pointed out, between pre-Conquest indigenous culture and the culture of the Conquistadores, a national trauma reflected in films such as *María Candelaria* (1943) and *Maclovia* (1948). We also need a comparative study of the ethnic and racial presence in the commercial entertainment traditions across the Americas. In both the United States and South America, for example, the advent of sound made possible the appropriation of Afro–American and Afro–Latin musicality. How might one compare the black presence (explicit or implicit) in the Hollywood musical as compared with the tango film in Argentina, the *chanchada* in Brazil, the cabaret film in Mexico and Cuba? (The first sound film from Latin America, *Tango* (1933), features a lone black women in a party sequence, in conditions that suggest a taken-for-granted non-discrimination.) Most Brazilian Hollywood-imitating *chanchadas* of the 30s and 40s foreground white stars, while relegating mixed-race musicians and dancers to the background, while black stars like Grande Otelo are generally featured only in subordinate comic roles.

One might also expand the study of the 'cinemas of slavery' by including Cuban films about black resistance – for example, Sergio Giral's *El otro Francisco* (*The Other Francisco*, 1974), *Maluala* (1979) and *Plácido* (1986) and Alea's *La ultima cena* (*The Last Supper*, 1976). One could also imagine a comparative study of the 'Amazon genre', which would analyze the films about the Amazon, from the Rondon Commission's documents of colonization in the teens of this century, to Lévi-Strauss's amateur films about Bororó rituals in the 30s, to the Brazilian animated cartoon *Amazon Symphony* (1953) through the recent explosion of fiction and documentary films about the Amazon (*The Green Wall, Fitzcarraldo, Mato Eles?, The Emerald Forest, Bye Bye Brazil, Iracema, Forbidden Dances* and *On the Playing Fields of the Lord*).[24]

Finally, in this period of reflection on the significance of the Columbus quincentenary, one might undertake a comparative study of the cinematic representation of 'discovery', conquest and resistance, especially privileging an indigenous perspective. How is indigenous resistance shown in films like the Cuban–Peruvian epic *Tupac Amaru* or in 'anthropophagic–modernist' films like *How Tasty was my Little Frenchman* (*Como era gostoso o meu francês*, 1971) with their 'cannibalist' critique of European colonialism? How is the European encounter with the indigenous peoples of the Americas portrayed in the Brazilian *Descobrimento do Brasil* (Discovery of Brazil, 1937), the German *Aguirre, Wrath of God* (1972), or more recently, the Venezuelan *Amerika; Terra Incógnita* (1987) and the Mexican *Barroco* (1988) and *Cabeza de Vaca* (1990)?

One of the most heartening recent developments is the emergence of films which relay a Native American perspective on the encounter between Europe and indigenous America, whether directed by Americans and Brazilians of European descent (Terry Turner, Andréa Tonacci, Sergio Bianchi, and even Kevin Costner) or by Native Americans such as Bob Hicks and George Burdeau in the United States or by the practitioners of 'indigenous media' in Brazil. Burdeau's *Surviving Columbus* (1990) recounts the first encounters between the Spanish and the Zuni Indians, giving pride of place to indigenous narratives and perspectives. In Bob Hicks's *Return of the Country* (1984) Euro–Americans suddenly find themselves in a situation where their language and culture are forbidden, where the courts, the congress, and the presidency are in indigenous hands. *Geronimo and the Apache Resistance* (1988) recounts the story of Geronimo through historical narration and through commentary by present-day members of the tribe. And in Brazil, the Kayapo people in the Amazon use video as a vehicle for resistance to domination, propagandizing internationally against the hydroelectric projects which would quite literally annihilate their culture.[25] My purpose here, in any case, has been to suggest the potentialities of a comparative, dialogical approach, which regards all the cultures and cinemas of the Americas as susceptible to 'mutual illumination', as deeply and mutually implicated in one another, economically, politically and culturally.

Notes

1. I place 'red', 'white' and 'black' in quotation marks because the identification of specific races with colors is ultimately a chromatic trope. Since racial categories are socially and historically constituted, I shall use Portuguese terms for the Brazilian context and English terms for the United States context.
2. The Olavo Bilac phrase is found in his *Poesias* (Rio de Janeiro: Alvez, 1964). The fundamental reference for Gilberto Freyre is *Casa Grande e Senzala*, published in English as *The Masters and the Slaves*, trans. Samuel Putnam (New York: Knopf, 1956).
3. I am grateful to Lula Buarque de Hollanda, who worked as a research coordinator on the project, for giving me a copy of the script of the proposed film.
4. 'Anthropophagy' refers to the presumably real cannibalistic practices of the indigenous Tupinamba peoples, who devoured their dead enemies in order to appropriate their force, and to the metaphorical extrapolation of these practices by the Brazilian modernists in the twenties, who call for cultural anthropophagy, a devouring of the techniques and information of the super-developed countries as part of a struggle against colonialist domination.
5. On the depiction of the 'Indian' in Hollywood see Edward Buscombe (ed), *The BFI Companion to the Western* (London: BFI/André Deutsch, 1988).
6. See Tom Engelhardt, 'Ambush at Kamikazi Pass', *Bulletin of Concerned Asian Scholars* (Winter–Spring, 1971), vol. III, no. 1.
7. See Doris Sommer, 'Irresistable Romance: The Foundational Fictions of Latin America', in Homi K. Bhabha (ed.), *Nation and Narration* (London: Routledge, 1990).
8. David Haberly argues that miscegenation was perceived as both blessing and curse by the Brazilian élite, who tended to project an 'Edenic metaphor' whereby Brazilians were driven from paradise by the 'sin' of mescegenation. See David T. Haberly, *Three Sad Races: Racial Identity and National Consciousness in Brazilian Literature* (Cambridge: Cambridge University Press, 1983).
9. The role of Jewish producers in Hollywood is the subject of Robert Sklar's *Movie-Made America: A Cultural History of American Movies* (New York: Random House, 1975) and Neal Gabler's *An Empire of Their Own: How the Jews Invented Hollywood* (New York: Anchor, 1989).
10. On the subject of the systematic substitution of European immigrants for the newly freed slaves, see Célia Maria Marinho de Azevedo, *Onda Negra/Medo Branco: O Negro no Imaginário das Elites Seculo XIX* (São Paulo: Paz e Terra, 1987).

11. See Warren Dean, 'O Village já Foi Brasileiro' (Greenwich Village was once Brazilian), *Folha de São Paulo* (13 May 1987).
12. For more on the Bakhtinian conception of 'polyphony', see Mikhail Bakhtin, *Problems of Dostoevsky's Poetics* (Minneapolis: University of Minnesota Press, 1984).
13. See Mario de Andrade, 'A Escrava que Não é Isaura', in *Obra Imatura* (São Paulo: Martins, 1944).
14. I further explore the analogies between São Paulo and New York, and between *Macunaíma* and *Zelig* in 'A Tale of Two Cities: Cultural Polyphony and Ethnic Transformation', *East–West Film Journal*, vol. III, no. 1 (December 1988).
15. See Mario de Andrade, *Poesias Completas* (São Paulo: Martins, 1972), pp. 203–4.
16. See Mario de Andrade, *Obra Imatura* (São Paulo: Martins, 1972), p. 266. For an excellent discussion of de Andrade's 'harlequinate' identity, see David Haberly, *Three Sad Races: Racial Identity and National Consciousness in Brazilian Literature* (Cambridge: Cambridge University Press, 1983). For a discussion of the racial question within Modernism, see Zita St Aubyn Nunes, *'Os Males do Brasil': Antropofagia e a Questão da Raça* (Rio: SIEC, 1989).
17. Some of the key texts in the comparative slavery debate are Frank Tannenbaum, *Slave and Citizen* (New York: Knopf, 1947); Stanley Elkins, *Slavery: A Problem in American Institutional and Intellectual Life* (Chicago: University of Chicago Press, 1968); Eugene D. Genovese, *The World the Slaveholders Made* (New York: Vintage, 1971) and *Roll, Jordan, Roll: The World the Slaves Made* (New York: Pantheon, 1974); and Herbert Gutman, *The Black Family in Slavery and Freedom* (New York: Pantheon, 1976).
18. See Carl N. Degler, *Neither Black Nor White: Slavery and Race Relations in Brazil and the United States* (Madison: University of Wisconsin Press, 1986).
19. Statistics cited in José Oscar Beozzo, *Situação do Negro na Sociedade Brasileira* (Petropolis: Vozes, 1984), pp. 563–4.
20. See 'Cem Anos, sen Quase Nada', *Veja* (20 April 1988).
21. See Zelbert Moore, 'Reflections on Blacks in Contemporary Brazilian Popular Culture in the 1980s', *Studies in Latin American Popular Culture*, vol. VII, (1988).
22. For analyses of Brazilian abolitionism, see Emilia Viotti da Costa, *Da Senzala a Colónia* (São Paulo: Diffusão Europeia, 1966), Robert Conrad, *Os Ultimos Anos da Escravatura no Brasil* (Rio: Civilização Brasileira, 1975). For black rebellion under slavery, see Clovis Moura, *Rebeliões da Senzala* (Rio: Conquista, 1972); João José Reis, *Rebelião Escrava no Brasil* (São Paulo: Brasiliense, 1986); María Helena P. T. Machado, *Crime e Escravidão* (São Paulo: Brasiliense, 1987); João José Reis and Eduardo Silva, *Negociação e Conflito* (São Paulo: Companhia das Letras, 1989); and Lana Lage da Gama Lima, *Rebeldia Negra e Abolicionismo* (Rio: Achiame, 1981).
23. See Décio Freitas, *Palmares: A Guerra dos Escravos* (Rio: Graal, 1974).
24. The Brazilian Cultural Organization of New York University (Catherine Benamou, Arlindo Castro, José Gatti, Marina Abs André) screened a number of these films as part of their multimedia presentation on the Amazon (26 March – 1 April 1990 in New York).
25. A number of films foreground the Kayapo use of media: *The Kayapo: Out of the Forest* (1989) and *Fight for the Forest* (1990).

ELDORADO AS HELL

*Cinema Novo and Post Cinema Novo – Appropriations of the
Imaginary of the Discovery*

ISMAIL XAVIER

Editors' Introduction

Long before the quincentenary, the conquest figured prominently in the
Latin American imaginary as a problematic, dystopian origin which enabled
contemporary nation states to emerge yet also eradicated the 'roots' upon
which these nations would attempt to base their identity. Ismail Xavier's
essay deals with the thematic re-emergence of the conquest as a migratory
process or dystopian journey in the Brazilian cinema of the 70s. While the
best-known studies of the Brazilian cinema have always linked the late
Cinema Novo films to the socio-political history of the nation, explaining
the appearance of a marked allegorical discourse after the 1964 coup and the
1968 coup-within-the-coup as a result of increased censorship and
repression, Xavier's analysis refuses this 'easy' explanation and explores the
complex symbolic negotiations that mark the intersection of historical forces
and cinematic practices.

Xavier, a professor of Cinema Studies at the Universidade de São Paulo
and prolific author and scholar, has already demonstrated the power of
subtle textual analyses in readings of Cinema Novo and Glauber Rocha (in
Sertão/Mar and various essays). Here, he evokes Octavio Paz and Eduardo
Galeano to exemplify the two markedly different approaches to the problem
of the historical explanation of 'national' culture in Latin America which
have echoed throughout the continent's cinemas. While Galeano's emphasis
on external economic exploitation reverberates throughout the films of the
early 60s (in Brazil and elsewhere), Xavier argues that Brazilian film-makers
began to look beyond the confrontation of national and foreign interests in
their search for appropriate historical explanations during a period of
accelerated traumatic change. The journey or migration is the central figure
of this new symbolic configuration, an echo of the dystopian originary force
of the conquest. Thus his essay traces the trajectory of the Brazilian cinema
as it rewrote the history of the nation as a succession of disasters, journeys,
and failed encounters by allegorising historical time spatially.

□

Latin America is a continent of nation states that emerged as the result of a historical process deeply marked by large-scale migrations. Migration provided the framework for the establishment of colonial rule and defined the nation states that came into existence after the nineteenth-century wars of independence. As post-colonial societies, these new nations have always questioned their identity as nations, their differences, characters, and destinies. Early in his classic book *The Labyrinth of Solitude*, Octavio Paz observes:

> All of us, at some moment, have had a vision of our existence as something unique, untransferable, and very precious. This revelation almost always takes place during adolescence.... The singularity of his being, which is pure sensation in children, becomes a problem and a question.... Much the same thing happens to nations and peoples at a certain critical moment in their development. They ask themselves: Why are we, and how can we fulfill our obligations to ourselves as we are? The answer differs in different situations, and the national character, which was thought to be immutable, changes with them.... To become aware of our history is to become aware of our singularity. It is a moment of reflective response before we devote ourselves to action again.[1]

Thus Paz argues that the so-called taciturn *pachuco* 'Mexican character' is not an essential national characteristic, but a response to a specific moment of Mexican history. There are, he says, specific reflective periods linked to historical conjunctures where an accelerated pace of transformation generates identity crises. More so than other periods, these moments of fast change demand historical assessments, the circulation of originary discourses, and the configuration of boundaries within which to encompass and preserve the imaginary unity of that which is inevitably changing.

Paz's analysis of Mexico in the 40s and 50s is also strikingly appropriate for Brazil in the 60s, a time of swift social and political transformations when artists intensified their efforts to question and demarcate the nature of a 'national reality' along the axis of identity. Like other Latin American countries, Brazil has a long history of debates about the 'national question'. Generally, these debates were focused on providing explanations for Brazil's economic shortcomings by linking poor performance in the production and commercial sectors to essential characteristics of the nation's historical formation. Especially towards the latter part of the 19th century, the highly positivist debate centered on the various ethnic groups that make up Brazilian society and on notions of racial hierarchies. Throughout this century, however, new historical theories were also attempting to define the place of Brazil within a world economy in relation to the legacy of colonialism and stressing the importance of different categories, such as social classes, modes of production and the international division of labor. This emphasis upon 'external domination' has indelibly marked nationalist thought, whether from the left or the right, since the 30s, linking questions of economic development with political emancipation (the control of decision-making). Left-wing nationalism, promoting a type of popular mobilization dubbed 'the integration of the masses into the nation's political life', peaked in the 60s, when its proposal seemed to have a concrete validity within the vicissitudes of the then reigning populist ideology. However, after the 1964 military coup, the collapse of this populist emancipation created a specific conjuncture where all nationalist debates were affected by the relationship between the nation's sudden economic and technological development and its repressive and authoritarian military dictatorship. The 1964 coup frustrated the belief that economic growth could only occur if it were linked to social projects democratizing culture and affirming national identity. The frustration of these projects of social transformation (primarily the left's) generated a widespread perplexity that highlighted the impossibility of providing answers to essentialist questions about the national character. For the left, history had not assumed its inevitable course, and it became necessary to explain the reasons for the derailment or, at the very least, to express a sense of helplessness about the unfolding events.

In this context, Brazilian political film-making in the 60s and 70s – Cinema Novo as well as the post-68 new movements – attempted to diagnose the 'state of the nation', utilizing representational strategies that positioned characters either as emblems of conflicting social forces (along the political – economic axis) or as the embodiment of the national character (along a behavioral axis). Thus, for example, in Joaquim Pedro de Andrade's *Macunaíma* (1969), the eponymous character is not really an individual, but a representative of the 'national character', a *malandro* or smart-alec crook who selfishly cons the system, avoids trouble, refuses work and manages to get everyone else to look after his interests. De Andrade's aim was to analyze this type of hero, common to Brazilian literature, in order to demythologize him and to expose his limits. With this film, Cinema Novo approximated the comedy of the popular *chanchadas*, but with a difference: *Macunaíma* tried to suggest the need for a different type of national hero attuned to ideas of work, solidarity, and the collective creation of a new social order. In other words, *Macunaíma* participated fully in the process of questioning the national characteristics that the left believed were responsible for the failure of the popular mobilizations of the 60s. In fact, since *Terra em transe* (*Land in Anguish*, Glauber Rocha, 1967), Brazil's 'tropical' tendency towards delirium and mystification had been linked to the maintenance of colonial structures of domination. Both films clearly express the need to locate discussions of the 'national' at cultural levels, first by positing the investigation of the formation of symbolic universes and national imaginaries as a necessary complement to analyses of economic domination and, secondly, by calling for self-criticism and for assessments of cultural practices that would link national identity and political processes in order to help explain the recent defeat. Rocha, for example, dealt with polemical questions that had once been the concern of traditional (conservative) intellectuals – national specificity and the effect of culture on politics – thus reinserting into public debate issues that progressive intellectuals of the 50s and 60s had abandoned. In other words, Rocha's agenda, despite the difference in content, is similar to that outlined by Paz: faced by a perplexing situation that complicated identity, his response was to ask, 'who are we?' and to assume the challenge of interpreting the nation in historical terms that go beyond socio-economic or political categories.

When I underline the fact that Paz and Rocha go beyond political economy when analyzing the national question, I do not mean to denigrate those films and essays which deal with the national question almost exclusively in terms of external economic exploitation. This approach retained a valid explanatory power throughout Latin America in the 60s and 70s, as is demonstrated by Miguel Littín's *Actas de Marusia* (*Letters from Marusia*), a film grounded in a tradition of political realism consolidated in the 60s, and Eduardo Galeano's book *Open Veins of Latin America*.[2] Published in Mexico in 1971, Galeano's book uses economic data about the extraction of wealth from Latin America during the colonial and neo-colonial periods to characterize the very identity of the continent as stemming from its 'open veins', a panoply of natural resources that distant powers systematically exploited so as to enrich themselves and transform the continent's inhabitants into mediators or allies. Latin American film-makers like Littín, Jorge Sanjinés, Fernando Solanas, Ruy Guerra and others, cinematically narrativized the pillages described by Galeano and the class conflicts thereby implied. Even Rocha cites Galeano, in *Land in Anguish*, using a reference to Faustus that appears in *Open Veins* to allude to the way the élite of the continent 'sold its soul for a pittance'.

However, this dominant discursive strategy which posited depredation and the foreign exploitation of resources as the most typical of Latin American experiences was displaced by several Brazilian films of the 70s. Rather than focus on the confrontation between foreign and national interests, they began to consider the processes of internal domination which the developmental plans adopted by the military regime had made much more visible. Jorge Bodansky and Orlando Senna's *Iracema* is the most brilliant example of this displacement. Filmed in 1974 and coinciding with the peak of the so-called 'Brazilian Economic Miracle' (1968–73), the film identifies the project to build the Trans-Amazon Highway as a perfect emblem for the nation. Iracema is a young indigenous girl who migrates through Amazonas from her village to a regional city (Belém), only to end up as a prostitute, unleashing a vertiginous process of personal destruction that leaves her destitute in a distant post of the highway, in the middle of the road, but lost in the jungle. Iracema becomes a symbol of the nation and its problems, caught within a predatory developmental model which produces battered forests, lumber contraband, the burning of the jungle, and the prostitution of young girls previously sheltered from 'civilization'. The 'open veins' of the Amazon, now part of the national project (the 'Greater Brazil' of the military regime), are here the result of a different process of domination than the one identified by Galeano as stemming from the colonial matrix. What is determining in the image of Iracema – especially highlighted in the last shots of the film where we see her defenseless, decadent, ailing, and abandoned in the middle of the Trans-Amazon Highway – is the notion that the detours, corrosion, alienation, and destruction of Brazilian life are directly linked to the idea of economic progress and to the arrival of civilization. *Iracema* epitomizes the Brazilian cinema's critique of the 'modernization' projects put in place by the military government after the 1964 coup.

So far I have provided examples of Brazilian films that assume two different positions vis-à-vis explanations of national reality: on the one hand, those that can be related to the spirit of the Galeano essay because of their emphasis on economic processes, and, on the other, those that can be linked to the Paz quotation and which, without slighting economic determinants, locate the discussion in terms of cultural and symbolic constructions. However, these are not mutually exclusive explanatory models, but simply two aspects of the political critiques circulated by Brazilian films between 1964 and 1974. Therefore, in this essay I shall not attempt to differentiate between the two but, instead, will highlight a characteristic that reoccurs both in the essays and in the films under consideration.

Both Paz and Galeano speak of a historical encounter marked by violence and domination that was, after all, the result of a process of migration: the mass movement of Europeans, their artifacts and slaves, that has Eurocentrically been called the 'discovery'. This is the essential *datum* that is central to both explanatory models, whether one focuses on the ethnic multiplicity of the national formation or on colonial domination and its consequences. The image of Latin America is indelibly linked to this intersection: a recurrent series of encounters, clashes, hierarchies, exterminations, wars and cultural shocks.

The power of this image is clearly evident in the representational strategies of Brazilian films that criticized the nation's political life between 1964 and 1974 through the matrix of colonial violence and in the experience of migration. The desire to produce global interpretations of the nation also led towards allegory, a mode of expression that promotes the spatial location of concepts, the remapping of experience as an adventure of spatial displacements where each location is associated with specific ideas or values. Thus contemporary historical events were signified, albeit spatially displaced, giving a *visible* configuration to the idea of *process*.

It is not surprising that the structure of these films reminds us of the Christian/mythological tradition in which the hero's journey/pilgrimage/search provides the opportunity for the discussion of values. My intention here is to mirror this process, focusing on the journey/trajectory of Brazilian cinema as it undertook the task of allegorizing historical time spatially. In other words, I want to focus on the changes that took place in the 'journeys' of heroes in the films of the 60s and 70s, considering the fact that the Messianic experience had been the matrix for the revolutionary ideals fueling Brazilian hopes in the early 60s.

MIGRATION AND THE 'DISCOVERY': FROM MESSIANISM TO ITS CRISIS

In *Macunaíma* the hero of the title leaves his home for the city, and his adventures in the land of technology are an exemplary instance of the confrontation between the modern and the archaic. *Iracema* repeats this movement, from country home to the city, but the eponymous character's wanderings along the Trans-Amazon Highway become an allegory for a nation that loses its identity as it caves in to predatory progress. In *Land in Anguish*, the migration is no longer a journey of the poor, but is associated with the power-

196

wielding dominant class: Rocha symbolically restages the arrival of European white men to the tropics and the conversion of the land to Christianity (the celebration of the first Mass in the 'New World'). This arrival, associated with the near-extermination of the indigenous population and the enslavement of blacks, functions as an allusion to a primal violence that the film presents as resurfacing in 1964 with a military coup that rearticulated the same paradigms.

In these and other films of the 1964–70 period, the recourse to an allegorical mode that globalizes the national destiny is dependent on the figure of a migrating character. Although it might be tempting to argue that the recourse to allegory was motivated by the military government's repressive actions in the period between the overthrow of João Goulart in 1964 and the gradual liberalization launched by General Geisel's government in 1974, it would be historically simplistic to do so. Without slighting the influence of censorship, the desire to describe the nation as a totality and to address the historical trajectory of the nation at a critical moment of transition was more determining. Before 1964, when the left believed that the nation would undergo a different kind of transition and that the contemporary moment was a dress rehearsal for the revolution, Cinema Novo had already demonstrated a tendency towards the allegorical. As Glauber Rocha's *Deus e o diabo na terra do sol* (*Black God, White Devil*, 1964), shot in 1963, demonstrates, allegory and the migrating character had already surfaced in Cinema Novo even while it enjoyed its greatest moment of creative freedom.

'. . . *the revolution as a process of migration* . . .' *Ioná Magálhães, Othon Bastos and Geraldo del Rey in* Deus e o diabo na terra do sol (Black God, White Devil, *Glauber Rocha, Brazil, 1964*)

Rocha's film recapitulates a century of peasant revolts in the *sertão* (backlands of north-eastern Brazil) through the journey of two peasants, Manuel and Rosa, who seek salvation from a world of drought, hunger, and extortion. First following the millenarian leader Sebastião and later the *cangaceiro* (bandit) Corisco, their journey is likened to the process of acquiring revolutionary consciousness and represented as a gradual overcoming of alienated forms of protest. Within a teleological scheme, these struggles function as necessary stages leading to a revolution represented by the formula, '*o sertão vai virar mar*', or 'the backlands will become the sea', the inevitable outcome of the peasants' journey. This future becomes concrete at the end of the film: after the death of the *cangaceiro* and after running around in circles throughout most of the film, Manuel and Rosa run through the *sertão* in a straight line and the screen is taken over by the image of the sea, reaffirming the certainty of the revolution. Manuel and Rosa's journey is a pilgrimage in search of justice, and the film defines this Utopian ideal and the constellation of values it represents in spatially concrete terms. The *telos* must be made visible: good and evil and suffering and happiness are linked to specific places. Thus, contrasting heaven and hell and the present (suffering) and the future (plenty), via the juxtaposition of the *sertão* and the sea, Rocha represents the revolution as a process of migration, a search for heaven on earth. This allegorical scheme is based upon a real historical experience: the constant migration of north-eastern peasants to the coast to escape the misery of drought. Thus the film individualizes this cyclical experience of misfortune and transforms it into a successful historical option for overcoming a given *status quo*.

Manuel's journey is fueled by his belief in impending salvation, and its imaginary is not unlike that of the European immigrants who came to the new world in search of riches and to live the 'American dream'. However, in 1963, the experiences of a north-eastern peasant could not be explicitly linked to the conquest of the Americas, since this event was seen as the original sin from which emanated the continent's ills. Colonial violence could only be interpreted as the realization of a teleology, of the colonizer's historical necessity, and the colonial heritage could only be figured as part of the 'other', of the conqueror that Latin American nationalist discourses posit as the first and most radical example of the external domination causing the economic underdevelopment and backwardness of the continent.

Although absent in *Black God, White Devil*, the reference to European migration appears in the later Rocha film *Terra em transe (Land in Anguish*, 1967) as part of the creative process of the exploitative white élite emblematically represented by the dictator Porfirio Díaz, an arch-conservative who engineers an anti-constitutional conspiracy to avoid the possible electoral victory of a populist leader. That the search for historical matrices through which to allegorize the defeat of contemporary politics leads to the appearance of European migrations in the post-1964 films is not coincidental. Defeat and disenchantment – the impossibility of believing that history would inevitably lead to freedom – had to be experienced before the imaginary of the 'discovery' could be rearticulated.

Thus, between 1964 and 1974, the Brazilian cinema, no longer motivated by the certainty and epic spirit of *Black God, White Devil*, assumes tropicality as the experience of continual pain and privileges a somber figuration of its specific geography. For example, in *Land in Anguish* Rocha constructs a baroque drama of Latin American crisis, centered on an intellectual whose political life is nothing but a senseless journey towards the abyss of meaningless death. Macunaíma's journey climaxes with the melancholic solitude of a hero betrayed by the very same tropical nature that created him. Finally, Iracema is allegorical not only because she destroys herself on the road that is bringing civilization to the jungle, but because her name is an anagram of America, reminding the spectator of José de Alencar's 19th-century novel. An ardent nationalist, Alencar narrativized the conquest/encounter as a romantic love story between a virginal Indian maiden and a Portuguese colonizer, with dire consequences for the indigenous girl. More crudely and with a strong dose of naturalism, Bodansky and Senna restage the encounter between native and colonizer as pure tragedy, precisely the explanation that is now a central theme of the protests against the more celebratory features of the quincentennial events. Reading against the grain of the conquest as victory, those who oppose the epic idea of 'discovery' underline the violence, oppression and extermination that accompanied the European imposition of a theological 'promised land' on to the 'new' continent. The 'promised land' carries with it a connotation of virginity (the virgin land) and the promise of an untamed nature. It is a territory that can be occupied, and its inhabitants are simply part of the landscape; the conquistador will control them just as he does the land. The price of the conquistador's liberation from the 'hell' of his native Europe (religious persecution, political struggles and poverty) is the annihilation of cultures and indigenous ways of being. Economically and religiously, Europe constructed an imaginary of salvation and of plenty as the *telos* of its spectacular migration to the tropics: Eldorado, earthly paradises, the promise of redemption in the New World, the American Dream.[3] It is precisely this imaginary, the result of an alliance between the Christian theology of salvation and a military mercantilist pragmatism, that the Brazilian cinema brings back on a different register between 1964 and 1974. Once associated with the ruling classes, these imaginary constructs are deliberately inverted, for film-makers argue that the concrete future defined by the Utopian voyages were, after all, a preamble to hell rather than to paradise.

The circulation of this anti-Utopian version of the discovery begins with *Land in Anguish*, where the nation is allegorically called Eldorado, but is figured as a place of suffering and hopelessness in which the dictatorship of the élite replaces the original colonial violence. In *Pindorama* (1970), Arnaldo Jabor also presents a despairing interpretation of life in the new lands (Pindorama was the first name given to the land later called Brazil). Pindorama is a place of violence against natives, of corrupt conquistadors and cynical merchants who lead a mock revolution against the Portuguese crown (the backdrop here is the film-maker's disillusionment with the national bourgeoisie's betrayal of the popular movement and complicity with the 1964 coup). The protagonist's journey follows a bitter trajectory from authenticity (impossible in this new land) to madness: at first loyal to the Portuguese crown, he realizes the true nature of the struggles he fought too late and is left,

199

without any order, condemned to isolation and to wandering throughout the vast emptiness of the 'new land'.

With these references to the first cultural shocks of life in the tropics, the cinema tends to define Brazil as a wilderness, a space of disintegration where the conqueror, to the same degree that he exercises his violent will over those he dominates, loses his credibility and his sanity (not unlike the operation of Joseph Conrad's *Heart of Darkness*). We see this not only in Cinema Novo, but also in the films of Cinema Marginal, where the identification of civilization and *barbarie* is radicalized. The journey here becomes a senseless gathering of hopelessly adrift characters who can only move in the direction of disintegration and defeat. In *Orgia* (*Orgy*, João Trevisan, 1970), 'civilization' becomes 'syphilization'. A group of heterogeneous pilgrims travels from the country to the city, repeating the familiar journey, but in an a-chronological world: their final destination outlines a 'first' encounter with civilization where the fake 'Indians' who accompany the entourage sing a hymn to 'syphilization', Europe's greatest contribution to Amerindian culture.

This countercultural representation of the encounter between European whites and indigenous peoples, common at the end of the 60s, leads film-makers to see Brazilian history as a sham, as a disqualified simulacrum. While audiences in the developed world saw this move as a critique of developmentalism and consumer society, in Brazil this critique was linked to the idea that 'civilization *is* the "other"'. In the tropics, civilization is the result of an illegitimate invasion which, imagined as a search for paradise, actually destroyed the well-balanced world of those living far from European culture.

Even when there is no direct reference to discovery Utopias, the films of this period always ironically refer to the harmony of the Garden of Eden. The titles of several Cinema Marginal films directly refer to the contradiction between the hellish experience of the conquest and the idea of the Garden of Eden. Thus, in Luiz Rosemberg's *O jardim das espumas* (*The Garden of Foam*, 1970) Brazil is the destination of extra-terrestrial beings who find only economic exploitation, guerrilla warfare, torture, and suffering. And in Neville D'Almeida's *Jardim de guerra* (*Garden of War*, 1970), the garden is a Kafkaesque space: the hero travels, but in a labyrinth where the source or purpose of the repression that surrounds him remains an enigma.

Other films emphasize the inevitability of the nation's infernal fate and the allegory becomes apocalyptic. *Brasil Ano 2000* (*Brazil Year 2000*, Walter Lima Jr, 1969) uses a post-nuclear parable to suggest the relationship between national identity and modernization: the developed nations destroyed themselves and have left the world to the underdeveloped. But this new favorable position resurrects the ghost of the peripheral nations' 'primitive' origins and congenital technological incompetence. Rogerio Sganzerla's *O bandido da Luz Vermelha* (*Red Light Bandit*, 1968) adopts the 'Boca de Lixo' ('red light') district of São Paulo as the site for its allegorical nation. The film constructs an ironic collage of modernist clichés that unveil the inconsistencies of a Third World city and defines the nation's crisis as an inevitable pull towards the abyss.

These films satirize the modernization of the nation through the apocalyptic interpretation of the national destiny. At that historical moment, economic development was linked with external domination, therefore the satire targeted the myth of *'Brasil Grande'* (*Greater Brazil*) promoted by the military government, with the intention of discrediting the promised happiness of the government's developmental projects as a grotesque version of consumerism.

In the early 60s, films had represented the much-hoped-for revolution in radical and Messianic terms that rarely addressed the nation's specific needs. By the early 70s, the critiques leveled at the government were perhaps no less mythical. But by figuring crisis as apocalypse and the tropics as hell, they articulated a radical challenge to contemporary historical events.

The bitter political climate also led to an identification with native Brazilians, those useful historical emblems of the downtrodden. Thus, early in the 70s, the Brazilian cinema begins to work out the migration matrix in melancholic terms, focusing on the experiences of indigenous peoples, their frustrated pilgrimages in search of paradise, and their loss of cultural references after 'encountering' the white man.

The melancholy of the defeated is represented, for example, in Gustavo Dahl's *Uirá, um indio em busca de Deus* (*Uirá, an Indian in Search of God*, 1974). Focusing on the story of Uirá's travels while searching for heaven and his encounter with white men, the film suggests that Uirá's loss of cultural identity and the frustration of eternal difference transform his search into a death wish. Julio Bressane's *Monstro Caraíba* (*Caraíba Monster*, 1973) organizes the hero's journey around a search for origins. An endless trek through different times and places, the hero's melancholic and decentered journey suggests the lack of a stable historical referent for the development of national identity. The 'encounter' of cultures brought about by the discovery is represented from a different perspective in Nelson Pereira dos Santos's *Como era gostoso o meu francês* (*How Tasty was my Little Frenchman*, 1971), which returns to the first years of the colonial period to tackle the issue of anthropophagy. Parodying the European discovery narratives that have served as the basis for much Brazilian historiography, Pereira dos Santos displaces them with a narrative that is at once idyllic – the representation of natural 'savage sinless life' – and melancholic, for the cannibalist rite which consumes the Frenchman is accompanied by a threat that seems a prophecy to the contemporary viewer: 'Soon my people will arrive in ever-increasing numbers to avenge my death and destroy you all.'

In this trajectory of Brazilian cinema, Arthur Omar's *Triste Trópico* (*Sad Tropics*, 1974) stands as a perfect synthesis of the themes and issues I have highlighted. Associating Messianism with traveling (the title alludes to Lévi-Strauss's Brazilian excursions, the protagonist is a traveler, a photo-collage documents the protagonist's trip to Europe), the film also links the melancholy of defeat with urban carnival festivities. Neatly inverting the millenarian hope of a film like *Black God, White Devil*, the search for paradise becomes a tragic quest. Professor Arthur, a physician who returns to Brazil after studying in France, ends up in the middle of the country as the leader of a traditional indigenous community. Because of his knowledge and daring medical experiments, he is believed to have magical powers. However, his migration and visionary experiences are not meant to interfere with the

'. . . *the representation of natural "savage sinless life"* . . .' Como
era gostoso o meu francês (How Tasty was my Little
Frenchman, *Nelson Pereira dos Santos, Brazil, 1971*)

progress of history: they neither inaugurate a new era nor save his followers.
Instead, his mysterious death and the anomalous decay of his corpse lead the
positivist scientists who later examine it to diagnose madness. That this was
the same diagnosis scientists used during the examination of the Messianic
leader Antônio Conselheiro does not escape the Brazilian audience. Conselheiro was the leader of Canudos, a Messianic community exterminated by the
Brazilian army at the end of the nineteenth century. It was he that coined the
Messianic prophecy 'the *sertão* will become sea' that Rocha so powerfully
evokes in *Black God, White Devil.*

In a circular operation, Omar's film refers to Rocha's and, simultaneously,
questions the brutal repression of difference in Western thought, alluding to
the endless violence of its most exemplary moment, the 'discovery' of the
'New World'. Synthesized as a recurring historical paradigm, the conflict in
Omar's film rests upon the contradiction between repressive reason (claiming
exclusiveness and always demanding more control) and alternative experiences, be they based on beliefs or social experiences. As the locale where
these differences intersect, Latin America could not but also be the site of
tragic conflict. Within this context, *Triste Trópico* also offers an interesting

202

rereading of carnival as the dionysian equivalent of Latin America's tragic destiny (the film establishes a parallel between Professor Arthur's trip to the interior and images of carnival celebrations in Rio de Janeiro filmed in such a way as to 'make strange' their ribaldry and masking). After equating the *sertão* and the sea and indelibly etching the omnipresent sadness of the tropics, Brazil is represented as the *locus* of a journey in a time when redemption is impossible.

Between *Black God, White Devil* and *Triste Trópico* the Brazilian cinema undertook a journey guided by the imaginary of salvation. Whereas Rocha's film (the beginning of the trip) affirms the possibility of a revolutionary Utopia, by the end of the journey (Omar's film) we find only the tragic representation of the failure of that experience. In other words, the cinema's journey to freedom begins with a hope-filled allegory where delirious experiences are a form of the 'astuteness of reason' (Hegel), but ends with the visionary hero's travels as approximations to the abyss.

In these final stages of the historical process I have attempted to delineate, history is seen from the point of view of the vanquished and is represented as a series of disasters: the 'great' historical events, like the voyages of the discovery, lose their victorious epic dimensions. By re-presenting the origins of the formation of Latin America, the Brazilian cinema found a way to express the defeat of 60s left agenda and its critique of contemporary politics. Privileging the cultural shock of the 'encounter', it sought to deny an idea of progress that, like the 'discovery', was nothing but the imaginary construct of the conquerors.

(Translated by Elizabeth Hill)

Notes

1. Octavio Paz, *The Labyrinth of Solitude* (New York: Grove Press, 1961), pp. 9–10.
2. See Eduardo Galeano, *Las venas abiertas de América Latina* (Mexico City: Siglo XXI, 1971), translated as *The Open Veins of Latin America* (New York: Monthly Review, 1983).
3. For a detailed elaboration of this 'imaginary of the discovery', see Sergio Buarque de Holanda, *Visão do paraiso* (São Paulo: Companhia Editora Nacional, 1985) and Juan Gustavo Cobo Borda, *Fábulas y leyendas de Eldorado* (Barcelona: Tusquets Editores y Círculo de Lectores, 1987).

IN THE BELLY OF THE OGRE

Cinema and State in Latin America

RANDAL JOHNSON

Editors' Introduction

Randal Johnson's extensive work on the Brazilian cinema (as co-editor with Robert Stam of *Brazilian Cinema* and author of *Cinema Novo × Five* and *The Film Industry in Brazil*) has helped make it one of the best-documented Latin American national cinemas in English-language scholarship. In this essay, Johnson expands the analysis of Brazilian state–cinema relations presented in *The Film Industry in Brazil* to explore more generally the complex nature of state–cinema relations in Latin America.

Although in agreement with Octavio Paz's description of the typical Latin American state as a 'philanthropic ogre', Johnson critiques the idealistic belief that any state (or cultural worker within it) can assume a position of neutrality. His overall argument is based on the paradoxical proposition that the historically uneasy partnership between the cinema and the state in Latin America must continue in order for culturally significant national cinemas to exist, even though state support has often made it impossible for such cinemas to develop consistently. Furthermore, Johnson posits the need to overcome the split between economistic and ideological theories of state cultural relations and proposes an approach that takes into account the status of films as commodities and symbolic goods by analysing what he calls, borrowing from Pierre Bourdieu, autonomous versus heteronomous principles. In other words, Johnson argues that state–cinema relations can only be successfully implemented (and well understood) when they are seen as accommodating both economic needs and aesthetic or ideological prerogatives.

☐

Government support of diverse modes of cultural production has existed for centuries and continues to exist in countries throughout the world, including advanced industrial democracies. Cultural policies in different national settings by necessity vary according to the set of cultural and social values at stake. Policies involving archaeology naturally have a greater weight in Mexico, Peru and many Arab states than they do in Argentina or Brazil. Language policy also takes on greater importance in some national contexts, especially in countries such as Bolivia and Peru, with significant non-Spanish-speaking populations.

Rationales for state cultural polices are often cast in terms of the notion that culture is an integral part of development and that as the ultimate guarantor of a nation's cultural unity and identity the state has a legitimate responsibility to protect society's cultural memory and heritage, to defend its cultural values, to stimulate cultural production, and to ensure that culture is not defined exclusively by market criteria. In other words, cultural policies are frequently designed to preserve the nation's cultural, artistic and historical patrimony (no matter how it is defined) and to mitigate what many see as the deleterious effects of the commercial mass media and the privately owned culture industry. To say that the state has a legitimate role to play in relation to culture, however, is a far cry from reaching a consensus about its nature and goals.

The relationship between culture and the state has rarely if ever been free of tensions and contradictions. A perfect example of the tensions engendered by cultural policies appeared in the early 1990s in the United States in the wake of the National Endowment for the Arts' support of the Robert Mapplethorpe exhibit. Episodes such as this call into question the precise nature of the state's cultural role. Should the state fund any kind of art or only that which does not offend what are taken to be the moral standards of some vaguely-defined social segment? How does one determine the social legitimacy of art, and thus the justification for public expenditures, and who should be the arbiter? Can government refusal to fund certain modes of artistic expression be considered a form of censorship? These are complex and often controversial questions for which there is no simple answer.

Cultural policies, normally formulated by social and political élites, tend to reflect the structure and concerns of the intellectual field of which they are part. Patrimonial aspects aside (for example, preservation of archaeological ruins), this often makes for a primary focus on support of élite cultural practices, especially those with scant commercial potential (such as classical music, the fine arts, dance, the cinema in many national contexts, and for a paternalistic conception of popular culture. This focus raises questions of canonicity and access. In most societies, with a mutiplicity of modes of production and consumption of culture, canonicity involves the question of *whose* cultural identity and historical patrimony are to be preserved, informed by *which* concept of the nation? *Whose* cultural projects are to be financed? Based on what criteria? What degree of access do different groups have to society's collective cultural (and economic) capital?

In its relationship to cultural production, the state is often, in Nobel laureate Octavio Paz's apt phrase, a 'philanthropic ogre'. Paz suggests that as a writer his duty is to maintain a marginal position in relation to the state, to political parties, to ideologies, and to society itself. At the same time, he argues that the state should increase its support of cultural production, but with no strings attached (*El ogro filantrópico*, 306, 314). Paz's position, although widely shared and espoused, is ultimately idealistic. In fact, the state, especially in developing countries, is rarely 'neutral' with regard to art and culture. Its relative emphasis on the philanthropic or the ogreish varies at different historical moments according to specific national characteristics and conjunctures.

States have their own interests and their own reasons for intervening, or not intervening, in support of different sectors of cultural production, and those interests may not always coincide with those of cultural producers. By its very nature, the state determines the parameters within which artists may act, and in most cases they have relative freedom as long as they stay within these parameters, which delineate what film critic Jean-Claude Bernardet calls a 'legal space' of cultural activity (Bernardet, 1979, p. 46).

The state also has a monopoly on institutional coercion and violence, which inevitably functions as a component of its policy toward culture. Although it can and often does control the distribution of cultural goods through censorship and repression, most states would normally prefer to control by indirect constraints and consensus: thus the existence, even in periods of repressive authoritarian rule, of governmental boards, agencies, commissions, and institutes designed to support different sectors of cultural production. Cultural policies are thus never simply a question of 'defending' a national identity or 'supporting' certain forms of cultural production.

Within such contexts programs of film industry support tend to be considerably more complex than they may at first glance seem. Two questions might initially be asked. First, can a culturally or aesthetically significant cinema survive in Latin America without state support? Second, can one survive *with* state support? The answer to the first is almost certainly 'no'. The answer to the second (which may seem facetious) may well also be negative. In tandem, a response can only come in the form of a familiar paradox expressing the double bind many if not most Latin American filmmakers have confronted over the last thirty years or so: they cannot live with it, and they cannot live without it.

This contradictory situation in no way implies that culturally or aesthetically significant *films* cannot be successfully produced in Latin America – with or without state support – but rather that, if the recent history of Latin American cinema is any indication, stable national film industries cannot exist without state support and that, given the way they are often conceived and carried out, state policies towards national film industries may ultimately have an effect diametrically opposed to their original intent.

Outside the United States, direct government support of national film industries is the rule rather than the exception.[1] Industries in Europe, Africa, the Middle East, Asia, Latin America, Canada, and Australia are supported in one way or another by the state. Even India, which has one of the largest and most successful commercial film industries in the world, producing over 700 films per year, has a government-sponsored Film Finance Corporation which makes the production of alternative, experimental or less commercially oriented films possible.[2]

In his seminal *The International Film Industry* (1969), Thomas Guback traces the development of state financial assistance to Western European film industries. Although many of the particulars of the situation he describes have changed in the 25 years since he wrote the book, its fundamentals have not. The essence of his argument is that without government assistance, most such industries would exist only under the most precarious conditions, always on the verge of insolvency. State support of film industries in Europe derives primarily from US domination of local markets and the resulting loss of foreign exchange. The extent and nature of state assistance reflect basic assumptions about the role of the state and may differ widely from country to country (Guback, 1969, p. 144).

If film industries in Western Europe have been unable to withstand the onslaught of American films without state assistance, the industries of economically weaker, dependent countries have been even less able to do so. Their markets have long been virtual appendices of Hollywood's domain. In many if not most instances, exhibition circuits were in fact constructed as a function of American (and to a lesser extent European) distributors.

In Latin America, Mexico, Argentina and Brazil are the countries with the strongest cinematic traditions, and their periods of success, however relative, have by and large been accompanied by considerable state support. Film production in Venezuela increased steadily in the 80s after the creation of the Fondo de Fomento Cinematográfico (FONCINE) in 1981. Feature films in Colombia were almost non-existent until the establishment of the Compañía de Fomento Cinematográfico (FOCINE) in 1978.[3] The strongest period in the history of Chilean cinema coincided with the Unidad Popular years and Allende's election to the presidency, when the cinema became incorporated into government policy. When state support has waned, as in Argentina after the overthrow of Perón in 1955, the strength of the industry has also decreased (Schnitman, 1984, pp. 39–40).

As in Western Europe, state protection and assistance have been necessary in Latin America primarily because of the United States' film industry's domination of local markets. Argentine film-maker Octavio Getino estimates that Latin America represents some 11 per cent of Hollywood's total income, or around 40 million dollars per year (Getino, 1988, p. 97). Using techniques of 'block booking' (a practice prohibited in the United States), American cinema accounts for nearly half of all films distributed throughout Latin America, and a considerably larger percentage of screen time.

In 1960, the American industry controlled at least 50 per cent of all screen time in every Latin American country except Mexico, where the state owned major studios and exhibition circuits. There US films controlled a mere 40 per cent. American films occupied 70 per cent of screen time in Brazil and 50 per cent in Argentina (US Department of Commerce, 1960). In 1982, its most successful year ever (in terms of percentage of screen time occupied), Brazilian cinema attained only 36 per cent of its own market. Yet even that figure is misleading, since it occurred at a time when the overall market was shrinking. Brazilian films thus received a larger slice of a smaller pie.[4] The same pattern has occurred in varying degrees throughout the continent. Unable to depend even on home markets for a return on investment, and lacking access to significant ancillary markets (television, cable, video), unprotected Latin American film industries have lacked the capital necessary to sustain continuous production on a large scale. Inevitably, the result has been the underdevelopment of most national film industries.

To fully understand cinema–state relations in such a context, however, one must look beyond the relationship of center to periphery and the US domination of local markets. Of course, one cannot deny or understate that presence, nor can one fail to recognize that the question of the 'occupied market' has been central to the development of governmental protectionist policies. But one must also understand the ways in which certain cinematic 'standards' have developed and become internalized and transformed into expectations by large sectors of the public.

Historically, the filmgoing public throughout Latin America has been conditioned by the standards of European and American cinema, which dominated local markets as early as the first decade of the century. These films displayed levels of technical perfection impossible for incipient national industries, and with that perfection they imposed certain cultural models of the 'proper' or preferred form of cinematic discourse. Audiences became accustomed to that form, and have been reluctant to accept alternative forms, even if produced locally. Latin American cinema has found itself in a double bind. On the one hand, it has not had the economic wherewithal to equal the technical achievements of advanced industrial countries, and on the other, it has often lacked audience support for introducing different modes of filmmaking.

To look only at the dichotomy between foreign and domestic influence, furthermore, is to oversimplify internal relations in specific national contexts as well as the relationship between the cinema and the state, often resulting in a primary focus on a quantitative analysis of the industry's development. In his well-researched study of Latin American film industries, for example, Jorge Schnitman argues that the protectionist policies of the Mexican government have helped create a strong film industry in that country, especially when compared with that of Argentina. That may be true, but what he does not deal with is the quality of Mexican cinema (Schnitman, 1984, especially Chapter 4). Mexican critic Alberto Ruy Sánchez, writing on the 'ideology of crisis' in the national industry, convincingly reveals state support to be essentially pernicious, creating a situation in which the film itself is the least important aspect of an industry plagued by corruption and the play of influences (Sánchez, 1981, p. 46). The place of the cinema in the broader field of social relations must also be taken into consideration without resorting to essentialist justifications of state support.

Cinema–state relations are a two-way street. Since at least the 20s, industrial groups or professionals in different Latin American countries have requested state protection and aid, and governments have responded in accordance with their own priorities and designs. One must thus also analyze the internal tensions and the diverse articulations between cinema and the state. Such an analysis clearly transcends the purely economic and the impact of foreign cinemas on the national film industry.

The modes of production, distribution, and exhibition of a film are shaped by a variety of industrial, economic, cultural, aesthetic, and ideological factors. As an industry, the cinema in Latin America is affected by state measures in ways not affecting other art forms. Since it depends largely on imports for virtually all production equipment, as well as raw film stock, it is sometimes dramatically affected by changes in import or exchange policies. Ticket prices are often set by government agencies, so the production sector has virtually no say in determining the market value of its product. Development has been hindered by foreign trade accords in which, bowing to pressure from Hollywood, governments have agreed to the principle of free flow of motion pictures across international boundaries (GATT, for example). In short, even without direct government protection or intervention, Latin American cinema is in many ways dependent on, or shaped by, the state and its policies.

Octavio Getino suggests that approaches to film practice and film industry development in Latin America have been shaped by two opposing strategies, one based on 'economism', which sees the film industry and its products in purely economic terms, the other based on what Getino calls 'ideologism', or a privileging of the ideological and cultural aspects of the cinema over commercial potential (Getino, 1988, pp. 13–16). This fundamental opposition is often at the root of tensions which have arisen within Latin American cinema over the last few decades and has often shaped state policies of support of local industries.

The opposition outlined by Getino can be recast in terms of competing and at times incompatible principles of legitimacy, which might be called, borrowing from Pierre Bourdieu, autonomous versus heteronomous principles.[5] The autonomous principle of legitimacy establishes a hierarchy according to the aesthetic realization or, depending on the specific context, the cultural or political configuration of the film object. The heteronomous principle establishes a hierarchy based on factors external to the filmic text *per se*, especially success in the market-place. Although there is often overlap between the two competing hierarchies, success in one does not imply (indeed, may even negate) success in the other. At the extreme, each one constitutes a reverse mirror image of the other. Specifically artistic consecration (for example, the 'art' film), as determined by peers or critics with similar values, may be interpreted by exhibitors as a sign of élitism and limited commercial appeal. Commercial success, on the other hand, may be seen by other directors and intellectuals as a sign of co-optation. In its support of the cinema, the state must navigate the waters of this often tense opposition.

In Brazil, for example, many films of the Cinema Novo movement were acclaimed at international film festivals and consecrated by specialized critics. Exhibitors, however, found them excessively 'intellectual' for a broad public and were reluctant to book them into their theaters. The reverse is also frequently the case. When Brazilian director Hector Babenco made *Lúcio Flávio, o passageiro da agonia* (*Lúcio Flávio, Passenger of Agony*) in 1977, he was accused by some critics of having sold out to a Hollywoodian aesthetic. Carlos Diegues (*Xica da Silva*, 1976; *Bye bye Brasil*, 1980) also faced frequent accusations of co-optation largely because of his films' popular success. That which is popular with a broad public seems only rarely to be popular with specialized critics.[6]

By its very nature a film industry produces objects which are both symbolic goods and economic commodities. In capitalist contexts without alternative exhibition outlets, the cinema's viability as a form of artistic expression depends on the availability of production financing, which in turn depends on the film's potential to attract a fairly wide audience and attain success in the market-place. The artistic and economic aspects are often intricately intertwined. In ideal terms, one might suggest that state policies toward national film industries have as their goal the creation of a situation in which the production of artistically or culturally relevant films is guaranteed through measures designed to strengthen the industry as a whole. The ideal, however, rarely becomes reality.

Jorge Schnitman distinguishes between restrictive, supportive, and comprehensive protectionist policies. A restrictive policy, which includes measures such as screen and import quotas, and high import tariffs and customs duties, is designed to give the local industry some breathing room by impeding a complete take-over of the local market by foreign concerns. A supportive policy includes direct state support of the industry in the form of bank loans and credit, prizes, production subsidies and other forms of film financing, assistance in reaching foreign markets, and training of film industry technicians. Restrictive policies provide indirect support of the industry while supportive polices lend direct financial support. A comprehensive state policy would include both restrictive and supportive measures (Schnitman, 1984, p. 46). But is that enough to guarantee stability? The dramatic decline of Brazilian cinema in recent years suggests that it may not be.

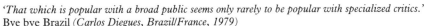

'That which is popular with a broad public seems only rarely to be popular with specialized critics.'
Bye bye Brazil *(Carlos Diegues, Brazil/France, 1979)*

Despite the existence of restrictive policies (notably a screen quota which ultimately reserved 140 days per year for national films) and increasingly aggressive supportive policies (subsidies based on box-office receipts, cash awards, low-interest loans and different forms of production financing) Brazilian cinema, long one of the strongest in Latin America, is back to square one, with production levels lower than any time since the 30s.

What happened? First of all, the crisis of the national economy, beginning with the petroleum crisis of the late 70s, sent shock waves through the industry. The so-called 'economic miracle' of the 1967–73 period, characterized by high growth rates and relatively low inflation, was replaced by an economic nightmare with a 100 billion dollar foreign debt and near hyperinflation. The economic crisis forced the government to impose severe restrictions on imports, making film production costs rise dramatically and accentuating what is often called the 'dollarization' of the film production process. Film production costs increased rapidly at a time when the market was shrinking, thus accelerating the process of decline, and ticket prices, which have long been controlled by the government, did not keep pace with inflation, further reducing the industry's income. The constant and massive presence of foreign (largely American) films in the domestic market served only to exacerbate the situation.

In addition, television, which was so successful during this same period (due in part to considerable infrastructural public sector investments in the telecommunications industry), provided Brazilians with inexpensive yet generally high-quality entertainment in the comfort of their homes. It did not, however, provide the national film industry with a significant additional source of income since historically there has been little integration between the two media.

Significantly, the relationship between cinema and the state was also a major contributing factor. In many ways, the decline of Brazilian cinema is the most evident result of the bankruptcy of the state-supported model of film production that led Brazilian cinema, in the mid-70s, to truly remarkable levels of success. The model did not derive from a far-sighted vision of the future of Brazilian cinema, and was authoritarian in many of its particulars, especially in relation to the exhibition sector, which has been virtually destroyed by the general economic situation and by the imposition of a plethora of measures supporting the production sector at its expense.

Although the state claimed that its goal was to make the cinema more competitive in its own market, the screen quota and the various forms of financial assistance it provided in fact suspended the rules of the market-place for national films, which ceased to compete against foreign films in the domestic market and began to compete against each other in the reserve market. Embrafilme became the major source of production financing, creating a situation of dependence between the state and so-called 'independent' film-makers, and in itself became a market-place where film-makers competed against each other for the right to make films. This, in turn, exacerbated tensions within the industry and created a situation in which the play of influences was often more important than the talent of the film-maker or the quality of the final product. As a consequence, public sector investments in

'. . . television . . . provided Brazilians with inexpensive yet generally high quality entertainment in the comfort of their homes.' Fernanda Torres and Thales Pan Chacon in Eu sei que vou te amar (Love Me Forever Or Never, Arnoldo Jabor, Brazil, 1986)

the cinema lost social legitimacy. Brazilian President Fernando Collor de Mello's dismantling of Embrafilme in 1990 represented the *coup de grâce* to a poorly conceived and misguided policy of state 'support'.

The state, through Embrafilme, ultimately failed to reconcile its cultural and industrial responsibilities via-à-vis the cinema and contributed greatly to the meteoric fall of the Brazilian film industry during the last several years. The policy failed, in short, largely because of its clientelistic nature, which led it to respond to the demands of clients who occupied dominant positions in the cinematic field rather than attend to the real needs of the industry and provide infrastructural support which might have strengthened the industry as a whole.

Octavio Getino argues that the ideological and cultural concerns of Latin American cinema in the 60s and 70s have given way to an overriding concern with survival. One can only agree with Getino that the very survival of Latin American cinema depends on the formulation and implementation of 'vigorous and lucid local policies of cultural and communications policy' (Getino, 1988, p. 19), but at the same time one must wonder if, in cases like that of Brazil, it may not already be too late.

Notes
1. One should not assume, however, that there is no state support of film production in the USA, no matter how secondary. Numerous films have been produced with funds from the National Endowment for the Arts and the Public Broadcasting

212

Service. Close links have also long existed between the American film industry and diplomatic policies.

2. In *Third World Film Making and the West*, Roy Armes describes diverse forms of state support of film industries throughout Latin America, Asia, Africa and the Middle East.
3. See Getino for a brief discussion of these organizations and their modes of film industry support, especially pp. 68–80. For more detailed accounts, see Aguirre and Bisbal on Venezuela and Alvarez on Columbia. Schnitman discusses the situation in Argentina and Mexico in some detail. For Brazil, see Johnson. On the situation in Cuba, see Chanan.
4. In 1975 the Brazilian market had a total of 275,380,000 spectators; by 1982 that number had fallen to 127,913,000 (it would reach a low of 89,939,000 in 1984). The total number of spectators for Brazilian films was 48,859,308 in 1975 (17.7 per cent of the market), but only 44,965,000 in 1982 (36 per cent of the market).
5. See especially Bourdieu.
6. Referring still to the case of Brazil, one might think of the *chanchada* (light musical comedy, often set at carnival time) in the 40s and 50s, the *pornochanchada* (soft-core erotic comedy) of the 70s, or the films of the Trapalhões comedy team, all of which have been immensely popular but disdained by critics.

Works Cited

Aguirre, Jesús María and Marcelino Bisbal. *El nuevo cine venezolano*. Caracas: Editorial Ateneo de Caracas, 1980.

Alvarez, Carlos. *Sobre cine colombiano y latinoamericano*. Bogotá: Universidad Nacional de Colombia, 1989.

Armes, Roy. *Third World Film and the West*. Berkeley: University of California Press, 1987.

Bernardet, Jean-Claude. *Cinema brasileiro: propostas para uma história*. Rio de Janeiro: Paz e Terra, 1979.

Bourdieu, Pierre. 'The Field of Cultural Production, or: The Economic World Reversed'. *Poetics* (Amsterdam), 12, no. 4–5 (November 1983): 331–56.

Chanan, Michael, *The Cuban Image*. London: BFI, 1985.

Getino, Octavio. *Cine latinoamericano: Economía y nuevas tecnologías audiovisuales*. Buenos Aires: Editorial Legasa, 1988.

Guback, Thomas H. *The International Film Industry: Western Europe and America Since 1945*. Bloomington: Indiana University Press, 1969.

Johnson, Randal. *The Film Industry in Brazil: Culture and the State*. Pittsburgh: University of Pittsburgh Press, 1987.

Paz, Octavio. *El ogro filantrópico: Historia y política*. Mexico: Joaquín Mortiz, 1979.

Sánchez, Alberto Ruy. *Mitología de un cine en crisis*. Mexico: Premia, 1981.

Schnitman, Jorge. *Film Industries in Latin America: Dependency and Development*. Norwood, NJ: Ablex Publishing Company, 1984.

United States Department of Commerce, Business and Defense Services Administration. *World Survey of Motion Picture Theater Facilities*. Washington, DC: Government Printing Office, 1960.

COLOMBIA

State Role in Film Production

PAUL LENTI

Editors' Introduction

Paul Lenti, *Variety* contributing editor for Latin America and expert on Colombian cinema, takes on Randal Johnson's call for more subtle and detailed analyses of state–cinema relations. Focusing on the case of Colombia, Lenti outlines the debates and arguments about state protectionism that led to the creation and transformations of the state cinema institute FOCINE. This state agency was preceded by a polemical experiment in protectionist legislation that directly funded the production of national shorts from a tax on box-office receipts and mandated their exhibition at first-run theatres – the so-called *ley de sobreprecio* or surcharge law. Under this law, Colombia's short-film production increased vertiginously in the mid-70s, but most of the films produced were 'quota quickies', designed to reap profits from the new law. It is interesting to see how, despite the debates over the *sobreprecio* legislation and practice and its ultimate demise, the Colombian state sustained its interests in the national cinema by shifting to feature-film production under the aegis of FOCINE. Lenti's account of how FOCINE has functioned over the last decade – its achievements, errors, and potential for the future – continues the debate begun by Randal Johnson's essay: on the one hand, the impossibility of sustaining a national cinema without state support and, on the other, the impossibility of surviving within it.

□

With the predominance of US cinema in most world markets, government funding of national film production has become a theme discussed seriously in almost all countries. Protectionist measures demanding domestic screen-time quotas for the preservation of national cultural expression have become the rhetoric of nations such as France, which boasts one of the world's oldest and most prestigious film histories. If this is the scenario in the First World, what about Latin America, where outside of Brazil and Mexico (which both boast sizable enough domestic markets to pay off hefty production costs), the national market alone is seldom sufficient to recoup investments? For a low-budget (US $200,000) national film to recoup investment within a country such as Colombia, the picture needs approximately one million spectators at an average 500 pesos (US $1) per ticket on initial release.

Addressing the subject of state intervention in Colombian cinema, Jorge Alí Triana, director of the 1985 film *Tiempo de morir* (*A Time to Die*), notes that,

in the first place, we must situate ourselves in the type of country in which we live. We can't even consider the development of Colombian cinema in an equal sense to the development of world cinema, nor can we even enter into this type of comparison such as to whether the state should intervene or not or if cinema should or should not depend on the private sector. We should begin with very precise things. This is an underdeveloped and dependent country and this is manifested in all organs of national life.

If we are trying to see concretely what is happening with national cinema we can observe our audience as a public that is dependent on the 500 or more foreign titles – mainly American – that are imported for us each year, resulting in a disfiguration of what could be the development of our own image within such an important mass communication vehicle as cinema is the world over. Or, it could be that, in the face of these 500 or 600 annual titles, we don't have a type of cultural presence before the public. And we

Filming Gabriel García Márquez's Tiempo de morir (A Time to Die, *Jorge Ali Triana, Colombia/Cuba, 1985*)

don't have one because cinema is a huge monopolistic industry and is a huge capitalistic industry, and it's an industry that is produced only in large centers of power on a distribution level.

There are examples of small developed countries such as Sweden, whose population I believe doesn't pass 10 million inhabitants and which doesn't have a major film industry, but it does have a state that is interested in showing a presence, a cultural profile in front of its own public and in front of the world. For this reason Sweden has produced a cinema such as that of Bergman and for this we know Sweden in Colombia and for this the world knows Sweden perhaps more through Bergman's cinema than for its commercial products.[1]

'What we have to ask ourselves in relation to Colombian cinema is: What is it we are looking for?' writes national critic Luis Alberto Alvarez:

A buoyant industry to compete with film monopolies is a naive illusion. . . . There are only two real reasons for the existence of Colombian cinema: to create a mirror of our own identity, and to create the possibility of artistic, personal and socially significant expression. These things demand the necessity and attitude of funding subsidy, a state philosophy that determines that cinema is important and makes its existence possible simply for that reason.[2]

Responding to the need to supply a national cinema infrastructure, Colombia's Federal Communications Ministry established the film governing entity FOCINE (Compañía de Fomento Cinematográfico) in 1978 in order to coordinate, produce, and promote national cinema, financed by money derived from an 8.5 per cent tax levied on cinema tickets. The idea was that the public should support the creation of a national cinema through its attendance at the mostly foreign (read American) films that dominate Colombian movie houses.[3] In the beginning, FOCINE provided production credits to film-makers, but when loan payments were not forthcoming the Fomento decided to become a full-time producer in 1983. Yet FOCINE's decisions were blocked by a muddled legal and financial sense of purpose leading it to protracted judicial battles and desperate economic measures. The government's lack of official concern can be seen in its selection of a series of entity directors with neither background nor interest in cinema: over the past decade, the political appointment of FOCINE directors have included everyone from singers to boxing promoters with no previous experience in film.

By 1988, when FOCINE celebrated its tenth anniversary, national film-makers felt there was little to cheer about. Even thought FOCINE marked the occasion by publishing an illustrated catalog touting its impressive body of work (some 200 features, medium-length and short films), since 1986 the company had barely managed to keep its doors open and, by 1990, FOCINE announced its decision to get out of the production business altogether. Yet, during the first decade of the Fomento's existence, Colombian film-makers received praise and prizes at international film festivals for works that for the most part were neither derivative nor imitative of other national models. (Their distinctiveness and variety of original themes sparked curator Larry Kardish to assemble a series of new Colombian films in 1990 at New York's Museum of Modern Art, which later toured other North American locations.)

Despite this decision, it is striking to find an extraordinary number of works by one-time feature film-makers, including award-winning directors such as Alí Triana, Luis Fernando Bottía, Sergio Dow, Víctor Manuel Gaviria, and Jaime Osorio Gómez. Outside of a few exceptions, notably Lisandro Duque and Carlos Mayolo, very few Colombian directors have had the opportunity to maintain a directing career. As FOCINE's role as producer waned in recent years due to lack of production funds, even these two film-makers have had to turn to national television, directing mini-series in order to sustain activity.

Ivan McCalester, former marketing vice-president of the leading exhibition chain Cine Colombia, notes that FOCINE's demise stems from its lack of business sense within the film industry.

In its first years [1980–2] the Fondo had received approximately 220 million pesos through the [8.5 per cent box-office] surcharge, from which it financed 17 productions. At that time the situation of FOCINE's roster was already cause for concern because it hadn't recouped more than 10 per cent of its loans from the film's producers and didn't possess real guarantees for the rest of the money. After having seen that it wasn't a viable business, from 1983 onwards FOCINE informed producers not to solicit credits, and instead it would act directly as producer ... [from 1983 to 1986] it produced an average of four films a year, of which said films haven't recouped even 6 per cent of their investment.[4]

To sustain production, the state upped its box-office tax to 16 per cent in 1985, causing exhibitors to rebel and withhold their entire quota, and the matter went to the courts for five and a half years. Points of contention were that Colombian exhibitors are saddled with the world's highest percentage of box-office taxes, in addition to being forced to screen product that it labeled 'non-commercial'. Led by Cine Colombia, which controls over 50 per cent of Colombia's cinemas, exhibitors boycotted FOCINE and, with bombs exploding in the streets due to Colombia's late-80s war with the drug barons, government efforts to crack down on exhibitors were given low priority. New directors at FOCINE became a common occurrence, staying only long enough to size up the problem before resigning in frustration.

Defending the exhibitors' actions, McCalester detailed the high taxes levied on Colombian exhibitors: 'Besides the normal taxes that the film exhibitor must pay – the same as any other national business –cinema tickets bear an exaggerated charge of 46 per cent that must be paid to four different entities, each requiring completion of specific collection requirements.'[5]

According to McCalester, eight separate taxes were levied on Colombian exhibitors, various of which have absolutely no connection with cinema:

1. *Fondo de Pobre* (Poverty Fund), equivalent of 10 per cent of the value of the ticket, created by Agreement No. 001 in 1918, for Bogotá. Other cities have similar taxes.
2. Tax created by Law 12 of 1932 and given to individual cities, equivalent to 10 per cent of the value of the ticket.
3. Tax created by Law 1 of 1967 of 10 per cent of the value of the ticket; this goes to Col ieportes, which funds Colombian sporting events.
4. FOCINE tax, created by article 15 of Law 55 of 1985, equivalent to 16 per cent of the value of the ticket.
5. Industry and commercial taxes, which are different for each city.
6. *Predial*, or property tax.
7. Rental tax.
8. Money order tax on film importation.

Besides high taxes, exhibitors also note that box-office receipts have fallen sharply in recent years (somewhere between 15 and 30 per cent) due in part to rampant video piracy and cheap contraband tapes imported illegally from Venezuela and Panama. Increasing violence and crime in some neighborhoods have also made Colombians think twice before venturing outside after dark, forcing cancellation of late-night screenings in poor neighborhoods.

FOCINE pursued legal recourses against exhibitors in a slow, methodic fashion while the debt grew to approximately four thousand million pesos in 1990, which exhibitors had held in escrow and for which they received full interest. In the meantime, Colombian production slowed to a trickle. Finally, after years of legal battles, several principal exhibitors eventually admitted their debt officially in 1990 and began making monthly payments. (In 1990, FOCINE collected around one thousand million pesos, which includes both debt payments and tariffs for the year.)

When the new administration of President César Gaviria took office in August 1990, it immediately set about resolving some of the country's major problems. Among new legal measures was a revised cinema law, which the state passed in December 1990. This law officially ended the government's near-six-year stalemate with domestic exhibitors by declaring a general amnesty on debt payments to FOCINE, virtually cutting this debt in half. Film-makers and producers thus feel that the amnesty reverses their hard-won battle. Terms dictated an almost 50 per cent cut in back taxes (from 16 per cent to the original 8.5 per cent), and awarded exhibitors favorable payment terms: exhibitors had between one and eleven months to make good their arrears. In addition, all interest accrued on this debt was likewise forgiven, and the new law also reduced FOCINE's future box-office tax from 16 per cent to 12 per cent.

The amnesty was made official in January 1991, when FOCINE's then pro-tem director Neftali Espinosa Rengifo signed a formal agreement with Cine Colombia director Munir Falh Issa. Similar agreements with other exhibitors followed. The new plan also relieved FOCINE of its role as tax collector. Instead, tariffs are now collected by the federal tax administration, which in turn passes this money on to FOCINE. One FOCINE official called this move 'an entirely new ball game. Since the federal government is collecting the money, they can always divert it to another project that they think has higher priority,' he said.

National film-makers also charge that rather than going to production, FOCINE's budget only finances the firm's oversized bureaucracy. Major restructuring efforts made by the organization in 1990 reduced FOCINE's permanent staff from 66 to 64 employees, while production funds went to completing post-production on only one film, a movie that had been shot in 1989.

Colombian film-makers find it ironic that while FOCINE has finally won its legal battles, it also decided to get out of the production business altogether. Future plans are for the state to act as middleman between film-makers and producers by stimulating domestic production through private sector loans. This plan includes granting credits and low-interest loans, subsidizing the exhibition of Colombian films, promoting national cinema, marketing Colombian films abroad and granting cash prizes to films that have received awards at film festivals.

As an incentive to make investment in film production a profitable venture, FOCINE has proposed granting credits for production coupled with a three-year low-investment loan to producers. Although this policy is still pending final definition, a FOCINE representative notes that nothing will be owed on the principal during the first year. Interest rates are to be set at around 16 per cent, considerably lower than the 42–45 per cent charged at private banks, due in part to the nation's approximate 25 per cent annual devaluation of currency against the dollar, coupled with an even higher rate of inflation – around 3 per cent a month. (Despite these figures, Colombia has one of the most healthy economies in Latin America.)

Yet film-makers charge that, despite the introduction of production credits, the new plan does not stimulate investment in cinema. Most of FOCINE's new measures reward films after the fact, they say, based on box-office performance or festival recognition. They claim the commercial success of a film such as Carlos Duplat's *Amar y vivir* (*To Love and Live*, 1990) was prompted by its being adapted from an already successful television soap opera and by the fact it received heavy promotion from the exhibition chain Cine Colombia, one of its producers. (*Amar y vivir* is Colombia's top-grossing national film to date, breaking all previous records set for a domestic film by selling 675,000 tickets through mid-May, 1991; *Batman*, a national blockbuster, sold 800,900 tickets.) Film-makers also charge that, even though retrospectives of national cinema may draw awareness to Colombian films, paucity of product (due to FOCINE's legal battles) have made producers wary.

As for the distribution of national films and the role of the state, film-maker Sergio Cabrera opines that the government should offer some sort of protection:

The state should play the role that a father plays with regards to his child, more or less. The state must advance the film industry, and afterwards it can defend itself. It's more that the state must make cinema viable as national television is. Inravisión [the state channel] is a financially viable institution. FOCINE could also be such if the state wanted, if there existed at least a minimum degree of protection. We don't have the means to compete. In one cinema they're showing a film by Spielberg that cost $80 million dollars, in which 20 airplanes and nine helicopters are destroyed, and it features major stars, and next door they're showing your film. It is very difficult to get people to want to see your film, and I understand them. . . . There must exist an industrial management of cinema to protect it as we protect our automobile industry.[6]

McCalester further adds that

this entire structure of intervention as applied to date has not given results: this can be noted in the closure of movie theaters. Each day the process of presenting a film to the public is more difficult, theaters have deteriorated for lack of credit sources, and because of the price control policies and excessive taxes. . . . No sort of production infrastructure has been created in the country, there are no efficient laboratories, there are no film studios, developed production companies do not exist; all individual efforts in this area have not been taken advantage of efficiently.[7]

Meanwhile, FOCINE is redefining its role in national cinema development and has been busy with a number of new activities to be funded by newly collected back taxes. These include:

– A retrospective of Colombian cinema. Between 19 February and 3 March 1991, FOCINE hosted a retrospective of national films produced between 1974 to the present in cooperation with the Teatro Libre de Bogotá. The retrospective also toured other cities outside the capital.
– The acquisition and distribution of short films. Since federal law dictates mandatory screening of domestic shorts with all features, Colombia boasts a steady production of short films. In 1991, FOCINE held several national competitions to purchase short films; winners received nine million pesos for one-year distribution rights at national cinemas.
– Control of the Colombian box office. National exhibitors have recently installed a new electronic ticket system to control the box office. In the past, exhibitors were accused of using what is referred to locally as 'the carousel system', where sold ticket stubs were resold again and again, making accurate box-office assessments impossible. This new system also streamlines operations and reduces personnel.
– Promotion of National Film Festivals. Colombia boasts two film festivals. The Cartagena International Film Festival, directed by Víctor Nieto, celebrated its 34th anniversary in 1992, and (with the future of the Havana Film Festival uncertain) present plans are to promote it as a major showcase for new Latin American cinema. There is also the Bogotá International Film Festival, directed by Henry Laguado, which held its ninth festival in October 1992.

Now that FOCINE has withdrawn from production, it is currently sending works from its catalogue to film festivals and other international forums. It is also distributing its works nationally, while new non-FOCINE productions receive no official support either as cultural representations or national presence at international arenas. With its financing finally resolved, its role in the future of Colombian cinema remains to be seen.

Notes

1. Jorge Alí Triana, 'En busca del cine perdido', *Gaceta*, no. 3, July–August 1989, pp. 23–4.
2. Luis Alberto Alvarez, 'Reflexiones al final de un período', *Arcadia Va al Cine*, no. 13, October–November 1986, pp. 33.
3. 'Creación y Estructura de Focine, 1978', *Hojas de Cine: Testimonios y Documentos del Nuevo Cine Latinoamericano*, vol. I., 'Centro y Sudamérica' (Mexico: Dirección General de Publicaciones y Medios/Secretaría de Educación Pública (SEP)/Fundación Mexicana de Cineastas/Universidad Autónoma Metropolitana, 1988), pp. 267–73.
4. Ivan McCalester, 'Bases para una política cinematográfica' (Bogotá: Compañía de Fomento Cinematográfico (FOCINE), 1987), p. 159.
5. Ibid., pp. 165–6.
6. Guillermo González Uribe, 'Las grandes obras de arte nacen de los grandes conflictos', *Cinemateca*, no. 9, June 1988, p. 7.
7. Ivan McCalester, op. cit., p. 161.

MEXICAN CINEMA COMES ALIVE

NISSA TORRENTS

Editors' Introduction

Mexican cinema since its 'Golden Age' of the late 30s and early 40s has developed in a stop–go fashion. From the early 50s, each presidential *sexenio* (six-year term of office) would witness the introduction of measures to 'save' the film industry; these measures would, on the whole, drive the industry further into crisis. The pendulum oscillated between complete liberalism and state monopoly. In this article, Nissa Torrents argues that the balance today seems about right and has led to a partial renaissance of Mexican cinema.

The state is a central actor in this current development. State intervention in cinema has been manifest in a number of ways, either by restricting foreign competition or by supporting local initiatives through loans and production subsidies. Paz has called the state a 'philanthropic ogre', pointing out the limitations imposed by having to work intimately in the shadow of power. Randal Johnson's earlier essay in this volume reveals the pitfalls as well as the advantages of state controls and initiatives. However, as Nissa Torrents rightly points out, with a deepening economic crisis throughout the subcontinent, state subsidies are declining everywhere and the chill winds of the market threaten to blow away many of the achievements of the last 30 years. By 1992 Mexico was the only country in Latin America with a relatively vigorous cinema production, producing a variety of different films, thanks to an enlightened state policy. Whether the model of financing can provide long-term solutions, or whether, as so often in the past, the Mexican giant is found to have feet of clay, remains the question for the 90s. Nissa Torrents saw grounds for optimism.

□

The year of Mexican cinema was 1991. Prizes were showered on it from diverse and multiple sources and the number and quality of output from old hands like Matilde Landeta (Mexico's pioneer female director), Marcela Fernández Violante, Jaime Humberto Hermosillo and newcomers such as Alfonso Cuarón and Juan Mora Cattlet was without parallel in the cinematographies south of the Rio Grande, which went through one of their worst years to date. Venezuela produced an outstanding film in *Jericó*, the first feature of Luis Alberto Lamata on the 'in' theme of the conquest, though highly original and off-beat, favouring as it does gentle comedy over the transcendental. Colombia previewed films made as far back as 1986 and Peru did the same, as not a single feature film was shot in the year. Cuba, without funds and just about recovering from the recent scandal of Díaz Torres's *Alicia en el Pueblo de las Maravillas (Alice in Wonderland)*, a mild criticism of government policies that was practically banned and required many public confessions of Communist faith by its director, provoking a shotgun marriage between ICAIC (Instituto Cubano de Arte e Industria Cinematográficos), IRT (Instituto de Radio Television – Radio and TV Institute) and the film section of the armed forces, had a predictably meagre year with only two films being completed. Brazil did not recover from the *coup de grâce* of President Collor's disbandment of Embrafilme, the state producing and distributing agency, and in Argentina, though 17 national films were previewed, the most successful, Javier Torre's *Las tumbas (The Tombs*, 1991) was only seen by 75,000 filmgoers. Cinemas continued to close and the high cost of tickets kept people at home in spite of a partial recovery of the economy.

In Mexico, however, after one disastrous and one near-disastrous presidential period, film under President Carlos Salinas de Gortari seems to be recovering its health with alacrity, though without relinquishing the 'artistic supervision' that many identify as a form of censorship, a supervision that starts when the project is presented and only ends when the film is publicly screened. Until recently – privatisation is as strong in Salinas's Mexico as it was in Thatcher's Britain – COTSA (Compañía Operadora de Teatros SA – National Exhibition Company), a state enterprise, was the largest owner of cinemas in the nation and as such had the final say on exhibition policies.

Not since President Echeverría's time (1970–76) had Mexican cinema been in such good health. In his period the film industry was run by his brother, a well-known actor who set up three state production companies and, with ample funds for the modernisation of studios and equipment, promoted the film industry at home and abroad, wresting its control from the hands of the private sector. These measures and a partial thematic 'opening' produced a second 'golden age' (the first being that of the 40s to 50s) and a new generation of film-makers made their mark at home and abroad, becoming the first 'auteurs' of national cinema. Among them are Sergio Olhovich, Jorge Fons, Alberto Isaac, Felipe Cazals, Arturo Ripstein and the best known of them all, Jaime Humberto Hermosillo, a leading director in the 80s and 90s.

Social and political themes were addressed, something unheard of since the 30s, the Cárdenas presidency (1934–40) included, but film-makers largely remained cautious, avoiding direct confrontation with the political, religious and military authorities. The displaced private sector made films to be shown on the other side of the border and in provincial towns with the usual themes of violence and as much female nudity as was permitted. This cinema did not

223

collect any international prizes, as did the state-backed cinema, but it won the battle at the box office, 'serious' films remaining notably unattractive to mass audiences.

The next President, José López Portillo (1976–82), put his sister Margarita at the helm of the industry and a wave of unparalleled nepotism and wilful ignorance almost did away with Mexican cinema. She had no sympathy for the policies of her predecessor or for cinema itself. She favoured the private sector and so-called 'family' pictures, though during her time more soft porn pictures were produced – by the private sector – than ever before. Call-girls, drug trafficking and extreme violence became the pattern: over 200 movies with narcotics traffic at the centre were made in the 80s; social conflict, private or public, was banished. Ambitious international co-productions were promoted with Spain's Carlos Saura and the USSR's Sergei Bondar-chuk, obvious prestige moves for an industry in a terminal state, but they proved to be expensive failures. She tried and failed to attract Fellini, but she did succeed in starting to dismantle those state institutions that financed film production, withdrawing support for the state companies, thus allowing TELEVISA, the giant commercial television conglomerate, to gain a foot-hold in the hitherto nationalised public sector. Some excellent films by Her-mosillo and Ripstein, among others, were exhibited in her time, but they were conceived in the previous administration.

The election of President Miguel de la Madrid (1982–8) was welcomed by film-makers, and his initial steps seemed to be a clear attempt to offset the disasters of his predecessor's sister. Alberto Isaac, a film-maker of known repute and a friend of the president, was named as the director of the newly created IMCINE (Instituto Mexicano de Cine – Mexican Film Institute), a state corporation that was to encompass production, distribution and exhibi-tion. At the time, Mexico's film studios were run down and the technical gap between them and Hollywood was becoming paralysing. Due to galloping inflation, costs had increased and it was almost impossible to recover invest-ment. Bourgeois audiences had deserted local productions and by 1987, though Hollywood films had seen a drop of 15 per cent at the box office, local cinema had lost 45 per cent of its audience nationally and 50 per cent in the United States, a main source of income. And then, there was video.

Alberto Isaac tried to revive the national industry and elevate its quality, notably with the 1985 experimental film competition that produced excellent screenplays from newcomers Diego López, a grandson of Diego Rivera, and Alberto Cortés, but the president was not interested in his project and he resigned, with great bitterness, in 1984, to be replaced by a minor PRI (Partido Revolucionario Institucional – Revolutionary Institutional Party) politician, ignorant of the medium and only interested in self-enrichment. The result was predictable. The private sector had a field day, using well-tried formulas of exploitative female nudity; extreme violence (preferably at the US border); indistinguishable drug traffickers and policemen, and bring-ing to the fore a new genre, the *albur*, a type of comedy based on sexual innuendo and very blue jokes, acted by well-known singers, radio and TV figures which satisfied the popular audiences. The problem of illegal immi-grants was just a pretext for more blood and shoot-outs and never a subject for serious analysis, except in the exceptional *Raices de sangre* (*Roots of Blood*, 1987) by Jesús Treviño, the only Chicano film ever to be financed by and shot in Mexico.

Independent film-making continued, and although directors like Marcela Fernández Violante and Paul Leduc made films closer to the national realities, their production hardly went beyond university and art cinema circles, though it was well received in festivals and by the specialised press abroad.

On taking power, the current president, Carlos Salinas de Gortari, intent on taking Mexico into the 21st century, was torn between the need to open to privatisation all state enterprises, a necessary step for entry into the North American Free Trade Area, and a desire for intellectual and artistic prestige which, in the film industry, could only be the result of state financial backing. His government has tried to mix public and private sector finance, thus enacting a mini-revolution in the sector. State enterprises such a CON-ACINE (Compañía Nacional de Cine – National Film Production Company) (production) and Azteca Films (distribution) have been sold and COTSA (exhibition) is also in the process of privatisation. The power of the official trade unions, which almost choked the industry in its ailing times, has been broken; some directors – as happened in Alfonsín's Argentina – have become their own producers and a few small but totally committed film producers have appeared on the market: Berta Navarro, the producer of María Novaro's successful films; the actor Héctor Bonilla, whose money and interest made possible Jorge Fons's controversial *Rojo amanecer* (*Red Dawn*, 1989) on the Tlaltelolco massacre of students in 1968; and the sons of Manolo Barbachano, the famous producer and friend of Luis Buñuel.

At the head of IMCINE the president placed Ignacio Durán, a film man and also (and this is central) a very able administrator not afraid of privatisation and competition. He has implemented a policy of co-financing films – the only policy possible given the financial position and the ideological stance of the presidency – that has given the Mexican industry a new lease of life. There is also an encouraging variety of themes and formal approaches being developed. The dogmatic positions of the 70s, the political correctness of form and content, have disappeared. The quantity and quality of the new-comers (another sign of euphoria that marked Argentina's film revival after the military dictatorship) together with the number of women film directors (six were able to film between 1990 and 1991) have no parallel in the Hispanic Americas. In 1991, IMCINE participated in the production of 15 feature films, although in only nine of them was its share of finance important. The quality of these films has been high.

If one were to compare Mexico's revival with that of Argentina after 1983, one impression would be difficult to avoid: Mexican cinema is obviously mainstream and, because it comes out of economic euphoria (however real or otherwise this may be) and not out of the nightmare of dictatorship, it is light, almost frothy, a cinema of private conflict and hope except, of course, in its inevitable contribution to the 1492 controversy. Many of the new directors, such as Carrera, Novaro, Sistach and Athié, came from state film schools, while others – for example, Cuarón, Lubeski or Buihl from the film

'. . . Mexico's favourite film star, María Rojo . . .' in Danzón (María Novaro, Mexico, 1991)

industry or TV (Doehner) and Echeverría – have spent many years of documentary film-making on indigenous themes for the state agency INI (National Institute for the Indigenous Peoples).

María Novaro has had great success in foreign festivals with *Danzón* (1991), in which she highlights an important element of popular culture. It is a pleasant reworking of a fairy tale, reworked with modern ingredients. The protagonist is a telephonist and a single mother. She is not particularly glamorous though played by Mexico's favourite film star, María Rojo, and her beloved is an old man, of no private means but an excellent dancer of that very Caribbean tune, the *danzón* of the title. There are fashionable transvestites and a whore whose heart of gold (a favourite with Mexican audiences) is hardened by circumstances. The hotel concierge is suitably soft-hearted and there is even a handsome young man whom the protagonist beds and leaves! The acceptable face of feminism? Certainly Novaro's previous film, *Lola*, about the confusions and ambiguities of a young mother, also a single parent, was more disturbing in its ambiguity. The same can be said of Marisa Sistach's film *Anoche soñé contigo* (*Last Night, I Dreamt of You*, 1991), which is dangerously close to acceptable soft porn. A film about a young boy's rites of passage, her handling of the theme and her chosen camera placements are indistinguishable from those of male directors, though in her first feature *Los Pasos de Ana* (*Ana's Steps*, 1990) a different handling of themes and forms was emerging. The second feature, like Novaro's, could be seen as a step backwards.

226

A homage to the popular film genre of masked wrestlers in the 50s and 60s is at the centre of José Buihl's *Historia de una máscara* (*Story of a Mask*, 1991), a gentle and humorous tribute to metaphorical violence. The influence of Tornatore's *Cinema Paradiso* is clear in Juan Antonio de la Riva's *Pueblo de madera* (*Wooden Village*, 1990), a tribute to that vanishing space, the village cinema. This influence reappears, together with that of Allen's *The Purple Rose of Cairo*, in Carlos García Agraz's *Mi querido Tom Mix* (*My Beloved Tom Mix*, 1991), a gentle comedy about an old lady and her love for the cowboy star.

Films within films, the influence of the comic strip and a wide range of post-modernist strategies softened by an awareness of a possible and desired audience are some of the key elements of the film. Not always sustained, it is a likeable comedy that eschews vulgarity and confirms the appearance of a new trend in Mexican cinema: the sophisticated comedy. Good examples are Hermosillo's *La tarea* (*Homework*, 1989) and Cuarón's outstanding *opera prima*, *Solo con tu pareja* (*Only with your Partner*, 1991). Hermosillo is a veteran film-maker who is well known abroad but his latest works, filmed originally on video in record time (some seven days) are not just brilliant comedies like *La tarea* or convincing dramas like *Intimidades en un cuarto de baño* (*Bathroom Intimacies*, 1989) but masterly examples of how to make films in countries where finance of conventional features has all but disappeared and shows no immediate signs of returning. His latest films continue to unmask social hypocrisy, especially in the field of sexual repression, and in *La tarea*, an extremely funny and *risqué* comedy with a twist, the inevitable María Rojo plays a film school mature student shooting her graduation film as a soft-core exercise. Some very simple devices, the video camera immobile on the floor and the single filmic space, are exploited by the director with

'Films within films. . .'. Ana Ofelia Murguía in Mi querido Tom Mix *(My Beloved Tom Mix, Carlos García Agraz, Mexico, 1991)*

humour. In *Intimidades en un cuarto de baño*, where the camera is hidden behind the bathroom mirror, the very same strategies are at the service of a low-key dramatic theme: the impotence of the male and the predatory nature of the female in the Mexican middle class, a role–gender division which has become familiar in the misogynist world of Mexico's premier film-maker.

Alfonso Cuarón's *Solo con tu pareja (Only with your Partner)* has fallen foul of a new type of censor. Its theme, which alludes to AIDS in a comic mode, was declared out of bounds by the new Torquemadas (inquisitors) who seem to have forgotten that art has always been able to laugh at that which we all fear. The film did eventually open, however, to great success in Mexico in December 1992. A brilliantly directed comedy with the pace of the best Feydeau, it is a modern bedroom farce about a promiscuous male advertising executive. He is the butt of a discarded lover's sinister joke, a nurse who takes her revenge by faking an HIV-positive test on the unfaithful lover. The women whom he 'betrays' are not helpless and constantly avenge themselves on the maladroit Don Juan.

It is also important that Mexican cinema has decided to acknowledge the existence of a 'yuppy' class, Americanised, well-heeled and oblivious to the need to repeat nationalist slogans and perpetuate traditional sexual behaviour. Actresses and actors are convincing in their portrayal of the men and women of a country that aspires to become one with the old enemy. By tackling the problem of AIDS within a comedy, Cuarón is not insulting those who have become infected by choosing a genre which will not alienate (by its Savonarola-like undertone) those most vulnerable to the disease. He is, simply, looking for a more direct way to reach them.

The comedy of manners, which in the United Kingdom has been identified with social climbers from the middle classes, in the Spanish-speaking world has more popular undertones. De la Riva's *Pueblo de madera* was a prime example of the continuity of the genre, as is Carlos Carrera's first feature, *La mujer de Benjamín* (Benjamin's Woman, 1991), a fine, low-key portrayal of a small village where boredom contributes to the aberrations of a machismo which is just so many words in the mouths of human wrecks but which still has the power to destroy people's lives. Routine and mediocrity are great killers and Carrera points out that, in spite of apparent stillness, something always happens even when the events are negative manifestations. Lack of personal freedom in the everyday ends up by confining people to invisible prisons that are as soul-destroying as the real ones.

Nicolás Echeverría and Juan Mora Cattlet have explored the theme of the shock of cultures that followed the arrival of the Spanish. After some eight years of wrangling and many changes of script, Echeverría, a well-known documentary film-maker of indigenous themes, managed to finish his expensive anti-epic, based on the account of a Spaniard who, after a shipwreck and a seven-year voyage, learned about the wisdom of the natives and the folly of his compatriots. It is difficult not to compare *Cabeza de Vaca* (1990) with *Dances with Wolves* as it shares with Kevin Costner's film some of the obsessions and some of the pitfalls. The original book, Cabeza de Vaca's 16th-century diaries of his journey, is almost forgotten in a treatment that owes more to hippy-derived alternative cosmologies than to the original work. The protagonist, body painted like an African tribesman Hollywood-style, wanders around meeting Buñuel-like dwarfs, and by some magically inverted curative powers curing all and sundry while putting on a convincing show of anorexia. Since Echeverría is a documentary film-maker, the natural settings are impressive but the story, and the history, fail to convince. Far more modest, Juan Mora Cattlet's *Retorno a Aztlán* (*Return to Aztlán*, 1990), spoken entirely in Nahuatl, takes place in a pre-Hispanic world. Its visual and story referents are the codices which account for the world that the Spaniards hoped to blot out. Mora and his archaeologist collaborators have attempted to re-create the pre-Hispanic world, giving voice and image to cultures that were denied by the conquest. Far removed from industrial film-making, Cattlet, convinced that the pre-Columbian cultures of Mexico were highly visual as well as oral, successfully transposes this belief into a curious, difficult and highly unusual film.

Finally, and also on the positive side, is the evidence of the beginnings of a decentralisation of Mexican film production. A film school is active in Guadalajara where Hermosillo likes to work. Novaro and de la Riva have also filmed in the provinces, making them the geographical centre of their work, and the province of Tlaxcala, following the example of Durango and Veracruz, is now offering substantial incentives to film-makers.

On the negative side, an old note: the scarcity of popular audiences for the new Mexican films. In 1991, the most popular films were those with 'light' themes. Films by famous pop singers or films like *La risa en vacaciones II* (*Holiday Laughs II*), Mexico's answer to Hollywood serial films, have continued to be great box-office success, as have the films of Rosa Gloria Chagoyán, a powerful young woman who is most accomplished on the battlefield and is the scourge of drug traffickers on both sides of the Rio Bravo–Grande. Even *Danzón* could not last more than one week in most cinemas which, because of the lack of expenditure on equipment, screen the films in such poor conditions that they can never be seen as the film-makers intended.

229

DEATH IS NOT TRUE

Form and History in Cuban Film

TIMOTHY BARNARD

Editors' Introduction

Many decades before 'difference', 'hybridity' and the 'other' were commonly used in critical discourses, the Cuban ethnologist Fernando Ortiz proposed a different model for thinking through questions of influence and North–South relations. The concept of transculturation, widely used by Latin American critics (such as Angel Rama, for example), does not insist on pure essences or originality for either the dominant or minority culture. Instead, Ortiz insisted that the colonial encounter unleashed complex historical processes of hybridisation and syncretism which made the culture of Cuba, a typical colonial crossroads, always necessarily transformative and adaptive.

Barnard's piece traces the significance of Ortiz's work for an understanding of contemporary Cuban culture and cinema. Despite the revolution's insistence on radical purity, despite the obvious and much publicised efforts to eradicate 'foreign', 'capitalist' influences from the island's cultural life, Barnard maintains that Cuban cultural history must still be understood as a process of adaptations and transformations. His argument is many-layered: on the one hand, he traces how even the cinema, the most perfect example of culture as immutable commodity, is subject to transculturation through alternative viewer habits (talking back to the screen, for example); on the other, he argues that the call for a radically new cinema aesthetic in Julio García Espinosa's well-known article 'For an Imperfect Cinema' also embodied an appeal for a transculturative synthesis of form and content which was used, in practice, to bring past and present together. Supported by an iconoclastic analysis that superimposes public billboards and details of individual films, Barnard finds that 'history' in the Cuban cinema is mediated through the present's ideological pressures, confounding past and present and formally dissolving the past.

Although Barnard does not make the connection, the reader may very well ponder about the relationship of this practice, that through historicity makes the historical disappear, and the well-circulated descriptions of the work of post-modernist culture, especially Fredric Jameson's arguments about post-modernist nostalgia and historicity. Can the Cuban examples be considered in the light of a 'post-modern' redefined to include a non-capitalist culture?

In this context, Barnard's closing question should perhaps also serve as a preface: 'What is the relationship between the insertion of a photograph of Fidel Castro into a film set in 1672 and the airbrushing, 300 years later, of discredited revolutionary heroes out of photographs where they appear at his side?'

□

'The true history of Cuba', the Cuba ethnologist Fernando Ortiz wrote in 1940, 'is the history of its extremely intricate transculturations.'[1] Ortiz went on to explain that 'transculturation' was coined to oppose the Anglo–American sociological term 'acculturation', which described a process of complete assimilation of minority cultures into dominant ones. Ortiz maintained that the process of cultural transformation set in motion by the meeting of races and cultures was better described as one of mutual influence resulting in new hybrids. The colonial era in the New World, of course, had provided the setting for the most extensive and sustained such 'encounter' in history. At its centre lay Cuba, a colonial crossroads, the site of a major New World port and a destination for peoples of vastly different cultures. The process of transculturation that took place there over the centuries was so extensive that Ortiz was led to claim:

> In Cuba, there were so many and such diverse cultures which influenced the formation of the Cuban people, and they were so geographicaly disparate in their origins and distinct in their characteristics, that the immense mixing of races and cultures there surpasses all other historical phenomena in importance. (*Contrapunteo*, p. 87, see note 1.)

Ortiz did not suppose that cultures entered into a free and equal exchange, a cordial and voluntary transculturation. Rather, he saw cultural transformation as a violent confrontation, the result of the 'shock' of social upheaval. Transculturation was in fact the third, syncretic phase of this process, following an initial 'deculturation', the traumatic and wholesale loss of culture during the initial encounter between stronger and weaker cultures, and the subsequent periods of 'inculturation', when the suppressed culture regroups and begins to infect the dominant culture. In Cuba, the arrival of the Europeans was so overwhelming – a 'hurricane of culture', Ortiz described it – and their genocide of the native population was so rapid that the deculturation–inculturation–transculturation cycle was carried out between the Europeans and their African slaves, with many other cultures added along the way. Ortiz reflected that this course of events could ultimately be seen as propitious for transculturation, remarking that all cultures were now 'foreign' to the island and that all, albeit disproportionately, had been 'torn' by the 'trauma of uprooting'.[2]

Although Ortiz's *Contrapunteo* (*Cuban Counterpoint*) approaches transculturation obliquely, through a novel study of the cultivation, trade and uses of sugar and tobacco in Cuba and around the world, he later extended his methodology to various studies of Afro–Cuban music, building on his earlier studies of black culture in colonial Cuba. Long one of the most diverse, dynamic and influential in the world, Cuban music presents tremendous opportunities for transcultural analysis, not just for historical research but for assessing its present-day relationship to other music. Significantly, the transcultural methodology has also proven invaluable to the continuing struggle in Cuba – both pre- and post-1959 – to defend and encourage continued hybridisation and experimentation. Before 1959 in particular, (white) cultural élitists periodically decried the black, foreign or popular contamination of their canon, blissfully unaware that the 'authentic' musical tradition they sought to preserve was itself almost invariably the product of such cross-fertilisation.[3]

After 1959, despite many progressive cultural changes, this fear of 'contamination' persisted, although the categories of 'authentic' and 'alien' were now redefined in keeping with the country's political transformation. Thus a concerted attack on Western pop music was launched in the mid-60s, the effect of which on a music industry whose lifeblood had always been foreign contact should not be underestimated. In any event, armed with the insights of Ortiz's and others' historical research demonstrating the fundamental role of hybridisation in the development of Cuban music, a group of Cuban intellectuals, musicologists and musicians in the post-1959 period has been able to hold at bay the periodic isolationism and xenophobia of Cuban cultural policy. Today Santana and Michael Jackson (not coincidentally strongly syncretic performers) can be heard from street-corner boom boxes. Furthermore, one of Cuba's most popular contemporary dance–pop bands is Irakere, which has joined the rhythms and instruments, including synthesizers, of ritual African and contemporary pop music.[4] One of Cuba's leading novelists and intellectual figures, Alejo Carpentier (1904–80), himself a musicologist, waded into the fray by stressing that a dichotomy between 'cultured' and 'popular' music was false, bourgeois and driven by racial prejudice. Carpentier also characterised Latin American music as the product of continuous 'grafts and transplants' which problematise its national character: 'if electronic music and synthesizers have no nationality, whoever uses them brings to them his own nationality'.[5]

In 1969, Cuban film-maker Julio García Espinosa proposed that the Cuban cinema should carry out a radically different synthesis. In his essay 'Por un cine imperfecto' he rejected US and European influences out of hand: 'Today a perfect cinema – one that is technically and artistically polished – is almost always a reactionary cinema.'[6] In a tone consistent with the cultural rhetoric of the post-1959 political leadership, which regularly proclaims that European culture is 'decadent' and 'sterile', García Espinosa continued:

When we look at Europe we rub our hands. We see the old culture today incapable of responding to the problems of art. What's really happening is that Europe can no longer respond in the traditional manner nor, at the

232

same time, can it easily do so in an entirely new way. (*Hojas de cine*, p. 71, see note 6 below.)

García Espinosa's essay makes no suggestion that some accommodation between imperfect cinema, a radical liberationist aesthetic, and European cinema can exist. Rather, a complete break is urged, a rapid revolutionary cultural reconstruction breathtaking in its scope: '[the revolution] will allow us to sweep away once and for all minority artistic ideas and practices' (*Hojas de cine*, p. 72).

What then was the synthesis that García Espinosa proposed? It was to be the formulation of a 'new poetics' which, together with sweeping political change, would bring about a Utopian merging of life and art: 'Art will not disappear into nothing. It will disappear into everything' (*Hojas de cine*, p. 77). García Espinosa sketched out some of the effects of this process: the role of professional artists would gradually be taken over by workers, who would produce films in consultation with 'sociologists, revolutionary leaders, psychologists, economists, etc.', bringing to an end the 'star' system of film directing and eliminating the quest for personal fulfilment on the part of the film-maker and the need for specialised film-making instruction (*Hojas de cine*, pp. 77, 73). Furthermore, the passive spectator would become a critical subject, a 'spectator–creator' rendering film criticism obsolete: 'imperfect cinema rejects the services of criticism. It believes the function of mediators and intermediaries to be anachronistic' (*Hojas de cine*, p. 77). New film-production technologies, higher levels of education and more leisure time would make film-making the activity of many and not just the few (*Hojas de cine*, p. 64). García Espinosa based his theory on his understanding that a successful resolution of the class struggle would precipitate 'the definitive disappearance of the specialised division of labour'. From this, he speculated that revolutionary culture would also put an end to cultural fragmentation and alienation: 'revolution is the highest form of cultural expression, because it will cause artistic culture as fragmentary culture to disappear' (*Hojas de cine*, p. 72).

García Espinosa's 'new poetics' was to be the aesthetic means to this end. While his comments about the form of this new poetics are vague, it is clear that it would rely on a strategy of radical synthesis: 'Imperfect cinema can use documentary or fiction techniques, or both. It can use one genre or another, or all' (*Hojas de cine*, p. 76). The result of this all-encompassing aesthetic would be a transparency, an aesthetic final solution: 'It is no longer a question of substituting one school for another, one "ism" for another . . . imperfect cinema can't forget that its essential objective is to disappear as a new poetics' (*Hojas de cine*, p. 77). Or again: 'This new poetics' true end, however, will be to commit suicide, to disappear as such' (*Hojas de cine*, p. 72).

Echoes of these ideas resurface in an essay published ten years later by Cuba's other leading film-maker and theorist, Tomás Gutiérrez Alea, who describes 'the process of an organic integration of form and content' as a dialectic 'in which both aspects are indissolubly united and, at the same time as they oppose each other, they interpenetrate each other, to the point where they can take over each other's functions'.[7] Rather than articulate the oft-

233

repeated dictum that revolutionary content must be accompanied by a revolutionary form, this statement implies a necessary synthesis of form and content: a form which embodies content and assumes diegetic functions.

A synthesis such as García Espinosa and Alea describe is discernible in some of the political billboards that decorate Havana streets. For example, in 1989–90 a long and narrow billboard featured at its centre a young Fidel and Raúl Castro striding towards us, arm-in-arm with Camilo Cienfuegos, the young revolutionary hero who disappeared in 1960 (neither his body nor the wreckage of the plane he was in were ever recovered).[8] On either side of these three, arm-in-arm in a line, are groups of three or four students, police, workers, striding smilingly towards us. But the police uniforms were introduced several years after Camilo's death; the construction mini-brigades, not until the 80s. The past has been brought into the present with a seamless stroke of the brush. 'Death is not true' (*La muerte no es verdad*), hero of the Cuban war of independence José Martí once wrote. Although I once thought of this as a way of saying 'one's deeds live on after death', one can also see in the phrase the billboard's propensity to confound past and present. Cuban cinema incorporated and further elaborated this synthetic aesthetic, creating in many of its historical fiction films a cinematic past–present tense via the conflation of documentary and fictional modes of addresses.

It is often said that with the popular revolution of 1959 and the founding of the national film institute, ICAIC, that same year, Cuban film 'started from zero'. If by this it is meant that before 1959 Cuba had no established feature film industry, and much less a tradition of 'social' or 'art' cinema, then this is certainly the case.[9] However, Cuba was a particularly large market for foreign films before 1959, and the young Cuban film-makers who began working in the 60s encountered well-established viewing habits which were to have a marked influence on the evolution of post-1959 film theory and practice, determining, for example, an insistence on the popular (the use of genres, the recourse to comedy and melodrama, the fast pace) which distinguished Cuban films from the other Latin American 'new waves' of the period.

Perhaps, by borrowing Ortiz's terminology, we could say that a process of inculturation had taken place in Cuba before 1959. For decades a cultural commodity, a finished industrial product seemingly closed to transculturation, is said to have had its way with Cuban audiences. Cinema even seemed to carry with it predetermined modes of consumption. But it was precisely at the level of consumption that Cuban audiences were able to carry out a remarkable inculturation of this foreign cultural commodity via 'audience participation': in theatres to this day, members of the audience speak to the screen, cajoling and chiding actors, and expressing shock and dismay. This is the manifestation of a virtual cultural imperative in Cuba, to make foreign culture 'Cuban', and an expression of the powerful legacy of transculturation in the formation of Cuban culture and identity. Here then is our first indication of a 'perforation' of narrative structures and a mingling of voices in the cinema.

These viewing habits are complemented by a typical Cuban custom. With the exception of the Cinemateca and ICAIC (which have fixed-schedule archival and retrospective screenings) cinema theatres project their daily programme in a continuous, uninterrupted loop. The programme generally consists of a five-minute newsreel, a ten- to twenty-minute documentary or animated short, and the feature. Cuban audiences, including the middle class at first-run shows in downtown cinemas, seem to wander in and begin watching the show whenever they arrive (which can never be predicted when travelling on Havana's erratic transportation system). Thus the feature is often interrupted, made to straddle the short films, and viewed out of sequence.

In the above-mentioned essay, Alea draws attention to this programme format but neglects entirely to mention this critical aspect of the mode of consumption. He contemplates how this format may influence formal strategies without considering how the viewing habits associated with it may determine them further:

> [This programme format allows viewers to] experience *various levels of mediation* [author's italics] . . . which can offer them a better understanding of reality . . . seeing various genres at one screening does not always have the greatest coherence. . . . Nevertheless, this possibility of connections throws light on what could be achieved here, *even if we are just considering the framework of a single film* [my italics] (Alea, 1988, p. 27).

We know that the recent introduction of the remote-control TV channel-changer in the West was a decisive factor, along with the roughly contemporaneous stylistic innovations of the music video, in the recent radical change in the style of television commercials. No longer certain of the viewer's attention, commercials are abandoning their 'narratives' in favour of bursts of rapidly edited images. Sellers hope that exposure to a few seconds of these images will continue to sell their product, that form can do the job that content once did. Did Cuban viewing habits established in the pre-1959 period help determine post-1959 formal strategies in a similar way? We have already noted the broad impact they had, the emphasis in Cuba on popular entertainment, the manipulation of generic codes. More specific formal questions should also be considered, such as the construction of the diegesis (how can closure operate under the viewing conditions described above?).

Historical features were among ICAIC's earliest productions, and at most times in the past 30 years have formed the bulk of Cuban film production.[10] One critic has described this genre as *cine rescate*, a way to correct the distorted images of Cuba's own history.[11] In the early 60s, Cuban films predictably enough turned to themes of the recent past, the years of revolutionary struggle. However, something curious happened as the young Cuban film-makers matured in the late 60s. The 1968–76 period, when Cuban cinema produced its greatest works, was dominated by historical narratives which reached even further into history, from the 30s to the earliest colonial times. It could be argued that this evolution was a logical extension of the film-makers' historical enquiries and that these new themes offered better opportunities for more subtle and profound analysis than the revolutionary themes, as indeed they did. Yet at the same time it is true that

'The 1968–76 period . . . was dominated by historical narratives which reached . . . to the earliest colonial times.' La última cena (The Last Supper, *Tomás Gutiérrez Alea, Cuba, 1976*)

many in Cuba expected that, as the topic of the revolutionary years ran its course, these talented young directors would set their sights on contemporary reality, and there is considerable evidence that the film-makers themselves attempted to move in this direction. That they were unable to do so was clearly the result of political pressure, as the doctrine of not casting a critical eye on contemporary Cuba was consolidated in those years.[12]

As it became clear that it was far easier to shepherd a historical theme through the ICAIC project-approval bureaucracy than a contemporary topic, this new generation of film-makers in a 'revolutionary' society worked overwhelmingly with topics from the distant past. We can expect that a complex depiction of the past would develop as a result, that the present might appear in phantom forms. Yet no doubt because widespread disillusionment with the political leadership was not yet evident in Cuba, an aesthetic of political allegory and irony through an 'encoded' depiction of the past did not develop (as it did during roughly this period in past of Eastern Europe). Two films from this period dealing with the recent past best illustrate how the present was submerged in the historical narrative. In Manual Octavio Gómez's *Ustedes tienen la palabra* (*Now It's Up to You*, 1974), a tale of corruption and opportunism is told in flashback. The conflicts and contradictions of that recent period are explored, but contrasted with present-day sequences, when these conflicts have been dissolved in a display of popular revolutionary unity and resolve. It is significant that the only images we see of the present are those of the trial which purges the corrupt elements from the community. In

Alea's *Memorias de subdesarrollo* (*Memories of Underdevelopment*, 1968), arguably the most ambivalent Cuban film produced, Alea's ambivalence is not
only filtered through the past (the Bay of Pigs invasion of 1961), it is embodied in the figure of Sergio, a representative of the national bourgeoisie, a
class dismantled, exiled and reviled by the time of the film's production. In
each film, the narrative is carefully constructed to ensure that the contradictions of the past are banished from the present.

In 1971 Alea filmed *Una pelea cubana contra los demonios* (*A Cuban Struggle
Against the Demons*, 1972), one of his least seen and most experimental works.
Based on Fernando Ortiz's account of a case of religious fanaticism in 1672,
the setting is the furthest back in history that Cuban film has reached. On
viewing Alea's treatment, one suspects that part of the story and the setting's
appeal lay in the opportunity to create a radical abstraction of form against
such a remote and delirious backdrop. Virtually every frame of the film is
animated by a moving camera which circles dinner tables and follows people
through buildings.

Alea's moving camera creates a structure which seems not so much stitched
together through montage as a continuous image, a two-hour zoetrope. The
surface image, described by some critics as 'fluid', could really be said to be
'liquid', a flowing river of images. Near the end of the film there is a scene of
a canoe being paddled along a still river. While a shaman speaks in trance off
screen, the screen goes black with leader and then flickers with brief, ethereal
black and white photographs of José Martí, Che Guevara and Fidel Castro.
The surprising thing is how little we are taken aback by this juxtaposition of
historical moments, so porous and elastic is Alea's image. Alea has created a
form which has allowed him not to depict the past but to foretell the future
from the vantage point of the past.

In Manuel Octavio Gómez's *La primera carga al machete* (*The First Charge
of the Machete*, 1969) a variety of techniques are used to produce a similar, if
less transparent, transposition of past and present. Something of a *cinéma
vérité* docu-drama on the war of 1868, when poor *mambís* fought the Spaniards armed only with their cane-cutting machetes, the film employs mostly a
jarring hand-held camera and is shot on a grainy, high-contrast black and
white stock. Among the film's 'documentary' techniques are battlefield interviews and a segment on the history of the machete, while the film is punc-
tuated with periodic appearances of a roving troubadour, Cuban folk-singer
Pablo Milanés. But the most startling segment, the one which most conflates
documentary and fiction, past and present, occurs on a Havana street when
an individual, described by Michael Chanan as an 'accomplice of the camera'
(Chanan, 1985, p. 248 – see note 9 below) accosts passers-by and asks them
their political views. A disturbance develops and Spanish soldiers arrive to
quell it; Gómez's camera has travelled into the past and taken an active role in
the history unfolding there.

In describing his approach to the film and the reasoning behind the use of
the hand-held camera and sequences like the one above, Gómez has said: 'we
set about trying to give the idea that we were developing the story as if it were
being filmed at that very moment, as if it had been possible at that time to use
a camera and recorder to collect the facts', to which Chanan, in citing these

237

comments, adds 'the net result of these techniques is not so much to transport the viewer of the film into the past as to bring the past into the present' (Chanan, 1985, p. 248). Again, a form has been created which does not just depict the past, it inhabits it and films it in the present tense. It is interesting to note that this film was put into production when another film of Gómez's with a contemporary theme was shelved six months into production.[13] The sequence described above is the invention of a young film-maker unable to take his camera out on to the streets of contemporary Havana. The spectator not only sees history presented with the immediacy and 'authenticity' of an on-the-spot newsreel; he or she also sees history and the present cohabit the film frame, uniting past and present, creating a revolutionary film tense which corresponds to the appropriation of Cuban history by the post-1959 political leadership and their own appeal to an 'eternal past' which has been brought to life by the revolution.

Yet another instance of the appearance of past and present in the same frame can be cited: in Manuel Herrera's *Girón* (1972), also a docu-drama reconstruction, this time of the Bay of Pigs invasion of 1961, battle participants speak to the camera as they re-create their activities during the invasion. In one scene, a combatant appears as a commentator only, standing upright in the battle zone beside comrades in trenches, somehow safe from enemy fire. 'At this point,' he says, pointing down into the trench at one of

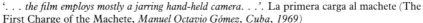

'. . . *the film employs mostly a jarring hand-held camera.* . . .'. La primera carga al machete (The First Charge of the Machete, *Manuel Octavio Gómez, Cuba, 1969*)

238

his comrades, 'X was hit in the shoulder', as we see X clutch his shoulder and grimace in pain, a few feet and ten years away.

Like *Primera carga*, *Girón* is a mishmash of styles, that 'one genre or all' that García Espinosa spoke of: we see in it direct address, interviews, dramatic re-enactments, voice-over narration, archival footage. There is even a brief 'romantic interlude' incongruous with the other footage: far from the muddy battlefield, a young couple stroll hand-in-hand on the beach in the setting sun, while a guitar softly strums on the soundtrack. By no means irrelevant to the narrative or without function in the film, this sequence recalls García Espinosa's call for a 'new poetics', an all-encompassing aesthetic which could contain elements of all forms and narrative strategies. [14]

Many important films (Humberto Solás's *Lucía*, 1968; Sergio Giral's *El otro Francisco*, 1974) and formal devices (the zoom, voice-over narration) have been overlooked in this brief survey of formal devices in Cuban historical narrative. While I drew attention to those instances where a cinematic past–present tense was clearly at work in specific films, a broader discussion might uncover other examples of the genre's radical formal experimentation and situate them within the framework of my argument: that these films developed formal means for embodying diegetic signification where the conditions for a more conventional construction of the diegesis may have been lacking, and that this process reflected currents and traditions in Cuban culture and society.

This is certainly a time for critical reappraisal of Cuban cinema: unable to build on the success of the first 15 years or to train a second generation of film-makers as talented as the first, Cuban film has been floundering now for more than half of ICAIC's existence. This is partly a result of the bureaucracy, gerontocracy and petty censorship which riddles Cuban society, but partly it may also be traced, paradoxically enough, to the success of the historical genre in those first 15 years. It is no coincidence that Cuban film in general declined when the historical genre showed signs of having run its course in the mid-70s, since Cuban film-makers had never really developed an aesthetic approach to contemporary life worthy of their talents. As the historical genre became a decadent, insipid shadow of its former self (Solás's *Cecilia*, 1981, and Enrique Pineda Barnet's *La bella del Alhambra* (*The Belle of the Alhambra*, 1989), come to mind) neither younger nor older directors were able to forge art out of contemporary reality. Even Pastor Vega's *Retrato de Teresa* (*Portrait of Teresa*, 1979), one of the most controversial Cuban films because of its topical subject matter of working women and machismo, is ultimately an extremely pedestrian film.

The idea for this essay grew out of my response to the work of a previous generation of foreign critics who saw greatly different things in Cuban film of this period, particularly, it seems, the spectre of Brecht at every turn. [15] While this is undoubtedly a valid critical perspective in many instances, when I viewed the films 20 years later, removed from the context of their production and from the fever of Brechtian analysis, I found instead that the range of formal devices these films employed conspired to the construction of an integrated, formal whole. Rather than being constructed to afford multiple readings, I found that many of the films spoke instead with one voice, that there was an ideological ventriloquism at work able to express itself through a wide variety of narrative and stylistic techniques. My general query, which this essay has only suggested, and that in a roundabout way, is: 'Are these films formal representations of an ideology which has set about to intervene in history in order to create a need for the present?' And I end with yet another unanswered question: 'What is the relationship between the insertion of a photograph of Fidel Castro into a film set in 1672 and the airbrushing, 300 years later, of discredited revolutionary heroes out of photographs where they appear at his side?'

Notes

1. Fernando Ortiz, *Contrapunteo cubano del tabaco y azúcar* (Havana: Editorial de Ciencias Sociales, 1983), rev. ed., p. 86. Unless otherwise noted, all translations are my own. For a general discussion of Ortiz and transculturation, see Jean Lamore, 'Transculturation: naissance d'un mot', *Vice versa*, no. 2, November 1987.
2. Fernando Ortiz, *Africanía de la música folklórica de Cuba*, (Las Villas, Cuba: Universidad Central de las Villas, 1965), rev. ed. For his studies of black culture, in particular, his trilogy *Los negros brujos* (1906), *Los negros esclavos* (1916) (Havana: Ciencias sociales, 1975), rev. ed., and *Los negros curros*, published posthumously (Havana: Ciencias Sociales, 1986).
3. See, for example, Leonardo Acosta's account of such a lament in the 19th century in 'From the Drum to the Synthesizer: Study of a Process', *Latin American Perspectives*, vol. 16, no. 2, Spring 1989, p. 35. I am indebted to Acosta's analysis of musical transculturation for my own comments here.
4. See Acosta, p. 43.
5. Alejo Carpentier, 'América Latina en la confluencia de coordenadas históricas y su repercusión en la música', *América Latina en su música* (Mexico: Siglo XXI, 1977), cited and translated by Acosta, p. 33.
6. Originally published in *Cine cubano*, no. 66–67, 1969. Reprinted in translation in *Afterimage*, no. 3, Summer 1971 in abridged form, and in *JumpCut*, no. 20, May 1979. Reprinted in Spanish in *Hojas de cine: testimonios y documentos del nuevo cine latinoamericano*, vol. II (Mexico: Fundación Mexicana de Cineastas, 1988). All page references are to the Mexican edition.
7. Tomás Gutiérrez Alea, 'Del espectáculo en su sentido más puro al "Cine de Ideas" ', *Dialéctica del espectador* (Havana: José Martí, 1988), p. 28.
8. A considerable death cult has grown up around Camilo Cienfuegos and to this day in Cuba, on the anniversary of his 'physical disappearance' (never his death) large numbers of people throw a single rose into the sea in his memory.
9. For an overview of early Cuban film history, see Michael Chanan, *The Cuban Image* (London: British Film Institute, 1985), and Paulo Antonio Paranagua (ed.), *Le Cinéma cubain* (Paris: Centre Georges Pompidou, 1990). These are the two most comprehensive publications on Cuban film.
10. In a recent poll of ICAIC's 'Artistic Committee', the 30 top films of the post-1959 period were selected. Of these, 13 were depictions of the recent past, from the 50s on, as time progressed; 8 were set in the distant past (I include *Lucía* here); and 9 addressed contemporary issues. Even these figures are unrepresentative, because the ICAIC officials were careful to represent each decade equally, even though the earlier films are by far more accomplished than the later ones, which tended to have contemporary themes (5 of the 8 contemporary themes can be found in films made between 1983 and 1985). See Paranagua (ed.), *Le Cinéma cubain*, p. 105.
11. See Chanan, *The Cuban Image*, pp. 247–9.

12. See Andrés Hernández, 'Film-making and Politics: The Cuban Experience', *American Behavioural Scientist*, vol. 17, no. 3, January–February 1974, for a reasoned account of censorship and political pressures at ICAIC in those years. There are many other indications of film-makers having problems getting productions off the ground and a certain amount of turmoil at ICAIC in those years: there is, for example, an interview with Solás in *JumpCut*, no. 19, pp. 27–31, where he describes a project with a contemporary theme, whereas his *oeuvre* consists of only one film with a contemporary theme, made before this interview and whose release had been delayed by ICAIC, and there is also a 1971 *International Film Guide* report whose list of upcoming productions bears no resemblance to that year's completed films.

13. Hernández, 'Film-making and Politics', p. 346.

14. It is interesting to note that, following his manifesto 'Por un cine imperfecto' in 1969 and until his appointment as head of ICAIC in 1982, Julio García Espinosa virtually ceased film-making and became a frequent co-author of Cuban film scripts, including those for *Primera carga* and *Girón*.

15. The literature on Brechtian influences in Cuban film is large; much of it can be found on three special issues of the US journal *JumpCut* in the late 70s, nos. 19, 20 and 22.

NATIONAL CINEMA AFTER GLOBALIZATION

Fernando Solanas's Sur *and the Exiled Nation*

KATHLEEN NEWMAN

Editors' Introduction

Exile is perhaps the word that best characterises the condition of the Latin American intellectual and artist: either by choice or political necessity, most have had to face the decentred and contrapuntal life of the exile. In recent decades, the Latin American cinema has had more than the usual share of exiles, as film-makers physically or spiritually left their 'nations' – Brazil in the 60s (see Xavier's essay), Chile and Argentina in the 70s, many others in between – in the wake of the repressive military dictatorships that swept over the continent. These diasporas had an unexpected side-effect in the case of the Chilean exile cinema: a prolific 'national' cinema produced outside the boundaries of the nation–state. In Argentina, the political exodus and subsequent return after the process of redemocratisation begun in the 80s was markedly different. Instead of Pinochet, the dictator we all loved to hate, Argentina had a 'dirty war', an insidious deterritorialisation of the nation that redefined citizenship and national belongingness.

Kathleen Newman's essay tackles the question of state–cinema relations already explored in economic and legislative terms by Johnson and Lenti from a different perspective that links the state of the nation to exile, and thus to the idea of a *cine nacional* or national cinema. Her essay focuses on two films by the Argentine exile film-maker Fernando Solanas – *Tangos: L'exil de Gardel* (*Tangos: El exilio de Gardel*; *Tangos: The Exile of Gardel*) and *Sur* – the former a film of exile, the latter one of national redefinition. While *Tangos* speaks of the hopes and fears of those who left the nation and seems to propose the need for the redemocratisation process to rebuild national political institutions, *Sur* 'conflates the return from exile with redemocratization itself [and] invents a nation that meets the expectations of those exiles'. *Sur* is ultimately invested in positing the continuing viability of a Peronist Argentine nation while revealing 'the extent to which globalization has already erased the nation as a viable political ensemble'. Thus Newman's analysis indicates that the Argentine nation (and its cinema), violently torn asunder by the dirty war, exile, and global

242

economics, survives as a fictional, if determinate, construct that exists in the nostalgia of nationalist political projects.

☐

In Latin American countries, national cinema has long competed with films imported from Europe, the United States and other Latin American nations for the attention of the citizenry. For this reason, it has been possible to consider cinema history for the region as a cumulative history of national cinemas. Even the region-wide New Latin American Cinema, despite its common political commitments and aesthetic practices, could be viewed as no exception to national categorization: in the 60s and 70s cinema production and distribution was still largely determined by the specific configurations of national film industries in countries such as Argentina, Brazil, Cuba and Mexico, on the one hand, and by the relative lack of sustained industrial infrastructures in Andean and Central American countries, on the other. Yet, while politically committed film-making in this period did mark commercial cinema as a contested cultural practice, it is clear that, by the end of the 80s, the binary opposition between political and commercial cinema within the nation–state had been altered irrevocably. The current diversity of film and video practices in the region is a response to adverse political and economic conditions and, necessarily, a distinct politics of cinema. Such 'diversity out of adversity' is evidence of the profound impact of capitalism's continuing globalization on the nation itself and, consequently, national cinema.

In the case of the nation in Latin America, after a first 500 years in which the political–economic competition between nation–states was a mechanism of integration of geographical regions into a world-economic system, capitalism has entered a second phase in which transnational practices overcome the pretenses of national sovereignty.[1] Though nation–states still mobilize and deploy the means of violence within and without their borders, and though the state still functions as the guarantor of class relations, the scale of systemic integration is such that almost any struggle is always already local, national, regional, and global. Thus struggles for self-determination and social justice, which numerous Latin American film-makers have taken to heart, are measured against a different scale of events.

In the case of national cinema in Latin America, there has been over the last 30 years a dislocation of film-maker and nation. Specifically, exile in the case of nations under dictatorship, and (seemingly national) economic crises in the case of nations with elected governments, caused many Latin American intellectuals to lead transnational lives. Hindsight shows this to be part of a massive reorganization of the intellectual sector, including film-makers, within and across nation–states in Latin America, as part of a reorganization of the world economy. Concomitantly, film production and exhibition in the region, always an expensive, collaborative project, by necessity had to improve on the international financial and distribution arrangements of previous periods. Thus, a nation, whether a film-maker's own or not, came to be

243

no longer necessarily the base from which films are made and distributed, and a national audience no longer necessarily the primary addressee. In fact, many of the recent feature films considered to be Latin American films, by reason of the nationality of the film-makers, are co-productions with European companies or institutions and first address an international audience. These co-productions have been sought by Latin American film-makers in response to a sharp decrease in national film financing due to debt crisis, and by European producers with an eye to an expansion of markets.

To explore the question of the current status of cinema and nation, I should like to discuss a co-production which is in many ways a treatise on the nation and national cinemas: Fernando Solanas's feature film *Sur* (1987), an Argentine–French co-production, which is most often discussed by critics as part of the cinema of redemocratization in Argentina, that is, as part of a renovation of a national cinema. Indeed, John King has observed that 'The trajectory of Solanas from 1968 to 1988, from *La hora de los hornos* to *Sur*, charts in microcosm the development of politically committed film-making in Argentina'.[2] I shall argue that while *Sur* itself does attempt to chart a new course for both Peronism and third cinema, it reveals in this attempt the extent to which globalization has already erased the nation as a viable political ensemble. In discussing Solanas's work and its relation to Argentina as a nation, it is important to recall a point about the impact on Argentine society of the most recent period of military rule (1976–83), during which some nine thousand citizens were 'disappeared' by the junta and by paramilitary forces. As Donald C. Hodges has observed in the preface to his recent book on Argentina's dirty war, 'Argentina has experienced domestically the hostilities that citizens of other states experience mainly in the area of foreign relations'.[3] The military coup of 1976 was a redeployment of a pre-existing authoritarianism in Argentine society, but it was different from all of the previous coups since 1930, even the coup of 1966 which Guillermo O'Donnell has argued marked the 'implantation' of a bureaucratic-authoritarian state,[4] in that this coup 'deterritorialized' the nation: the abstract guarantee of protection of life for citizens within their own national boundaries was revoked and citizenship was redefined. In fact, the coup and the dirty war signalled a redefinition of the state. As an abstract institutional ensemble constituting all citizens as subjects of a nation, the state is the essential binding of citizen to citizen in solidarity which is expressed through governance itself, that which we recognize in daily life in its more concrete manifestations as government institutions and political regimes. Yet, as the theoretical work of Nicos Poulantzas and Michel Foucault[5] of the same period of Argentine military rule has shown, this abstract, essentially democratic relation among citizens is, under the modern capitalist state, concretized in violence. Argentina's military coup actualized the potential for violence at the heart of all states within the capitalist world economy, very simply because nations serve to sustain, within this ever expanding economic system, social divisions of labor that are not equitative. The historical development of Argentina's political economy in linkage with a world economy produced, at this conjuncture, such antagonistic political projects for the nation, from socialism to Peronism to Fascism – and much in between – that 'violence at the heart of the state' was mobilized. The return to civilian rule in Argentina in the early 80s did not diminish the systemic capacity for state terror, but rather deferred its deployment. The nation as a political ensemble, then, is at once the lived experience of citizenship, country, and government, and, as well, a dynamic, systemic set of relations that, potentially, can eradicate all three. I will argue that Solanas's cinematic work in the 80s, beyond his own political theories and the national political project he advocates, registers a change in the very set of relations that is a nation.

NATIONALIST ALLEGORY AND THE RETURN FROM EXILE: 1985

Much of what *Sur* is in terms of style and politics was announced in Solanas's *Tangos: El exilio de Gardel* (*Tangos: The Exile of Gardel*, 1985), his previous Argentine–French co-production. A film of great emotional impact, perhaps the best-known film of Latin American exile, *Tangos* explored the anguish of a group of Argentine exiles in Paris involved in the invention of a *tanguedia*, a theatrical piece about their specific exile, based on tangos, which is at once tragedy and comedy. The film itself is explicitly a *tanguedia*, a new dramatic genre announced in the film and then parodied by the film to serve Solanas's political goals. Filmically, Solanas pays homage to European political films and the US dance-musical, and creates for himself as auteur signature patterns of framing and camera movement to express, respectively, memory as praxis and the circularity of violence. He also introduces into this film language a diegetics of theatrical space derived from Latin American political theatre, which will enable a Peronist, nationalist allegory within the film which is not expressed at other levels of the text.

Though much of the film takes place inside a cavernous rehearsal hall, with the curved balustrades and support columns of the mezzanine defining, through the use of the tiers and shadows in shot composition, the socio–political order the diegetic *tanguedia* seeks to examine, the chapters of the films are successively structured to have the narrative culminate in quite a different space, that of the small tableau for a political *acto*. The opening section of the final chapter, 'Volver' ('Return'), which takes its title from the classic song expressing the desire to return to one's homeland, is staged beneath the high central vault of a trade center and is presented as a dream sequence of Gerardo, the exiled intellectual who now works as a guard. In the sequence, Gerardo converses with General San Martín, a leader of the war for independence from Spain, and Carlos Gardel, the renowned tango singer, both of whom died in lands distant from Argentina. The immensity of the space, lighted for night, is used in the first part of this sequence to locate the three characters in a Utopian space beyond both everyday politics and the nation–state, to measure their small contribution to the greater cause of the nation. In the second part of the sequence, at the end of cross-cut medium shots constructing an easy intimacy between the three men as they converse about *la patria*, the camera dollies back from the three characters to suggest a tableau. With San Martín and Gardel seated in the semi-darkness to the left and right, respectively, of Gerardo who, in white bedclothes on white sheets, centrally framed and lighted, is made the focus of the words of the tango 'Volver'. The characters have been listening to the tango on a record-player,

245

'The film itself is explicitly a tanguedia, *a new dramatic genre announced in the film. . .'.* Tangos: L'exil de Gardel, Tangos: El exilio de Gardel (Tangos – Gardel's Exile, *Fernando E Solanas, France/Argentina, 1985*)

but the increase in volume during the dolly back breaks with the diegesis. The scene becomes recognizably a set common to political theater of the generation of the 60s. The combination of all these elements serve to have the lyrics of the tango directly apply to the character of the intellectual, and therefore it becomes an explicit evaluation of the political activism of Solanas's generation. The tableau insistently prefigures not merely the return of the exiles to Argentina, but the renovation of Peronism, as we shall see below.

Readers familiar with the film will recall that the character of Gerardo has played a relatively minor role until this point. The film is principally concerned with a female dancer, the lead in the *tanguedia*, who suffers great depression because of exile and memories of her husband, a professional who was 'disappeared' by security forces during the dirty war, and her lover, another exile, who is the composer of the *tanguedia*. The chapters of the film are also structured by musical street performances, of 'the children of exile', who after a number of years find themselves emotionally between countries and, in some ways, more French than Argentine. The memories of the various exiles of their friends, family and homeland, the daily confrontations between the tragic and the absurd (mannequins in the dance hall representing the disappeared and the tortured; stylized exploding or deflating bodies literalizing the emotions of the troupe), and the dances of the diegetic *tanguedia*, energetically delineating the expressive patterns of the tango itself, all in all do *not* require, at the level of plot, an ending which focuses on the traditional intellectual (such as journalists or university teachers or students)

246

for whom print is the principal medium of expression, rather than the artists in the film. Yet no other character could serve the political purpose of Solanas's tableau. In this tableau, the political genealogy is Peronist, extending from the military founding father, San Martín, to the singer Gardel (here recuperated not merely as an icon of mass culture but a figure of political populism) to the left intellectual who had seen his country lost to authoritarianism.[6] Here, as is common in Peronist art, a military *prócer* or leader is read as the prefiguration of Perón, Gardel as an expression of the desires of the laboring classes whose union activities have sustained Peronism for some forty years (to the date of the film's release) through both civilian and military regimes (some Peronist, some not), and the intellectual-who-writes as a synecdoche of the militant political theorist. The militant intellectual was a crucial figure in the leftist political parties of the 70s, one often involved in party leadership. Yet most parties, including left Peronist parties, did not foresee the coming state terror, or the ways in which their own actions would expose their membership and the populace at large to the violence of the dirty war. The political theory under which the activists of Solanas's generation operated was not adequate: it underestimated the reaction of the rightist military and civilian leadership and did not understand the nature of the state, particularly when and how violence is mobilized against the citizenry (though, it should be stressed, this latter lack of attention to state theory was a common problem among the left in many countries in the 60s and 70s).

When the ghost of San Martín enters this scene, emerging from the swirling night fog to the sound of distant cannon fire, the spatial relations serve to emphasize the enormity of the historical undertaking that is the founding of a nation. In the second half of the scene, during the conversation with Gerardo and Gardel, the reduction of the space to a patriarchal trio allows for the conflation of the entirety of Argentine political history under the banner of Peronism with its particularly odd combination of populism, militarism and vanguardism. In English-language cinema studies, it is not widely recognized that the Third Cinema described by Solanas and Octavio Getino in the 60s would become by the 70s an explicitly Peronist cinema, albeit one very critical of the rightist elements within historical Peronism. Solanas's political theory of the period, which advocated elements of Marxist theories of class struggle at the same time as it espoused a contradictory vision of labor struggles enabled by Peronist government leadership, was anti-imperialist and nationalist, the latter of which included an epic vision of Peronist creation of the nation based on social justice. The evaluation of the exiled militants' political theory in this scene is ultimately a reaffirmation of this epic nationalism rather than its critique. After noting the fear involved in confronting one's past life, the lyrics of 'Volver' employed in this scene to cover the tableau end with the following lines: 'y aunque el olvido que todo destruye haya matado mi vieja ilusión, guardo escondida una esperanza humilde que es la fortuna de mi corazón/Volver . . .' ('and although my old illusions have been killed by oblivion that destroys everything, I keep hidden a humble hope that is the fortune of my heart/Return . . .'). To say in this context 'although my old illusions have been destroyed by their passage into time' (here suggested by 'oblivion' or erasure) is not to critique the basis of

247

those illusions. The humble hope in this context is only humble in the sense that it is meant to associate the three figures of the tableau with popular sectors (*gente humilde*) and to suggest that the return of those political militants who had to go into exile will signal the renewal of the nation itself. While Argentine redemocratization did propose a renewal of national political institutions, the process included many more sectors of the citizenry than Solanas included in *Tangos*.

A cinema of redemocratization did emerge in the five years that followed Argentina's return to civilian rule. With significant support from the Instituto Nacional de Cinematografía, these films of the redemocratization period examined the causes and consequences of the dictatorship and the dirty war. Though a noticeable trend in feature films, this cinema did not overshadow, in terms of national cinema production, the many comedies and action films released at the same time, and, as in the past, films imported from the United States and Europe tended to dominate the market. However, the cinema of redemocratization did earn for Argentina a different status in the international market and at international festivals, which had a concomitant impact on its reception by national audiences. The award of the Oscar for Best Film to *La historia oficial* (Puenzo, *The Official Version*, 1985) increased the international interest in Argentine film, as did the release in the same year of *Tangos* and *Hombre mirando al sudeste* (Subiela, *Man looking South-East*), and renewed international attention to the torture and murder committed under the dictatorship. The promotional materials for the restrospective of Argentine cinema at the Institute of Contemporary Art in Boston in 1990,[7] though misleading, are not atypical of writings on Argentine film after redemocratization:

Argentina lays claim to one of the oldest and most influential film industries in the world, one that has been subject to the vicissitudes and upheavals of that country's political and social history. In the 1950s and 60s, the *nuevo cine* (new cinema) and *cine liberación* (liberation cinema) were in the vanguard of third-world cinema movements. Under the military dictatorship that lasted from 1976 to 1983, artistic expression and scores of filmmakers went underground or into exile. With the return of democracy in 1983, the floodgates opened and what followed was a veritable renaissance of film production.... Including more than thirty films, CINE ARGENTINO celebrates one of the most vital and engaging national cinemas in the world.

This summation suggests, erroneously, that the years of the dictatorship, in terms of both film and social history, were a period of decreased cultural activity, a lull between two periods of intense activity. In fact, the dictatorship was a moment of rupture, a sundering of social contracts, a period of state terror and bureaucratic authoritarianism in which some fifty years of social organization came to an end. Likewise, the films of redemocratization were not in any way the resumption of the aesthetics and politics of *nuevo cine* or the Peronist cinema of the 60s and early 70s but rather a response exactly to the violent sundering. It was impossible in the 80s to return to a politics

248

that had not foreseen the retaliatory vengeance of the dirty war against not only political militants but against the populace as a whole. Furthermore, it suggested that Argentine film might regain a former aesthetic or political preeminence (or both) internationally because the conditions which undermined such preeminence have been overcome. Though there was resistance to the dictatorship within the nation, the return to democracy was made possible by the self-destruction of the military leadership by means of disastrous long- and short-term economic policies and the instigation of the Malvinas–Falklands War. Briefly, the return to civilian rule, under Radical Union Party leadership, did not undo the imbalance of power between the military and civil leadership and did not forestall the impact of the foreign debt incurred by the military rulers on the quality of life. Ultimately, though members of the junta were tried for their crimes, the civilian government did not redress fully the murder of Argentine citizens by other Argentine citizens in the dirty war, that is, did not take all the steps necessary to prevent a recurrence of state terrorism. What sense of revitalized national cultural production existed in the first years of civilian rule had evaporated by 1989 when Carlos Saúl Menem assumed the presidency six months earlier than scheduled in a moment of severe political–economic crisis. The obviously deepening divisions within the electorally victorious Peronist party between Menem's centrist and rightist supporters, on the one hand, and *la renovación peronista* (Peronist renovation), a wing seeking to recapture the dynamism of the left-Peronist commitment to social change of the 70s, on the other, augured the two years of ever-increasing severity of economic problems leading to the dollarization of the Argentine economy in April 1991. If anything, Argentine national cinema from 1983 to the end of the decade did not register the emergence of a new cinema movement nationally or internationally, as suggested above, but rather the ever-increasing difficulty of film production and a shattering of previous political alliances within Peronism.

In this context, *Sur* was Solanas's explicit intervention in Argentine national politics. Solanas's return to Argentina from exile in France coincided with the first phase of Peronist redefinition after the return to civilian rule. Whereas *Tangos* chronicled the various fates of Argentine exiles in Europe and their sense of the ways in which they had both lost and preserved the true Argentine nation, *Sur* invented a nation that met the expectations of those exiles, a nation to which their return would be crucial. The story of the return home of a political prisoner released from prison in the south of Argentina on the eve of return to civilian rule, *Sur* conflates the return from exile with redemocratization itself, thus omitting what was widely discussed at the time, the history of the two distinct yet inseparable Argentinas, one belonging to those who stayed during dictatorship and one to those who had to leave. Historically, in both Argentinas, individuals and groups continued the struggle for human rights and social justice. Solanas, however, chooses a version of redemocratization which overlooks the political resistance inside Argentina in the period of the dictatorship in order to see redemocratization as the revitalization of Peronism.

It could be argued that this version is not disingenuous. Argentine sociologist María del Carmen Feijoó considers the film, released in 1987, to mark a shift in Peronist cultural politics. For Feijoó, *Sur* correctly concentrates on the specific experiences and private life of political activists as opposed to a more exemplary, but more deadly, sacrificial heroism of the films of the second period of Peronism (1973–6). From the perspective of cultural history, Francine Masiello argues, on the other hand, that *Sur* expressed a Peronist nostalgia, seeking a story of political origin in labor struggles prior to Perón's first presidency (1946–55) that would exonerate left-Peronism of the political mistakes that fed the violence of the dirty war and the rise of Fascism in Argentina.[8]

Solanas's cultural imprimatur is of the magnitude that, though not a direct representative of the Peronist party, he is a considerable political force in national politics. In his fourth incarnation as a film-maker at the time of *Sur* – the first three incarnations involving, first, clandestine film-making under the first phase of bureaucratic authoritarianism (*La hora de los hornos (Hour of the Furnaces)*, 1968); second, a bleakly celebratory nationalism during Peronist government (*Los hijos de Fierro (The Sons of Fierro)*, 1975); and third, film-making concretizing the time spent in France (*La mirada de otros (The Gaze of Others)*, 1980), and *Tangos: El exilio de Gardel (Tangos: The Exile of Gardel)*, 1985) – Solanas had the political stature during redemocratization to redefine political debates. Solanas supported Menem in the latter's election campaign, but as Menem's presidency evolved, Solanas denounced corruption in Menem's administration (which, in one case, Solanas felt had undermined the project to purchase the Galería del Pacífico for a cultural center) as did a number of other leading figures.[9] On 22 May 1991 gunmen shot Solanas as he left the sound studio where he had been working on the film *El viaje (The Journey)*. Though Solanas recovered from the leg wounds he received, the attack was believed to signal the willingness of the paramilitary to resume, at any time, the violence that had previously forced Solanas and so many others into exile. Significantly, in an interview subsequent to the attack, Solanas said that the protagonist of all his films was Argentina itself[10] and it is this question of the nation as protagonist to which I shall now turn.

REDEMOCRATIZATION AS FRATERNAL ROMANCE: 1987

Recent work on the relation between fiction and the nation stresses that the construction of a national culture is part and parcel of the continuing con-figuration of nationality and state formation.[11] In these simultaneous pro-cesses, citizens are constituted by their relation to the state, the abstract ensemble in which all members are defined as equal, but socially positioned by the concrete manifestations of nation and government which, usually, ensure the continued functioning of unequal political and economic relations, particularly in the case of capitalist states.[12] Citizens are inscribed within the nation in an ensemble, 'the people', whose collective action is neither predict-able nor easily described. Homi Bhabha has termed this a rhetorical strategy:

> The people are not simply historical events or parts of a patriotic body politic. They are also a complex rhetorical strategy of social reference where the claim to be representative provokes a crisis within the process of

250

signification and discursive address. We then have a contested cultural territory where the people must be thought in a double-time; the people are the historical 'objects' of a nationalist pedagogy, giving the discourse an authority that is based on the pre-given or constituted historical origin or event; the people are also the 'subjects' of a process of signification that must erase any prior or originary presence of the nation–people to demonstrate the prodigious, living principal of the people as that continual process by which the national life is redeemed and signified as a repeating and reproductive process.[13]

In a country such as Argentina, the contested 'cultural territory' for some 60 years has been the public sphere itself, given the alternation of civilian and military rule since the first coup of 1930. This means that what must be constantly redeemed is democratic government and legitimate representation, and that the political struggles of 'the people' for egalitarian relations among citizens is principally a contest over the definition of the nation itself.

This struggle is allegorized in the film *Sur* as Project Sur, a worker's project (which Solanas invents for the film) conceived in the generation before Peronism: it is a southern hemisphere project seeking the legitimate representation of 'the people' in opposition to the northern hemisphere version of government, that is to say, the Argentine military and upper class aligned with US imperialism. In a humorous interrogation scene in a 'national' library[14] – part the exploration of Don Quixote's library, part Borges's 'Biblioteca de Babel' (the Library of Babel) – an elderly militant responds to his military questioners that, if they do not understand Project Sur, it is because they are aligned with the North. Like the tableau of *Tangos*, the interrogation of the *dirigente* allows Solanas to reposition the politics of this film in order to once again conflate all of Argentine political history with the renovation of Peronism. On the surface, the film seems to concern issues of redemocratization. The plot treats the return of a working-class political prisoner, Floreal, released on the eve of democratic rule, to his wife, Rosi. He is accompanied on his night's journey by El Negro, the ghost of a friend who was a labor leader. Floreal must come to terms not only with the tragedies of the dirty war but with his memories of his wife's affair with his best friend, Roberto, while he was in jail. Yet, in a typically epic gesture by Solanas, this love triangle becomes the new base on which the Project Sur will stand – as soon as it can be reduced to a binary, patriarchal relation. *Sur*, for all Solanas's broad gestures, subtly addresses an issue that *Tangos* did not: the relation between the gender system and the state.

The promotional materials for *Sur* presented the film as an offering from Solanas to the Argentine people, a gift of the returning exile. The record cover, for example, states that this is 'a film to carry in one's heart', and the video presents a message from Solanas indicating the political significance of the love story he has constructed:

I want to tell you that *Sur* is a love story. It is the love of a couple and the story of love for a country.
It is the story of a return.

251

Sur reminds us of those Argentines who I have called in the film the ones of 'the table of dreams'.

They, beyond their political convictions, gave us, as our heritage, their work and their commitment.

Sur speaks to us of reunions and friendship. It is the triumph of life over death, love over resentment, freedom over oppression, desire over fear.

I also want to tell you that *Sur* is an homage to all of those who, like my character The Stutterer, knew how to say 'no'. They were the ones who maintained dignity. They said 'no' to injustice, to oppression, to the surrender of the country.

Dear friends, here is *Sur*. It was made from the heart and now it belongs to you.

The affirmation of life and love after all of the deaths and separation occasioned by the dirty war could be considered a first step toward the renewal of a democratic culture, but Solanas intertwines his stated principal love story, between a couple who were young adults in the days of political militancy prior to the military coup, with two other narratives: the sacrificial death of the generation of the grandparents of his principal couple and of the more politically active members of this couple's generation. The 'table of dreams', around which sit the militants of the generation of Emilio Rasatti and Project Sur, is said by Solanas to bequeath the current generations an inheritance combining their work, that is, their struggles, and the example of their political commitment.[15] In film, however, Emilio also bequeaths the example of his death, which the male protagonist Floreal, sitting alone at 'the table of dreams', appreciates, saying that Emilio really knew how to die. The meanings created by the scene of the death of Emilio and his wife, which is presented as poignant though representing paramilitary violence, are further complicated by the implicit comparison with the other death Floreal has witnessed, that of El Negro.

Near the beginning of the film, with El Negro as his Virgil in this night of memories of the hell of the dirty war, Floreal watches El Negro reenact his own death: the security forces in the standard Ford Falcon pull the political leader from his home and shoot him down in the street. As Floreal watches horrified at the loss of his friend, El Negro jumps back up and comments on his own foolishness. The scene comes very close to comparing our memories of the dirty war to the comedy of a film run backwards. When Emilio and his wife hear the thugs arrive outside their home at night, Emilio makes a barricade across the central hallway of their home with a large chest and prepares to shoot the intruders with a pistol when they break through the front door. Ignoring Emilio's entreaties to hide, his wife fetches two glasses of wine with which to toast their life together. They die bravely together under a volley of shotgun blasts, the carnage of which the audience does not have to witness because the bodies are behind the chest. The pet bird flies up into the air at the shots and curses the assassins.

The purpose of this heroic, Hollywood death is exactly to create a 'triumph of life over death' and to find the 'dignity of those who resisted' in the lottery of massacre and terror that was the dirty war, yet Solanas is very close to

252

insulting those who died in the dirty war: his insistence that there is such a thing as a dignified death or an honorable death suggests that, at some deeper level, he believes a dignity must be invented for and assigned to these deaths. Solanas has constructed this film in such a way that Emilio's death is suggested to have been a sacrifice worthy of his life of activism, and therefore El Negro's activism and death is judged in the film as not as worthy. Here Solanas is very close to blaming the victims of the dirty war for their victimization, and, specifically, blaming the left political actors of his own generation who fell victim to state terror. This is quite different from a critique of the political theories operating in the period. As a consequence of the film's comparison of the two characters, those who were not part of Argentine society during the dictatorship, such as Floreal in prison, or those who were able to reach exile, are exonerated from the responsibility for the political failures of the period.

The two love stories which here receive approval are also made the model of the greater heroic gesture, in terms of narrative as a communicative act, of the love of storyteller for audience, film-maker for nation. For example, the space in which Emilio and his wife die, the long corridor, prefigures the space of the reunion of Floreal and Rosi at the very end of the film, another long interior corridor. In this final sequence, as Rosi looks at Floreal through the panes of a window, the camera reveals Floreal's reflection covering her face such that the two images merge. Solanas, in the book of interviews on the film published in 1989 (and advertised as a 'biography' of *Sur*), stated that he wishes to continue in *Sur* the formal experimentation he had begun in *Tangos*:

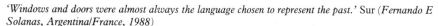

'Windows and doors were almost always the language chosen to represent the past.' Sur *(Fernando E Solanas, Argentina/France, 1988)*

In *Sur* I wanted to continue reframing images, treating the images through the other elements that break down the frame. My purpose in *Sur* was that of 'glimpsing' memory, and almost all the shots are filmed through doors, windows, or various modifications of the classic rectangular frame. Windows and doors were almost always the language chosen to represent the past. Still shots seen through something. For the present, in contrast, the scenes with Floreal were moving shots, great long shots filmed in a lengthy single take, almost always tracking shots. In the scenes of Rosi waiting in the house, I wanted the multiplication of her image in the mirrors or reflections in the window panes, in a stationary shot.

Whereas camera movement was foregrounded in *Tangos*, framing and shot composition are made to bear 'the burden of history' in *Sur*. The reunion of Rosi and Floreal, the gender politics of which will be explored shortly, is the intersection of past and present where, ironically, it is the prisoner who has been living in memories of the past who represents the present and the woman who has been active in the present who represents the past. Rather than the multiplication of images which had suggested the complexity of Rosi's dilemmas as a person living under dictatorship or in a love triangle, the two faces that blur together in the pane of glass reduce the possibilities of interpretation of this scene, in a sense, limiting the present because it limits the future. Solanas's plan to spy on memory, to glimpse the past, while an effective technique to suggest the elusive nature of memory, becomes in the film's final sequence a rejection of the past, an erasure of the events that led to the reunion. What one glimpses is a triumphant return to the present, in contradiction to all the past adversity and all past mistakes.

The reunion is part of the fourth and final section of the film, 'Morir cansa': Dying is wearisome. Significantly, Solanas described this section in the above-mentioned book of interviews in terms of what the protagonist, Floreal, came to understand about the differences between the politics of Floreal's dead guide and 'the people:

> '*Dying is wearisome*'. . . . It is the protagonist's confrontation with social reality, unemployment, and the decay of an economically perverse society. It is the protagonist's understanding of the real meaning of his parents' struggle. It is El Negro's self-criticism of the triumphalism and sectarianism of the [political] leadership and his understanding of the silent leadership of the people. 'One learns in defeat . . . dying is wearisome . . . how many things have died in these years and I with them . . . I, who gave my life as a leader, because of my triumphalism, ended up not understanding the silence of the people. . . . The people were not conquered: they survived by defending what little they had.'
> In all, it is the final confrontation of Floreal with the true country which will make him understand the importance of concentrating his anger and his energy in order to change reality, to defend and realize his dreams.

The quotations at the end of the first paragraph are fragments of dialogue of El Negro. He confesses that he never understood 'the people', who were not vanquished but rather survived defending the little they had. The triumphalist position of the Peronist leadership caused these leaders not to recognize the direction 'the people' were taking, and not to 'hear' what they should have heard. While the Peronist leadership did make numerous mistakes, to have this one leader, murdered in the streets, stand for all that happened in the days of political militancy prior to the dirty war, the deaths of militants from various non-Peronist left and centrist parties and of citizens who had no political involvement, is a dismissal of the human dignity Solanas stated he wished to affirm. Ultimately, Floreal's understanding of the struggles of his parents is Solanas's dismissal of the members of his own generation who could not return, because they, unlike Solanas, never left the political present of the dictatorship, rather they died because of it or lived through it. In the latter case, these people changed in ways Solanas does not choose to recognize; were he to do so, it would undermine his political agenda for the nation.

The resolution of the love triangle between Rosi, Floreal and Roberto has a bearing both on the question of the responsibility for the conduct of politics in the present and the past and on the question of legitimate representation in the future. Rosi and Roberto end their affair in the film and Roberto (a French immigrant who is lame in one leg, or *rengo*, in the best Arltian literary tradition) chooses to return to France. El Negro tells Floreal just before Floreal's reunion with Rosi that Rosi had never left him: she had chosen him again. Yet before this reunion is presented, there is an enactment of Roberto, seated at his own café table in the Utopian space of Floreal's night journey through the streets past the 'table of dreams', facing the camera, speaking to Floreal. Roberto tells Floreal that though Floreal was a prisoner, he was always able to maintain this freedom in ways Roberto could not. Though this would appear to be another rejection of the activism of Solanas's generation, the narrative resolution of this triangle is not the subsequent visualized reunion of the married couple. If Rosi never left Floreal but awaited his return, the connection between them was never broken. The principal return is Floreal's to Roberto, the fraternal embrace is not represented on screen because it need not be. The Utopian night space through which Floreal has travelled is masculinist: his relationship with his wife and his brief affair with a woman while in hiding prior to his arrest are secondary to Roberto's motorcycle rescue of Floreal early in the film, a trope often repeated in the film outside the frames of the past, dissolving freely in the narrative to the roar of the cycle's engine on the soundtrack. Whereas Rosi has embodied Argentina, to the extent to which the narrative has been an allegory of return, and Roberto embodied France, in the final sequence when Rosi's face is covered by Floreal's there is a transference of nationality from female to male. Roberto and Floreal return to their respective homelands and all is renewed. It is implied that Floreal will be the next labor leader to hear the 'people' and, thus, patriarchal Argentina is recovered. The freedom from constraint which Roberto appreciates in Floreal is reaffirmed as a masculinist freedom of political action, a freedom only possible outside of history.

I am not arguing that Solanas's inability to admit into *Sur* and *Tangos* aspects of Argentine political history that would contest a Peronist teleology demonstrates that there is no possible reconciliation between political actors

255

in contemporary Argentina. Neither is *Sur*'s masculinist political imaginary merely an example of Solanas's individual rejection of the public sphere, as currently constituted, in favor of a better patriarchal past. Instead, these two films (*Sur* in particular) are part of the rhetorical strategy of a nation of which Bhabha wrote. They are, if you will, part of the discursive formation of citizenship constitutive of the nation. They indicate that the Argentina in which Solanas now works is no longer a nation in the same sense that it had been for most of this century. In fact, Solanas's political intervention, his 'story of love for a nation', which on the surface seems inclusive of all Argentines and of the breadth of Argentine political history, is only cohesive as a narrative in the diegetic Utopian space of his characters outside the story of a return to the nation. The film registers in its formal elements the dissolution of the nation, the continuing exclusions of sectors of the citizenry, and the further sundering of the abstract ties that bind citizens as members of the same nation. Solanas's allegory of return from exile, which as a political project is an attempt to heal the wounds of the nation when 'the violence at the heart of the state' was mobilized in the 70s, is in fact evidence of the fictionality of the nation as a political unit. The pane of glass that divides Rosi and Floreal at the end of the film, but permits at once the fusion of their faces and the superimposition of Floreal's image over Rosi's, eradicates *both* the Utopian space of Floreal's journey home and the realist space of the nation's political future. Space is reduced to reflection and reflection to the impossibility of intimacy and reunion. Rosi's final non-synchronous laughter on the soundtrack is a laughter which evokes both past and future but registers instead the impossibility of the political present: the gendered transference of the embodiment of the nation promises, at the level of allegory, a future for the nation, yet, given that the language and politics of the film are those of exclusion and distanciation, *Sur* exemplifies national cinema after globalization. The nation, necessary to the previous period of capitalism, exists in the nostalgia of nationalist political projects: *Sur* may express Solanas's desire that nation should triumph over the restructuring of all political relations at this conjuncture, but the film itself is evidence that the one exile that will not return to Latin America in the 90s is the nation itself.

Notes

1. What I have presented as an initial phase of capitalism, Roland Robertson considers to be constituted by five phases. See his 'Mapping the Global Condition' in Mike Featherstone (ed.), *Global Culture: Nationalism, Globalization and Modernity*, (London: SAGE Publications, 1990), pp. 15–30. See also Christopher Chase-Dunn, *Global Formation: Structures of the World-Economy* (Oxford: Basil Blackwell, 1989).
2. John King, *Magical Reels: A History of Cinema in Latin America* (London and New York: Verso, 1990), p. 95.
3. *Argentina's 'Dirty War': An Intellectual Biography* (Austin: University of Texas Press, 1991), p. ix.
4. See among O'Donnell's other works 1966–73, *El estado burocrático-autoritario: Triunfos, derrotas y crisis* (Buenos Aires: Editorial Belgrano, 1982).
5. For their principal arguments, see respectively, *State, Power, Socialism*, trans.

Patrick Camiller (London: Verso, 1980), and *The History of Sexuality, Vol. I: An Introduction*, trans. Robert Hurley (New York: Pantheon Books, 1978).

6. For a history of Peronism and the Argentine state, see William C. Smith, *Authoritarianism and the Crisis of the Argentine Political Economy* (Stanford, Calif.: Stanford University Press, 1989).

7. The retrospective, CINE ARGENTINO, was curated by Julie Levinson and Juan Mandelbaum. The poster and program notes were by Pat Aufderheide and Andrés Di Tella.

8. Papers read at the Latin American Studies Association National Meeting, Washington DC, April 1991.

9. For a brief overview of the charge against Menem, see Alma Guillermoprieto, 'Letter from Buenos Aires', *New Yorker*, 15 July 1991, pp. 64–78.

10. *La Nación*, 26 May 1991.

11. See, for example, Doris Sommer, *Foundational Fictions: The National Romances of Latin America* (Berkeley: University of California Press, 1991).

12. See, for an elaboration of the nature of the capitalist state, Bob Jessop, *State Theory: Putting Capitalist States in their Place* (University Park, Pa.: Pennsylvania State University Press, 1990), or David Held, *Political Theory and the Modern State* (Stanford, Calif.: Stanford University Press, 1989).

13. Homi K. Bhabha, 'DisseminNation: Time, Narrative and the Margins of the Modern Nation' in *Nation and Narration* (London and New York: Routledge, 1990), p. 297.

14. In Gabriel García Márquez's *Clandestino en Chile*, exiled Chilean film-maker Miguel Littín tells the anecdote of the great impression it made upon him when, upon returning in secret to his country, he discovered that his mother had preserved his study, his desk, his books. Like the concern of the character Gerardo in *Tangos* for his library left in Argentina, the rescue of Littín's study is emblematic of the loss of political and intellectual history that was one of the results of state terror in these Southern Cone nations. It is not gratuitous that Solanas should place principal confrontation in *Sur* between the forces of oppression and the exemplary militants in a library. The sheaves of papers that circle through the air in this scene, matching the flyers which drift on the wind in the scenes of the street demonstrations of redemocratization in the film, are emblematic of the circulation of knowledge essential to the functioning of a democracy as well as to the bureaucracy of print that permits the functioning of the modern state, that is, the disciplining of its citizenry, the control and register of each individual.

15. See Fernando 'Pino' Solanas, *La mirada: Reflexiones sobre cine y cultura*, interview by Horacio González (Buenos Aires: Puntosur Editores, 1989), for Solanas's discussion of Argentine politics in this generation.

REGARDING RAPE

Fictions of Origin and Film Spectatorship

JULIANNE BURTON-CARVAJAL

Editors' Introduction

Julianne Burton-Carvajal has been a central figure in English-language Latin American film studies and one of the most faithful promoters of Latin American film in the USA. Her annotated bibliography (*The New Latin American Cinema*) and anthologies (*The Social Documentary in Latin America* and *Cinema and Social Change in Latin America*) have become indispensable texts. In this essay, she takes a very different look at the always problematic question of gender relations in Latin American film. Rejecting the usual critical boundaries of the 'national' and 'national specificity', Burton-Carvajal's analysis productively addresses Stam's call for comparative approaches to the study of Latin American cinemas. More specifically, her analysis is partly motivated by the work of Doris Sommer, who studies the erotic rhetoric of patriotic Latin American novels in her *Foundational Fictions: The National Romances of Latin America*. Burton-Carvajal argues that, unlike the patriotic novels which use 'foundational romances' to represent national unity through the figure(s) of heterosexual love, the Latin American cinema echoes the strategy of the great Boom novels of the 60s and 70s and is marked by anti-foundational features crystallised in figures of violation, illegitimacy, and usurpation. Her analysis focuses on the representation of rape in six films from Mexico and Cuba that span five decades and coincide with each nation's post-revolutionary consolidation: *Doña Bárbara* (1943), *La negra Angustias* (1949), *El* (1952), *Lucía 1895* (1968), *The Other Francisco* (1974), and *Up to a Certain Point* (1984). She finds that, although the figure of rape continues to reappear as an originary, defining force, either as the narrative explanation of identity or as catalyst for transformation, the more recent Cuban films have begun to complicate their representational strategies, implicating the spectator and his or her positioning at different levels.

☐

258

History (that is, the new viewing subjects that history creates) changes films in curious and sometimes confounding ways. The Cuban feature *Memories of Underdevelopment* (Tomás Gutiérrez Alea, 1969) has been part of my annual teaching repertoire for nearly 20 years. In the last three, disconcertingly, student discussion has immediately, avidly, tenaciously anchored itself to 'the rape sequence'. People familiar with the film who find themselves asking '*What* rape sequence?' are, literally or metaphorically, coming from a different place than my students. The concept of date rape, and the accompanying insistence that only yes means yes, provokes my students to read what was initially read as a mutual seduction – Sergio (Sergio Corrieri) by Elena (Daysi Granados) and Elena by Sergio when the two visit his apartment for the first time – as sexual abuse by an older, experienced, privileged man who has targeted a younger, poorer, less experienced (and avowedly emotionally unstable) woman.

This new reading is both heartening and troubling. Heartening because of the passion with which students of both sexes criticize the kind of conflicted and hypocritical sexual manners so characteristic of the 50s and early 60s and so indelibly captured by the director, the screenwriter (Edmundo Desnoes) and the actors in *Memories*. Troubling because this clear-sighted optic blinds these same students to the criticism that the film is leveling against the mores of its era and the social strata who embrace them, either to their advantage (Sergio's privileged class and gender) or to their detriment (the unfortunate Elena and her modest, contentious, self-defeating family). Troubling too because this reading robs Elena of both agency and responsibility, because Elena, at the apparent instigation of her family, *does* eventually take Sergio to court on an accusation of rape, but neither the desperation of Elena's stratagem nor the eventual resolution make sense if we believe that her complaint (that Sergio 'deceived' and 'took advantage of her'[1]) is a valid one. Sergio, who expected to be the target of this 'people's court', is instead exonerated, but as he exits the courtroom he muses, 'For once justice triumphed. But was it really like that? There is something that leaves me in a bad position. I've seen too much to be innocent. They have too much darkness inside their heads to be guilty.'

Though I remain convinced that the term 'seduction' is the only accurate way of naming what transpires in that disturbing sequence between a jaded middle-aged man and a confused young girl full of longing for another kind of life, the challenges posed by these discussions are one of the factors that prompt me to reflect on the numerous unequivocal instances of rape in Latin American films. Another impetus comes from Doris Sommer,[2] who asks, 'What was it ... about the notoriously obsolete programmatic brand of [earlier] Latin American fiction that haunted the Boom [writers]?' She finds her answer in 'a rather flagrant feature that has nevertheless gone unremarked ... the erotic rhetoric that organizes patriotic novels' which she sees as the result of 'the positivist tradition in which national projects [were] coupled with productive heterosexual desire' (Sommer, p. 2). She goes on to argue that 'The great Boom novels rewrite, or un-write, foundational fiction as the failure of romance, the misguided political erotics that could never really bind national fathers to mothers, much less the *gente decente* to emerg-

259

ing middle and popular sectors' (Sommer, pp. 27–8). The example she invokes is Carlos Fuentes's *La muerte de Artemio Cruz* (*The Death of Artemio Cruz*, 1962) which offers a dual vision of the foundational moment, first as romance and later as rape, a rape that was retroactively 'refigured' as romance by the principals in order to disguise the violent origins of their ongoing union. She might have also, if somewhat more problematically, invoked the novel which Fuentes himself acknowledges as the simultaneous origin and greatest achievement of the Boom, Juan Rulfo's *Pedro Páramo*, in which the hauntingly anomalous Susana San Juan is herself haunted by fragmentary associations of romance (Florencio), abduction and potential rape (Pedro Páramo) and incest (her father Bartolomé San Juan).[3]

A survey of Latin American cinema reveals a corresponding number of (anti)foundational features in which an aberrant figure of coupling – prostitution, incest, sterilization, orphanhood, love triangle, rape – substitutes for the mutually committed heterosexual pair (and the resultant patriarchal nuclear family) around whom the literary foundational romances revolved. Emilio Fernández's monumental *María Candelaria* (1943) figures the prototypical 'indigenous' couple (Dolores del Río and Pedro Armendáriz) as fated never to couple because of the 'original sin' bequeathed María by her long-deceased mother. The villagers revile María as they once reviled the *mala mujer* who gave birth to her. Their internal (intraracial) hostility (exacerbated by the cross-cultural insensitivity of the creole painter whose reluctant reflections frame the film) in the end destroys the Edenic couple. Brazilian director Ruy Guerra's *Eréndira* (1982), the first García Márquesian superproduction, uses prostitution as its figure for the chronic exploitation of the region, as does Brazilian Jorge Bodansky's *Iracema* (1974), a cinéma-vérité-style allegory of Amazonian development as the ecological prostitution of the region.

Incest, much rarer, has been figured through the union of a holy father (priest) and one of his parishioners, as in *O Padre e a Moça* (*The Priest and the Young Woman*, Brazil, Joaquim Pedro de Andrade, 1965) and María Luisa Bemberg's *Camila* (Argentina, 1984). The narrative design of the landmark Bolivian feature *Yawar Mallku/Blood of the Condor* (Jorge Sanjinés and the Grupo Ukamau, 1969) is driven by the surreptitious sterilization (both fictional and factual) of indigenous Bolivian peasant women by medical teams from abroad. Orphanhood is the theme that motivates *La historia oficial* (Argentina, Luis Puenzo, 1984), a feature which cries out for a new foundation and lays the responsibility for the nation's moral bankruptcy at the feet of the father, a collaborator with both the repressive military regime and manipulative outside interests. Tizuka Yamasaki's *Patriamada* (Brazil, 1985) is a neo-foundational romance with a feminist bias; here the traditional dyad becomes a triad and the heroine is not compelled to chose between her two lovers. The final shot of the three protagonists situates them at a political rally for progressive presidential candidate Tancredo Neves. Lina (Deborah Bloch) is flanked by the middle-aged industrialist Rocha (Walmor Chagas) and the young film-maker Goias (Buza Ferraz), each with a hand upon her bulging belly, which metaphorically promises to bring forth 'the new Brazil'. Here paternity remains deliberately unspecified in order to emphasize new figures of collaboration over traditional nuclearity, potential parental nurturance over the paranoia of positive paternity.

Romance and rape stand at opposite ends of the narrative spectrum that figures national unity through (hetero) sexual union. As Doris Sommer so eloquently and eruditely argues, romances are generated out of historical periods which encourage reconciliation, collaboration, amalgamation. An era or a social sector that perceives itself subject to threat is not characterized by such generosity, but recurs defensively to figures of violation to express its own desperate urge to reassert the legitimacy of its own claim to command. Rape is also a figure of illegitimacy and usurpation, because the body that is brutally violated presumably 'belongs' not to itself, though that would certainly be enough, but to a socially-sanctioned other. Rape thus has to do with the breaching of boundaries, the disordering of prior regimes of order.

I initially intended not to address rape as subjective trauma, expression of social pathology or mechanism of social intimidation, but instead to examine rape as a literary and cinematic theme, to consider what motivates this recurrent figure. To the degree that the female body is made (both socially and symbolically) to represent purity and innocence, passivity and defenselessness, rape is the violent defilement of a 'powerless' vessel, a vessel which, if not female to begin with, is inescapably feminized by the experience of violation. Textual rape arguably represents for the female character that same liminal moment that death conventionally represents for the (textual) male. In that sense, rape is 'a fate worse than death' for the woman who undergoes it.

In many societies, rape and the threat of rape is as potent a form of social control as death and the threat of death. Reviewing nine books linking psychoanalysis and feminism, Phyllis Grosskurth wonders why castration and not rape is the governing figure of sexual assault in Western culture.[4] Castration, infinitely rarer in statistical terms, is given prominence through mechanisms of projection (male on to female) and numerous popular idioms. Rape, more prevalent in countless societies than most officials and individuals are willing to admit, is elided by a multitude of concealing practices – personal and interpersonal, legal, linguistic, textual. But since that elision, like any repressive process, is inevitably incomplete, rape 'figures' numerous texts, foundational and otherwise. The conclusion offered in Lynn Higgins and Brenda Silver's important collection of essays, *Rape and Representation*,[5] is that there is a direct, inseparable relation between the textual and the experiential: 'The politics and the aesthetics of rape are one,' they assert.

In their introduction, Higgins and Silver characterize references to originary rape as a 'recurring trope', 'an obsessive inscription and an obsessive erasure of sexual violence against women' (p. 2). They note 'a conspicuous absence: a configuration where sexual violence against women is an origin of social relations and narratives in which the event itself is subsequently elided' (pp. 2–3). They call for readers, writers and critics 'to confront the naturalization of "prior" erotic violence and rape in ... founding tales: to reveal them as myths that simultaneously articulate and hide the socially constructed story of male and female sexuality, difference, and power that makes women "essentially" vulnerable and mute' (p. 5), thereby 'unraveling the

261

dynamics, the mechanisms, by which aesthetic conventions and critical traditions continue to inscribe and displace rape as a founding event of art' (p. 7) –and, we can legitimately add, nationhood.

In order to look at how rape is figured in Latin American cinema, I would ideally address three Mexican and three Cuban films which, together, span five decades, splitting neatly into two periods which correspond to post-revolutionary processes of national consolidation in their respective countries. *Doña Bárbara* (Fernando de Fuentes, 1943) is arguably Latin America's most (in)famous antiheroine, an archetype of vengeful voraciousness who transcends both the Venezuelan origins of her novelistic incarnation and the Mexican origins of her cinematic embodiment. Matilde Landeta's *La negra Angustias* (*Angustias the Black Woman*, 1949), set during the early stages of the Mexican revolution, and Luis Buñuel's *El* (*This Strange Passion*, 1952), a psychological melodrama of upper-class urban life, are less well known. Of the Cuban triad, *Lucía 1895* (Humberto Solás, 1968, the first part of a trilogy) is by far the most pivotal, but the subsequent *El otro Francisco* (*The Other Francisco*, Sergio Giral, 1974), also set in the 19th century, and the contemporary love story *Hasta cierto punto* (*Up to a Certain Point*, Tomás Gutiérrez Alea, 1984) also highlight the issue of rape.

In four of these – *Doña Bárbara*, *La negra Angustias*, *El*, *Lucía* (and arguably in *Hasta cierto punto* as well) – rape is the originary moment, the true beginning, presented as the narrative 'explanation' of identity or history. Regarded carefully, the explanation itself begs explanation.

In both *Doña Bárbara* and the initial segment of the three-part *Lucía*, the anomalous, transgressive nature of a major character is 'explained' through an account of her rape. Both accounts are secondary in the sense that they are related to the protagonists in flashback by more minor characters. In *La Negra Angustias* and *El*, frustrated rapes are the occasions at which the narratives (and the narratees) take a new turn. In both these instances, the attacks are depicted directly, as part of the primary diegesis, rather than mediated through flashbacks anchored in the consciousness of characters who lack direct experience of the events recounted to them. In both these Mexican features, the victim throws off her attacker and, fortified by her own successful resistance, goes on to invert the established order that had shaped and sheltered her antagonist. In this pair of examples, then, rather than the explanation of essence, rape functions as the catalyst for transformation. Arguably, if less obviously, this is also the case in *Hasta cierto punto*. *El otro Francisco* is unusual in that it figures rape three times – once as 'documentary', once as melodrama, and once as metaphor for materialist socio-economic analysis.

Intriguingly, it is with *Doña Bárbara* that Sommer draws the line between the patriotic, positivist traditions according to which 'national projects [were] coupled with heterosexual desire' (Sommer, p. 2), and their 'militant "populist" revisions'. This Venezuelan *novela de la tierra*, written in 1929 by Rómulo Gallegos, the man who would be president, was brought to the screen nearly 15 years later by one of Mexico's greatest film-makers, Fernando de Fuentes, in a fully collaborative project.

Space limitations compel me to forgo the analysis of Gallegos' notably more

'. . . frustrated rapes are the occasions at which the narratives (and the narratees) take a new turn.'
Arturo de Córdova and Delia Garcés in El (*Luis Buñuel, Mexico, 1952*)

convoluted representation of the rape of his (anti)heroine, which is deferred
until the third chapter of the novel. Like the novel, the film begins with men
in a boat travelling down river toward the vast plain where the action will
transpire, the plain where the monstrous *cacica* Doña Bárbara rules unchallenged – though not for long. In the film, Santos Luzardo (Julián Soler),
returning, city-educated heir to a local estate – who will eventually tame the
legendary gender aberration by, among other strategies, civilizing and win-
ning the love of Bárbara's cast-off daughter and sole offspring – hears from a
boatman the story of what made *la devoradora de hombres* so devouring. The
brief flashback sequence which accompanies the launch captain's narration is
subjectively anchored to Santos Luzardo by a prolonged close-up which
dissolves into a long shot of the river (which in turn dissolves into shots of
other rivers, successively named by the voice-over narrator). A close-up of
María Félix dissolves into a medium long shot of another, somewhat larger
boat, an insert of five sailors (the narrator says there are six), a cut to a girlish
María Félix happily preparing their food, and an establishing shot of the
arrival of a handsome young male passenger. The camera reveals a special
rapport between Bárbara and the newcomer. Cutaways to another corner of
the same craft reveal the crew conspiring to preempt her chosen partner.
They gamble for first privilege, attack the unsuspecting pair, knife the young
man and toss him overboard, then turn their attention toward the vulnerable
Bárbara, who recoils, shields her eyes, and demurely faints dead away. In the
next shot, the inert body comes back to life, adjusts her skirt and her
neckline, and then stares severely into a close-up camera, a 'changed' woman.
   This narrative elision conforms to a prevalent paradigm frequently

observed in the *Rape and Representation* anthology. As Susan Winnett writes in 'The Marquise's "O" and the Mad Dash of Narrative',

> The rape will achieve representation only through the narrative of its consequences, and this narrative will necessarily focus on the mind and body of the (unconscious) victim rather than on the mind and body of the rapist. . . . To the extent . . . that the reader 'knows' about the rape without having had to encounter it in the text and thereby experience it affectively, s/he complies in . . . broader cultural processes that relegate to 'the heroine's plot' particular untold stories of male violence. (Higgins and Silver, p. 70)

The only woman who can (temporarily) beat men at their own game has been (un)made (unmaid?) by them; she is their creation/perversion, and so her originary rape which, as the novel subtly suggests, replicates that of her indigenous mother in an almost incestuous way, subjects her to an ultimately male authority which the remainder of the novel works to reassert. In this sense, then, the framing flashback at the beginning of the film functions very much like a similar framing device in Emilio Fernández's *María Candelaria* (1943): to underscore the fact that the representation of the female has been appropriated by the male discourse/s. Both framing narrations 'capture' and fix the protagonist as a male consumer might wish her. The painter confronts María Candelaria on his canvas, 'frozen' in innocent unawareness of the violent, recapitulative death that awaits her. The boatman 'captures' Bárbara in her last moment of innocence and purity. Both frames compel the viewer to regard the female character as object rather than subject, and more specifically as an object that can be conjured up for the 'information' of another character (the journalist/biographer in *María Candelaria*, Santos Luzardo in *Doña Bárbara*) who is clearly a surrogate for the viewer.

What is also notable about the rape sequence in *Doña Bárbara* is the deliberate de-realization of its representation. The sequence of parallel shots – the boat crew leering and conspiring, the maidenly Bárbara seated at the feet of her sweetheart, raptly listening to words the viewer does not hear – only make narrative sense if read as two contiguous portions of a shared and confined space, the boat on which all travel. Yet the lighting is starkly differentiated: the shots of the boat crew seem to take place at night, the shots of the young lovers is sparkling sunshine. Fernando de Fuentes is too much of a master to tolerate such continuity 'errors'. Instead, he seems to be intent on undercutting the impact of the violation on the viewer through a style which foregrounds the Manicheism at work here on multiple levels.

The rape retold and reinvisioned in Part I of *Lucía* displays a very different set of narrative and representational strategies, to very different ends. In the first of a series of parallel occurrences which link the upper-class Lucía (Raquel Revuelta) to the insane street-dweller Fernandina (Idalia Anreus), Lucía's clandestine sewing circle is interrupted by a commotion in the streets. The bored but dutiful seamstresses (they are sewing hammocks and shirts for the rebel troops who are fighting for Cuba's independence from

Spanish colonial rule) welcome the distraction and rush to the windows, where they glimpse the frenetic Fernandina haranguing a scraggly bunch of Spanish soldiers who are returning from the battlefield. Turning their attention once again on each other, several of the women propose different explanations for Fernandina's crazed state until Rafaela (Herminia Sánchez) silences them all with the promise of an authoritative version of Fernandina's downfall.

The intricate editing of this extended sequence intercuts three sets of shots. First, shots of Rafaela coyly unraveling her tale – pausing, primping, provoking her anxious listeners to beg her to get on with it, all the while displaying an unbecoming gusto in the telling of what are understood to be traumatic events. Second, reaction shots of her circle of listeners, first urging her to proceed, later reacting, each in her own way, to the events Rafaela is relating. As the narration intensifies, close-ups of the teller and of her listeners begin to predominate. The third visual 'thread' consists of the representation of the events which Rafaela recounts. These cutaways to a darkened, smoke-filled battlefield, instantaneous at first, then appearing in increasingly longer segments, are characterized by several devices: hand-held camera, high contrast which makes the features of the actors hard to identify, frequent cutting, and an expressionistic auditory amalgamation of pseudo-electronic sounds and human sighs. Fragmentation of the soundtrack parallels the fragmentation of the image track: Rafaela's voice may be heard over the images of the battlefield, or conversely, the sounds of the nuns being attacked by soldiers may be heard over reaction shots of Lucía's friends. The predominantly but not exclusively feminine sighs and sobs and moans frequently 'float' independently of the images. The sequence culminates in a juxtapositional montage which pairs Fernandina and Lucía in three separate sets of 'mirroring' close-ups. The profile of Fernandina's rapist is still visible in the frame; her attacker has not yet released her. Lucía, 'facing' Fernandina from the opposite side of the succeeding frame, shakes with sobs.

Abrupt cut to an extreme high angle: the 'girls', decked in mantillas and kneeling in a small chapel, fan themselves briskly while reciting a litany to the Virgin Mary – in pious expiation of their unbridled fantasies, or so the cutting, along with the monotonous drone of their voices, seems to suggest. The uniformity of their comportment in church retrospectively emphasizes the range of their responses in the previous sequence: titillation, fright, revulsion, grief. Lucía and Rafaela demarcate the extremes of this self-positioning vis-à-vis Fernandina's rape. Rafaela keeps her controlling, manipulative distance. The tale she tells empowers her. If she inserts herself within her narrative to any degree, it is to identify with the soldiers when she exclaims, eyes sparkling suggestively, 'Ahora viene lo bueno' ('Now for the good bit') and, later, 'Allí mismo comenzó la fiesta!' ('That's where the fiesta began'). Lucía's response is the polar opposite of Rafaela's alienated irony. Lucía identifies with the pious nun so innocently blessing 'dead soldiers' who then rise up from their feigned demise to violate her and her sister nuns by envisioning herself as one of them. Careful viewing of these chaotic sequences reveals numerous shots of Raquel Revueltas, who plays Lucía, being stripped of her robes and struggling against the attacks of more than one Spanish

265

soldier. Repeated viewings confirm that other members of Rafaela's audience also fantasize themselves into Fernandina's situation.

The telling of this tale is a modeling of the polarities of spectatorship – engaged or aloof, 'othering' or identificatory. Solás, in registering the differing reactions and, more significantly, in the almost subliminal corporeal interpellation of the listeners into the scenario verbally reconstructed for them, reminds us that spectatorship is not neutral, that we all choose a position from which to 'see' the experience of others as it is recounted to us. For Rafaela, Fernandina remains an abstract 'other', an outsider to her own subjectivity, beyond the possibilities of empathy. (The vicarious pleasure taken in the suffering of others is echoed in the sequence in which the girlfriends come *en masse* to call on a heartbroken Lucía who has taken to her bed upon learning that her fiancé is already married.) Lucía's emotional stance, in contrast, figures a slippage between the 'object' of Rafaela's story and her own subjective self-positioning. Lucía's ability to identify with the most 'othered' element of her rigidly hierarchical society provides her, in the end, with the solace of the one figure who can fully empathize with her betrayal and loss because the story of the one 'mirrors' that of the other.

These echoes reverberate throughout the segment: in the narrative, in the editing, and even, towards the end, in the physiognomy of the actresses. The shift to permanent high contrast that ensues with Lucía's realization of the personal and historical consequences of Rafael's betrayal, combined with her disheveled state, erratic movements, and crazed expression, produce an uncanny resemblance between two actresses who have formerly exhibited no physical resemblance. Though, at the conclusion of this first, autonomous segment of the trilogy, both Fernandina and Lucía inhabit a space of mad-

'. . . *spectatorship is not neutral* . . .' Lucía (*Humberto Solás, Cuba, 1968*)

266

ness outside the society to which they once belonged, their alliance also figures a future nationhood bound together by the treachery and suffering that result from colonization.

Matilde Landeta's *La negra Angustias* balances attempted rape and repeated threats of rape with a retributive castration sequence, visually framed amid spiked maguey plants and sombreroed guitarists, and aurally framed (with sweet perversity) by the only love song on the soundtrack. The climax of Luis Buñuel's *El* is Francisco's (Arturo de Córdova) attempted meta-rape of his wife Gloria (Delia Garcés) whom he suspects of impropriety. Characteristically, Buñuel leaves it to his spectator to deduce just what Francisco intends to do with the macabre implements he has assembled: cotton, needle, thread, rope. The assumption of the female as male property, on which the 'privilege' of rape depends, has seldom been figured with greater clarity or revulsion.

The Other Francisco first figures rape as part of a documentary-style mini-essay on female sexuality under slavery. Sexual aggression and violation are presented as one component of a sexual economy in which females are scarce, infant and child mortality high, overwork and violent physical abuse rampant. The refusal of reproduction through self-induced abortion is shown to be a logical response. What is striking about this brief depiction is its refusal to symbolize the female; no overlaid baggage of signification is imposed upon this montage of (some of) the deplorable conditions which governed Afro–Cuban female sexuality under slavery. In contrast, the rest of the film elaborates a romance between slaves which is disrupted by a jealous and spiteful master, and simultaneously deconstructs that romance. Dorotea (Alina Sánchez) is twice raped by her master Ricardo (Ramón Veloz), or rather, her rape is given two separate representations. In the second, Ricardo's aggression is echoed and interrupted by industrial sabotage: the simultaneous insertion of a blade into the gears of the mechanical sugarcane press recently imported from England to accelerate the exploitation of the enslaved cane cutters.

Tomás Gutiérrez Alea's *Hasta cierto punto*, its stylistic and thematic debt to Sara Gómez's *De cierta manera* (*One Way or Another*, 1974) vouchsafed in its title, takes on the issue of machismo in all its ramifications: double standards, marital infidelity, the sexual consequences of inequalities of class and social possibility, single motherhood, models of childrearing, the parameters which limit genuine female independence. No less interesting for its flaws and failures, this film also deserves acknowledgment for confronting the issue of what Americans have termed 'date rape'. There is no terminology that I know of in Spanish for this concept, but the phenomenon is explicitly depicted in this film, though most reviewers chose not to comment on this incident in which a displaced boyfriend lays claim to what he thinks of as 'his'. Though the tendency to reduce and confine the female within a hackneyed symbology persists in *Hasta cierto punto*, which concludes with shots of seagulls in flight to connote Lina's (Mirta Ibarra) 'escape' to a different life in another part of the island, what is even more notable in the Cuban films, cumulatively, is the increasing, if unsteady, effort to align narrative perspective and spectatorial identification with female subjectivity and, yes, vulnerability, and with actual rather than purely symbolic transformations. Increasingly, foundational features seem to imply a politics of spectator identification which foregrounds the connections between textuality and actuality.

Notes

1. No member of Elena's family even makes a direct accusation of rape to Sergio; the issue for the family seems to be defloration. Her brother accuses him of 'ruining her'. Her mother insists, 'Girls must go to the altar as virgins! That's the greatest treasure a woman can bring in marriage,' and later recalls tearfully how her daughter had told her that she had come home late that night, her underwear stained with blood, a statement which Sergio immediately and vehemently denies. The father admonishes Sergio against 'making fun of' his daughter. They demand that Sergio marry Elena, and he does not refuse but, characteristically, neither does he act upon his promise. They then take him to court, where the legal charge becomes rape of a minor. As part of his deposition, Sergio states, 'It isn't true. I have had relations with her, but they were voluntary. There was no abuse and certainly no rape. All this is a lie.' In his concluding statement the bailiff states, 'In the facts proved as true there are no grounds to sustain the crime of rape as charged by the district attorney.' All the quotations derive from Tomás Gutiérrez Alea and Edmundo Desnoes, 'Memories of Underdevelopment' and 'Inconsolable Memories' (New Brunswick: Rutgers University Press, 1990).
2. Doris Sommer, Foundational Fictions: The National Romances of Latin America (Berkeley: University of California Press, 1991).
3. For an early assessment of gender and sexuality, see my 'Sexuality and the Mythic Dimension in Juan Rulfo's Pedro Páramo', Symposium, vol. 28, no. 3, Fall 1974, pp. 228–47.
4. Phyllis Grosskurth, 'The New Psychology of Women', New York Review of Books, vol. XXVIII, no. 17, 24 October 1991, pp. 25–32.
5. Lynn A. Higgins and Brenda R. Silver, Rape and Representation, (New York: Columbia University Press, 1991), p. 1.

ZOOT SUIT

The 'Return to the Beginning'

ROSA LINDA FREGOSO

Editors' Introduction

'The secret fantasy of every *bato* [is] to put on the zoot suit and play the myth.' When, in a moment of great cinematic reflectivity, the zoot-suited Pachuco in Luís Valdez's *Zoot Suit* addresses the audience with this statement, he identifies himself as *the* emblem of Chicano identity, linked to the projects of Chicano politics and embodying desire, myth, and history. What interests Rosa Linda Fregoso in this piece is precisely how this notion of Chicano identity (prevalent in the Chicano movement and the arts) reveals the deep-seated and problematic ambivalences of identity politics in Chicano cultural nationalism.

Drawing on the work of Stuart Hall and other contemporary theorists of 'difference' and cultural identity, Fregoso challenges many of the commonsensical assumptions that have provided a framework for Chicano politics, film-making and other critical practices. She argues that *Zoot Suit* demonstrates not only that the search for Chicano identity has been framed as an essentialist 'archaeological project' seeking legitimacy and authority in the pre-Columbian (Aztec and Mayan) past, but also that it has been couched in exclusive patriarchal terms. In her analysis, *Zoot Suit*, despite its self-reflective elegance and obvious political importance, contributes to the masculinisation of Chicano identity. It posits an equivalence between male desire ('the secret fantasy of every *bato*') and desire as such, thus negating the possibility of a Chicana desire other than the desire for the Pachuco, much as the Chicano movement itself marginalised the women within it. Her final call for an awareness of the work of representation in the formation of 'alternative' cultural identities is worth noting in relation to all the 'other' practices we have addressed in this collection.

□

This is 1942 or is it 1492? . . . Something inside you creates the punishment, the public humiliation, the human sacrifice? There's no more carnal pyramids, only the gas chamber.

EL PACHUCO, *ZOOT SUIT* (1981)

INTRODUCTION

In a 1989 article, Stuart Hall emphasizes that cultural identity is 'always constituted within, not outside, representation' (Hall, 1989, p. 69). Underscoring the productive rather than the simply reflective nature of cinematic representation, Hall's insights about the role of representation in the production of cultural identity challenges certain positivist assumptions about the nature of identity. As Hall puts it, film is a 'form of representation which is able to constitute us as new kinds of subjects and thereby enable us to discover who we are' (p. 80).

No account of Chicano and Chicana film practices would be complete without examining the articulation of identity within cultural politics. For the most part, the political task of Chicano cultural nationalism centered on the search for the 'origins' of Chicano identity. In this respect, the clever numerological permutation cited above – 1942 and 1492 – captures the continuity that cultural nationalists envisioned between Chicanos and pre-Columbian (Aztec and Mayan) societies in the Americas. For over three decades, cultural nationalists have continually revised history, forging a linear historical continuity between the oppression of 20th-century Chicanos in the USA and that of the indigenous nations under Spanish domination. In cinematic representation, the first Chicano film, *I Am Joaquín* (1969), eloquently reflects this revision, for the film is emblematic of the quest for the 'origins' of cultural identity. It is fitting that our most prolific and commercially successful Chicano film-maker to date, Luís Valdez, launched his career with 'the "return to the beginning"' of cultural identity.

Valdez's artistic productions emerged within the social formation of Chicano cultural nationalism. Not only did he direct the collective ensemble, El Teatro Campesino, he also took an active role in shaping the ideology of Chicano nationalism. He was one of the four authors of the Plan Espiritual de Aztlán, the blueprint of nationalist ideology for the liberation of the Chicano nation (Muñoz, 1989). His first intervention in film was the visual adaptation of *I Am Joaquín*, a Chicano movement poem by Rodolfo 'Corky' Gonzales which narrates, in epic form, the history of Chicanos beginning with the conquest of Mexico by the Spanish conquistadores. Yet, like the poem, the filmic version subsumes multiple Chicano identities into an authority enunciated by the singular historical subject, Joaquín. This particular version of identity politics would continue to inform Valdez's subsequent film projects. As we inaugurate the 500 years since the Conquest (or the 'Discovery' as many Spaniards and 'Hispanics' would have it), I should like to reflect upon the ambivalences of identity politics in Chicano cultural nationalism. I shall focus on the manner in which Valdez's *Zoot Suit* represents a major treatise on masculine notions of identity within the representational practices of Chicano cultural nationalism.

270

An adaptation of its earlier stage performance, *Zoot Suit* (1981) was Valdez's first feature film.[1] The film recounts the Sleepy Lagoon trial of 1942, the first case in US history of imprisonment on charges of conspiracy (Mazon, 1986). While the film's overt subject deals with the trial, incarceration, and appeals process of the 38th Street Club members, exposing racism towards Chicanos during the Second World War, *Zoot Suit* is as much about cultural identity as it is about the Sleepy Lagoon case. An examination of how the narrative is framed reveals its implicit concern with cultural identity.

The narrative unfolds through a fictitious psychological struggle between two main characters, Hank Reyna and the Pachuco, two protagonists whose representation reverses the negative position of the Chicano 'gang' member in dominant discourse. One of the two main characters, Hank (Daniel Valdez), is based on the actual leader of the 38th Street Club, Hank Leyvas, whereas the Pachuco (Edward James Olmos) represents an imaginary/mythical figure, one whose visual presence is accessible solely to Hank and the audience.[2] Yet it is in this relation, the structural contrast the film establishes between Hank and the Pachuco, that Valdez theorizes on the nature of cultural identity.

In the opening scene of *Zoot Suit* we witness the mechanism by which cultural identity is produced within representational discourse. *Zoot Suit* visually renders the fantasy, the myth, and the multiple registers occupying the myth, especially as these elements are inscribed on to the body of the Pachuco. The Pachuco is first and foremost the film's omnipresent narrator. In the opening segment of the film, for instance, the Pachuco uses a switch-blade to tear apart a full-screen image of a newspaper and addresses viewers with the following words:

> Ladies and gentlemen. The *mono* [slang for 'movie'] you're about to see is a construct of fact and fantasy. But relax, weigh the facts and enjoy the pretence. Our *pachuco* reality will only make sense if you grasp their stylization.
> It was the secret fantasy of every *bato* [guy] living in or out of the *pachucada* [*pachuco*, or street-youth, reality] to put on the zoot suit and play the myth. *Más chucote que la chingada, órale.'*

As the Pachuco begins his monologue, a shot–reverse-shot pattern is established between the character and the audience. Yet the only discernible audience members are rendered in a single two-shot of a father–son couple. Thus, the self-reflectivity of the film, as expressed by the Pachuco, that is to say, its disclosure of the mechanism by which cultural identity is produced, also signals the extent to which a masculine content governs the production of identity. This film is about men; the Pachuco personifies the 'myth' of Chicano manliness.

Within the film's corpus of narrative action, we are privy to the way in which *Zoot Suit* foregrounds the male subject by essentializing male desire as the Pachuco. For, 'the secret fantasy of every *bato*', as the opening statement clearly puts it, is 'to put on the zoot suit and play the myth.' As the narrative

'. . . the secret fantasy of every bato is to put on the zoot suit and play the
myth.' El Pachuco (Edward James Olmos) welcomes the audience in Zoot
Suit (Luís Valdez, USA, 1981)

unfolds, we discover the ways in which the Pachuco 'plays out' a male-
centered fantasy about the *pachuco* reality.

At the same time, the Pachuco functions as Hank's unconscious: he is a
character which only Hank can speak to and see. If for Lacanian psychoanalysis the 'other' is part of the construct of the unconscious, rather than an
identity with the referent, in Valdez's formulation the 'other' appears in a
dual role: as an internal as well as an external entity to Hank. The Pachuco is
simultaneously an identity with the referent and the construct of Hank's
unconscious. As Hank's 'other', the Pachuco represents the literal embodiment of Hank's desire and imagination. However, it is important to single
out that this representation of subjectivity derives less from psychoanalytic
insights about the fractured nature of identity than it does from the director's
earlier efforts in theater. As Broyles-González's recent study of El Teatro
Campesino documents, members of the ensemble were highly influenced by
Mayan and Aztec philosophy. Consequently, the film's intelligibility requires
knowledge of Valdez's studies in indigenous philosophical systems principally because it encapsulates the convergence of a particular brand of mysticism and unconventional characterization.

As readers may recall, El Teatro Campesino was a theater collective ensemble that supported the organizational efforts of the United Farmworkers Union headed by César Chávez. In addition to their commitment to class-based struggle, members of the theater collective were also driven by identity politics (Muñoz, 1989). Towards this aim, Teatro Campesino members undertook extensive spiritual training in Mayan and Aztec philosophy.[3] According to Yolanda Broyles-González, the Pachuco is a stock character from the Teatro's repertoire of stock characters that were created collectively through improvizational techniques. However, the Pachuco character is also illustrative of Valdez's application of studies in Mayan and Aztec mysticism, particularly the Mayan religious principle of *In Lak'ech*, or 'you are my other self'. Reminiscent of the Rastafarian notion of 'I and I', (Barrett, 1977)[4] *In Lak'ech* reconfigures identity as inextricable from the notion of the Chicano collective. Indeed, the premise behind *In Lak'ech* is one of identity as a subject which is self-identical to an-other, and this other identity occupies a relation to the referent as much as it is a part of the collective unconscious. The narrative application of the native or Mayan principle within cinematic discourse takes concrete form in the conflict depicted between two characters. Symbolizing two sides of the same coin, Hank and the Pachuco represent indissoluble unity, that is to say, together, they are one.

Thus, the notion of identity as a struggle between the self and the 'other' is reproduced by the conflict between the Pachuco (as thought) and Hank (as being). The Pachuco signifies Hank's wish-fulfillment; the Pachuco acts out and verbalizes what social codes and conventions would sanction in Hank (such as making disparaging sexual comments towards women, incessantly smoking a joint, or sitting rather than standing when the judge enters the courtroom). Moreover, the character's capacity to effect cinematic transitions in time and space with the snap of a finger, to be present in multiple spaces, as well as his inordinate power for moving narrative action forward or backward, couples him with memory. Thought, fantasy, myth crystallize in the Pachuco's persona whereas Hank embodies the concreteness of being. The temptation to praise the film's conscious disclosure of the mechanisms by which cultural identity is produced is extraordinary. *Zoot Suit* does in fact lucidly reconstitute the relation between the self/Hank (the identity with the referent) and the 'other'/Pachuco (the construct of the unconscious) as non-homologous, as disruptive. However, this production is simultaneously regressive in nature, turning against itself. *Zoot Suit*'s notion of cultural identity is first and foremost grounded in an archaeology, in a return to the pre-Columbian origins of cultural identity.

THE 'RETURN TO THE BEGINNING'

Stuart Hall notes that nationalist critiques of dominant discourse refashion alternative nationalist and cultural identities that deconstruct the explicit racism of dominant discourses of representation. Often, the first stage of anticolonial and anti-imperialist discourse involves the reconstruction of national and cultural identities based on a political model of subjectivity that is grounded in a notion of a fixed self or essence. In this formulation, cultural identity is expressed as an authentic essence, located in a core subject, that is to say, as an identity of unity and coherence. Accordingly, the 'real' self, as Trin T. Minh-ha explains, 'remains hidden to one's consciousness'. Its emergence 'requires the elimination of all that is considered foreign or not true to the self, that is to say, not I, the other' (Minh-ha, 1990, p. 371). As Hall indicates, the rediscovery of cultural identity in this view depends on the 'unearthing of that which the colonial experience buried and overlaid, bringing to the light the hidden continuities it [colonial powers] suppressed' (Hall, 1989, p. 69). In Hall's estimation, this notion of cultural identity is grounded in an archaeology for, as he suggests, the rediscovery of an 'authentic' core self is predicated on the search for the 'fixed *origin*' of cultural identity, an origin predating colonialization and subjugation.

During the 'Marihuana Boogie' scene of *Zoot Suit* we are privy to the notion of cultural identity as an archaeological project. It is in this instance that the permutation in the Pachuco's ironic remarks, 'This is 1942 or is it 1492?' is made to reference the European conquest of the Americas. Valdez further imbues the Pachuco with pre-Columbian significance by choosing for the Pachuco's zoot suit the colors black and red, thereby imputing the association with the Aztec deity, Tezcatlipoca (Broyles-González, forthcoming). Furthermore, the film reconfigures cultural identity as the 'search for origins' in the climactic scene of the movie, the Marine beating of the Pachuco.

In a scene with clear reference to the Zoot Suit Riots of 1943, a group of Marines gang up on the Pachuco, violently beating him and stripping him of his zoot suit. Hank witnesses the action and, gesturing assistance, approaches the Pachuco. The body of the man lying in a fetal position, weeping, turns out to be Hank's brother. Puzzled, Hank makes a second attempt to assist his brother. This time, however, the image of the Pachuco displaces that of the brother. Defiantly rising, the Pachuco has reappeared dressed in the groin cloth of an Aztec warrior. His image moves to the foreground, towards the Aztec sun as a musical score of native rhythms accompanies the over-the-shoulder shot of Hank facing the Pachuco. Thus, the superimposition of two characters (the Pachuco and Hank's brother) signifies the symbolic convergence of two historical events: the Marines' attack on *pachucos* (1943) and the Spanish conquest of the Aztec nation (1519). Reconstituting first the Zoot Suit riots and subsequently the conquest on to the Pachuco's body propels the notion of identity as an archaeology, for the authenticity of the more recent historical event rests on the 'authority' of the more distant Aztec past. Furthermore, by inscribing the Aztec warrior on to the body of the Pachuco, multiple identities are collapsed into one subject. His confinement in jail had already marked him as a *pinto* (ex-convict). In sum, the Pachuco is essentially all of the identities of the revolutionary subjects envisioned by cultural nationalism: he encapsulates the fusion of the *pinto*, the Aztec warrior, and the *pachuco*.

ESSENTIAL CHICANISMO

During the 60s the new political subject of an alternative identity surfaced as the central tenet of Chicano cultural nationalism, mirroring the project of various 20th-century nationalist movements (Chatterjee, 1986). In artistic practices like poetry, mural painting and film, Chicano and Chicana cultural workers experimented with alternative Chicano subject-identities. By reversing the previously negative position of Chicanos in dominant discourse, the counter-discourse of Chicano cultural nationalism produced 'new' Chicano subjects. Cultural nationalists reclaimed as the 'revolutionary role models' for the 'new' Chicano identity precisely those subjects that the dominant discourses of representation positioned as socially 'threatening'. Moreover, Chicanos and Chicanas nurtured by the political activism of the Chicano movement rejected the assimilationist thrust of previous generations of Mexican–Americans. Rather than conforming Chicano/a identity into the melting-pot ideology, they reaffirmed precisely the identities that the dominant order had positioned as the 'other.' Chicano movement intellectuals positively valorized the identities of those subject-ed by the dominant culture and Mexican–American middle-class intellectuals to the realm of the 'inferior': the *pintos* (ex-convicts), the *pachucos* (street-youth), and the (mostly Aztec) warriors of indigenous peoples. In poetry, mural paintings and theater, Chicanos and Chicanas therefore systematically figured the *pachuco*, the *pinto* and the Aztec

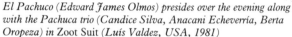

El Pachuco (Edward James Olmos) presides over the evening along with the Pachuca trio (Candice Silva, Anacani Echeverría, Berta Oropeza) in Zoot Suit *(Luís Valdez, USA, 1981)*

warrior as the 'new' Chicano subjects of the counter-discourse of Chicano liberation. In sum, Chicano movement activists affirmed the identities derived from histories, partially in working-class forms and practices, but also from a non-European legacy of the Mexican people. However, these new identities were problematically predicated on the politics of simple reversal. The new Chicano subjects of cultural nationalism were primarily cast into a highly schematic binary relation, Anglo versus Chicanos (or 'bad' versus 'good'). Yet the major ambivalence of the project of cultural nationalism centered on its systematic elision of women as subjects of its discourse, an ambivalence clearly rendered in *Zoot Suit*.

Prior to narrative closure, in the solitary confinement scene, Hank undertakes an inward journey to the psychic realm of the self. Appearing fully transformed at the end of the film, Hank emerges as desire, embodies the myth of *pachuquismo*. In so doing, the film reproduces the central problematic of cultural nationalist discourse, namely that Chicano brotherhood, existing to time immemorial, involves the symbolic elevation of the Pachuco as a form of desire. The cultural nationalist strategy rearticulated in *Zoot Suit* consequently interpellates all subjects, Chicanas and Chicanos, into new discursive relations, into inhabiting the brotherhood of *Chicanismo* by privileging the masculine. The Pachuco-as-desire normalizes a masculine content for cultural identity; in the configuration of an oppositional discourse, the female desire is essentially a universal male desire.

Zoot Suit ultimately offers a masculine discourse which masks itself as politics. Indeed, the film transforms the negative positioning of the Chicano male in dominant discourses into a new Chicano 'positive' subject. The transgressive nature of Chicanos as 'gang members', formally articulated as a threat to dominant culture, is rearticulated into the positive masculine attributes of brotherhood and Chicanismo. Yet by positing Chicano desire as a universal one (as in the final lines of the film, 'The Pachuco, the myth, still lives'), the film marginalizes the female subject as well as the members of the Chicano collective who do not desire this myth. Thus, the film's strategy of simple reversal culminates by positing an essential Chicano cultural identity with masculine attributes. Valdez was not, however, isolated from more general currents in Chicano cultural politics. As Angie Chabram has noted, cultural nationalist discourse generally configured the male as the essential subject whereas the identity of the Chicana was relegated to the status of split subject (Chabram, 1991). In representing the Chicano as an essential Pachuco, Aztec warrior, or *pinto*, cultural nationalists marginalized the Pachuca (the female counterpart). The discourse of cultural nationalism positioned the Chicana as the subject whose object of desire was also the Pachuco, subsuming the female subject within a universal Chicano male cultural identity.

CONCLUSION

To the extent that Valdez was an exponent of the ideological premises of cultural nationalism, he was also deeply motivated by the broader formulations for decolonizing Chicano consciousness from dominant ideology (Johansen, 1979). The cultural nationalist configuration of the new Chicano subject for revolutionary practice by way of a journey to the authority and authenticity of the pre-Columbian past led many cultural nationalists to the study of ancient Aztec and Mayan rituals.[5] Rediscovering the 'authentic' indigenous traditions became not just a way of reconstructing an 'authentic' Chicano, but also of thinking about identity as an essence. In its most extreme formulations, the true 'essence' of the Chicano lay buried deep within the inner psyche (Fregoso and Chabram, 1990). As his words make evident, Valdez was clearly a part of a broader phenomenon in search of mythical origins:

> Most of us know we are not European simply by looking in a mirror . . . the shape of the eyes, the curve of the nose, the color of skin, the texture of hair; these things belong to another time, another people. Together with a million little stubborn mannerisms, beliefs, myths, superstitions, words, thoughts . . . they fill our Spanish life with Indian contradictions. It is not enough to say we suffer an identity crisis, because that crisis has been our way of life for the last five centuries (Valdez, 1968).

However, contrary to the attempts at rediscovering Chicano subjects in the 'authority' of the past, cultural identity could only be reconstituted in the present. Chicano cultural identity was not an essence but a positioning of Chicanos as certain subjects within discourse. Despite the archaeological project of cultural nationalism, representational practices like poetry, art, drama and film function as sites for the reproduction of alternative subject positions, for while alternative notions of identity are available through practices and memories of resistance, the process of their production entails a 'retelling,' performed in the present. As Stuart Hall's theoretical reflections on the problem of cultural identity remind us:

> This 'return to the beginning' is like the imaginary in Lacan – it can never be fulfilled nor requited, and hence is the beginning of the symbolic, of representation, the infinitely renewable source of desire, memory, myth, search, discovery – in short, the reservoir of our cinematic narratives (Hall, 1989, p. 80)

Notes

1. In 1979 Valdez obtained a budget of $2.5 million from Universal Studios to produce a filmed version of the highly successful theatrical performance of *Zoot Suit*.
2. The Pachuco has three narrative functions: as cinematic technique, as narrator, and as Hank's unconscious. In his role as cinematic technique, the Pachuco supplants traditional film-editing devices. For instance, rather than resorting to the more conventional techniques of dissolves or slow-motion shots to signal transitions in time or memory/dream effects respectively, Valdez employs the Pachuco as a literal visual marker of time passages. With a snap of his finger, the Pachuco freezes narrative action, particularly those involving violence. The Pachuco is also used to signal transitions in narrative space. In an early jail scene, the Pachuco marks a transition to a previous narrative event. As Hank begins to

tell the defense lawyer about the events leading up to the Sleepy Lagoon incident, the camera cuts to a medium shot of the Pachuco who snaps his finger. The camera then cuts to the dance scene. And while the Pachuco's figuration is, according to Luís Valdez, inspired by cinematic techniques, his function as the film's narrator is taken from Brechtian theater. The opening segment of the film establishes the Pachuco's function as *Zoot Suit*'s narrative voice.

3. For an in-depth account of the spiritual and philosophical training of El Teatro, see Y. Broyles-González, *El Teatro Campesino: An Oral History of the Ensemble* (Austin: University of Texas Press, forthcoming).

4. As Barrett writes in his account of Rastafarian philosophy: 'The existence of the I and the speaking of I are one and the same thing. When the primary word is spoken the speaker enters the world and takes his stand in it. . . . [T]he language of the Rastafarians is a soul language in which binary oppositions are overcome in the process of identity with other sufferers in the society' (p. 144).

5. Among many Chicanos and Chicanas during the 60s, the revival of hermetism or the occult sciences (currently termed 'New Age') was particularly evident in those who followed the teachings of Don Juan, but also in practitioners of Aztec ritual dance.

Works Cited

Barrett, Leonard. *The Rastafarians*. Boston: Beacon Press, 1977.

Broyles-González, Yolanda. *El Teatro Campesino: An Oral History of the Ensemble*. Austin: The University of Texas Press, forthcoming.

Chabram, Angie. 'I throw punches for my race *but* I don't want to be a man: Writing Us Chicanos (Girl/Us)/Chicanas into the Movement Script'. *Cultural Studies: Now and in the Future*. Eds Cary Nelson, Lawrence Grossberg and Paula Treicher. New York: Routledge, 1991.

Chatterjee, P. *Nationalist Thought and the Colonial World*. London: Zed Books, 1986.

Fregoso, Rosa Linda and Chabram, Angie. 'Reframing Alternative Critical Discourse: an Introduction'. *Cultural Studies* 4, 1 (October 1990).

Hall, Stuart. 'Cultural Identity and Cinematic Representation'. *Framework* 36 (1989): 68–81.

Johansen, Jason. 'Pensamientos'. *Chicano Cinema Newsletter* 1, 4 (June 1979).

Mazón, Mauricio. *The Zoot Suit Riots: A Psychology of Symbolic Annihilation*. Austin: University of Texas Press, 1986.

Minh-ha, Trin T., 'Not you/Like you: Post-colonial Women and the Interlocking Question of Identity and Difference.' *Making Faces, Making Soul*. Ed. Gloria Anzaldua. San Francisco: Aunt Lute Foundation Books, 1990.

Muñoz, Jr., Carlos. *Youth, Identity and Power*. London and New York: Verso, 1989.

Valdez, Luís. 'The Tale of La Raza'. *Bronze* 1, 1 (25 November 1968).

'TRANSPARENT WOMEN'

Gender and Nation in Cuban Cinema

MARVIN D'LUGO

Editors' Introduction

Although narrowly focused on a small group of Cuban films, Marvin
D'Lugo's essay synthesises many of the issues and concerns addressed by
other essays in this collection. Like Barnard, for example, he proposes
different readings of 'classic' Cuban films based on a reassessment of the
cinema–state relationship. Like Burton-Carvajal, he is interested in how
women are represented and in issues of gendered spectator positioning.
Finally, like Newman, he is concerned with expanding our understanding
of the relationship between the cinema and the nation. His essay analyses a
curious phenomenon: since the 60s, Cuba has produced a series of films that
articulates the hopes, ideals, and developments of the new revolutionary
nation via narratives focused on female characters. Puzzled by this insistent
equating of the nation with women, D'Lugo analyses what he terms the
'transparency' of the logic of this female figuration. From *Lucía* (1968)
through to *Hello Hemingway* (1990), he finds that the Cuban cinema has
asked its audience to read the discourse of nation *through* female characters
and that this allegorical strategy has itself become so naturalised as to be
transparent. In other words, the texts do not demand allegorical readings
and the female characters provide a position for the audience (or, following
Stanley Fish, the interpretive community) to 'participate metaphorically in
the process of national self-realisation'. D'Lugo's analysis traces the
development of this strategy, arguing that the logic of female figuration has
evolved and has been used to promote a critical interrogation of the
development of Cuban society, especially in Tomás Gutiérrez Alea's *Hasta
cierto punto*, Jesus Díaz's *Lejanía* and other recent films.

□

*Lucía is not a film about women; it's a film about society. But within that
society, I chose the most vulnerable character, the one who is most transparently
affected at any given moment by contradictions and change.*

HUMBERTO SOLÁS[1]

The female figure has long been identified with the emergence of a truly national cinema in Cuba, that is, with the expression of the narratives that embody and circulate the values of the revolutionary community. During the first decades of operation of the Cuban Film Institute, and in films as striking as Humberto Solás's *Lucía* (1988), Sara Gómez's *De cierta manera* (*One Way or Another*, 1974), and Pastor Vega's controversial *Retrato de Teresa* (*Portrait of Teresa*, 1978), the ethos associated with a revolutionary national identity was elaborated in fictional films through an insistent focus on the narrative destiny of female characters. The mobilisation of 'female narratives' on behalf of the nation were, of course, much more complex than merely the structuring of stories about women. The underlying objective of such films was to develop a form of address to, and identification by, the Cuban audience through the mediation of a new revolutionary mythology rooted in the female figure.

In the last decade that line of development has intensified, but with a distinctive feature. While the allegorical condition of women as embodiments of a concept of nation has been sustained, the female figure has emerged in Cuban films as the agency through which a new range of critical discourses about Cuban culture in general and the revolution in particular are enunciated. Evolving as a series of responses to the development of contemporary Cuban society, the cinematic representation of women retains the one cardinal feature that Humberto Solás had designated as the essential feature of the female characters of *Lucía*: transparency.

For the three female protagonists in *Lucía*, transparency meant at once the social condition in which male characters did not so much see women as see *through* them. Solás's repertory of heroines were all socially marginalised beings, 'unseen' within the patriarchal power structure before and after the revolution. But beyond that diegetic notion of transparency, the film was configured discursively in such a way as to motivate the audience to read into the narrative destiny of the three heroines the larger panorama of a century of the struggle for national liberation and self-realisation. This 'propensity' to read the nation through the transparency of the female allegory of *Lucía* was no mere accident but derived from the cluster of textual practices Solás employed that defined the cinematic text not merely as a reflection of social reality, but also as the occasion of a particular type of audience engagement. In *Lucía* the female figure, rather than functioning simply as the mimetic representation of gender or class struggle, thus became the 'site' in which the audience participated metaphorically in the process of national self-realisation.[2]

Cuban film has undergone intense transformation since Solás's landmark film, just as Cuba itself has undergone important historical and political change. Yet as the films of the last decade attest, despite such change, that fundamental notion of transparency – the textual motivation of the audience to read the discourse of nation through female characters – has remained an indelible constant.

Tomás Guttiérez Alea's *Hasta cierto punto* (*Up to a Certain Point*, 1988) is perhaps the most striking example of the ways in which this type of cinematic tradition and innovation converge in Cuban film of the 80s. Conceived as a homage to Sara Gómez's 1974 film, *De cierta manera* (*One Way or Another*), *Hasta cierto punto* understandably holds a conceptual similarity to the earlier film's feminist thematics and to its interweaving of documentary footage and fictional narrative. Gómez's film grows out of the twin thematics of feminism of the late 60s and 70s in Cuba: the centrality of women within the revolutionary activity of the nation, and the rebuke of persistent machismo. These were themes that enjoyed the prestige of official support with the formulation of the Family Code in 1975. Yet popular cultural attitudes about the status of women in Cuban society were slow to change, as evidenced, for instance, by the ferocious polemics that surrounded Pastor Vega's 1979 film, *Retrato de Teresa* (*Portrait of Teresa*), and the official position was clearly at odds with popular cultural attitudes about the status of Cuban women. Though made nearly a decade after the *De cierta manera*, *Hasta cierto punto* inscribes much of that same polemical discussion into the formulation of the film.

The most striking formal feature of Alea's film and the principal element borrowed from Gómez's film is the staging of an on-screen audience within the film who comment on and assess the themes that shape the film's narrative. From the very beginning of *Hasta cierto punto*, a pre-credit documentary sequence establishes that dramatised audience as an essential paradigm. The sequence consists of a brief interview with a young male black dockworker in Havana who appears to be responding to a question posed by an off-screen voice about how the revolution has changed his machista attitudes. The dockworker says:

> Oh, they've managed to change my attitudes on that score. I've certainly changed up to a certain point (*hasta cierto punto*). I'm probably at 80 per cent now. Maybe they can work on me and get me up to, say, 87 per cent. But they will never get me up to 100 per cent, no way. That thing about equality is OK but only up to a certain point.[3]

This is followed by a series of five other brief documentary interviews interspersed within the narrative. These interviews at first appear to be ironic self-referential counterpoints to the story of Oscar, a Cuban intellectual involved in directing the videotaping of interviews with Havana dockworkers as background for a film on proletarian attitudes toward machismo. As scriptwriter for the proposed film, Oscar is attempting to corroborate the thesis of the film's director, his friend, Arturo, that machismo in Cuba remains a vestige of pre-revolutionary thinking in the working classes. In the process of videotaping, Oscar is forced, however, to confront his own machista attitudes.

But beyond their immediate function as an ironic counterpoint to the narrative, the interviews serve a more fundamental social function in depicting the larger cultural community as the source and arbiter of the social meanings presented and contested within the filmic narrative. In *De cierta manera*, the status of this community was even more pointedly depicted as the audience of a workers' council hearing, in which the guilt or innocence of a worker was to be determined. While serving as a form of direct address, the device of dramatised on-screen audiences also reinforces the theme of the community's participation in the maintenance of revolutionary values. This radical narrational aesthetic coincides with Stanley Fish's notion of 'interpretive communities'. According to Fish, interpretive communities are made up of:

> those who share interpretive strategies not for reading (in the conventional sense) but for writing texts, for constituting their properties and assigning their intentions. In other words, these strategies exist prior to the act of reading and therefore determine the shape of what is read rather than, as is usually assumed, the other way around. . . . The ability to interpret is not acquired; it is constitutive of being human. What is acquired are the ways of interpreting and those same ways can be forgotten or supplanted or complicated or dropped from favour.[4]

This staging of the interpretive community within the film helps reinforce in the viewer a sense of audience as nation.[5] The narrational dynamics of *Hasta cierto punto* thus suggests a self-conscious effort to align cinematic spectatorship with the interpretive community of the nation and thereby to engage that audience in the full appreciation of the revolutionary meanings attributed to the female within Cuban society.

Tellingly, the dockworkers who constitute the on-screen interpretive community of the film, all of whom are non-professional actors speaking in spontaneous, unscripted interviews, effectively enunciate a sense of individual and collective identity by defining a view of women within the home and workplace pointedly at odds with Arturo and Oscar's contention. An additional important scene takes place outside the context of the videotaping, in which Oscar and Arturo meet informally with several of the men they have already filmed in order to continue discussing the status of machismo and the social role of working wives. This scene serves as a bridge between the documentary interviews and the fictional narrative of *Hasta cierto punto*, in effect collapsing the neat divisions *petit-bourgeois* intellectuals like Oscar and Arturo have about machismo in the working class and the reality of the workers' views on this subject. What the dockworkers tell the two men when they are off camera further points up the discrepancy between social reality and the views of intellectuals.

The two final interviews in the series do not focus on issues of gender but rather on the question of pride and commitment that particular individuals have to their work. The final clip is a statement by one worker, an older black man, about efficiency and his sense of personal commitment. Taken as individualised expressions of a unified discourse on gender and society, these documentary interviews can readily be identified by the off-screen audience as part of a larger national effort to define social and personal identity in terms of work. Machismo, in this light, is viewed as debilitating the work force by undermining the female's potential for contributing.

282

'A relationship develops between bourgeois, intellectual Oscar and the proletarian dockworker . . .' Oscar Alvarez and Mirta Ibarra in Hasta cierto punto *(Up to a Certain Point, Tomás Guttiérez Alea, Cuba, 1988)*

Indeed, what passes for an innocent plot in *Hasta cierto punto* is continually subjected to intense scrutiny and critique through the agency of the interpretive community, both on screen and off. At a union meeting of the dockworkers that Oscar attends at the beginning of the film to get more documentary footage, he meets Lina, a female dockworker who protests about the hazardous conditions to which the workers are subjected. Lina is the unmarried mother of a small boy. A relationship develops between bourgeois, intellectual Oscar and the proletarian dockworker, which produces a crisis in Oscar's marriage with Marianne. The film ends ambiguously as Lina appears to depart by plane from Havana for Santiago.

Lina functions as the catalyst for Oscar's confrontation with the confining patterns of his own consciousness. Having come to the docks to discover hard-core machismo, he encounters in her a woman who tells him from experience that much of the heavy macho bravado he has videotaped 'is just talk'. From the very start of their relationship, in fact, Lina seems unimpressed by Oscar's view of machismo as the problem. When she tells him that she had a child out of wedlock by choice and that her parents were not happy with the mulatto father of her son, Oscar's reactions appear to expose for the audience his own implicit class bias.

In Alea's conception, Lina turns out to be not the expression of the long-suffering Cuban woman as often depicted in Cuban films of the 60s and 70s, but a more expansive expression of broader cultural values of the revolution, values that transcend the conventional notions of gender to which Oscar is himself bound. Alea identifies Lina metaphorically with a bird in flight, both through the images of gulls we see in the port area and also in the inclusion of a Basque song that serves as an epigraph to the film. The song's lyrics include

283

the verse: 'I could clip her wings if I liked/ Then she couldn't fly/ and she'd be mine/ but what I love is the bird.' By consciously imaging Lina as a bird, the film reinvests in the female the soaring aspirations of an earlier generation's revolutionary exuberance.

The song's words also sum up the problematic nature of Oscar's relation to Lina. On a formal level that problematic is transposed to the chain of documentary interviews which, by the film's end, has shifted from talk about machismo to reflections on the individual's dedication to those revolutionary ideals that have become reified with the passage of time. In this context the female figure constructed by the narrative is recognised as transcending her identity as either sexual object or subject and becomes more clearly the cipher of a revolutionary ethos badly in need of rededication. We can read that inscription of the meaning of the nation in the final documentary interview that follows the scene in which Lina breaks off the relationship with Oscar.

That last videotape, in which an old black worker speaks of his need to continue to struggle on behalf of the revolution, even in the face of the faltering dedication of his fellow workers, is now viewed by Arturo and his wife in their home. The feelings expressed by the worker coincide with the values of dedication and vigilance within the revolutionary community expressed by Lina from her very first appearance in the film. The logic of this admittedly eccentric sequencing of what in a more clichéd genre film would be the melodramatic ending draws the viewer's attention to the essential linkage between the narrative's female figure and the interpretive community within which that figure circulates.

LEJANÍA

Alea's development of Lina reveals another critical dimension of transparency that to varying degrees is a common factor in the subsequent treatment of female narratives, namely, the effort to bring the audience to read into these female characters narratives of the nation. The bulwark of that allegorising process is its very discursive transparency, that is, the way in which it has been naturalised within the cultural practices that situate cinema within a particular political and cultural context in revolutionary Cuban society.[6] In such a context we come to recognise the logic of the female figuration as an effort to forge a complex rhetorical strategy of social reference whereby the textual claim to be representative of the national community is based on a process of identification between the audience and the fictional character.

One of the most striking examples of this process is Jesús Díaz's *Lejanía* (*Parting of the Ways*, 1985), in which the female figure is used not merely to embody a static concept of patriotism but rather to problematise issues of national identity around one of the most emotional contemporary cultural themes: the return of Cubans who had emigrated to the United States. The film chronicles the return to Havana of Susana, a woman who ten years earlier had left her son with relatives when the rest of the family fled to Miami. Now, thanks to the recent agreement with the US government, she returns for a brief visit only to receive her son's rebuke and recriminations from his wife.

Originally filmed for television, *Lejanía* is modestly scaled to the television medium with a limited number of sets, characters, and actions. Michael Chanan argues that this reduction of space and time of action to one day, that of Susana's arrival at the Havana apartment where she once lived and which is now occupied by her son Reinaldo and his wife Aleida, along with the film's thematic emphasis on the exile and reunion of Cubans, inevitably establishes an allegorical quality within a social–spatial discourse.[7] The reduction of the setting to the space of the apartment operates, as it often does in theatrical works, to promote the audience's reading of the space of action as a symbolic *mise en scène*. In this instance, a Cuban audience is led to read a decisive historical intertext through the presence of Susana who discovers in objects and spaces of her former home a nostalgia for a Cuba that exists only in her mind.

This allegorical dimension is foregrounded by the reduction of the film's dramatic conflict to a tension embodied in the film's three female characters, Susana, Aleida, and Ana, Reinaldo's cousin who has accompanied her aunt on this painful return. All three women are seen as figuring social and historical positions that transcend their status either as women or as representative members of a family. The Cuban audience is thus engaged in the simulation of a polemic not unlike that inscribed into the interpretive communities of earlier films. Here, the axis of dramatic tension lies squarely in the conflict between emotionally compromised positions and intellectually

'. . . *an allegorical quality within a social-spatial discourse.' Beatriz Valdés and Jorge Trinchet in* Lejanía (Parting of the Ways, *Jesús Díaz, Cuba, 1986*)

and politically 'correct' postures with regard to Susana, whom we are brought to see either as an anguished maternal figure or as political enemy.

The audience's culturally determined ambivalence toward Susana is never resolved within the film, nor apparently can it be within the social world to which the film alludes.[8] In one sense the entire film revolves around Susana's contradictory status. She embodies the unfulfilled 'historical' desire for a reunion among the two parts of the allegorical family of the nation but, as the narrative suggests, that union cannot be achieved simply by bringing the parties together.

Although there is scarcely a reference made in the dialogue to political questions, Susana voices the social and cultural prejudices that clearly mark the differences between the old Cuba, supported by the USA, and revolutionary society under Castro. One brief but telling dialogue between mother and son crystallises this condition of the text. Susana is alone with Reinaldo and begins a painful conversation about their past by asking her son about his wife. 'Why did you marry a divorced woman? She has black blood. She's mulatto. We've never had one in the family.' Voicing the classist and racist positions that are synonymous both with pre-revolutionary society and with the popular characterisation of the US society in which she has resided for ten years, Susana leads the audience to transpose the figure of Aleida from the initial realist presentation of the wife meeting her husband's mother for the first time into a symbolic field in which conspicuously she emblemises the egalitarian aspirations of revolutionary society that Susana's mentality and values have historically opposed.

That condition of Americanised values is pointedly depicted through a visual intertext early in the film. Susana has brought a home movie of the 'family' in Miami for her Cuban relatives to see. In this brief sequence the family is depicted as proto-typical American suburbanites who have so successfully integrated themselves into American culture that they have even assumed American names, thus making them indistinguishable from 'the enemy'. The home movie, in effect, establishes the basis for the off-screen audience to break any emotional bonds with friends and relatives whom they once viewed as countrymen. The exile family has been metamorphosed into Yankee capitalists.

Two other sets of visual intertexts further delineate that cultural cleavage. The first of these occurs in a scene in which Ana, Reinaldo's childhood sweetheart, returns to the apartment and an awkward conversation ensues. Ana turns on the television set, which just happens to be showing a musical programme. Omara Pontuondo, a popular black singer, is singing 'Veinte años atrás' (Twenty Years Ago), which describes the separation of two lovers and the impossibility of rekindling their love. The song's lyrics aptly describe Ana's relation with her cousin, but the allusion to 'twenty years ago' seems to imply a larger historical context of separation for the Cuban audience, roughly the period of the massive flight of middle- and upper-class Cubans during the early 60s. The presence of the black singer prefigures Susana's later conversation regarding Aleida's racial background and speaks to the larger schism that both time and cultural values have erected as barriers to the reunion of the two generations.

That cultural schism defined by race is reiterated in a later scene when Susana responds disapprovingly to a scene from Alea's film *La última cena* (*The Last Supper*, 1976), which is being shown on television. In this instance, the cinematic intertext serves to align Susana's cultural mindset with that exploitative tradition that for centuries enslaved and exploited the Cuban people. Both scenes, while underscoring the racial dimensions of Cuban identity, also serve as modes of subject address, establishing for the audience the dichotomy between Cubanness and alien 'otherness' in terms of class, race and, ultimately, national history.

As critics have often noted with regard to *Lejanía* and as critical reaction in Cuba has reaffirmed, the film's insistence upon the problematic status of the mother as the enemy produces the intolerable situation in which Reinaldo is seen rejecting the *emigré* population. While such a painful polemic has no simple solution, *Lejanía*'s enunciative strategy is revealing of the shifting nature of female figuration, for here the audience is forced to engage in a painful debate focalised around the most intimately emotional female image, that of motherhood. Yet, tellingly, the female figure is used not simply to reaffirm cultural beliefs but also to promote in the audience a critical interrogation of contemporary society and values.

RECENT FILMS

Lejanía's discursive structure reflects the increasing stylistic penchant among a number of film-makers of enunciating the theme of nation through patterns of allegory. Yet this allegorising tendency is not as static and unoriginal as it may at first appear. In Carlos Tabío's highly self-conscious comedy *Plaff!* (1988), for instance, the tradition of allegorising the nation through female characters is intentionally parodied. The film focuses on two women, Concha, a widow in her fifties who explicitly embodies the revolutionary values of the 60s, and Clara, her daughter-in-law, a chemical engineer, who is the spokesperson for a younger generation that sees the pervasive patterns of waste and inefficiency in Cuba as the result of the ways of the previous generation, particularly people like Concha.

That generational schism is reiterated through the film but never more pointedly than in the juxtaposition of scenes in which Clara is first seen receiving a prize for her development of a new polymer made from turtle excrement, and then Concha is given an award at a block party held by the local committee for the Defense of the Revolution. What is particularly striking about Tabío's film is the way in which it avoids the heavy-handed moralising style of an earlier tradition of Cuban film-making that also dealt with important themes of the conflict and critique of contemporary society. Indeed, the self-consciousness of the comedic elements of *Plaff!*, which includes the comic reduction of recent Cuban history to the conflict between mothers and daughters-in-law, clearly functions as a way of addressing and engaging a Cuban audience in serious national issues.

Another use of allegory is to be found in the collective film *Mujer transparente* (*Transparent Woman*, 1990), developed under Solás's general direction, and conceived of as an update on the progress of women in Cuban society through its choice of five stories of representative women of different ages and social strata. While the five stories attempt to provide a social panorama of the lives of contemporary women, it is perhaps most pointedly in the last episode, Ana Rodríguez's 'Laura', where the potential for audience engagement is most fully realised. 'Laura' deals with the ways in which the protagonist prepares to reunite with a childhood friend visiting from Miami in one of the so-called 'community' trips following the Mariel exodus. Laura's reminiscences of the two decades she has known her friend, Ana, thus sketch a more generic history with which a whole generation of Cubans can easily identify. The most powerful moment of the story occurs when Laura comes to the tourist hotel where she will meet Ana and is ignored by the desk clerk, thus making her feel that she is an alien in her own country and bringing an audience of both men and women to identify with Laura's sense of marginalisation.

That same effort to address and engage the audience in a reflection on the themes of national identity is the motivational force of Fernando Pérez's 1990 film, *Hello Hemingway*, a film which historicises the female figure by situating its protagonist in the Havana of the final year of the Batista dictatorship, thereby aligning the notion of female identity with the revolutionary concept of struggle. The film's plot is developed in much the same spirit as Solás's original *Lucía*, that is, as a way of looking through the transparency of the vulnerable female to the larger image of the nation's struggle.

Set in 1956, during the Batista dictatorship, in the Havana suburb in which Hemingway resided, *Hello Hemingway* tells the story of Larita, the illegitimate daughter of a kitchen maid who has been recommended by her high school teacher for a scholarship to study English in the USA. First, however, she needs to collect the various letters of support from members of the community and to pass a series of interviews. The film traces Larita's efforts as she slowly comes to realise the impossibility of achieving her goal given her humble background and her precarious financial resources.

The process through which Larita reaches that consciousness, fails to proceed with the application, and finally resigns herself to remain in Cuba is structured around her contact with three women: her grandmother, Josefa, her teacher, Dr Martínez, and 'Miss Amalia', the representative of the American Embassy who interviews candidates for the scholarship.

As allegory, *Hello Hemingway* functions in a complex manner, for not only does the narrative involve the schematisation of political and cultural scenarios through female characters that has, by this time, become a staple of Cuban cinema, but it is also built upon a subtle historical theme in which the fairly familiar view of Batista's Cuba as 'bastard child of the USA'[9] is re-imaged through the protagonist of Hemingway's novella, *The Old Man and the Sea*. In this intricate structure Larita is seen first as the economically oppressed, socially marginalised Cuba of the neo-colonial period, her desire to go to the United States reflecting precisely the kind of mental colonisation in which the objects of individual desire and of social aspiration are those of the American cultural empire. In such a context the proper Miss Amalia, who voices unsubtle classist comments about Larita, embodies the evil of the USA.

What saves the narrative from such a simplistic schema, however, is that gradually Larita undergoes a transformation when she reads *The Old Man and the Sea*. Instead of identifying with Hemingway, the author, she comes to identify with his creation, the fisherman Santiago, whose indomitable spirit will lead her on. The film thus displaces the historical Hemingway by the image of a Cuban fisherman whom Larita views at Cojimar where *The Old Man and the Sea* is set. When she stands on the rocks at Cojimar and views the old fisherman casting his net, we understand that Larita is replicating the identical situation of the little boy, Manolín, in Hemingway's story, who also deeply identified with Santiago's indomitable spirit. That moment, which ends the film, makes apparent not only the repatriation of the Hemingway narrative into a Cuban context, but also, strikingly, its regendering into a female narrative.

Thus Larita's failure to go to the USA is figured as part of a grander design in which she will become heir, as the film implies, to the struggle that will shortly lead to revolution's triumph. In this, Pérez's script appears to follow the Utopian reading of the past in which the contemporary audience of the 90s is conditioned to view in Larita's character a precursor to the revolutionary ethos that connect her with them. Even Hemingway's theme, stated by Dr Martínez as a translation exercise for her English class – 'a man may be destroyed, but he cannot be defeated' – is recuperated into the political struggle against Batista that serves as a historical background to the film.

In this way, *Hello Hemingway* re-semanticises Hemingway's writings as a form of national mythology and, in addition, a spiritual precursor to the revolutionary spirit of post-1959 Cuba. Like Solás's 'historical' heroines in *Lucía*, and the other 'transparent women' who have followed in her wake, Larita is ultimately understood as a figure gestating towards the future, and the audience is once again given the opportunity to ponder that future through her struggle.

Notes

1. Marta Alvear, 'Every Point of Arrival is a Point of Departure', *JumpCut* no. 19, as quoted by Michael Chanan in *The Cuban Image: Cinema and Cultural Politics in Cuba* (London: BFI Publishing, 1985), p. 226.
2. Homi K. Bhabha, 'DissemiNation: Time, Narrative, and the Margins of the Nation', in Homi K. Bhabha, *Nation and Narration* (London: Routledge, 1990), p. 297.
3. As quoted by James Roy Macbean, 'A Dialogue with Tomás Gutiérrez Alea on the Dialectics of the Spectator in *Hasta cierto punto*', *Film Quarterly*, vol. 38, no. 3 (Spring, 1985), p. 22.
4. Stanley Fish, *Is There a Text in This Class?: The Authority of Interpretive Communities* (Cambridge, Mass.: Harvard University Press, 1980), pp. 171, 172. In describing the function of interpretive communities in a cinematic context, Rick Altman notes how 'a specific interpretive community arrests the free play of a text's signifiers and freezes them *in a particular way*, thus producing a meaning proper to the particular community in question by foregrounding certain patterns the recognition of which leads to an apprehension of that particular meaning'. See Rick Altman, *American Film Musical* (Bloomington and London: Indiana University Press, BFI Publishing, 1987), p. 2.

5. Gerardo Chijona, 'El cine cubano, hecho cultural de la revolución', *La cultura en Cuba socialista* (Havana: Editorial Letras Cubanas, 1982), p. 221.
6. As Fish observes of the cultural contexts that inform allegory, allegorising as an interpretive act may be performed on such a deep level of consciousness that 'it is indistinguishable from consciousness itself'. See Fish, p. 272.
7. Michael Chanan, 'Algunos prefieren proyectarse', *El nuevo cine latinoamericano en el mundo de hoy* (Mexico: UNAM, 1988), p. 92.
8. In an interview with US film critics, Díaz acknowledged the painful ambivalence many Cuban audiences felt towards the character of Susana. See Dan Georgakas and Gary Crowdus, 'Parting of the Ways: An Interview with Jesús Díaz', *Cineaste*, vol. 15, no. 4 (1987), p. 23.
9. Richard Fagen, *The Transformation of Political Culture in Cuba*, Stanford Studies in Comparative Politics (Stanford: Stanford University Press, 1969), pp. 6–10.

o Plaff: Demasiado miedo a la vida (Plaff! or Too Afraid of Life, *Juan Carlos Tabío, Cuba, 1988*)

SELECT BIBLIOGRAPHY

This is a selected guide to the most accessible, largely English-language, sources on Latin American cinema. A more specialist bibliography can be found in the footnotes, and in Burton's bibliography of the New Latin American Cinema, quoted below.

Almendros, Néstor, *A Man with a Camera*, Faber and Faber, London 1985.

Armes, Roy, *Third World Film Making and the West*, University of California Press, Berkeley 1987.

Aufderheide, Patricia, ed., *Latin American Visions: Catalogue*, The Neighborhood Film/Video Project of International House of Philadelphia, Philadelphia 1989.

Bradford Burns, E., *Latin American Cinema: Film and History*, University of California Press, Los Angeles 1975.

Barnard, Tim, *Argentine Cinema*, Nightwood, Canada 1986.

Burton, Julianne, 'Film Artisans and Film Industries in Latin America, 1956–1980: Theoretical and Critical Implications of Variations in Modes of Filmic Production and Consumption', The Wilson Center Latin American Program, Working Papers, no. 102, Washington 1981.

— , 'Marginal Cinemas and Mainstream Critical Theory, *Screen* 26, nos. 3–4, 1985.

— , 'Seeing, Being, Being Seen: *Portrait of Teresa* or the Contradictions of Sexual Politics in Contemporary Cuba', *Social Text* 4, 1981, pp. 79–95.

— , 'The Hour of the Embers: On the Current Situation of Latin American Cinema', *Film Quarterly* 30, 1,1976, pp. 33–44.

— , *The New Latin American Cinema: An Annotated Bibliography of Sources in English, Spanish and Portuguese: 1960–1980*, Smyrna Press, New York 1983.

— , ed., *The Social Documentary in Latin America*, Pittsburgh, University of Pittsburgh Press 1990.

— , ed., *Cinema and Social Change in Latin America: Conversations with Filmmakers*, University of Texas Press, Austin 1986.

Chanan, Michael, *Chilean Cinema*, BFI, London 1976.

— , ed., *Santiago Alvarez*, BFI, Dossier 2, London 1980.

— , ed., *Twenty-five Years of the New Latin American Cinema*, BFI, London 1983.

— , *The Cuban Image*, BFI, London 1985.

Coad, Malcolm, 'Rebirth of Chilean Cinema', *Index on Censorship* 9, 2, 1980, pp. 3–8.

De Usabel, Gaizska S., *The High Noon of American Films in Latin America*, UMI Research Press, Ann Arbor 1982.

Downing, John H., ed., *Film and Politics in the Third World*, Autonomedia, New York 1987.

Fusco, Coco, ed., *Reviewing Histories: Selections from New Latin American Cinema*, Hallwalls Contemporary Arts Center, Buffalo, NY 1987.

Gabriel, Teshome, *Third Cinema in the Third World: The Aesthetics of Liberation*, UMI Research Press, Ann Arbor 1982.

García Márquez, Gabriel, 'Of Love and Levitation', interview with Holly Aylett and Patricia Castaño, *Times Literary Supplement*, 20–26 October 1989, pp. 1152 and 1165.

— , *Clandestine in Chile*, Granta, Cambridge 1989.

García Riera, Emilio, *Historia documental del cine mexicano, Epoca sonora*, 9 vols, Era, Mexico, 1969–78.

Georgakis, Dan and Lenny Rubenstein, *Art, Politics, Cinema: The Cineaste Interviews*, Pluto Press, London 1985.

Getino, Octavio, *Cine latinoamericano: economía y nuevas tecnologías audiovisuales*, Fundacíon del Nuevo Cine Latinoamericano, Havana/Mérida, 1987.

Gutiérrez Alea, Tomás, *The Viewer's Dialectic*, José Martí Editorial, Havana 1988.

Hadley-García, George, *Hispanic Hollywood: The Latins in Motion Pictures*, New York, Citadel 1990.

Henebelle, Guy and Alfonso Gumucio Dagrón, eds., *Les Cinémas de l'Amérique Latine*, L'Herminier, Paris, 1981.

Johnson, Randal, *Cinema Novo × 5*, University of Texas Press, Austin 1984.

— , 'Brazilian Cinema Novo', *Bulletin of Latin American Research* 3, no. 2, 1984, pp. 95–106.

— , *The Film Industry in Brazil: Culture and the State*, University of Pittsburgh Press, Pittsburgh 1987.

— , 'The Nova República and the Crisis in Brazilian Cinema', *Latin American Research Review*, vol. XXIV, no. 1, 1989.

— , and Robert Stam, eds, *Brazilian Cinema*, Associated University Press, New Jersey 1982.

Keller, Gary, *Chicano Cinema: Research, Reviews and Resources*, Binghampton, NY, Bilingual Review/Press 1985.

King, John and Nissa Torrents, eds. *The Garden of the Forking Paths: Argentine Cinema*, BFI, London 1987.

King, John, *Magical Reels: A History of Cinema in Latin America*, London, Verso 1990.

Kolker, Robert, *The Altering Eye: Contemporary International Cinema*, Oxford University Press, New York 1983.

López, Ana, 'The Melodrama in Latin America Films: Telenovelas, and the Currency of a Popular Form', *Wide Angle* 7, 3, 1985, pp. 4–13.

— , 'A Short History of Latin American Film Histories', *Journal of Film and Video* 37, 1985, pp. 55–69.

— , 'Towards a "Third" and "Imperfect" Cinema: A Theoretical and Historical Study of Film-making in Latin America', Ph.D. dissertation, University of Iowa, 1986.

Maciel, David R., *El Norte: The US–Mexican Border in Contemporary Cinema*, San Diego, Institute for Regional Studies of the Californias (San Diego State University) 1990.

McBean, James Roy, *Film and Revolution*, Indiana University Press, Bloomington 1975.

Martínez Pardo, Hernando, *Historia del cine colombiano*, América Latina, Bogotá, 1978.

Mattelart, Armand, *Multinational Corporations and the Control of Culture: The Ideological Apparatuses of Imperialism*, Harvester Press, Brighton 1982.

— , ed., *Communicating in Popular Nicaragua*, International General, New York 1986.

Minstron, Deborah, 'The Institutional Revolution: Images of the Mexican Revolution in the Cinema', Ph.D. dissertation, Indiana University, 1982.

Monsiváis, Carlos, *Amor perdido*, Era, Mexico, 1977.
— , *Escenas de pudor y liviandad*, Grijalbo, Mexico, 1988.
Mora, Carl J., *Mexican Cinema: Reflection of a Society, 1896–1980*, University of California Press, Berkeley 1982.
Myerson, Michael, ed., *Memories of Underdevelopment: The Revolutionary Films of Cuba*, Grossman, New York 1973.
Noriega, Chon A. (ed.), *Chicanos and Film: Essays on Chicano Representations and Resistance*, New York, Garland 1992.
Orellana, Margarita de, *La mirada circular: El cine norteamericano de la revolución mexicana*, Joaquín Mortiz, Mexico 1992.
Oroz, Silvia, *Melodrama: O cinema de lágrimas da América Latina*, Rio Funda Editora, Rio de Janeiro, 1992.
Paranagua, Paulo Antonio, 'Women Film-makers in Latin America', *Framework* 37, 1989, pp. 129–38.
— , *Cinema na America Latina: longe de Deus e perto de Hollywood*, L & PM Editora, Porto Alegre, 1984.
— , ed., *Le Cinéma brésilien*, Centre Georges Pompidou, Paris, 1987.
— , ed., *Le Cinéma cubain*, Centre Georges Pompidou, Paris, 1990.
— , ed., *Le Cinéma mexicain*, Centre Georges Pompidou, Paris, 1992.
Pettit, Arthur G., *Images of the Mexican American in Fiction and Film*, Texas A & M University Press, College Station 1980.
Pick, Zuzana, 'Towards a Renewal of Cuban Revolutionary Cinema: A Discussion of Cuban Cinema Today', *Cine-tracts* 7–8, 1979, pp. 21–31.
— , 'Chile: The Cinema of Resistance 1973–79', *Cine-tracts* 9, 1980, pp. 18–28.
— , 'The Cinema of Latin America: A Constantly Changing Problematic', *Cine-tracts* 9, 1980, pp. 50–55.
— , 'Chilean Cinema in Exile (1973–1986)', *Framework* 34, 1987, pp. 39–57.
— , ed., *Latin American Filmmakers and the Third Cinema*, Carleton University, Ottowa 1978.
Pines, Jim and Paul Willemen, eds, *Questions of Third Cinema*, BFI, London 1989.
Ramírez, Gabriel, *Lupe Vélez; la mexicana que escupía fuego*, Cineteca Nacional, Mexico, 1986.
Ramírez, John, 'Introduction to the Sandinista Documentary Cinema', *Areito* 37, 1984, pp. 18–21.
Ranvaud, Don, 'Interview with Fernando Solanas', *Framework* 10, 1979, pp. 34–8.
— , 'Interview with Raúl Ruiz', *Framework* 10, 1979, pp. 16–18.
Reyes, Aurelio de los, *Cine y sociedad en México, 1896–1930: Vol. 1. Vivir de sueños (1896–1920)*, UNAM, Mexico, 1983.
Reyes Nevares, Beatriz, *Trece directores del cine mexicano*, SEP, Mexico, 1974, translated as *The Mexican Cinema: Interviews with Thirteen Directors*, University of New Mexico Press, Albuquerque, 1976.
Rios-Bustamente, Antonio, *Latino Hollywood: A History of Latino Participation in the United States Film Industry 1913–1945*, Encino, Floricanto Press 1991.
Rocha, Glauber, 'History of Cinema Novo Part 1', *Framework* 11, 1980, pp. 8–10.
— , 'History of Cinema Novo Part 2', *Framework* 12, 1980, pp. 18–27.
— , 'Humberto Mauro and the Historical Position of the Brazilian Cinema', *Framework* 11, 1980, pp. 5–8.
— , *Revisã ocrítica do cinema brasileiro*, Civilização Brasileira, Rio de Janeiro, 1963.
Sanjinés, Jorge and El Grupo Ukamau, *Teoría y práctica de un cine junto al pueblo*, Siglo XXI, Mexico, 1979.
Schnitman, Jorge, *Film Industries in Latin America: Dependency and Development*, Ablex, New Jersey 1984.
Schumann, Peter B., *Historia del cine latinoamericano*, Legasa, Buenos Aires, 1986.
Stam, Robert, 'Censorship in Brazil', *JumpCut* 21, 1979, p. 20.
— , 'The Fall', *JumpCut* 22, 1980, pp. 20–21.

—, 'Slow Fade to Afro: The Black Presence in Brazilian Cinema', *Quarterly Review of Film Studies* 36, 2, 1982–3, pp. 16–32.

—, 'Hour of the Furnaces and the Two Avant Gardes', *Millennium Film Journal* 7–9, 1980, pp. 151–64.

Trelles Plazaola, Luis, *Cine y mujer en América Latina*, Editorial de la Universidad de Puerto Rico, Rio Piedras, 1991.

—, *South American Cinema: Dictionary of Filmmakers*, Editorial de la Universidad de Puerto Rico, Rio Piedras, 1989.

Usabel, Gaizka D. de, *The High Noon of American Films in Latin America*, Ann Arbor, UMI Research Press 1982.

Xavier, Ismail, 'Allegories of Underdevelopment: From the "Aesthetics of Hunger" to the "Aesthetics of Garbage"', Ph.D. dissertation, New York University, 1982.

—, *Sertão/Mar: Glauber Rocha e a estética da fome*, Brasiliense, São Paulo, 1983.

A number of film journals – *Afterimage, JumpCut, Cine-tracts, Framework, Cineaste, Screen* – either publish regular articles on Latin American cinema or have published special issues on this topic; see Burton and the footnotes to this book for references. The trade journal *Variety* has also produced an annual 'Latin American and Hispanic Market Survey' over the past fifteen years. *Hojas de cine: testimonios y documentos del nuevo cine latinoamericano*, vols I–III, SEP, Mexico City 1988.

302

301

300

INDEX

Tangos: L'Exil de Gardel, Tangos: el exilio de Gardel (Tangos: The Exile of Gardel, *Fernando E. Solanas, France/Argentina, 1985*)